# AMERICA'S
# POLISH HERITAGE

# AMERICA'S POLISH HERITAGE

## A Social History of the Poles in America

by

JOSEPH A. WYTRWAL

DETROIT

1961

97763

Library of Congress Catalog Card Number: 60-15742

*To*
## DR. CLAUDE A. EGGERTSEN

# ACKNOWLEDGEMENTS

During the long process of research and composition, a large number of individuals gave the author valued and liberal assistance which is herewith gratefully recorded. Dr. Claude A. Eggertsen and Dr. Peter A. Ostafin helped to plan the initial stages of research. Clark Mills read the entire manuscript and gave both general criticisms and detailed suggestions. Henry Archacki prepared the maps which have been used in the book. Rev. Alexander J. Wytrwal prepared the index. Mrs. Lottie Kuliga Peczynski and Mrs. Edith Fucinari typed the successive drafts and prepared the manuscript with competence and care.

In gathering the material, I enjoyed the facilities and courtesies of the following libraries: the Jagiellonian University Library in Krakow, Poland; the Alliance College Library in Cambridge Springs, Pennsylvania; the Polish National Alliance Library in Chicago, Illinois; St. Mary's College Library in Orchard Lake, Michigan; Columbia University Library in New York City; New York University Library in New York; the University of Warsaw Library in Warsaw, Poland; and the Ossolineum Library in Wroclaw, Poland. I wish to thank the various staffs of the libraries mentioned and I am particularly appreciative of the helpful efforts of Rev. Joseph Swastek, Edward Kopielski and Zbigniew Sowinski.

I am especially grateful to Dr. Joseph L. Lichten for writing the Foreword to this book.

J. A. W.

Detroit, 1960

# Foreword

"One part Declaration of Independence; one part the Constitution; one part love for apple pie; one part desire and willingness to wear American shoes and another part pride in American plumbing will make an American out of anyone."—FRANKLIN LANE

"The problem of this study arises from the recognition that the culture of the United States, carried along from its origins and crossed and blended, is neither English, nor any one of the other numerous ethnic cultures that have been brought to the country. It is rather a new culture."
—JOSEPH A. WYTRWAL

These two quotations characterize most vividly the progress made in our approach to the problem of integrating new immigrants into the stream of American life and also to the role which various ethnic groups play in the American community. *America's Polish Heritage* makes a unique and important contribution to the proper evaluation of these fascinating processes which have taken place in the American society from the very moment of this country's foundation.

The secret of America is that it represents a nation of people with vivid memories of old traditions built anew. The country is the product of this dynamic and continuing process which began 300 years ago. President Franklin D. Roosevelt was literally correct when he greeted a convention of the Daughters of the American Revolution with the words, "Fellow immigrants."

The significance of Dr. Wytrwal's book is twofold. First, it represents an up-to-date study of the processes of acculturation and the analysis of the pluralistic society. Secondly, the book gives us a social history of one of the most important ethnic components of this society—namely, Americans of Polish descent. These two elements are so interwoven that it would be impossible to comprehend the value of this entire book if we stressed only one of these elements, despite the fact that the main purpose of *America's Polish Heritage* was to evaluate the role and present the life of America's Polonia.

The discussion about integration in Dr. Wytrwal's study would remain in a sphere of theory or even hypothesis if not documented by a detailed historical and sociological study of American Poles. Moreover, this study could never have been executed with such lucidity and brilliance if the author had not a sufficient background to perceive and understand the cultural substratum, that is, the philosophical and sociological basis of the concepts of integration and the pluralistic society.

Scholars from various walks of life presently devote a lot of time and space to discussions on the concept of the pluralistic society in which we live. They rightly see in this concept probably one of the best answers to harmonious living, founded not upon the arbitrary standards of co-existence, but on the principles of an integrated community life.

These scholars tend, however, to underline racial and religious components with much less or no accent upon the ethnic aspects of a multifarious society. With great satisfaction, we acknowledge that the proper understanding of various races and faiths and their roles in our social life is responsible for a significant progress in lessening tensions, eliminating prejudices and bringing about a better understanding among people. At the same time, it would enhance our understanding of the concept of a pluralistic society if we would remember that also the process of acculturation of diverse nationality groups is still developing before our eyes. As Dr. Wytrwal so convincingly proved, we mean not only the changes within the well established ethnic groups, but also in the life of newer arrivals and their contributions and growth.

Dr. Wytrwal stated that when Thomas and Znaniecki studied the Polish immigrants in the United States from 1914 to 1919, they were convinced the first generation immigrants alone had been capable of preserving Polish cultural patterns. They foresaw that the second generation would drift away from the heritage of their fathers. When Znaniecki returned to the United States in 1939, however, he was amazed to discover there had been an almost

cyclical alternation between the urge to assimilate with the larger
culture and desire for a militant assertion of the identity with
the sub-culture. If Znaniecki could see the Polish-American organizational life of today, he would undoubtedly discover another
cycle in the history of Polonia, perhaps of different dimensions
and aspirations, but still the same process of acculturation as vivid
as ever.

Dr. Wytrwal is perfectly right when he says that since immigration to the United States has been curtailed for nearly a generation, the composition of the immigrant group is characterized less
and less by the immigrant. Rather, it indicates more and more the
influence of the descendants of the immigrants.

At the same time, on many pages of this fascinating book the
reader will find the names of individuals who came to these shores
during the last two decades, and have significantly contributed
to both the American and Polish-American communities. The
reader will also note that several new organizations and scholarly
institutions were established by these new arrivals. The role of
this new group, within and outside of the Polish-American community, must not be underestimated.

Dr. Wytrwal in his approach to the problem of integration
supports "the middle course (which) means the conscious preservation, in the midst of the American environment, of the basic
and permanent values of the old cultures which must be preserved neither to maintain eternally active loyalty and affiliation
with the native land, nor for the perpetuation of hyphenated
Americans. These values must be preserved rather to the end
that the maximum of what is true and of eternal value in the old
cultures may be conserved and contributed with a minimum loss
to the expanding content of the evolving American culture."

America's Polish Heritage with its scholarly method and style,
incredibly large source material, and with its case study of the
two largest Polish-American organizations is able to destroy several myths about problems of integration and the nature of American ethnic groups. We touched upon the mythical solutions of
the "Melting Pot" theory, and another myth, that since the cur-
tailment of immigration to the United States, ethnic groups do

not play much of an important role in the life of the American
community.

Still another myth derives from misusing the terms "political"
and "economic" immigration. This concept, describes only the
reasons *why* immigrants had come to the country. Some, unlike
Dr. Wytrwal, are often of the opinion that "economic" immigrants differ from "political" immigrants, mainly because the
former were mediocre individuals, lacking education, with no
great interest in organizational life and not great understanding
of their own past.

Dr. Wytrwal's short history of Poland which underlines several elements will be of interest to the American reader, and will
prove that the Polish immigrant, "political" and "economic" not
only had an important cultural past, but was conscious of it. For
example, the Polish-Lithuanian Commonwealth became the strongest and most progressive state in Eastern Europe. Poland for centuries had an immigration of her own, i.e., Germans, Armenians,
Tartars, Scots and Jews settled in Poland. One of the reasons for
the comparatively small participation of Poles in the original settlement of America was due to religious and political freedom
in pre-partitioned Poland. In the context of Polish history, Dr.
Wytrwal's book was primarily concerned with Poland prior to
1918.

In reference to Poland's guarantee of religious and political
rights it is worthwhile to mention that in the first constitution
of 1880, the Polish National Alliance committed itself to a program of "toleration of all creeds in the spirit of Poland's ancient
constitution."

In view of the fact that not only Poles, but also many other
citizens of different nationality or faith, like Jews, were immi-
grating to America from Poland, Dr. Wytrwal acknowledges also
their contributions to the American culture. His first reference
was to Polish-born Haym Salomon.

The foreword would be incomplete if we did not at least
mention the most interesting case history of the two largest Polish-
American organizations which are covered in the book. They are
the Polish National Alliance and Polish Roman Catholic Union.

This opus is a pioneering work, giving us not only historical facts, but a deep social insight into the life of the Polish family, parish and organizations in the United States.

Far from an apology for American Polonia, the book is an objective study written by an erudite author who performs his delicate analysis like a veteran surgeon with a scalpel. Sometimes he presents the brutal truth, but always it is done with the sincere intention of grasping the existing trends and signs of the future.

At the same time, Dr. Wytrwal works on his subject with great admiration and understanding of a son, writing about the home of his parents and grandparents.

Finally, it would not be an exaggeration to say that *America's Polish Heritage* is not one, but two books. Here, we mean the "Notes" and the "Bibliography" are of no lesser interest than the text. And we strongly urge the reader not to skip over them with a glance.

With commanding modesty, the author stated that he "has no idea that his labors are definitive." On the other hand, nothing is ever definitive in the lives of humans. The book is however a *tour de force* which successfully blends high level scholarly approach with a frank and detailed presentation of Polish-American social history.

It was a privilege to write the foreword to Dr. Wytrwal's book.

JOSEPH L. LICHTEN

New York City, 1960

No man may love the beauty of his race
Unless he knows the path by which he came,
Unless he knows that blood-soaked, hallowed place
Where histories of the ages call his name;
Where footsteps of his fathers traced the soil
From sun's arising to the last moon's wane,
With hieroglyphics attesting the toil
Of harvesting and sowing of the grain.

O knowledge born of beauty, bearing love,
O threefold, priceless heritage of man,
Man fit to arm and wear the bright shield of
Wisdom—and walk among her royal clan!
Unless he touch his fingers to the pain
Can man have knowledge—nor be born again.

—VICTORIA JANDA: *The Heritage*

# Table of Contents

CHAPTER | PAGE

*Foreword,* by Dr. Joseph L. Lichten — vii

*Introduction* — xv

1 POLAND: HISTORICAL BACKGROUND — 1

2 PIONEER POLISH IMMIGRANTS 1608-1776 — 19

3 POLITICAL IMMIGRANTS 1776-1870 — 36

4 ECONOMIC EMIGRATION 1870-1929 — 77

5 CAUSES FOR POLISH EMIGRATION TO AMERICA — 106

6 THE ORGANIZATION OF POLES IN AMERICA — 148

7 ACTIVITIES OF THE POLISH NATIONAL ALLIANCE — 191

8 ACTIVITIES OF THE POLISH ROMAN CATHOLIC UNION — 212

9 THE PNA AND PRCU COMPARED — 227

10 DISSOLUTION ANB ASSEVERATION — 236

11 AMERICAN POLONIA DURING WORLD WAR II — 260

12 POLISH-AMERICAN CULTURAL RELATIONSHIPS — 276

13 JAMESTOWN REVISITED — 287

*Bibliography* — 295

*Appendix* — 310

*Index* — 331

# LIST OF TABLES IN THE APPENDIX

I    The Distribution of Poles in 1790.

II    Number of Poles in the United States According to the Census of 1860 and 1870.

III    Distribution and Density of the Polish Population in the United States in 1903.

IV    Distribution of Money Brought by Immigrants to the United States in 1903.

V    Polish Foreign-Born Population of the United States by Country of Birth, 1860-1930.

VI    Nine States Having the Largest Polish Population (Census 1940).

VII    Nine States Having the Smallest Polish Population (Census 1940).

VIII    Poles Re-entering Poland from the United States 1919-1923.

IX    Earning Power of Immigrants until World War I.

X    Average Annual Income of Immigrants Before World War I.

XI    Per Cent of Males Among Immigrants 1899-1909.

XII    Earliest Fraternal Societies in America.

XIII    Fourteen Polish Organizations in the United States.

XIV    Distribution and Relationship of Polish Parishes, Clergy, and Attendants to the Total Catholic Set-Up in the United States in 1903.

XV    Polish Immigrants in the Cities of the Great Lakes Area.

XVI    Juvenile Membership and Juvenile Insurance in Force January 1st, 1944 in Polish Organizations.

XVII    Changes in Adult Membership and Total Insurance in Force in 1943.

XVIII    PNA and PRCU Lodges, Membership by States, January, 1944.

XIX    Statistical Chart of the Polish National Alliance Growth, 1880 to December 31, 1954.

XX    Immigrants Who Departed From the United States 1908-1931.

XXI    Membership in the Largest American Polish Organizations since 1955.

XXII    Polish Press in America in January 1915.

XXIII    The Slavs in 1950.

# Introduction

From the beginning of recorded history, territorial mobility played a significant part in shaping the characteristics which a society may possess. Although modern man understands a fixed place of residence as the normal situation, it is very probable that tribes, war bands, and armies had seared plains and valleys with their trails and roads and launched their boats on the trackless seas before the era of modern man. Even today, in isolated parts of the earth, it is possible to find pastoral groups to which a migratory way of life is normal. Individuals and groups tend to move from localities in which the prospects for a decent livelihood are poor to sparsely settled areas where, it is believed, a better existence can be pursued.

Henry P. Fairchild has classified the different types of population movements as follows: (1) invasions, in which more primitive civilizations overcome those better developed, (2) conquests, in which people of a more complex culture take the initiative and attack less well developed areas, (3) colonizations, in which well established states send bodies of their citizens to settle specified localities under their political control, and (4) immigrations, or movements of people, individually or in families, acting on their own initiative and responsibility, without official support or compulsion, who pass from one well-developed country to another with the intention of residing there permanently.[1]

Of these types of human movement, the last two, colonization and immigration, are the processes which have most affected the culture of the United States. History has witnessed few treks comparable to the flood of humanity sweeping across the Atlantic Ocean from the older European nations to the United States. In little more than a century, between 1820 and 1930, over 62 million people uprooted themselves from their native lands to seek a better life in newer lands around the globe. Almost two-

---

[1] Henry Pratt Fairchild, *Immigration,* (New York, 1925), pp. 1-30.

thirds of these enterprising souls came to seek new homes in the vast and empty spaces of the United States. The establishment of a large body of culturally different people in the midst of a population tends to create problems of adjustment. When the people of one culture move into another, they often have to shed layer after layer of old habits and ways of thought, much as one peels an onion. This was true to some extent of Europeans who came to America, and especially so of those peasants who ex-changed their rural life for American city life. But the danger inherent in the peeling of the onion, that so many layers will be removed that nothing is left, was no threat to the great majority of immigrants; most of them retained a number of their traditional habits. The problem of this study arises from the recognition that the culture of the United States, carried along from its origins and crossed and blended, is neither English, nor any one of the other numerous ethnic cultures that have been brought to the country. It is rather a new culture, which is slowly and steadily evolving and expanding in a rich, variegated pattern as a result of the interaction of people of various ethnic and national back-grounds in the process of adjusting to a new physical and social environment. Inherent in this situation is the problem of culture change. Today, people of any given ethnic or national group find themselves either adjusting to, or reacting against the culture of other ethnic and national groups with which they are in im-mediate contact in the United States. As a result, regional cul-tures are emerging which are determined in part by the following forces: (1) the physical environment and economy, (2) the first settlers and the subsequent immigrants, (3) the polity and social arrangements, and (4) the impact of a variety of stocks shaping the amalgam of the new American society.

This interaction of sub-cultures or particular nationality groups involves changes in the original pattern of a group and pushes the emergent culture pattern of the community farther along the road toward a relatively homogeneous and harmonious culture, especially an "American Way" of life.[2] Douglas G. Mar-

---

[2] Douglas C. Marshall, "Nationality and the Emerging Culture," *Rural Sociology*, XIII (March, 1948), p. 41.

shall states that there is no doubt that the original values and idea systems of these groups have been modified. Most of these modifications can be traced to the fact that if people live and work together, they cannot help but be influenced in how they do things, no matter how impervious they might appear to social change. These modifications have been accepted at varying rates because certain ethnic groups have values which are not too far removed from the accepted dominant values of a community. Other ethnic groups have experienced more difficulty in conforming to a socially acceptable way of life, but are eventually "infected" by the dominant groups. Consciousness of kind is not only corroded by time but by the inability of most groups "to live unto themselves."[3]

There are two general stimuli to changes in culture. Through the process of migration each of the immigrant groups have come in contact with a new physical environment. To the extent that this new physical environment is different from the native environment of the respective immigrants, it will initiate a more or less extensive reorientation of the knowledge, attitudes, and behavior patterns of the immigrants. The changes resulting from the new physical environment are aspects of the general process of culture change. The second general stimulus to culture change is that resulting from the need to adjust to a new social environment. This is the aspect of culture change which has been designated as acculturation. The concept of acculuration is defined in anthropological literature as the process of cultural change which takes place when a people are exposed over a long period of time to a culture different from their own.[4] Robert Bierstedt defines acculturation as the process of acquiring the culture of a different society from one's own.[5]

Acculturation can be seen on a grand scale in the millions of European immigrants who settled the continental United States and became assimilated to an American culture. Within three generations, the family of the Polish immigrant is indistinguishable, except perhaps by name, from an immigrant family from France.

---

[3] Ibid., p. 47.

[4] M. J. Herskovits, Acculturation, (New York: 1938), pp. 14-15.

[5] Robert Bierstedt, The Social Order, (New York: 1957), p. 154.

Both families pledge allegiance to the same flag, send their children to the same college, and belong to the same welfare organizations. From the encrustration of shared experiences they form "cliques"; from common leisure and recreation activities, they form clubs, whose chief ties are an interchange of tastes and experiences. In this way, the two families manage to achieve a functional set of social relations with like-minded people, the core of which is not propinquity of place or ancestry but community of interests, vocation, preferences, and tastes. Many writers refer to this process as the "melting pot"; in sociological terms it is acculturation.[6] This process is not always smooth and easy and some groups are acculturated more easily than others, but it never fails to develop when people of two cultures have social relations for an extended period of time.[7] Acculturation, like education, is a constant process in society. Education is the process by which we acquire the culture of our own society. Acculturation is the process by which we acquire the culture of a contemporary society other than our ancestral heritage. Acculturation is the result of the contact of cultures.

In his discussion of the concept of acculturation, Linton holds that it was first used to designate the process of change which was taking place among the immigrant groups who had settled in the United States.[8] He limits the use of the concept to situations where two societies are brought into a close relationship as wholes. Specifically, he applies the concept only to those phenomena which result when groups of individuals having different cultures come into continuous first-hand contact, with subsequent changes in the original culture patterns of either or both groups.[9] According to this definition acculturation is to be distinguished from culture change, of which it is but one aspect, and assimilation, which is at times a phase of acculturation. It is also to be differentiated from diffusion, which, while occurring in all instances of

---

[6] *Ibid.,* p. 155.

[7] American students can understand this phenomenon more readily than students of other nationalities, for all of them, unless they are of Indian descent, have a history of acculturation in their own families.

[8] Ralph Linton, *The Study of Man,* (New York: 1936), p. 335.

[9] Ralph Linton, *Acculturation Among Seven American Indian Tribes,* (New York: 1940), pp. 463-464.

acculturation, is also only one aspect of the process of acculturation.[10]

Assimilation is a psychological process dealing with the individual and personality, while acculturation is a sociological process dealing with the group and culture change. The one cannot
exist without the other, but it is entirely possible to isolate and
study the processes separately. The dividing line between personality and culture is so minute that the processes seem to treat
of two aspects of the same thing. However, they are really com-
plementary to each other, as neither can exist without the other.
In the process of assimilation, certain elements of the original
culture lose specific meaning and cease to be values. This loss of
meaning involves the forgetting of elements which slowly disappear from the cultural horizon of the individual. In this manner,
ideas, languages, skills and customs are forgotten and cease to be
a part of the culture of a given social group. The assimilated individual loses and acquires culture. However, the process of
acquisition and loss is of a psycho-social nature and involves the
individual and his personality. These ideas may be summed up
as follows.

| Process | Discipline | Unit | Subject |
|---------|-----------|------|---------|
| Assimilation | Psychology | The Individual | Personality |
| Acculturation | Sociology | The Group | Culture |

Under these conditions, acculturation becomes a reciprocal
process between two groups in continuous first-hand contact
through which elements of both cultures are combined into a
new dynamic culture which may include elements that are new
to both interacting cultures.

Acculturation must be evaluated in terms of the attitudes of
the individual members and in terms of the value system of the
ethnic group. Attitudes are the manifestation in the individual
member of the value system of the group and conversely, the
value system of the group is abstracted from the attitudes of
its individual members. Attitudes and values constitute the inter-
related parts of any social situation, which involves three kinds of
data: (1) the totality of values which at the given moment affect

----

[10] *Ibid.*, p. 464.

directly or indirectly the conscious status of the individual or the group, (2) the pre-existing attitudes of the individual or the group which at the given moment have an actual influence on the behavior of the individual or group, and (3) the definition of the situation, that is, the more or less clear conception of the conditions and consciousness of the attitudes.[11] The total culture of a society is not known or expressed by any individual member of the society. Similarly, an emerging culture is not expressed in its entirety by any single member. But the emerging culture can be deduced from observations of the innovators and leaders in the society.[12] In modern society, the emerging culture is incorporated in part, into recommendations for school curricula, civic projects, and other official and semi-official acts. Thus the emerging culture is not the same as the new culture. It is only an approximation of the new culture, which is the ultimate end product of the acculturation process.

This process of acculturation has changed the orientation of the immigrant groups. Except in rare instances the immigrant groups do not retain their strong nationalistic attachment to the country of origin, since most of them have accepted the responsibilities of citizenship in the new country. Also, since immigration to the United States has been curtailed for nearly a generation, the composition of the immigrant group is characterized less and less by the immigrant and more and more by the descendants of the immigrants. However, for the present study, the significant point is that even after their outward manifestations, such as language and names have disappeared, many groups still retain their ethnic identity and a number of their traditional habits. The groups retain an orientation which sets them apart and makes them distinguishable, one from the other. They develop certain social values and attitudes peculiarly their own. These virtues and attitudes tend to crystallize into social heritages and, as such,

---

[11] W. I. Thomas and Florian Znaniecki, *The Polish Peasant in Europe and America*, (Boston: 1918), I, p. 68.

[12] It would seem that the innovators take up new elements for reasons of utility and prestige. The innovator adapts the new element to the existing culture and adapts the pre-existing culture to include the new element and, by this process, in the single instance, gives the society a preview of the emerging culture, to which the other members of the society can and do react.

condition the behavior of nationality groups in their new cultural settings.[13] The members of the group are aware of their identity as a distinct group. They are Americans, true, but they are not just Americans. They are Polish-Americans, German-Americans or Irish-Americans. Niles Carpenter and Daniel Katz expressed these phenomena clearly in 1927.

> There is evidence of gradually decreasing knowledge of Polish tradi-
> tions and gradually increasing knowledge of American traditions.
> Thus out of a possible 100, the foreign born Poles made a score of
> 87 for Polish traditions and legends, as against 72 for American;
> whereas the native born of mixed native and foreign parentage have
> an average score of 72 for Polish traditions and legends as against 99
> for American. However, there is not so much loss of knowledge of
> Polish traditions and legends as one would expect, that is, the gain
> in knowledge of American legends and traditions is much more than
> the loss of Polish traditions and legends, and whereas, after three
> generations, the Polish-Americans in this group show a very respectable
> knowledge of American traditions and legends, they show only
> slightly less knowledge of Polish traditions and legends. This circum-
> stance suggests the fact that culture traits are much more easily ac-
> quired than they are dropped. It also suggests the fact that certain
> immigrant groups are maintaining a kind of culture dualism. In other
> words, they are quite satisfactorily "Americanized" so far as this term
> connotes familiarity with American traditions and history, but they
> are not correspondingly "de-Polandized."[14]

According to Dr. Wood, of the Polish families in Ham-
tramck, Michigan, in 1927, with fathers who were born in Poland, 1.3 per cent spoke only English at home; while 47.7 per cent spoke Polish only in the home and 50.0 per cent spoke English and Polish.[15] When a new appraisal was made on this point in the school census of 1945, including nearly 8,000 families, it was discovered that 49.3 per cent of the Polish families were shown to use only Polish in the home, and 50.7 per cent both Polish and English.[16]

---

[13] George W. Hill, "The Use of the Culture Area Concept in Social Research," The American Journal of Sociology, XXXVII (July, 1941), pp. 14-24.

[14] Niles Carpenter and Daniel Katz, "The Cultural Adjustment of the Polish
Group in the City of Buffalo; an experiment in the technique of social investigation,"
Social Forces, (September, 1927), p. 80.

[15] Arthur Evans Wood, Hamtramck Then and Now, (New York: 1955),
p. 36.

[16] Ibid., p. 36.

These groups have a sense of belonging together that set them apart from other groups whether immigrant or old American stock.

Francis views ethnic groups as a variation of the community type of association and states that the pattern of social inter-action characteristic of the group permits its extension under cer-tain conditions to a larger, locally less well-defined, and culturally less homogeneous group. We may, for instance, think of a peasant village as the ideal primary group. Now, under certain conditions, the "we-feeling" of this community can be made to include the natives of the valley or of a wider region, even a whole country. Thus, a larger, but secondary group may form which presents most of the characteristics originally attached to the primary group. In this way, we may say that the ethnic group is the most inclusive, cumulative, and realistic type of secondary community.[17]

This conception of the ethnic group approximates to a rather marked degree the pattern of association which characterizes the immigrant groups in this country. The process of immigration severed the connections of the individual with his native village and to some degree with his family. The "we-feeling," which has been attached to this primary group, was not transferred directly to the neighborhood or community in the new country where he took up abode. It became associated rather with immigrants from the same region, though not necessarily from the same community. This process of transference of allegiance or of the "we-feeling" from the community of origin to the community of immigrants is implied, if not expressly stated, in the research of Thomas and Znaniecki dealing with Polish immigrants in America.[18] It is through this process of identification that numerous ethnic groups, which together characterize the cultural landscape of the United States, have emerged. Every ethnic culture tends to assure the survival of the group which bears it. In the process, however, of making adjustments, which are necessitated by the new environ-ment, the culture may be changed vastly. Hence, it is the group and not the culture that persists. The culture consists of the tech-

---

[17] E. K. Francis, "The Nature of the Ethnic Group," *The American Journal of Sociology*, LII (March, 1947), p. 399.
[18] Thomas and Znaniecki, *op. cit.*

niques of the members of the group whereby they assure their survival. The culture changes as new techniques are worked out or as old techniques are discarded to meet the requirements of a changed environment.

Economic determination cannot fully explain the rise of thirty-five hundred fraternal orders in the United States in the period between 1865 and 1910.[19] In these decades of transition, when Americans were moving from an old to a new civilization, the rapidity of social change, the permissiveness of the state, the openness of an open society and the newness of the surroundings increased the sense and fact of insecurity for multitudes of individuals. There was a definite need to bring together people of diverse ethnic groups, or conversely, of their huddling together inside a separate ethnic tent until they could be assimilated. These voluntary fraternal orders performed a crucial function by bridging the transition between the closed hierarchical society of the Old World and the fragmented individualism of the New World. Besides the limited protection which these fraternal orders offered in the form of insurance or mutual aid, certainly one of the drives behind "joining" was the integrative impulse to form ties with like-minded people and thus find status in the community. For not only did the fraternal orders satisfy the nostalgic longings of strangers in a foreign land, but they were also instrumental in achieving a fuller life by helping their members to "get ahead," to "meet people," to "make contacts," to "get something done," to learn something, and to fill their lives.[20] These early fraternal orders were organized by workers of certain trades; by nationality groups; and by religious organizations. The "Czechoslovak Society of America" was organized in 1854; the "Order of the Railway Conductors" in 1868; the "Free Sons of Israel" in 1871; the "Polish Roman Catholic Union" in 1873; and the "Polish National Alliance" in 1880.

The last two fraternal orders, the "Polish Roman Catholic Union" and the "Polish National Alliance" are the fraternal

---

[19] For the earliest fraternal orders in the United States see Table XII in the Appendix.

[20] Ralph Henry Gabriel, *The Course of American Democratic Thought*, (New York: 1956), pp. 200-201.

orders investigated in this study. These two organizations are referred to as "nationality leadership groups" denoting a category
of "special interest groups.[21] Their primary purposes and aims,
and the structures for implementing their objectives, are studied
to determine their role in the acculturation process of the Polish
immigrants to American life. These two organizations, do not
exist in a vacuum. Having a combined membership of almost
600,000, their activities embrace almost the gamut of Polish group
life and offer a key to a better understanding of the Polish past.
In immediate contact with the Polish immigrants and Americans
of Polish and non-Polish descent, they contribute to American
culture. Hence the process of culture-change, as it is observed
among immigrant ethnic groups, is not merely a reciprocal inter-
action, but includes the process of adjusting to the emerging
"American culture," which includes elements from many sources.

The major hypothesis of this study is that these two organizations functioned as a type of special interest group or "nationality leadership" group, and that in the process of implementing
their aims and objectives, their activities have facilitated the acculturation of Poles in America. Of interest to the hypothesis is
the fact that these two organizations presented two different
approaches to the problem of improving the cultural and social
well-being of Polish immigrants in America. The Polish Roman
Catholic Union implemented its program through the Polonia
parish system, dominated naturally by the Polish-American hierarchy; the Polish National Alliance, in order to avoid any religious control, implemented its program through local secular
institutions and agencies. Cultural traits associated with the economic and physical aspects of everyday life can perhaps be expected
to change more readily than traits associated with its religious
and social aspects. It may be that the authoritarian orientation
found in the Polish parish system had retarded culture-change in

---

[21] In this study, the term "special interest group" refers to a voluntary association of persons who pursue activities which they deem to be in their own interest.
The prime orientation of their program is the welfare of their particular group. The
term "nationality leadership group" is used to refer to a type of special interest
group whose common bond of interest is the welfare and status up-grading of a
particular ethnic element of the American society, in the present study, the immigrant Pole or the American of Polish descent.

all areas of culture. Since both organizations have been exposed to the "American culture" over the same period in history, and with comparable intensity, both organizations should have adopted the same views and motives, if we take other factors as equal, marked differences in the extent to which the groups have accepted specific culture elements in the "American culture" give an indication of what Linton refers to as "compatibility or incompatibility with the preexisting culture."

To study this problem satisfactorily in relation to the role of the AmericanPolish nationality organizations in the acculturation of the Polish immigrant, a review of the history of Polish immigration in America seems imperative. Attention must also be focused on the cultural, national, and religious factors responsible for the rise of the American Polish nationality organizations. The factors that influenced American Polish nationality organizations in America must also be traced. And finally, the effects of these American Polish nationality organizations on the acculturation of the Polish immigrant in America must also be appraised. To accomplish this purpose, the writer made an examination of the causes for Polish emigration to the United States; the acculturation processes of each group; and the background and character of the specific immigrant groups which founded the Polish National Alliance and the Polish Roman Catholic Union. The writer also tried to ascertain if a need existed for organizations to which Polish immigrants could turn for material, social, and cultural benefits; and if it were important to have institutions organized on nationality and linguistic lines in order that the immigrant might communicate his needs and receive a feeling of security and a sense of belonging. Furthermore, the writer tried to determine whether consciousness of kind and the need for mutual assistance were the two most important factors which favored the founding of the Polish National Alliance and the Polish Roman Catholic Union. The activities of these two organizations are also studied to determine whether they remained within the limits of our democratic system of values, that is, whether both organizations, the PNA and the PRCU, have exemplified themselves as loyal American organizations by giving freely of their time, money, and personnel, wherever it was in the interest and welfare of the United States. And lastly, the writer tried to determine if the Polish National Alliance and the Polish Roman Catholic Union functioned to define, articulate, and reflect by their activities the needs, values, and objectives of the Polish immigrant groups.

The subject has been approached in a chronological order, as far as possible. For background, it is useful to know the political and social history of the immigrants' native country, since this will explain, in part, their defensive mechanisms, and their tenacious loyalty to religion and language, both of which hindered accultura- tion and caused a delay in Americanization and naturalization. The best source material for this study is the generation that gave us the immigrant. This generation is rapidly dying out, and with that group are disappearing irreplaceable primary sources. Many, however, were available to serve the purpose of this study. In obtaining the necessary information about the programs and activ- ities of the PNA and the PRCU, major consideration has been given to the official published literature. The two organizations publish official organs: for the Polish Roman Catholic Union, *Narod Polski,* for the Polish National Alliance, *Zgoda.* These publications serve a useful purpose, even if they do not treat the subject from the point of view of this study. In addition to these two official organs, the annual reports of each organization, and the special bulletins, the directives to lodges, pamphlets, folders, and letters were sources of information. These sources have been supplemented by secondary materials. Personal interviews were also held with officials of these organizations in Chicago and Cambridge Springs, Pennsylvania. To arrive at a neutral and ob- jective point of view, the histories and writings of M. Haiman, K. Wachtl, F. Barc, S. Osada, and K. Piatkiewicz were also considered.

Although the study reaches as far back as 1608, to the be- ginning of Polish colonial immigration, it is, in reality, an inquiry into the economic immigration which actually began in 1854 with the Panna Maria settlement in Texas. Little has been written in the English language about immigration. Marcus Lee Hansen con- tributes the following explanation why American scholars have avoided this subject:

Like other aspects of history whose significance is primarily sociological, immigration was for a long time neglected by historians because of their pre-occupations with political matters. Moreover, during
the first hundred or more years of our national past, and of our historical literature as well, there was an intense concentration on domestic
expansion, accompanied by a desire to assert the nation's independence of the rest of the world and to establish its uniqueness. Such a
mood was hardly conducive to a proper appreciation of the inter-
relation of European and American development.[22]

It is still correct to say that the history of immigration in the
United States, especially in its relation to other phases of hisory,
has been, comparatively speaking, sadly neglected in detail and
in general.

The Polish pioneer and political emigration did not present
any special problems. The study of the two emigrations has been
included, nevertheless, not only to round out the history of the
Poles in America, but above all to contrast it with that of the
Polish economic emigration. Although, no direct study of the
role of American Polish nationality organizations in the acculturation of the Polish immigrants has been completed in English or
Polish numerous monographs in the field of social sciences consider this problem. Many documents and primary source materials dealing with the Polish immigrant have been published in
the United States and Poland. Since territorial mobility often
creates problems which are readily observed, the tendency in the
past has been to analyze immigration in terms of problems. Because the immigrant groups were usually members of the lower
economic classes, such things as poor housing, illiteracy, and
other social ills associated with poverty were evident. In cities,
immigrants were often segregated from the dominant culture and
were confined to a cultural island composed of their fellow-
countrymen. Hence, in the past, countless studies have been made
concerning the problems created by the immigrant. Not the least
of these is Ross's study which has been valuable in demonstrating the assimilability or unassimilability of the various nationality
groups.[23] A number of studies have been made to explain the

---

[22] Donald Sheehan, *The Making of American History,* (New York: 1950), I,
p. 267.
[23] E. A. Ross, *The Old World in the New,* (New York: 1914).

cultural demoralization of specific immigrant groups. The most notable of these is W. I. Thomas and Florian Znaniecki's *The Polish Peasant in Europe and America*.[24] Thomas and Znaniecki attempted to explain the actions of the Polish immigrants in the United States in terms of cultural conflict. Personal histories, records, letters, case studies, and similar materials were the basis of their analysis. They concluded that the behavior of the Polish immigrants can be explained by the fact that the individual does not feel himself backed in his dealings with the outside world by a strong, organized society.[25] Another study of the same type was completed by Robert E. Park and Herbert A. Miller.[26] In this study the behavior of the immigrant groups is explained through conflict situations involving the cultural heritage of the migrant and that of the new situation in which he moves. Personal history documents were the sources analyzed in this study. Mary B. Kedzierska analyzed culture conflict situations that arise in an immigrant family, having children born and reared in the United States, who are endeavoring to reconcile American institutions with culture patterns of their foreign-born parents.[27] Kedzierska's study provides concrete examples of bewilderment of both parent and child in their effort to adjust to the American milieu. The activities and contributions of the Polish immigrants have been recorded by Miecislaus Haiman[28] and Father Waclaw Kruszka,[29] Oscar Handlin[30] and Paul Fox,[31] and Waclaw Gasiorowski.[32] Brown and Roucek[33] and Robert Schermerhorn[34] have also analyzed the activities and contributions of the Poles in America, and Dr. Wachtl has traced the

---

24 W. I. Thomas and Florian Znaniecki, *The Polish Peasant in Europe and America*, (Boston: 1918).

25 *Ibid.*

26 Robert E. Park and Herbert A. Miller, *Old World Traits in the New*, (New York: 1921).

27 Mary B. Kedzierska, "The Polish Family—Problems of Adjustment," (unpublished Master's thesis, Fordham University, 1941).

28 Miecislaus Haiman, *Polish Past in America*, 1608-1865, (Chicago: 1939).

29 Waclaw Kruszka, *Historya Polska w Ameryce*, (Milwaukee: 1905).

30 Oscar Handlin, *The Uprooted*, (Boston: 1951).

31 Paul Fox, *Poles in America*, (New York: 1922).

32 Waclaw Gasiorowski, *Ach! Te 'Chamy' w Ameryce!*, (Warszawa: 1935).

33 F. J. Brown and J. S. Roucek, *One America*, (New York: 1945).

34 Robert S. Schermerhorn, *These Our People*, (Boston: 1949).

historical accounts of Poles in American communities.[35] A limited literature exists on the acculturation of Polish immigrants in selected areas. Niles Carpenter and Daniel Katz have completed a monograph which considered the Buffalo community.[36] The authors selected Buffalo because of the large Polish population and because of its strong and well maintained cultural identity. The Carpenter and Katz study gives an insight into immigrant groups, which although thirty or forty years in the United States, still tend to cling to old traditions and customs, to hold to certain opinions and attitudes that vary from those of American institutions, while later generations although considerably within the influence of their predecessors, tend to show a marked deviation from the norms of living accepted by their forefathers. The study emphasizes the role of time as a great neutralizing force in the process of assimilation of the immigrant stream. It also stresses the fact that a richer American culture caused by the absorption and amalgamation of various European cultures will enrich the lives of Americans of tomorrow.[37] In 1919, Charles E. Coulter wrote *Poles of Cleveland* for the Americanization Committee, which had become interested in the history of the immigrant groups in the City of Cleveland.[38] Another larger and more detailed study was made by Norman Lyon.[39] Florentyna Kurpiewska's study deals with the history and progress of two Polish

---

[35] Dr. Karol Wachtl, *Polonja w Ameryce*, (Philadelphia: 1944).

[36] Niles Carpenter and Daniel Katz, "Study of Acculturation in the Polish Group of Buffalo, 1926-1928," *University of Buffalo Studies*, VII (1928-1929).

[37] Because the first study of 1926 dealt with a relatively small sample (sixty-four), it was, therefore not satisfactory. Another study was initiated in 1928 and it included 186 individuals. The former study demonstrated the possibility of an objective approach but failed to differentiate between native-born and foreign-born Poles twelve years of age or over. Consequently, the study tended to be limited to Poles born in America eighteen years of age or over. A period of two months was spent on the former survey, while the later one of 1928 was performed in seven months from July, 1927, to February, 1928. Another factor which facilitated the gathering of data was that social workers and students of Polish extraction were utilized in the actual work of interviewing and filling out the schedule forms. They had full advantage of using the Polish language. Niles Carpenter and Daniel Katz, "Study of Acculturation in the Polish Group of Buffalo, 1926-1928," *University of Buffalo Studies*, VII (1928-1929).

[38] Charles Coulter, *Poles of Cleveland*, (Cleveland: 1919).

[39] Norman T. Lyon, *History of the Polish People in Rochester*, (Buffalo: 1935).

parishes in Greenpoint, Brooklyn.[40] It is an attempt at inter-
preting the importance of the Polish parish not only as a religious
institution, but also as a center for cultural and social life. Reverend Joseph Swastek,[41] Sister Mary Remigia Napolska,[42] Peter
A. Ostafin,[43] and Stefan Wloszczewski also contributed important studies on the acculturation of the Polish immigrant in
America.[44] Robert E. Park in his study considered the Polish
press.[45] Arthur Evans Wood completed a study of Hamtramck,
a well established Polish community in Michigan.[46] These are the
foundations on which the final historiographical monument to
American Polish immigration will be built. But these studies,
despite their merits, are not comprehensive; there is a widespread
awareness that Polish-American history is in need of synthesis
to combine the results of research with literary eloquence. Generally the sociology of American Poles is still in its swaddling
clothes. Associational activities have hardly been treated. There
is, therefore, a great need for a series of monographs on the
history and present status of each of the multitude of organizations which dot the American landscape.

We are not even aware of the important role these organizations played in catering to Polish group needs. Many general
histories do not even mention this subject; while considerable
information can be culled from the Polish American press, there
are practically no monographs on any one organization in English.
At present there is not the slightest appreciation of the value of
constitutions, minute books, program materials, and other documents that emanate from the various organizations. People feel
that since these have no literary value, they can be discarded.

---

[40] Florentyna Maria Kurpiewska, A Study of the Polish Parishes in Greenpoint,
Brooklyn, (unpublished Master's thesis, Fordham University, 1936).
    [41] Reverend Joseph Swastek, "The Poles in South Bend to 1914," Polish
American Studies, II (July-December, 1945).
    [42] Sister Mary Remigia Napolska, The Polish Immigrant in Detroit to 1914,
(Chicago: 1946).
    [43] Peter A. Ostafin, The Polish Peasant in Transition. A Study of Group
Integration as a Function of Symbiosis and Common Definitions, (unpublished Ph.D.
dissertation, University of Michigan, 1948).
    [44] Stefan Wloszczewski, History of Polish American Culture, (Trenton: 1946).
    [45] Robert E. Park, The Immigrant Press and Its Control, (New York: 1922).
    [46] Arthur Evans Wood, Hamtramck Then and Now, (New York: 1955).

There is as yet no sense for Polish-American sociology as a science or a community discipline.

In this social history, *America's Polish Heritage,* an attempt has been made to give a faithful account of the contributions of two American Polish organizations to the development of the Polish immigrants in America, and of the general forces that have been and are at work in moulding the destiny of the American-Polish element in American life. It is a story of achievement and progress made possible by adherence to the democratic way of life.

Frederick Jackson Turner made the statement: "We shall not understand contemporary United States without studying immigration historically." If this book contributes one brick to the great structure of American history and if it helps a growth of understanding of the background of the Polish immigrants, their persistent use of the Polish language, and their devotion to the Roman Catholic Church, the author will consider his efforts abundantly rewarded. The author would also like to state that the task of writing a social history of Americans of Polish descent is one of such magnitude that the author has no idea that his labors are definitive. The interpretations presented are far from final; they are, rather, to be tested by further research. Thus he hopes that they may furnish suggestions to other historians who will explore this field in the future.

# AMERICA'S
# POLISH HERITAGE

# CHAPTER ONE

# Poland: Historical Background*

As a result of the international agreement reached without Poland's participation at the Yalta Conference of the Big Three, the area of the present-day "People's Republic" of Poland is approximately 121,000 square miles, or some 30,000 square miles less than the area of its prewar predecessor, the gains in the west having fallen short by this amount of losses in the east. The country nevertheless continues to rank among the larger European states. It has more than twice the area of its Czechoslovak neighbor, and, excluding the Soviet Union, is surpassed only by France, Spain and Sweden. Neither West Germany nor East Germany is as large as Poland.

If we exclude the period since September, 1939, Polish history can be divided into five periods, each characterized by a different political structure: the Piast period of the national state resisting the German "Drang nach Osten", the Jagiellonian period of the multinational commonwealth; the period of elective kings and of ultimate political decay; the period of the partitions; and the recent interwar period of the rebuilt First Polish Republic.

In racial classification the Poles are Slavs.[1] They form the westernmost branch of the Slavic race, the so-called Nordic group, which is characterized by tallness, an oblong shape of the skull and face, fair hair, and blue eyes. Following the legendary breaking up of the old Slavonic family, their country has been in central Europe since prehistoric times: a vast land east and west of the most important Polish river, the Vistula, extending between the Baltic Sea and the Carpathian mountains. The earliest information about the Slavonic tribes of that area is to be found

---

* The reader of non-Polish origin may find it useful to glance at a history of Poland in synopsis, as background for the study that follows.
[1] See Chart XXIII.

1

in the first and second century writings of Pliny and Ptolemy, which mention such names as Kalisz and Vistula. Sixth-century records also locate Slavonic tribes along the banks of the Elbe, Oder, Vistula, Dnester, and Dnieper rivers. By virtue of Poland's position, the Poles came in contact with both the Byzantine and the Roman civilizations, which have greatly influenced the forma-tion and development of the Polish character and national life.The wealth of the people at that time is demonstrated by the consider-able quantity of silver objects found in excavations. In Great Poland, in the region of Poznan, over a hundred such treasures (sixteen to twenty pounds of silver) have been found; in Pomera-nia, ninety. And in Podlasia a treasure of Roman gold coins of the third century A.D. has been discovered.

The agricultural character of the Polish tribes is attested by the origin of their name, which is derived from the word "Pole" or field. The Polanie, later Polacy, which signifies dwellers in the fields, have left their name to the whole Polish nation. Their ter-ritory, the region of Gniezno, the first capital, and that of Poznan, the seat of the first bishop, became the nucleus of the pristine Polish state. Among the other tribes that became subject to the Polanians were the Silesians and the Masovians. Eventually the tribes of the upper Vistula, with Krakow, were absorbed by the Polanie tribes.

A peasant, named Piast, was the first king of Poland. The Piast dynasty, which became the first national dynasty of Poland, governed the whole of Poland until 1370. The Piast rule was characterized by free peasant proprietorship and the extension of Polish territory through the heart of which ran the river Vistula. Piast's grandson, Mieszko I, in 962, married Dabrowka, a Bo-hemian princess, who had been a Christian for some time. Through her influence, Mieszko introduced Christianity into Poland. Con-verted to Christianity, the Polish church was brought under the jurisdiction of the Holy See. And as a result monks came from Italy; Jan, the first bishop of Wroclaw, was an Italian. The Cister-cians, as well as other orders and several bishops, came to Poland from France. The first Polish chronicler of the twelfth century, Gallus Anonymus, was a Frenchman. Even Ireland and Spain furnished Poland with monks. In his acceptance of Christianity from Bohemia, Mieszko deprived the Germans of the religious pretext of converting pagan Slavs. The Roman Catholic Religion brought Poland into the orbit of Rome; the eastern Slavs embraced the Greek rite, alphabet, and culture. This division became a permanent factor which deeply influenced the history of east-central Europe.

The rule of the early Piasts coincided with continuous struggles along the western border in defense of Polish suzerainty. Boleslaus Chrobry, surnamed the Brave, crowned King of Poland in 1025, was one of the greatest Polish monarchs; he united into one state Poles, Czechs, Slovaks, and Lusatians. Also, after sixteen years of war with Emperor Henry II, he managed to establish the Polish frontier along the Elbe and Elster in the West, along the Danube in the South, and along the Baltic in the north. Boleslaus also incorporated within the Polish state Red Ruthenia, the Lwow area, and the Kiev; he also retained Moravia throughout his reign. In addition, Boleslaus secured an autonomous ecclesiastical hierarchy in the archbishop of Gniezno. And under his direction, a powerful permanent army was organized for the Polish State. In the international field his power was acknowledged through the marriage of his sister to Sven, King of Denmark, who used Polish troops in the invasion of England in 1013. Boleslaus's sister won Sven over to Christianity; their son Canute became king of Denmark, Norway, and England. Boleslaus's daughter married a grand duke of Kiev, and Adelaida, mother of St. Stephen and sister of Mieszko I, married the Hungarian Geza, and influenced his conversion to Catholicism.

Boleslaus left his heritage to his son, Mieszko II. He was followed by Casimir I, the younger son of Mieszko II, who resumed his great-grandfather's work of organization. He left a well consolidated state to his eldest son, Boleslaus II, called the Bold. Like his glorious ancestor, Boleslaus the Bold made Poland completely independent of the Empire, and like Boleslaus the Brave, had himself crowned King of Poland at the Christmas of 1076.

The reign of Ladislaus Herman, who followed Boleslaus II, lasted twenty-three years. He was followed by Boleslaus III, whose reign is memorable for his heroic defense of Silesia. The imperial army suffered such severe defeats under the walls of Glogow and

before Wroclaw that it was forced to retreat, leaving Boleslaus III, the Wrymouth, master of the entire Polish region. The Polish border along the Oder, Bober, and Quels Rivers marked the limits of the Polish tribes and formed at that time an almost impenetrable defense line running twenty miles east of the western Niesse.

Boleslaus III established in his testament the rule of seniority to regulate the succession in the Piast dynasty, by which the eldest sons were to preside over the brothers, all of whom had hereditary provinces. His eldest son, Ladislaus, received Silesia; the second, Boleslaus, Masovia; the third, Mieszko, the principal part of Great Poland; the fourth, Henry, the region of Sandomierz to the east of Krakow, which eventually Casimir, for whom no portion had been provided, inherited. After the death of Boleslaw III, in 1138, his son Boleslaus IV succeeded to the throne. He was followed in 1173 by young Casimir, son of Boleslaus, the Wrymouth.

Surnamed the Just, Casimir united in his hands all the center and east of Poland. He also reestablished the Polish influence in the borderland principalities of Wolynia and Halicz. In 1180, Casimir convoked at Lenczyca the lords of his territories, as well as the bishops of the whole of Poland, and made them recognize that Krakow and the supreme power were to be henceforth hereditary in his house. This reform was sanctioned by the Pope and the Emperor. After the death of Casimir the Just in 1194, his eldest son, Prince Leszek, surnamed the White, inherited the throne. He was followed by Boleslaus V, surnamed the Chaste.

The brilliant efflorescence of medieval culture in the thirteenth century of St. Louis, was an epoch of struggles and hardships in Polish history. The following disasters oppressed the development of the Polish state: wars with jealous neighbors; internal political and religious reaction and disorganization; struggle for supremacy among the princes, resulting in the decrease of monarchical power; Tartar invasions from the east; Teutonic ravages, which under the pretext of converting Poland to Christianity had been responsible for great outrages, murders, and destructions of life and property. These ill-fated disruptions coincided with the destruction of the Slavs of the Elbe: the Slavonic Branibor became Brandenburg; and Barlin, Berlin; thus the German frontier ran

along the Oder instead of the Elbe and the German Empire acquired a common frontier with Poland. Due to the heavy losses
inflicted on towns by the Tartars, Polish princes promoted the
migration of Germans and Jews to Poland. Also, as the weak
principalities were unable to defend their borders against the
heathen Prussians, a tribe akin to Lithuanians and Latvians, the
prince of Mazovia brought Teutonic Knights to Poland to assist
him in converting the Prussians. The Knights ruthlessly destroyed
the Prussians, took over their lands, and over the years built the
powerful state which captured Pomerania and Danzig, and ultimately threatened the very existence of the Polish state.

During this period, Poland was ruled by Henry IV of Wroclaw, Przemysl II, and Ladislaus the Short, who united Poland in
1320. Under his rule and that of his son, Casimir the Great,
Poland achieved internal stability and prosperity and regained her
power. The reign of Casimir the Great ushered in the dawn of a
new era. His merits were so remarkable that of all the Polish
kings he was the only one who won the title of "Great." He
expanded the Polish borders in the southeast, created a central
administration and stabilized the currency. He incorporated mer-
cenaries into the army and imposed military duty on every land-
owner. He established a uniform law for the entire kingdom.
He extended his protection to the Polish towns, for which he
created a special tribunal and whose commercial interests he
carefully safeguarded. He protected the peasants against ill treatment and succored them during famines. He gave special protection to the Jews. In addition he covered the country with new
villages to which he granted extensive liberties. A great construc-
tor, he built, besides numerous churches, approximately forty
fortress towns to protect the frontiers (hence the popular saying
that the king had found Poland in wood but left it in stone).
He also established a university in Krakow, in 1364, which was
organized on the model of Italian universities.[2] With the death

---

[2] Before the establishment of a university in Krakow, Poles had had to go
abroad to study; the majority went to Bologna and Padua, some to Paris, and others
to Prague, where a university has existed since 1347. During the first thirty years of
the existence of the Jagiellonian University, 4,300 students enrolled in it, of whom
800 were from abroad—Hungarians, Silesians, Germans, and Swiss. Within the
fifteenth century the number of students exceeded 18,000, among them 8,000

of Casimir the Great, the four-hundred-year-long Piast period came
to a close.

During this period, the economic, social, and political development was progressive in character mainly because the peasants possessed a large measure of freedom. The knights, occupied
with military service and offensive or defensive warfare, did not
concern themselves with agriculture; they depended for their
livelihood chiefly on the rents of their peasants, which were paid
in kind as well as in money. This form of rental facilitated the
development of trade and the growth of towns where the knights
and peasants exchanged their agricultural surplus for the wares
made by craftsmen or imported by merchants.[3] Until the discovery of America, two world trade routes crossed on Polish
soil; one was the north-south route from the Baltic to the Mediterranean, the center of medieval world trade, and the other was the
west-east route from Western Europe to the Black Sea, Turkey,
and reaching as far as India. These routes caried a highly profitable trade, both export and import, and, as the Polish knights
rarely descended to robbing merchants, the trade flourished. Krakow, situated at the crossroads, became a very important center
for this trade and, though far from the sea, became a member of
the Hanseatic League. There was a steady flow of goods by road
and by water to and from Krakow, along the Vistula to Danzig
and the Baltic, whence Polish ships sailed to all parts of Europe.

The Jagiellonian dynasty (1386-1572), which followed the
Piasts, introduced into Poland the Eastern element, which subse-
quently was to play an important role in the history of Poland.
The Jagiellonian period opens with the union of Poland and
Lithuania through the marriage of the Polish queen Jadwiga, the
daughter of Louis of Anjou, who in Hungary was Louis the
Great, to the great duke of Lithuania, Jagiello, in 1385. Lithuan-

---

foreigners. Among the professors there were several outstanding scholars, while
counted among the student body were such famous men as Nicholas Copernicus, Jan
Dlugosz and the German humanist Celtes.

[3] From the fifteenth century, however, the role of the knights and their relationship to the state was altered. In consequence of the invention and application of
gunpowder, methods of warfare were fundamentally changed and the famous Polish
Hussars became useless. From then on, there was a general levy of knights only in
case of emergency and gradually having hitherto despised agricultural occupations,
the knights returned to their manors and began to organize their estates.

ians in 1253 formed a kingdom which expanded immensely south-
ward toward the Black Sea and included Ruthenia. As Lithuania
remained heathen, however, the Teutonic Knights raided her
territory under the pretext of spreading Christianity. The Polish-
Lithuanian union was established primarily to defend both states
against German pressure. Lithuania accepted Christianity through
Poland and Jagiello founded the Jagiellonian dynasty. The first
bishopric, founded at Wilno, at once received privileges analogous
to those of the church in Poland. The first chapter of privileges
was simultaneously granted to the Lithuanian boyars; it proclaimed the principle by which the boyars were to obtain all the
rights enjoyed by the Polish nobility. The Polish-Lithuanian Commonwealth became the strongest, largest, and most progressive
state in eastern Europe, spreading from the Baltic to the Black
Sea and from Silesia to the vicinity of Moscow. In included among
its cities Poznan, Warsaw, Danzig, Riga, Krakow, Lwow, Wilno,
Minsk, and Smolensk, and nearly all the provinces drained by
the Dnieper River. The University of Casimir the Great, in
Krakow, under Queen Jadwiga's patronage, was renovated; the
Sorbonne with its brilliant theological department was taken as
a model. In the battle of Grunwald, on July 15, 1410, the Teutonic Order was utterly defeated and its power was broken
forever by the combined Polish-Lithuanian army in one of the
great battles of the Middle Ages. Jagiello's son, Wladyslaw, became the King of Hungary; he tried to crush the Turkish power
and remove that danger to Christendom, but he lost his life at
Warna, in 1444, at the head of a combined Polish-Hungarian
army. Under his brother, Casimir, the Commonwealth achieved
prosperity. The gentry, which at that time constituted ten per
cent of the nation, were accorded voting privileges. In the war
with the Teutonic Knights, Poland regained Danzig and Pomerania, incorporated part of East Prusia, and extended her suzerainty over the remainder of the country, which became her fief.
Casimir also secured the crown of Bohemia and Hungary for his
son. The Jagiellonian dynasty thus ruled over all east-central
Europe. This period in Polish history is also characterized by the
introduction of humanism, the spread of the Renaissance move-

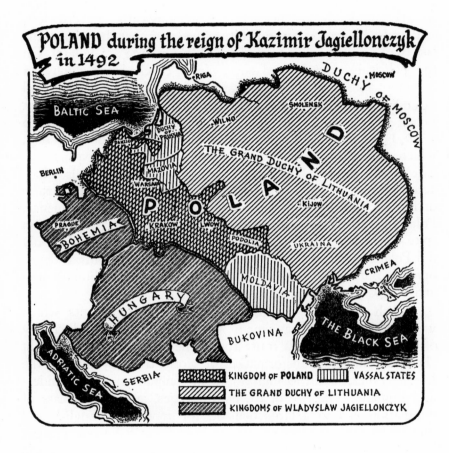

POLAND during the reign of Kazimir Jagiellonczyk in 1492

KINGDOM OF **POLAND** · VASSAL STATES
THE GRAND DUCHY OF LITHUANIA
KINGDOMS OF WLADYSLAW JAGIELLONCZYK

ment, the spread of the Hussite movement, and the secularization and the supremacy of the State over the Church.

The beginning of the sixteenth century was marked by the introduction of the parliamentary system, in which the Parlia-ment (Sejm) had to approve all important decisions of the kings. In the sixteenth century, the Commonweath, nevertheless, achieved such prosperity and cultural progress that the reign of the last two Jagiellonians is termed the "Golden Age" of Poland. On the political scene Poland successfully checked the duchy of Moscow; agreed to the secularization of the Teutonic Order; and extended her borders in Inflanty (Latvia), as that province sought Polish protection against the duchy of Moscow and Sweden. In 1569, Poland and Lithuania entered into a close union at Lublin, which unified both nations under one king and one parliament. The rule of the last Jagiellonian, Sigismund August, is also char-acterized by a religious tolerance almost unknown in other parts of Europe, which was torn by religious wars. As a consequence, Poland gave asylum to many Scottish and French Protestants, in spite of the Roman Catholic majority in the country. Not only did Poland reach in that century the climax of its political devel-opment, but also it experienced material prosperity, literacy and artistic glory, and international influence.

Polish prosperity was directly influenced by events which were taking place at that time in Western Europe. The discovery of America and the sea route round the Cape to India brought about a complete transformation of world trade by making the Mediterranean basin less important in comparison with Flanders and England. The rise of towns and cities, and the increase of population, led to a large demand for foodstuffs. English and Flemish merchants went to seek grain in Eastern Europe. Danzig became a flourishing center for the export of grain, livestock, and timber; and the peasants and merchants of Poland began to draw large profits. As a result a passion for bourgeois comfort spread everywhere. In Krakow, stories were added to houses and the number of rooms was increased. The entrance hall was abandoned as a sleeping place. Beds took the place of pallets; plate and furniture accumulated. Contentment with primitive simplicity gave way to the quest for material goods.

Seeing the possibility of wealth in the export of agricultural products, the nobles, who lived in comfortable manor houses on broad acres, secured a dominant position in the grain business.[4] Faced, however, with an almost insurmountable difficulty, the absence of labor, they secured a limitation of the personal freedom of the peasants to prevent them from moving from the soil on which they lived and worked to the free land which was available in eastern Poland.[5] As land without the peasant's labor was worthless, it was the interest of the nobles to hold him fast to it, thus making the peasant virtually a part of real property and depriving him of the opportunities available through migration. The struggle of the gentry against the peasants and burghers as well as the king for complete supremacy in the state was the turning point in Polish history. The aims of the nobles were threefold: (1) the concentration of all land in their hands and the creation of large estates for the production of grain for export; (2) the commuting of the rent system into serfdom in order to obtain sufficient labor; and (3) the direction and control of the state.

With the death of Sigismund, in 1570, the Jagiellonian dynasty became extinct, and kings of the Polish Commonwealth were to be elected by the electors, an assembly of nobles and higher dignitaries of the church. Each elected king had to sign the "Pacta Conventa," a plege to maintain the liberties of the Commonwealth. Every attempt to limit the influence of the nobles was doomed to failure; especially since any power exercised by the king was discontinued during the interregnum following his death; during which nobles, the wealthier members in particular, controlled the destiny of the Commonwealth. Since it was easier

---

[4] When the nobles acquired the monopoly of the grain export, the share of the towns in trade dwindled to nothing. It consisted of the import of luxury goods for the nobles and the export of goods manufactured in the towns, enough to maintain the population, but not enough to bring any prosperity to the towns. In 1493, the nobles acquired the right to import goods, duty free, for their own consumption. This privilege of exemption from import and export duties is almost unique in the history of Europe.

[5] In 1466, the nobles acquired the right to expropriate the peasants from their holdings on payment of a compensation according to the value of the land. Later, however, in the process of consolidating their estates, they frequently exercised this right without any compensations. In 1633, a law was passed which transformed into a serf every colonist who lived at least one year on the nobleman's land.

to impose terms of the "Pacta Conventa" on foreigners, the great majority of the Polish kings after the sixteenth century were of foreign blood. In the year 1573, the throne of Poland was offered to Henry of Valois, Duke of Anjou, afterwards Henry III of France.[6] His reign was followed by Stephen Batory (1576-86) who turned out to be one of the wisest and bravest of the Polish kings. He strengthened Polish authority in Danzig, and he conducted three victorious campaigns against Ivan the Terrible, thus winning back Polotsk and insuring Poland's rule over the whole of Livonia. In internal affairs, his greatest deeds were the creation of courts of appeal, which made the organization of jurisdiction more efficient and the founding in 1579 of a university in Wilno. Stefan Batory also struggled against the autocracy of the gentry, though generally without success. On one occasion he said to a gentleman named Kazimierski: "Silence, you clown!" He received the following answer: "I am not a clown, but I elect kings and I do away with tyrants!"[7] What would have been the fate of a French or Spanish gentleman of the time, had he dared to answer his king in this manner?[8]

Stefan Batory was succeeded by the members of the Swedish House of Vasa, who were in turn followed by Michael Wisniowiecki, John Sobieski, August I, Stanislaus Leszczynski,[9] August II, and Stanislaus Augustus Poniatowski.

---

[6] When the throne of Poland was offered to Henry of Valois, twelve Polish ambassadors accompanied by 150 young nobles arrived in Paris on August 19th, overwhelming the French inhabitants with the splendor of their appeal. They occupied fifty carriages, each drawn by four or six richly harnessed horses, and wore loose-flowing robes of Oriental appearance, caps trimmed with fur and scimitars studded with precious stones. When they were presented to Prince Henry in the Louvre, they wore robes of cloth of gold. What amazed the French was that they were able to converse in Latin, French, German, and Italian as well as in their own language. John Murray Gibbon, Canadian Mosaic, (New York: 1939), p. 267.

[7] Manfred Kridl, A Survey of Polish Literature and Culture, (New York: 1956), p. 41.

[8] This liberal and democratic principle, unfortunately, concerned only one social class, which consistently and stubbornly refused to grant rights to burghers and peasants. The Polish gentleman was one of the freest men in Europe, and he was proud of the fact that he owned nothing to his king except a realty tax, war duty, and the use of the royal name in court summons. The concept of divine right, of the king annointed by God, which still prevailed in the rest of Europe, had disappeared in Poland a long time before. Together with the fall of monarchical power, worship of the king, who was only a nominal ruler, also disappeared.

[9] The daughter of King Stanislaus Leszczynski, Marie Leszczynska, married King Louis XV of France in 1725. King Stanislaus, after he lost his throne in Poland, became the Duke of Lorraine in France.

During the Vasa period, Poland fought long and bloody wars against the duchy of Moscow, Sweden, Turks, Tartars, and Cossacks, who rebelled against the Polish magnates in the Ukraine.[10] In 1596, the religious union was concluded between the Catholic and Orthodox churches in Poland, as a result of which the Orthodox population became Catholics of the Greek rite. The devout Catholic attitude of Sigismund III, however, prevented his son from being elected Czar of Russia, and thus the eventual union of Poland and Russia was frustrated.

Polish-Turkish wars during the reign of John Sobieski reached a peak with his victory over a huge Turkish army besieging Vienna in 1683. His victory, inspired by the defense of Christendom, brought the liberation of Hungary, and marked the beginning of Turkish retreat in Europe. With the death of Sobieski also dies the power and glory of the Old Commonwealth. Nothing was done to better the status and condition of the peasantry. As the seventeenth century wore on, their situation grew worse. The following conversation quoted by a contemporary writer gives a witty idea of their lot.

> A gentleman said to a peasant: "You poor thing, you work so hard in this world; surely you will go to Heaven after you die." The peasant replied: "And who would chop the wood for the Lord and make his fire in hell? There is no other way, I must follow him there too."[11]

In the eighteenth century, Poland declined steadily under the rule of the Saxon kings. Culture and learning reached their lowest level. The degeneration of the parliamentary system was brought about by the "Liberum Veto," a rule by which all laws had to be passed unanimously. Financial mismanagement caused the reduction of the standing army. Religious intolerance of the kings, decline of towns, the supremacy and selfishness of magnates, and

---

[10] In the Pereyaslav Treaty in 1654 the Cossacks submitted themselves to the duchy of Moscow. In the following period, known in Polish history as "The Deluge," Poland was attacked by Sweden, duchy of Moscow, and Transylvania. Polish territory was almost completely occupied. Soon, however, Poland regained her position and the army led by Czarnecki drove out the enemies. The Ukraine was to become, through the Union of Hadziacz in 1658, a third autonomous part of the Commonwealth, but agreement was cancelled by the Ukrainian-Turkish alliance.

[11] Kridl, op. cit., p. 98.

the pauperization of the country for the sake of the vain foreign kings and aristocrats characterize that period. The decline of education brought indifference and apathy among the gentry. Suffering from these and other defects, the Commonwealth could not long resist the invasion and interference in the internal

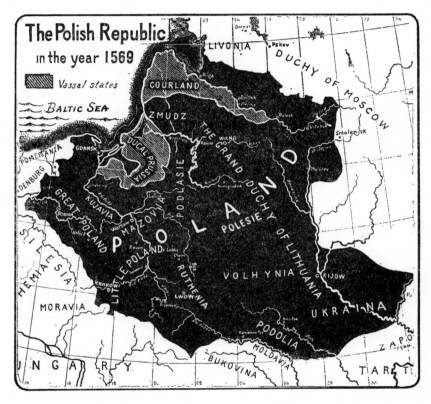

Polish affairs of outside powers who excelled each other in aggressiveness and in their territorial greed. However, the first partition of 1772, brought a revival on a greater scale as the spirit of indifference was shaken.

The revival began when educational reforms were attempted under the last Polish king, Stanislaus August Poniatowski. Among the reforms was the first establishment in Europe of an official board of education, stronger government, and extension of privileges to towns. The Four-Year Parliament also enacted a progressive constitution on May 3, 1791, which was adopted without bloodshed. Based on the American and French democratic ideas, the constitution aimed at the revival of Poland and reformed her political structure. As those challenged the foreign interfer- ence and influence, they brought on the second partition of Poland

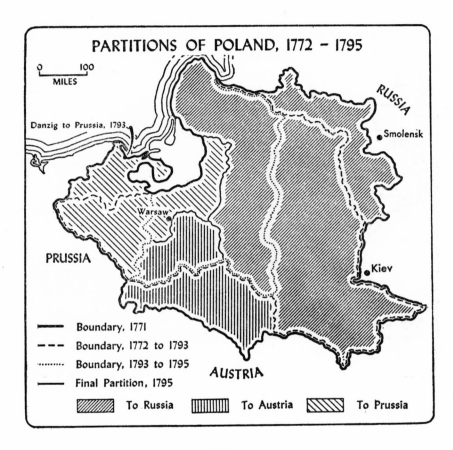

PARTITIONS OF POLAND, 1772 – 1795

in 1793 between Prussia and Russia. When the partition reduced Poland to the status of a protectorate, a national uprising began in 1794. In spite of the many valiant attempts and struggles of men like Kosciuszko and others, Poland was overrun finally by its hostile neighbors and the third partition, which erased Poland from the map of Europe, followed in 1795.

The reform of the Constitution of 1791 inspired future generations in their struggle for Polish independence. The hopes of the
partitioned Polish nation were tied to the emerging military
power of France under Napoleon Bonaparte. In the course of
Napoleon's war with Prussia and Austria, Poland was recreated
as a small duchy of Warsaw. The 1812 disaster of the French army
in Russia, supported by a Polish army of 80,000 shattered all
hopes of the Polish nationals for the rebuilding of the Polish state.
The Congress of Vienna of 1815 formed a small Kingdom of Poland in a personal union with Russia out of parts of the duchy of
Warsaw, while the residue of Poland was annexed by Russia, Prussia, and Austria. The material and social progress of the kingdom
was, however, marred by the tyranny of the Grand Duke Constantine, brother of Czar Alexander I. The ascent of absolute and reactionary Nicholas I on the Russian and Polish thrones resulted in
political tensions and in the desire for independence. While Polish
leaders abroad tried to tie the Polish cause to all major international
conflicts, the patriotic elements in Poland prepared the 1830 and
1863 insurrections. The collapse of the insurrections resulted in
the wholesale emigration of the military and intellectual elite of
Poland to western Europe where they hoped to rebuild Poland
in an alliance with similar western movements. Thus Poles took
part in all the revolutions of the period from 1830 to 1871.

The oppression of the Russians and Prussians and the heavy
losses sustained in armed efforts to regain independence, resulted
in the spread of positivistic theories which stressed improvement
of economic and social conditions. The turn of the nineteenth
century brought the development of political organizations which,
although united in the final goal, approached it in different ways.
Two political orientations emerged during World War I. The
majority of Galician parties, led by Pilsudski and the Socialists,
advocated action against Russia; the National Democrats, led by
Dmowski, wanted to achieve independence with Russian support
against Germany. The Western powers, allied with Russia, could
not openly support the Polish claims for independence. The Western Powers officially recognized the Polish National Committee
headed by Dmowski only after the Russian revolution which
recognized Polish rights to independence. When President Wil-

son officially made the independence of Poland one of the Fourteen Points on which peace could be concluded, other Allied powers followed suit and Poland was recognized as an Allied nation.

At the close of World War I, the Polish Republic was established in Warsaw with Pilsudski, as a temporary chief of state. While the western frontiers were delimited by the Treaty of Versailles and the Silesian plebiscite, the eastern frontiers were fixed only after the Soviet-Polish war of 1919-21. Polish borders received recognition by the Council of Ambassadors in 1923 and thus Poland was able to concentrate on her internal problems. During the twenty years of independence, Poland modernized and expanded her industry, and achieved marked progress especially in removing the effects of the uneven economic development of the country as a result of over a century of occupation. That progress, however, was checked by the German invasion of Poland which caused World War II and abruptly terminated the independent life of Poland.

# CHAPTER TWO

# Pioneer Polish Immigrants 1608-1776

The Poles are not strangers to America, even though there never was a New Poland on a map of America to match the New Spain or New England claimed for those countries.[1] Polish roots reach to the very formative times of the Republic, for in one way or another, Poles played a part in the building of the new continent. They came in their greatest numbers in the years between 1880 and 1910, when the "opportunity line" thinned out in partitioned Poland and grew bolder in America; but in reality, their kinfolk had gone to America much earlier. They were among the sailors who discovered its shores, among the explorers who traced its many contours, among the builders who constructed ships, among the workers who helped to level the forests, among the farmers who struggled to clear fields and remove the tremendous roots of virgin forests, and among the soldiers who fought for the independence of the new country. They knew how to endure adversity; they could fight when fighting was needed; and they had an instinct not only for exploring new paths but also the strength and ingenuity to build new communities out of the virgin forests. These early Polish pioneers did not find gold in America, but they found perhaps a rarer and more valuable ore—opportunity. They had come here to realize a fuller life as individuals, and in the belief that America had a future which human effort might shape. American conditions proved that they were not wrong. For there was in America a system of opportunity that gave scope to their energies and managed tolerably to give aspiration its outlet, talent its stimulus, and ability its reward. It was opportunity that was missing in Poland after its

---

[1] Duke Jacob of Courland purchased from Holland two small islands of Tobago and St. Andrew in the Carribean. These two and only Polish colonies in the American hemisphere, which were settled in 1652, remained in Poland's possession until 1737.

partition, and it was opportunity that they found in America. And it was their accomplishments and ideals which have given a hint of the contributions which Poles in the future may make to the sum of human happiness and American culture.

The accounts of Polish immigration to America usually begin with a mention of John of Kolno (a town in Masovia, north central Poland.) A Polish seafarer and explorer, he was in the service of Christian, King of Denmark, and is said to have piloted a fleet of Danish ships which touched the coast of Labrador and then sailed down to the mouth of the Delaware River in 1476. If the tale be true, about which there is a persistent tradition in Polish lore, a Pole was in America sixteen years before Columbus crossed the Atlantic Ocean.[2]

Francis Warnadowicz, a Pole, who settled in Cadiz, Spain, under the name of Francisco Fernandez, is said to have taken part in Columbus' voyage of 1492; however, there is no documentary evidence to support this fact. It is known that a Fernandez was left at Hispaniola by Columbus. He later perished at the hands of the Indians, thus becoming the first European to claim such an unrewarding distinction.[3]

When did the Poles begin to arrive in America? Sources that might supply the answer are meager. There are no records of the arrival in what is now the United States of the first Polish nationals. But it seems certain that at an early date Poles appeared in the various streams of colonization primarily as individuals. One must remember that it was not until the nineteenth century that the world became seriously interested in the nationality and language of a person. The medieval period had thought only in terms of allegiance to a given monarch or to some supernational state which embraced persons of many tongues and origins, united in a common loyalty. This held true for the first two centuries of American settlement and must be taken into account. It is

---

[2] Miecislaus Haiman, *Polish Past in America 1608-1865*, (Chicago: 1939), pp. 5-6. Ks. Waclaw Kruszka, *Historja Polska w Ameryce*, (Milwaukee: 1905-1908), I, p. 52. His second edition, published in 1937, devotes pages 20 to 27 to John of Kolno. Jacek K. Furdyna "Scolvus' Discovery of Labrador," *Polish American Studies*, IX (July-December, 1952), pp. 68-78. Jerzy Pertek, *Polacy Na Szlakach Morskich Swiata*, (Gdansk: 1957).

[3] Ks. Waclaw Kruszka, *Historja Polska w Ameryce*, (Milwaukee: 1937), I, p. 32.

barely possible that the first Polish immigrants to settle permanently in North America were pitch burners, who disembarked in
1585, in Roanoke, North Carolina, with Sir Walter Raleigh, who
wanted to establish a center for the production of pitch with
the aid of these Polish specialists. The objective of this venture
was to make England independent of Poland's monopoly.[4]

It is an established fact, however, that when Captain Christopher Newport anchored his colonial ships, "Mary and Margaret,"
off the Jamestown shore of Virginia, on October 1, 1608, he had
on board the following Poles: Michael Lowicki, a Polish nobleman;
Zbigniew Stefanski, a glass production specialist; Jan Mata, a
soap producer; Jan Bogdan of Kolomyja, pitch, tar, and ship
building expert; Stanislaw Sadowski, and Karol Zrenica.[5] These
skilled pioneers proved to be such an asset to the first English
colony that more of their fellow-countrymen were invited to settle
in Jamestown.[6] Eventually the following Poles made their homes in
Virginia: Mateusz Gramza, Michal Korczewski, Herman Kromka,
Jan Kulawy, Ignacy Machowski, Jedrzej Malaszko, Eustachy
Micinski, Thomas Mietus, Gwidon Stojka, Mikolaj Syrynski,
Wlodzimierz Terlecki, and Karol Zrenica. Within a few years,
fifty Poles were living in Jamestown.[7]

Captain John Smith expressed in his manuscript, *True Travels*,
now located in the Folger Shakespeare Library, Washington, D.C.,
great respect for and satisfaction with the Poles in his colony.[8]
He gave recognition to the Poles as good soldiers against hostile

---

[4] Jerzy Zubrzycki, *Polish Immigrants in Britain*, (Hague: 1956), p. 195.
Henry Archacki, "The Search for Clues in Sir Walter Raleigh's 'Lost Colonies,'"
*Polish American Journal*, (January 31, 1959), p. 2.

[5] Arthur L. Waldo, *First Poles in America* 1608-1958, (Pittsburg: 1956),
p. 5. Ks. Waclaw Kruszka, *Historja Polska w Ameryce*, (Milwaukee: 1937), I, p.
70. Albert Q. Maisel, *They All Chose America*, (New York: 1957), p. 207.

[6] Adela Lagodzinska, *The Polish Heritage and the Future of Chicago*, (Chicago: 1953), p. 3.

[7] Alvin Duke Chandler, "The Poles at Jamestown," *The Polish Review*, II
(Autumn, 1957), p. 4.

[8] Captain John Smith has reason to respect and admire the Poles. Only a few
years before, in Europe's war with the Turks, he had been captured by the Turks
and enslaved. Upon his escape, he found himself in Poland. In his manuscript,
Captain Smith describes how he crossed Poland, aided every foot of the way by
a people unmatched in his experience for, as he said it, "respect, mirth, content and
entertainment," who insisted on loading him with gifts before sending him on to the
next town.

Indians; as saviors of the Virginia colony; and as good crafts-men. According to Captain John Smith, "they and the Dutchmen were the only ones who knew what work was!"[9] It is recorded that in 1609 when the Indians set an ambush to kill him, the Poles saved his life and captured an Indian chief.[10]

As was the custom then, almost all of the colonists had worked out their passage by pledging themselves to labor for the company that owned the settlement. Within two to three years, the Polish immigrants had repaid the company for the passage by ship from Europe, and became free citizens of the community. Immediately upon their arrival they set to work to build a glass furnace on a tract of land alloted them about a mile from the fort. They also cut down trees for wood manufacturers. When the English ship was ready to sail for England across the Atlantic Ocean, it carried a full line of samples the glassmakers were prepared to turn out in commercial quantities, as well as a cargo of pitch dis-tilled from Virginia's pine trees, and other products of the field and forest which the Poles had manufactured. These were in fact the first products of American industry.

These Polish immigrants to Jamestown were among the first champions of American civil liberties. Colonial records of Virginia reveal a group of Poles somewhat disturbed and bestirred during the session of the first Virginia assembly. On the 30th day of June, 1619, when the House of Burgesses ushered in representa-tive government in America, the Poles appeared upon the scene as political dissenters protesting an undemocratic wrong which was being perpetrated in Jamestown, the cradle of democracy. Because they were not of English descent, they were disfranchised by the company authorities. In protest, the Poles refused to work until accorded the same voting privileges as those enjoyed by the English settlers; so they suspended operations in the glass factory, the tar distillery, and the soap establishments.

Thus it happened that those summer days of 1619 were to wit-

---

9 William Seabrook, *These Foreigners*, (New York: 1938), p. 250. Captain John Smith, *True Travels*, (Richmond: 1819), I, p. 240.

10 Robert H. Ferrell, "The United States and East Central Europe Before 1941," *The Fate of East Central Europe*, Stephen D. Kertesz, Editor, (Notre Dame: 1956), p. 21.

ness not only the first popular assembly in America but also the first labor walkout. Governor Yeardley and the legislature were not long in undoing this political injustice; they quickly realized that if the colony sent empty ships to England, the consequences could be very unpleasant. Except for the few pounds of tobacco the English colonists were beginning to export, practically all of the profits realized by the London Company came from the re-sale of the products of the Polish industries. The governor gave the following account of the incident in the *Virginia County Court Book*.

> Upon some dispute of the Polonians resident in Virginia, it was now agreed (notwithstanding any former order to the contrary) that they shall be enfranchised and made as free as any inhabitants there what-soever: and because their skill in making pitch and tar and soap ashes shall not die with them it is agreed that some young men shall be put unto them to learn their skill and knowledge therein for the benefit of the country hereafter.[11]

From the excerpt, it is evident that this first strike in America was conducted not for higher wages and better working conditions, as is so often the objective today, but for democratic rights.

The joint or collective protest of the Jamestown Poles suggests that they had settled together as a group and were looked upon by the early settlers as an ethnic group. Whether or not attempts were made to form distinct Polish colonies, both in the colonial as well as in the political immigration periods, cannot be determined. Not one study or research treatise has brought this possibility to light. Such an establishment would not be surprising. Such was the tendency at the time. The Swedes had their New Sweden; the Dutch their New Holland; and the English their New England.

Social and economic relations between Poland and Sweden during the seventeenth century were very close.[12] Thus it is not

---

[11] Susan Myra Kingsbury, *An Introduction to the Records of the Virginia Company of London*, (Washington, D. C.: 1950), I, p. 251. Haiman, *op. cit.*, pp. 14-15.

[12] Political relations between Poland and Sweden, during this period especially, were very unfriendly. The Swedes were in control of both Livonia and Estonia. Desiring to make the Baltic a "Swedish Lake," they were in continuous warfare with Poland. Swedish representatives were deeply involved in negotiations

surprising that there were Poles in the colony of New Sweden, the area in which the traditionally American form of the log cabin seems to have originated, a form reminiscent of the architecture of the East Baltic Slavs.[13] The organizer of the South Company for Swedish colonization of America, William Usselinx, made a tour through the northern provinces of Poland in 1627, to raise funds for his unredeemed project. When the Swedes eliminated the first Dutch settlement around Fort Casimir, they founded in 1641 their own Fort Christina and sent over a population of Swedes, Germans, Poles, and Finns. The presence of the Poles in New Sweden is attested by a mention of the children of Paul Malich, "the little Pole," who evidently became orphaned and received aid in clothes, food, shoes, and other articles in 1655, from a charity fund established by Governor Rising.[14]

During the sixteenth and seventeenth centuries, Poland also conducted a lively trade with Holland. This resulted in the formation of strong cultural ties between the two countries. In addition, during the seventeenth century, Amsterdam harbored a numerous Polish Protestant colony; in fact, the city became an important intellectual center of the Polish Arians, or the Polish Brothers (Fratres Poloni), who were expelled from Poland because of their guileful behavior during the Swedish invasion of Poland in 1655 and 1656. Thus it is not surprising that as early as 1659, Governor Stuyvesant, to prevent the English from disrupting the Dutch beaver-trade in America, tried to induce the Directors of the West India Company in Holland to send him twenty-five to thirty families from Poland. This request became urgent especially after the New Englanders endeavored to settle near Fort Orange, at the mouth of the Wappinger Creek in 1659. To prevent the English from settling in the neighborhood of the Dutch settlers, the Directors of the West India Company replied that they would make efforts to get some Polish farmers; they

with the Kozaks who were in almost constant state of revolt against Poland. Because of the Polish-Swedish conflicts, Sweden was unable to protect her American possessions. As a result Sweden ultimately lost her "New Sweden" colony in 1655.

[13] Clarence A. Manning, A History of Slavic Studies in the United States, (Milwaukee: 1957), p. 4.

[14] Miecislaus Haiman, Poles In New York in the 17th and 18th Centuries, (Chicago: 1938), p. 51.

would turn to the Polish nobleman, Lodem Rachio and others for help and assistance.[15]

This episode was not the only case of direct intercourse between the West India Company and Poland. For example, Hendrick Hendricksen of Elbingh, in Poland, is mentioned as being in correspondence with the Directors of the Company in 1657. A certain William Janse van Danstick is also mentioned in 1699. A very great obstacle in identifying Poles in documents pertaining to New Holland is the old Dutch custom of using patronymics instead of family names. To this must be added another difficulty, that of Hollandizing Polish names. Nevertheless, many distinct traces of Poland's connections with the colony have survived.

Among the early Polish settlers to reside in New Amsterdam at the tip of Manhattan Island was Daniel Litscho. He is first mentioned in documents as father of a daughter, Anna, baptized in the Dutch Church in New Amsterdam, on June 6th, 1647. Litscho's wife was the Dutch widow of Jan Jansen Swaartveger, a soldier in the Dutch service in Brazil. It is probable that before coming to New Amsterdam, Litscho also served in Brazil and that he came there with Christopher Arciszewski, Admiral in the Dutch service and famous Polish seafarer and South American explorer. He is mentioned for the first time in 1648, as tavernkeeper at New Amsterdam: later references to him as tavernkeeper are very numerous.[16] Litscho's tavern played a prominent part in the life of New Amsterdam. It stood on the site now occupied by the building at No. 125 Pearl Street. It consisted of a large house and a quarter of an acre of land with a small orchard. In 1651 he leased this house and built a new tavern in Wall Street, just outside the city gate, but eventually he returned to the old place and lived there till his death.

Business did not interfere with Litscho's military duties. In 1651 he participated in Stuyvesant's expedition against the Swedes on the Delaware, and on July 30th signed, with some others, a deposition of the Indians pertaining to the sale of land to the Swedes. During Stuyvesant's dispute with Van Slechtenhorst for the sovereign rights of Rensselaerswych, Litscho accompanied

15 *Ibid.*, pp. 28-29.
16 *Ibid.*, pp. 30-31.

the Governor up the Hudson. Acting on his orders, he entered Van Slechtenhorst's house with a detachment of fourteen soldiers and, after firing a volley, hauled down the patroon's flag from the staff and hoisted the colonial colors. This episode, according to O'Callaghan, "released the germ of the present city of Albany from feudal jurisdiction."[17] In 1653, Litscho is mentioned as Senior Sergeant, commanding the fourth company of burgher corps of New Amsterdam. In December, 1654, Stuyvesant advanced him to the rank of "Lieutenant in the Burgher Companies." His last military services seem to have been in 1655, when he took part in war preparations against the Swedes. The expedition ended with the capture of Fort Casimir in the summer of 1655.[18]

Litscho was considered one of the most influential burghers. He often participated in the deliberations of the Council of Burgomasters and Schepens. Usually he aligned himself with the party of Governor Stuyvesant. On March 4, 1649, he voted with them against Adriaen van der Donck, the leader of the popular party. He also was present at the Council on November 11, 1653, when Stuyvesant was forced to yield to the popular demands for liberties. In 1652, when the New Hollanders, fearing an attack of the New Englanders, began to fortify their city feverishly, Litscho contributed 100 guldens towards improving the defenses of the city. Litscho was also fire inspector, but resigned from this office on December 20, 1658, because of his "bad sight and other inconveniences." Lieutenant Litscho died in 1661 or 1662. In his will, dated December 26, 1661, he assigned four hundred florins in "good strung wampum,"to his stepson, Hermanus Jansen Swaartveger, who was born in Castel Rio Grande, in Brazil, and to his daughter, Anna Litscho, also four hundred florins. These sums were to be paid them when they became of age and married.[19]

---

[17] *Ibid.*, p. 32.

[18] Fort Casimir was the first geographical place in the New World bearing a Polish name. It was built by Governor Stuyvesant in 1651, after demolition of the Swedish Fort Nassau. It was named after John Casimir who reigned in Poland at that time. At the time of the construction of Fort Casimir, Sweden began preparations for an invasion of Poland and it is very possible that Stuyvesant gave it the name of the Polish King to irritate the Swedes. Fort Casimir was renamed Fort Trinity upon seizure by the Swedes in 1654, New Amstel after the Dutch conquest of New Sweden in 1655, and New Castle when the British captured New Netherland.

[19] *Ibid.*, p. 34.

Anna married Colonel William Peartree, who was Mayor of the City of New York between 1703-1707. She was the grandmother of William Peartree Smith, also prominent in the history of New York City. Her will of 1730, showing much affection for her grandson who early became an orphan, reveals her as a benevolent and intelligent woman.

Of greater importance to the small colonial Dutch city was the appointment, in 1659, of the Polish schoolmaster, Dr. Alexander Karol Kurczewski (Curtius) to the position of teacher.[20] He was to provide education for the youth in the New Amsterdam community. Peter Stuyvesant was delighted with Dr. Kurczewski, and after a short period of service, recommended to the Amsterdam Chamber that he be given an increase in salary. In his report to the Company, Stuyvesant made the following observation.

> As to his service and diligence we must truly testify that his industry is astonishing and the progress of the young people remarkable.[21]

A teacher of languages, Dr. Kurczewski tried to teach Russian and Polish to the New Amsterdam citizens, but they preferred their native Dutch.[22] Dr. Kurczewski is also credited with founding the first Latin School in what is now New York City.[23] With the exception of Harvard University, this academy was the oldest institution of its kind in the present United States.[24] In addition, besides being a schoolmaster, Dr. Kurczewski was also one of the New Amsterdam's first physicians.[25] In the history of American education, he is known as Alexander Curtiss.[26]

John Rutkowski and Casimir Butkiewicz also had been engaged as teachers in New Amsterdam. Wojciech Adamkiewicz was a successful builder in the old Dutch city.[27] Captain Marcin

---

[20] Henry H. Kessler and Eugene Rachels, *Peter Stuyvesant and His New York*, (New York: 1959), p. 208. Ks. Waclaw Kruszka, *Historja Polska w Ameryce*, (Milwaukee: 1937), I. pp. 85-86.

[21] *Ibid.*, p. 208.

[22] Sigmund J. Sluszka, "America Had a Slavic Language Problem Long Before the Coming of the Mayflower in 1620," *AATEEL Bulletin*, (June 4, 1953), p. 1.

[23] Kruszka, *op. cit.*, p. 85. Lagodzinska, *op. cit.*, p. 4.

[24] Sister Mary Remigia Napolska, *The Polish Immigrant in Detroit to 1914*, (Chicago: 1946), pp. 20-21.

[25] *Ibid.*, p. 21.

[26] Curtiss High School on Staten Island, New York City, was named in honor of the first academy founder and foreign language teacher, Kurczewski.

[27] Kruszka, *op. cit.*, p. 85.

Krygier had been elected co-Burgomaster of New Amsterdam in 1653. He served an additional term in 1654, and was elected to serve again in 1661. Krygier, Governor Stuyvesant's most trusted administrator, commanded also one of the town's forts named "Casimir."[28]

Besides those mentioned, other Poles, though less prominent, lived in New Holland. A certain John Bembo is mentioned in 1654, as a member of the garrison at Fort Orange. Jurriaen Hanouw, or Hand, thirty-four years old, from Great Poland, served as a soldier at Fort Casimir in 1656. On September 22nd of that year he appeared before the Council and requested that his bans be proclaimed so that he could enter into matrimony. Peter Targotsky, or Fergotsky, was stationed at Fort Casimir after the Dutch conquest of New Sweden.[29] Paul Palczowski, a graduate of the University of Padua, was among the most eminent Polish travellers of the seventeenth century to have visited America. Unfortunately the descriptions of his sixteen years of travel have come down to us only in part.[30]

In 1662, an exiled Polish nobleman, Olbracht Zaborowski, who claimed descent from King John Sobieski, settled in New Amsterdam and later acquired a large tract of land in the present County of Bergen, New Jersey. Haiman states that by 1682 his estate extended from the Hudson River on the east, to the Hackensack River on the west. Known as a trader, friend of the Indians, and interpreter,[31] Zaborowski held positions of authority, being among other things the first Justice of the Peace for Upper Bergen County, New Jersey.[32] He married Machtelt Van der Linden of New York on December 17, 1676. He was one of the founders of the Lutheran Church at Hackensack, New York, and for many years its leading member and chief supporter, though in 1680, for a

28 Edmund L. Kowalczyk, "Dr. Alexander Curtius," *Polish American Journal,* (October 10, 1959), p. 2.

29 Haiman, *Poles in New York in the 17th and 18th Centuries, pp.* 50-51.

30 Boleslaw Olszewicz, *Poland and the Discovery of America,* (Poznan: 1931), p. 28.

31 His signature as interpreter is found affixed to an Indian contract of purchase in 1679. Lagodzinska, *op. cit.,* p. 4.

32 Rev. Antoine M. Bochenski, S.T.L., O.M.C., "Our Youth and Its Polish-American Heritage," *Polish American Studies,* I (January-December, 1944), p. 49.

brief period, he joined the Dutch Church of Bergen. Olbracht died at Hackensack, where he settled permanently, on September 11, 1711. His widow died in 1725. His five sons intermarried with the most prominent colonial populations and were soon merged in the general population.

Of Olbracht Zaborowski's eldest son, Jacob, it is said that when seven years old, he was kidnapped by an Indian chief who took a liking to the boy. The sachem afterwards disclosed his deed to the father, with whom he lived on very friendly terms, and asked him to let the boy stay with the Indians. In that way he might acquire their language and learn their customs, and thus serve as arbitrator and interpreter between the Indians and the colonials, should disputes arise in the future. The father agreed and Jacob remained with the Indians for several years.[33]

John Zabriskie, grandson of Olbracht Zaborowski, filled the office of justice in New Jersey. In 1774, he was elected a member of the Bergen County Committee of Correspondence, which was organized for common action against the acts of the British parliament. When the Revolutionary War started, John Zabriskie was Colonel of militia of Bergen County. Choosing loyalty to the Crown, he resigned his commission. For this he paid later with the loss of his estate. It was confiscated by the revolutionary authorities and by an act of December, 1783, given to Major General Baron de Steuben.

> New Jersey gave to Steuben the life lease to a forfeited estate of John Zabriskie, lying in the County of Bergen, township of New Barbadoes, at the New Bridge, and in the immediate neighborhood of New York; but Steuben, when informed that Zabriskie, in consequence of that confiscation, was left without means, did not accept the gift, and interceded in behalf of Zabriskie.[34]

The documents also mention Albert Zabriskie, a loyalist, whose estate at Hackensack, consisting of approximately 143 acres, was confiscated June 10, 1779, because he had enlisted in the British army in December, 1776.

There is no record of the exact time when the Zabriskie family

---

[33] Haiman, *Poles in New York in the 17th and 18th Centuries*, p. 43.

[34] Miecislaus Haiman, *Poland and the American Revolutionary War*, (Chicago: 1932), p. 111.

took up residence in Passaic, New Jersey, but deeds recorded in the land office for Passaic County at Paterson, New Jersey, reveal purchases of land in Passaic County by Henry J. Zabriskie in 1816, by Christian B. Zabriskie in 1824, and by Abraham Zab-riskie in 1832.[35] Abraham Zabriskie built a dock in Passaic and operated a fleet of boats sailing to New York. He tried to improve the navigation facilities of the Passaic River and spent fifty thou-sand dollars for this purpose; the project was unsuccessful and brought about his financial ruin. Another member of the family, Dr. John B. Zabriskie, was licensed to practice medicine and surgery in New Jersey on November 4, 1826. Unable to make a success of his practice, he moved to New York and later settled in Jersey City. Still another descendant, Christian B. Zabriskie, took part in the planning of a bridge to be erected at some point between Zabriskie's Landing and the Dundee Dam before the Civil War, but the undertaking proved a failure.[36] Christian A. Zabriskie, who was born on March 14, 1829, was considered one of the oldest residents of Passaic. John C. Zabriskie, also from Passaic, took part in the Civil War.[37]

About the middle of the nineteenth century the name "Zbor-owski" was used. Martin Zborowski studied law in New York devoting himself particularly to the real estate branch of that profession, soon building up an immense and lucrative practice. Martin Zborowski later married Anna E. Morris, a member of Gouverneur Morris Family. At the outbreak of the Civil War

---

[35] Sister M. Gaudentia, Felician, "The Polish People of Passaic," *Polish American Studies*, V (July-December, 1948), p. 74.

[36] *Ibid.*, pp. 74-75.

[37] In the latter part of the 19th century, the Zabriskies of Passaic maintained close connections with some of Passaic's leading business concerns, particularly the Anderson Lumber Company, with whom Simeon T. Zabriskie was closely affiliated. Zabriskie A. Van Houten was a candidate for Freeholder of Passaic County in 1930, and during the campaign he spoke openly of his Polish ancestors. Recently Christian A. Zabriskie of New York donated Chopin's manuscript Impromptu in F sharp major to the Frederic Chopin Institute in Warsaw. The presentation was made at Madison Square Garden in New York City during the National Antiques Show. The gift was made in memory of the late Frances Hunter Zabriskie, who was a collector of historical memorabilia and an accomplished musician. Gifts made by the Zabriskie family to various institutions include collections of rare Civil War letters and manuscripts given to Harvard and Yale Universities and to the United States Military Academy at West Point. In 1951 Christian Zabriskie gave an 850-acre tract of land to Bard College.

he had already acquired a great deal of valuable real estate in New York City. By shrewd investments this estate had been greatly increased in value. Occupying as it does many holdings on Upper Broadway, the estate now exerts a powerful interest in New York business life. At the death of Elliott Zborowski his fortune was estimated at over $10,000,000.[38] The Zborowski family is very large, with many widely separated branches.[39] Several of the oldest families in New York, Brooklyn, and eastern New Jersey number Olbracht Zaborowski among their ancestors.[40] Among the early Americans of Polish stock, men outnumbered the women ten to one; thus many married the daughters of Dutch or English families and eventually their children did the same. In time the Polish language was largely forgotten; but the Polish names, though often with a few y's, sz's, and cz's dropped for the convenience of their neighbors, were proudly perpetuated.

Poles settled in the Delaware Valley as early as 1650. There was also a thin trickle of Polish immigrants into Pennsylvania and Virginia throughout the next hundred years. In the early years of the eighteenth century, when the European continent was swept by a wave of religious persecutions, following the revocation of the Edict of Nantes in France, a small group of Polish Protestants, attracted by fertile land, settled in New Jersey.[41]

Pennsylvania archives reveal that Polish immigrants have been a part of that colony since the days of its founder, William Penn. Pennsylvania colonial documents also mention Andrew Sanduski (Sadowski). In 1746, he possessed a "Plantation and a parcel of

---

[38] The violent death (April 1, 1903) in the automobile hill-climbing race between Nice and Laturbie, France of the New York society leader and famous polo player and horseman, Count William Elliott Zborowski, recalled the fact that Zborowski is the original Polish form of the name Zabriskie, which is so well known in America on account of the social prominence of so many members of the family. Louis E. Van Norman, *Poland The Knight Among Nations,* (New York: 1907), p. 342.

[39] At the fourteenth anniversary of the Polish Insurrection of 1830, there were present Zborowski descendants of Poles who settled in the United States one-hundred-and-eighty-years before.

[40] From this Olbracht Zaborowski came Chancellor Zabriskie of New Jersey and Dean George Gray of Harvard University. And there are strains of the same blood, according to Miss Emily Balch Green of Wellesley, in the American families of Astor, Bayard, Jay, Morrison, and Gouverneur Morris. Emily Greene Balch, *Our Slavic Fellow Citizens,* (New York: 1910), pp. 206-207.

[41] Zubrzycki, *op. cit.,* p. 195.

land," in Amity Township, Berks County.[42] The plantation was bequeathed by George Boone of Exeter, grandfather of Daniel Boone, to his son Jeremiah by his will of November 18th, 1753.[43] Besides the Sadowskis, the following of supposedly Polish origin lived in Pennsylvania: Jacob Brucki, Charles Gaski, Joseph and Mary Latzcho, and John Henry Kaekglosco.[44]

Polish pioneers also participated in the French and Indian War. Many served with New York Provincial troops during the French and Indian War. One of them was Christian Passasky, born at Albany, who enlisted in the County of Albany for Captain Robert McGinnis' Company, on March 31st, 1756, and reenlisted in Captain Stephen Schuyler's Company on May 3rd 1760. John Syrotjack, a weaver, who enlisted at Albany on May 19th, 1761, and Peter Collosha, laborer, who enlisted from Westchester County on May 15th, 1761, were perhaps of Polish origin, too. Joseph Galik was an English prisoner captured during the war.[45]

Many highly educated Poles rendered useful services to America in the delimitation of her boundaries. George Wenceslaus Golkowski made surveys of the territory around Nazareth and other settlements in Pennsylvania.[46] Captain Charles Blaszkowicz, a surveyor in the British service prior to the Revolutionary War, surveyed the coast of New England and drew the first map of that territory. Two of his maps are in the British Museum of London. The map of 1772 is entitled: "Coloured Plan of the Coast from Pleasant River to the Penobscot Bay, surveyed in 1772 by Charles Blaskowitz and James Grant, deputies to Surveyor-General Samuel Holland." The undated map bears the following title: "Coloured Plan of the Sea Coast from Cape Elizabeth on the West side of Easco Bay, of St. John River in the Bay of Funday, etc. Surveyed by Ensigns George Sproule, James Grant, Charles Blaskowitz and Thomas Wright, deputy surveyors." Another map, in the possession of the Russell Family of Plymouth, Massachusetts, bears the following inscription in Blaszkowicz's handwriting: "Plan of

42 Miecislaus Haiman, *Polish Pioneers of Pennsylvania*, (Chicago: 1941), p. 41.
43 *Ibid.*, p. 27.
44 *Ibid.*, p. 38.
45 Haiman, *Poles in New York in the 17th and 18th Centuries*, p. 54.
46 Bochenski, *op. cit.*, p. 49.

Plymouth, including Bays, Harbors and Islands etc., by Charles Blaskowitz, one of Deputy-Surveyors for North America and by him presented to Edward Winslow, June 1774." Blaszko-wicz's skill as cartographer is generally acknowledged.

> In 1876, Mr. Henry Mitchell of the United States Coast Survey, who was then stationed at Plymouth, made a partial sketch of the original Blaskowitz map, still in an excellent state of preservation, for the sake of making a scientific record of its early information upon Plymouth Harbor, its channels, soundings, etc., as they existed before the American Revolution. Mr. Mitchell in his official report, said: "In its topographical features the original plotting made by Blaskowitz from his survey of Plymouth is remarkable for accuracy and beauty"; "the details were admirably executed upon the original with pen and brush;" the map was "generally faithful."[47]

During the Revolutionary War, Blaskowicz remained loyal to the British flag. During the conflict he advanced to the rank of Captain in the British army. Evidently, during the conflict, he performed the duties of his profession. The following map was published at London in 1777: "A Topographical Chart of the Bay of Narragansett, in New England, taken by Charles Blasko-witz, and dedicated to Lord Percy, Lt. Gen. of his majesty's forces, showing the several works and batteries raised by the Amer-icans, with the banks, shoals and rocks." Sharing the fate of the Loyalists, he was transferred after the war to Canada. He remained in the British army as Captain on the staff of the Quartermaster General and in 1802 returned with half pay. He was summoned to duty during the War of 1812; he is mentioned in the docu-ments of 1812 and 1813 as Captain of the Royal Newfoundland Fencibles.

Casimir Theodore Goerck, perhaps the most influential among the Poles in New York City, was appointed surveyor for the city on April 6th, 1785.[48] In this position, which he held until his death, he made surveys and maps of many parts of New York City. On May 9th, 1787, he was also appointed one of two com-missioners "for the Direction and Management of the Real Prop-erty belonging to the City Corporation."[49] In 1797, be began

---

[47] Haiman, *Poland, and the American Revolutionary War*, p. 107.
[48] Haiman, *Poles in New York in the 17th and 18th Centuries*, p. 57.
[49] *Ibid.*, p. 57.

work on a general map of New York City, but death prevented him from completing it. Goerck married Elizabeth, sister of Cornelius Roosevelt, a merchant of New York and a great-great-granduncle of Theodore Roosevelt, and consequently, a blood tie connects a Polish immigrant with two presidents of the United States.[50] He had two children with Elizabeth, Henrietta and Theodore, who were still minors at the time of his death, which occurred some time before November 12, 1798. He fell victim to a malignant fever which raged throughout the country at that time. During his life, he resided at 67 Gold Street in New York City.

Among the Poles in colonial America were also typical backwoodsmen who adventurously explored the remote and uninhabited wilderness. The most prominent Polish frontiersman was undoubtedly Anthony Sadowski, a nobleman who came to Philadelphia before 1714. A daring individual, he became an Indian trader and interpreter in the colony. In 1735, he pushed into the wilderness beyond the Alleghenies into Ohio, Kentucky, and Tennessee, anticipating systematic white colonization in these regions by a hundred years. He established a trading post that is said to have been the forerunner of the busy industrial City of Sandusky (a corruption of the name Sadowski), Ohio.

When Sadowski was killed by Indians in Virginia, his pioneering ventures were continued by his descendants, the Sandusky boys, who became trailblazers in the Middle West. In the history of Kentucky, his sons, Jacob and James, are known as "long hunters, skilled Indian fighters and traders." They became companions of the famous Kentucky pioneer Daniel Boone.[51] In 1774 they became co-founders with Boone of Harrodsburg, the oldest town in Kentucky. Jacob and several companions are said to have made a canoe voyage in which they reached New Orleans by the Cumberland, Ohio, and the Mississippi Rivers, the first white men from the English colonies to descend those rivers.[52]

---

[50] Mondello, op. cit., p. 108.

[51] Haiman, Polish Past in America, 1608-1865, p. 20. Theodore Roosevelt, The Winning of the West, (New York: 1908), I. p. 193.

[52] Haiman, Polish Past in America, 1608-1865, pp. 19-22. Roosevelt, op. cit., I, p. 193.

Reverend Post, born in Chojnice, Poland, in 1710, also played an important part in opening up the West to English settlement. One of the scattered members of the Polish Moravian Church, he came to America in 1742. While in the service of the colonial authorities, as a Moravian missionary, he explored Pennsylvania, New York, Connecticut, and Ohio. In the year 1743, he did religious work among the Iroquois Indians of upper New York. In 1759, he published in London a pamphlet entitled *The Second Journal of Christian Frederick Post on a Message to the Governor of Pennsylvania on the Indians of Ohio.*[53] In the sixty-seven page pamphlet, he describes his activities among the Indians of Ohio. Largely through his efforts, the British were able to arrange an alliance with the Indians and to force the French to abandon Fort Duquesne. He was married three times; his first two wives were baptized Indian maidens.[54] He died in Germantown, Pennsylvania in 1785.

The pioneering successes of the Poles in the eighteenth century stimulated interest in the Poles to establish colonies in the New World. Paul Mostowski, an eighteenth-century Polish statesman, entertained plans for the founding of a Polish colony in the southern part of North America, to be called "New Poland." But political misfortunes, which were to bring the independence of the old Polish state to an end, prevented the Mostowski enterprise from maturing.[55]

---

[53] The title page of Reverend Post's notes actually was added to the end of a work by Charles Thompson entitled, *An Enquiry into the causes of the Alienation of the Delaware and Shawnee Indians.* Reverend Post and Thompson were sent by the British government to confer with the Ohio Indians and they were able to arrange a British alliance with the Indians.

[54] Edmund L. Kowalczyk, "Poles in America," *Polish American Journal,* (September 26, 1959), p. 2.

[55] Sister Mary Benedicta Kolat, Felician, O.S.F., *Father Dabrowski, the pioneer priest, and his significant contribution toward Catholic American School System,* (unpublished Master's thesis, Wayne, State University, 1950), p. 2.

# CHAPTER THREE

# Political Immigrants 1776-1870

The American struggle for independence beckoned many Polish patriots to the shore of America to participate in the colonial struggle for freedom. Advantageously for America, the fight for independence coincided with political events in Poland, which gave impulse to and favored immigration to America.[1] In contrast with the colonial immigrants, among these political exiles were men of distinction: soldiers, noblemen, poets, musicians, and educators. They contributed substantially to the building and expansion of the United States. Many were soldiers well versed in the science of war. Chief among these were Kosciuszko and Pulaski who brought enthusiasm as well as ability to the defense of the American cause.

Kosciuszko came to Philadelphia in 1776, bringing to the Continental army a professional training gained in the military schools of Poland and France. Appointed colonel of engineers and assigned to the northern army, he organized the defenses of Ticonderoga, Mount Independence, and West Point. He also contributed to the decisive victory over Burgoyne by the construction of the defenses at Bemis Heights. Kosciuszko's engineering skills were an extremely important factor in the achievement of American independence. His greatest services in aiding the American cause were in strengthening the fortifications at Saratoga, where the British surrendered to General Gates on October 17, 1777. Following the English defeat at Saratoga, where Kosciuszko's adequate fortifications played an important part, France agreed to conclude an alliance with the Americans. When General Greene

---

[1] The three partitions of Poland in 1772, 1793, and 1795 by Russia, Austria, and Germany; the rise and fall of Napoleon and the high hopes attached by Poles to his military ventures; the revolutionary crises of 1846-1848 in Europe; and the unsuccessful insurrections of 1830 and 1863 in Russian-Poland, all contributed their quota of political immigrants in the period 1776-1870.

became commander of the southern army, Kosciuszko joined him as chief-of-engineers. For his distinguished services, Congress awarded him American citizenship, a pension with landed estates in Franklin County, Ohio, and the rank of brigadier-general.[2] At the termination of the war, Kosciuszko was also elected, like George Washington, a member of the Society of Cincinnati, a rare honor for foreigners. General Greene, who considered him a "master of his profession," always spoke of him with the warmest praise.

> One of the most useful and amiable among my comrades-in-arms was Colonel Kosciuszko. His zeal for public service seems to be incomparable and in the solution of complicated problems, which we had to meet from time to time in the intermittent but active war, there could have been nothing more useful than his opinion, his watchfulness and his constant application to the task at hand. In the execution of my orders he has always been willing, competent, inaccessible to any temptation of pleasure, not fatigued by any labor, intrepid in any danger. He is incomparably modest. He has never expressed a desire for anything in his favor, and has never omitted an opportunity to commend and reward the services of others.[3]

In addition to being an excellent professional engineer; Kosciuszko was an outstanding humanitarian, and a forerunner of the movement to abolish slavery in the United States and serfdom in Poland. Before his second departure for Europe, Kosciuszko drew a will on May 5, 1798, in which he expressed his humanitarian views.

> I, Thaddeus Kosciuszko, being just on my departure from America, do hereby declare and direct that, should I make no other testamentary disposition of my property in the United States, I hereby authorize my friend Thomas Jefferson to employ the whole thereof in purchasing Negroes from among his own or any other and giving them liberty in my name; in having them instructed for their new

---

[2] Kosciuszko's account for services rendered to the United States amounted to $12,280.54, which Congress recognized. Under the warrants issued to Revolutionary soldiers, he selected five 100-acre lots in the nineteenth range in the United States Military Survey, for which President Adams issued him a patent in April, 1800. These lots constitute a tract on the eastern side of the Scioto River, in Franklin County, near the Delaware, Ohio, county line. Carl Wittke, Ph.D., *We Who Built America*, (Ann Arbor: 1957), p. 419.

[3] Haiman, *Poland and the American Revolutionary War*, p. 20.

condition in the duties of morality which may make them good neighbors, good fathers and mothers, husbands and wives, in their duty as
citizens; teaching them to be defenders of their liberty and country,
of the good order of society, and in whatsoever may make them happy
and useful.[4]

Kosciuszko also gave freedom to Agrippa Hull, a Negro presented
to him while at West Point by General John Patterson. Hull
settled on a farm in Stockbridge, Massachusetts after receiving
his freedom.

At the age of thirty-nine, Kosciuszko returned to Poland. In
1789 he became a major-general of the reorganized Polish army.
When the struggle over the Constitution of the 3rd of May, 1791,
broke out, Kosciuszko supported the Constitution, holding the
rank of lieutenant-general in the Polish forces. He left the country
when the Russian forces overwhelmed the Polish army. The Revolution of 1794, to restore the Constitution and Polish independence, brought Kosciuszko back to Poland, where he became
commander-in-chief of the army and virtually dictator. It is reasonable to assume that his experience in America and his knowledge of revolutionary France influenced him to break an ancient
tradition and lay the foundation of later Polish nationalism. This
may be observed from Koscisuzko's methods of action; his system of organizing the Polish armed forces; and his manifesto, a
modified echo of the Declaration of Independence, promising
freedom to all who will take arms for the fatherland. In this
struggle, Kosciuszko carried a sword which was a gift to him
from George Washington. The sword had the following inscription: "America cum Vashington suo Amico T. Kosciusconi."[5]
The sword, which came into the hands of the Russians after the
Battle of Maciejowice, was located in the Polish National Museum
at Warsaw after World War I.[6] The insurrection ended in failure;

---

[4] Anthony O. Shallna, "Adjudication of General Kosciuszko's Wills," *The
Massachusetts Law Society Journal*, XX (December, 1949), p. 123.

[5] Haiman, *Poland and the American Revolutionary War*, p. 9.

[6] There are two pistols of Kosciuszko, richly ornamented with gold and
bronze, in the Polish National Museum in Krakow. They possess the following
inscription: "G. Washington 17 E Pluribus Unum 83 Th. Kosciuszko." Another
Washington gift to Kosciuszko was an antique cameo mounted on a ring which
the French Society of the Cincinnati presented to Washington who in turn gave
it to Kosciuszko. The latter made a gift of it to Baron de Girardot who served
in the Polish Chevau-Legers of the Imperial Guard. *Ibid.*, p. 9.

the Polish forces were defeated by the more numerous and better equipped armies of Russia and Prussia. Kosciuszko was wounded and made prisoner. After two years of captivity, he was released by the young Czar Paul and given an extensive estate. He died in Switzerland in 1817. His final resting place is in the vaults of the kings of Poland, beside that of John Sobieski, the deliverer of Vienna and Prince Joseph Poniatowski, his friend and patriot compier, on Wawel Hill in the ancient city of Krakow.[7] Before his death, Kosciuszko wrote *Manoeuvres of Horse Artillery* for the United States Army. It was the first instance in which American artillery was authoritatively supplied with a general system of instructions. The "War of 1812" was fought by artillery in accordance with the *Manoeuvres of Horse Artillery*.

Abundant proof has been brought to light in recent years to show that the idea of a revolution did not suddenly spring into being, but rather that it was preceded by decades of preparation before crystallizing in the great outburst of 1776. That the Constitution of the United States and that of Poland were ratified only four years apart was not a mere coincidence; but indicates that many opinions of freedom must have been exchanged between the backers of both of these great documents. Their thoughts

---

[7] The esteem in which the Czar Alexander held Kosciuszko is shown by his ordering that funeral ceremonies should be conducted in all the churches of Poland. These imposing ceremonies were celebrated not only by the Roman Catholics but by the Greeks and Protestants, and also by the Hebrews and the Moslems in the bounds of Poland. The Czar also appointed Prince Anton Jablonowski to proceed to Soleure, obtain a special conveyance, and escort the remains to Krakow. The prince procured a costly carriage from Paris and removed the body to the ancient capital of Poland.

In the environs of Krakow, on an elevated piece of table-land, is an immense mound of earth, raised as a monument to Kosciuszko; it is three hundred feet in diameter, and one hundred and fifty feet high. The nucleus of this monument was laid by General Pozkowski in 1819, who wheeled a barrow full of earth and bones from the battlefield of Wraclawice and deposited it at the center; he next deposited in a marble coffin, a bust of the Polish chief, with his biography, and placed by its side an urn, containing some of the earth from the field of Maciejowice, where Kosciuszko fell. Then the spectators, who had assembled in tens of thousands, all contributed to raise the mound by voluntary labor; earth was brought from every battlefield in Poland and so great was the enthusiasm that wounded soldiers brought earth in their helmets, and women in their slippers, pilgrims from afar brought earth from their homes in sacks, and on this mound was unfurled a banner, amid the acclamation of assembled thousands, with the simple but soul-stirring inscription: Kosciuszko, the friend of Washington. A. W. W. Evans, *Memoirs of Thaddeus Kosciuszko, Poland's Hero and Patriot.* (New York: 1883), pp. 40-41.

ran in similar channels. Bishop Wawrzyniec Goslicki, Senator and Chancellor of Poland, wrote a world-famous political treatise, *De Optimo Senatore,* which created much comment and a lively interest. This basic work was so revolutionary, that its first two English editions were suppressed by the British authorities.[8] It was read and studied by Sydney, Locke, Helvetius, Montesquieu, Rousseau, and Bellarmine and others. They readily accepted and embodied in their writings many of the ideas and principles contained in Goslicki's work. Many principles found in the Declaration of Independence can be traced to this monumental work.[9] The principles expounded by Goslicki were also embodied in the Polish Constitution of May 3rd, 1791. They also influenced constitutional and legislative enactments in the United States.[10] Another treatise, widely read, was Frycz Modrzewski's *De Republica Emendanda* (On Amending the Republic).

Of all the Polish officers who took part in the American War of Independence, Count Pulaski was the most romantic and professionally the most prominent. He joined the American forces as a volunteer and eventually rose to command four regiments of cavalry: the First Continental Regiment of Light Dragoons; Sheldon's Connecticut regiment; Baylor's regiment, the Third, made up largely of men from Virginia and Maryland; and Maryland's Fourth regiment, made up of men from Maryland and Pennsylvania. Later he resigned this command to organize a mixed body of light infantry and cavalry with lances. During the recruiting of the Legion, Pulaski visited Bethlehem, Pennsylvania, where he ordered from the Moravian Nuns a banner for his Legion. This incident served as a theme for Henry Wadsworth Longfellow's well-known poem, "Hymn of the Moravian Nuns of Bethlehem at the Consecration of Pulaski's Banner." For this

---

[8] Rev. Antonine M. Bochenski, S.T.L., O.M.C., "Our Youth and Its Polish-American Heritage," *Polish American Studies,* I (January-December, 1944), p. 58.

[9] Sister Mary Benedicta Kolat, Felician, O.S.F., *Father Dabrowski, the pioneer priest, and his significant contribution toward Catholic American School System,* (unpublished Master's thesis, Wayne University, 1950), p. 2. Bochenski, *op. cit.,* p. 58.

[10] Wienczyslaw J. Wagner, Arthur P. Coleman, Charles S. Haight, "Laurentius Grimaldus Goslicius and His Age," *The Polish Review,* III (Winter-Spring, 1958), pp. 37-58.

banner, now preserved by the Maryland Historical Society of
Baltimore, Pulaski paid out of his own funds, just as he gladly
bore many other costs of the equipment and sustenance of his
Legion.[11] The "Pulaski Legion," which became a model for Lee's
and Armand's Legions, performed valuable service in the southern
campaign. Among the many Americans who served in the Pulaski
Legion was Light-Horse Harry Lee, father of Robert E. Lee. The
following Poles served in the Pulaski Legion: Captain Joseph
Baldeski, Lieutenant Colonel Baron de Botzen, Lieutenant Jerzmanowski, Captain Kotkowski, Captain Charles Litowski, Captain Matthew Rogowski, Jacob Terlecki, Captain Frederick
Paschke, Thomas Sznayder, Joseph Gabriel, Jonathan Sadowski,
Gottlieb Niemirycz, and Julian Zielinski who was killed during the
siege of Savannah on September 25, 1779.[12]

Pulaski proved his military abilities to such an extent that he
has often been called the "Father of the American Cavalry."[13] It
was by bold cavalry attacks that Pulaski saved Washington's
Army from destruction at Brandywine and at Warren Tavern;
and it was at the head of his own "Legion" that he marched in
1779 into South Carolina and lifted by sheer bravery the impend-
ing siege of Charleston.[14] In the defense of Savannah, 1779, Count
Pulaski was mortally wounded; he died on board the United States
brig *Wasp* where he had been taken for treatment.[15] His heroic
death made his name even more popular in America than Kosciuszko's as is attested by the number of memorials erected to his
memory.[16] Recognition of General Pulaski Day has also been wide-
spread throughout the nation; a dozen or more states have made
it officially a day of celebration. New York holds enthusiastic
festivities culminating in an impressive parade down Fifth Avenue;

---

[11] Captain Baldeski, paymaster of the "Pulaski Legion," stated that "Count
Pulaski has laid out for the Legion at least $50,000 of his own money" without
any expectation of a refund. Haiman, *Poland and the American Revolutionary War*,
pp. 29-30.

[12] "Odds and Ends," *Polish American Journal*, (July 19, 1958), p. 2.

[13] Joseph A. Wytrwal, "Twelve Governors Issued Pulaski Proclamations,"
*Dziennik Zwiazkowy* (March 12, 1955), p. 4.

[14] Roman Dyboski, *Poland in World Civilization*, Ludwig Krzyzanowski, editor,
(New York: 1950), p. 112.

[15] H. H. Fisher, *America and the New Poland*, (New York: 1928), p. 48.

[16] Joseph A. Wytrwal, "Pulaskiana in America," *Polish American Studies*, XIV
(January-June, 1957), pp. 1-11.

Detroit, Chicago, and Savannah also observe the day with great pomp and ceremony. Even Poland has for some years observed the day with commemorative luncheons, articles in the press, and speeches in Warka, Pulaski's birthplace.

Kosciuszko and Pulaski were not the only Poles who made outstanding contributions to America's history during the Revolutionary War. Haym Salomon, an acute businessman, helped to raise the money to keep the Continental army in the field. He made frequent loans out of his own pocket and died in poverty as a result. Anthony Polaski (Poliskie), who together with Cornelius C. Roosevelt, a merchant of New York, was witness to the last will of Frederickus Muzelius of Orange County, in 1782, served as private in the Second Regiment of Militia of Orange County during the Revolutionary War. In 1790, during the first federal census, he still lived in Orange County and his family consisted of one white female. Pelham Polaski (Poloske) was one of the eight-thousand American soldiers who were imprisoned on the British prison ship "Old Jersey" at New York during the war.[17] According to Miecislaus Haiman,[18] Poles from Connecticut,[19] Delaware,[20] Georgia,[21] Maryland,[22] Massachusetts,[23] New Hampshire,[24] New Jersey,[25] New York,[26] North Carolina,[27] Pennsylvania,[28] and Virginia,[29] also participated in the Revolu-

---

[17] Haiman, *Poles in New York in the 17th and 18th Centuries*, p. 55.

[18] Miecislaus Haiman, *Poland and the American Revolutionary War*, (Chicago: 1932), pp. 57-65.

[19] John Barsk, George Bekas, Andrew Broga, Jesse Icaisky and Solomon Luske.

[20] John Dusky and John C. Fabricius.

[21] Thomas Masney and Peter Zawadooski.

[22] Joseph Chalupetzky, John Deskey and Jacob Tilliskey.

[23] Frederick O. Bluskey, Samuel Desko, Michael Franko, James Laskey, John Laskey, Nathanial Laskey, Frederick Obleffisikie, John Pasko, Robert Pesko, Donder Rosonoschy.

[24] August Isaki.

[25] Leman Deaskey, Andrew Malick, John Malick, John Zabriskie and Yost Zabriskie.

[26] Simon Balyca, Peter Burcky, Conrad Burdjat, Heronimus Carareych, Caessimgir Rinas Jeefe, Nicholas Kaghaatsko, Godlieb Krak, Michael G. Kuraw, Joseph Kushel, John Malick, Anthony Polaskie, Elham Poloske, John Sohake and John C. Zabrisky.

[27] Peter Bakut, George Laskey and Moses Lovick.

[28] John Bonia, Henry Bonita, John Bolich, Peter Bolich, Alexander Bozec, Casimir Delwich, Joseph Dolo, John Doman, Mark Doman, Henry Donich, Adam Garney, Jacob Knias, Samuel Kokogai, Jacob Kowan, Henry Kracolo, Barnados Kusky, Sigmond Leshinskey, George Levasvick, Samuel Midera, Conrad Mitsco, Godlieb Niemerich, Richard Stach and Frederick Yaneletz.

[29] Thomas Cisko, Francis Copera, John Hallicia, Jacob Koslow, Andrew Rey,

tionary War. Twenty-five Poles from Pennsylvania alone, volunteered to defend the American cause during the Revolution. This
number was large, for according to the census of 1790 only thirty-
two families were of Polish origin or descent in Pennsylvania
during this period.[30] The names of many had been shorn of "ski's"
and "wicz's," but as least a thousand of unmistakably Polish descent can be identified in the muster rolls of the Continental
Army.[31] The records of Massachusetts regiments reveal more than
sixty different Polish names, each often borne by several members
of a single family.[32] The prolific Laski's of Salem and Marblehead
alone contributed more than thirty men.[33]

Captain Felix Miklaszewicz, a true swashbuckler in the boldest
tradition of the sea,was among the few foreigners who served on
the seas under the American flag during the Revolutionary War.[34]
Miklaszewicz's privateering expeditions were so successful that
he was able to purchase his own vessel, "Scotch Trick," and send
it to pursue the British in 1782. On March 18, 1783, he appeared
before the Council of Massachusetts Bay as proprieter and Captain of an additional vessel to cruise against the enemies of the
United States; he gave $20,000 in Continental and States Bonds
for his Letter of Marque.[35] The new vessel, a two-masted schooner,
christened "Prince Radziwill," was sent out to sea like her predecessor, but the news of the armistice between the United States
and England interrupted her activities.

Besides the American Continental army, the militia, and

---

Jacob Sadowsky, Jonathan Sanduskie, Anthony Sandusky and James Seduskey.

[30] Miecislaus Haiman, *Polish Pioneers of Pennsylvania*, (Chicago: 1941), p. 65.

[31] Albert Q. Maisel, *They All Chose America*, (New York: 1957), p. 209.

[32] *Ibid.*, p. 209.

[33] *Ibid.*, p. 209.

[34] With the termination of the hostilities, he settled in Georgia, where his name
appears frequently among the records of property deeds of Liberty County. These
references cover the years 1785-1795 and indicate that he was quite wealthy. In 1789,
his brother-in-law, Rev. John Albertrandi, librarian to King Stanislaus August Poniatowski, tried to get him appointed Consul for Poland in the United States. This did
not materialize. In 1790, he was residing in Charlestown, South Carolina. His household consisted of two free white males over sixteen years of age, and one free white
female and two slaves.

[35] Haiman, *Poland and the American Revolutionary War*, pp. 69-74. Edmund
L. Kowalczyk, "Poles in America," *Polish American Journal*, (August 15, 1959), p. 2.

privateering, there was yet another field in which the Poles fought for the independence of the United States, namely, the French army sent to America by King Louis XVI in 1780. Captain John Kwiryn Mieszkowski, Lieutenant Count Michael Grabowski, and Lieutenant George Uzdowski served under General Armand Louis de Gontaut Biron, Duke de Lauzun. His corps, known in American history as the "Legion of Lauzun," was officially called "Volontaires Etrangers de la Marine."

The papers of the Duke de Lauzun and the documents in the historical and administrative archives of the French Ministry of War at Paris contain abundant information concerning Captain Mieszkowski. He was born of a noble family in Karczew, Poland, on March 30, 1744. At twenty-two he enlisted as a volunteer in the French "Regiment de Conflans." He was promoted to the rank of Lieutenant in the same regiment on March 1, 1767. During his service in France, Mieszkowski became united by bonds of friendship with the Duke de Lauzun. With Duke de Lauzun, Mieszkowski made the campaign in Senegal in which he acquitted himself so well that the King made him "Chevalier of the Order of St. Louis," on June 25, 1779. On the eve of his departure for America, April 1st, 1780, he was commissioned Captain Commander of the Second Squadron of the Hussars of the Legion of Lauzun. Captain Mieszkowski distinguished himself by exceptional bravery during the siege of Yorktown. For his services, the French king, Louis XVI, sent him a commendatory letter and an award of 400 pounds, besides 800 pounds as compensation for his horse lost in battle. When Captain Mieszkowski returned to France, he became Duke de Lauzun's adjutant. Eventually he attained the rank of Brigadier General, Marechal de camp.

French documents regarding Count Michael Grabowski are rather scant. The record of service, written by Grabowski in 1814, and now in the administrative archives of the French Ministry of War, does not include the place of his birth. There are many noble families of that name in Poland, but the title Count allows for the supposition that he was a relative of John Grabowski, major-general of the Polish army, whose widow was secretly married to King Stanislaus Augustus in 1784. Grabowski entered the French service in January, 1774, as a volunteer in "la

Legion Royale." He was transferred to the "Regiment of Royal Dragoons" in 1776 and commissioned second lieutenant the following year. On November 1, 1778, he was appointed second lieutenant in "Volontaires Estrangers de la Marine." Lieutenant George Boncza Uzdowski was born in Warsaw, April 29, 1754. He began his French service in the same "La Legion Royale," but a year later than Grabowski. It is possible that there were still other Poles in the ranks of the "Legion de Lauzun" and Rochambeau's army.

After gaining its independence, in 1783, the newly recognized United States needed financial assistance. The war had left an aftermath of debt and the obligations of the government sold at a figure below their value. But the future of the new nation, with its untouched resources, was assured, if only financiers had the imagination to grasp this opportunity to make profitable loans. Peter Stadnicki, a wealthy Polish banker who settled in Amsterdam, was the first financier to look with favor upon American investments.[36] In 1780, he contributed to the American loan. Six years later, with faith in the future of America, he began to speculate in the securities of the United States. Eventually he became the chief banker for the United States in Europe. Thomas Jefferson, in 1788, considered him the "principal broker," of the United States. In 1792, Stadnicki organized the Amsterdam bankers into a "Club of Three" for speculation in undeveloped lands in the United States.[37] Later the firm was reorganized into the famous Holland Land Company, which eventually became the owner of five million acres of land in New York and Pennsylvania.[38]

A distinguished Pole who came to America during this post war period was Julian Ursyn Niemcewicz, who had been Secretary to the Polish Senate, adjutant-general of Kosciuszko in the latter's struggle for Polish independence and his companion in

---

[36] Henry S. Lucas, Netherlanders in America, (Ann Arbor: 1955), p. 24.

[37] Haiman, Polish Past in America 1608-1865, pp. 52-54. Roman Dyboski, Poland in World Civilization, (New York: 1950), p. 112.

[38] Few memorials of the work of the Holland Land Company in western New York remain. By 1810, the name of the village of New Amsterdam, on Lake Erie, had been changed to Buffalo. Seven of its avenues, as shown on the first plans of the village had been named for the chief figures of the company: Stadnicki, Willink, Vollenhoven, Van Staphorst, Cazenovia, Susti, and Schimmelpenninck; later these names were also dropped.

captivity at St. Petersburg. A celebrated poet and a noble, he so-journed in America from 1796 to 1804. During his stay, he made an extended tour of the country, which he described in his writ-ings.[39] He was probably the first Pole to visit Niagara Falls, of which he left one of the oldest descriptions. He also visited Boston around 1799 and his diary mentions a Polish Unitarian library, the "Bibliotheca Fratrum Polonorum" in Harvard, of which nothing is now known.[40] He spent two weeks at Mount Vernon as Washington's guest, an event he described in poetry and prose. During his stay, he often spoke with his host about the fate of Poland. One of his poems commemorates a touching episode in-volving Washington, who on hearing his narrative of Poland, wept over her misfortune. According to his notes in his memoirs, once during such a conversation Washington declared: "I always wished well to her (Poland) and that with all my heart." To the same Niemcewicz, Washington again disclosed his sentiments on Poland.

> That your country is not as happy as her efforts were patriotic and noble, is a misfortune which all lovers of sensible liberty and rights of men deeply deplore; and, were my prayers during that hard struggle of any good, you would be now "under your own wine and fig tree," to quote the Bible, as happy in the enjoyments of these de-sirable blessings as the people of these United States enjoy theirs.[41]

After his visit at Mount Vernon, Julian Ursyn Niemcewicz wrote Washington thanking him for the kind reception which he had received at his home. Washington in response stated:

> The satisfaction which our family had from the sweetness of your company in this solitude may only be compared with the sorrow which we felt on your departure and with our wishes that if you ever again visit this part of the United States you will not pass by the shadows of Mount Vernon without enjoying their coolness.[42]

--------

[39] Julian Ursyn Niemcewicz, *Podroze Po Ameryce 1797-1807*, Emil Kipa, Editor, (Wroclaw: 1959). Eugene Kusielewicz and Ludwig Krzyzanowski, "Julian Ursyn Niemcewicz's American Diary," *The Polish Review* III (Summer, 1958), pp. 83-115. Julian Ursyn Niemcewicz, *Pamietniki Czasow Moich*, Waclaw Zawadzki, Editor, (Warsaw: 1957).

[40] Manning, *op. cit.*, p. 6.

[41] Haiman, *Poland and the American Revolutionary War*, pp. 12-13.

[42] *Ibid.*, p. 176.

He married Suzanna Kean, through whom he came into relationship with some well known American families, and for some time
settled on a farm near Elizabeth, New Jersey.[43] He was known
to have been on intimate terms with Jefferson and Franklin, and
other dignitaries of the times.[44] While in Poland on a visit in
1802, he published at Warsaw, *A Short Story of the Life and
Activities of General Washington*. One of the first original
biographies of Washington, it was an excellent contribution to
the cause of international good-will. When Napoleon formed the
Grand Duchy of Warsaw, he returned to Poland, where he became actively engaged in his native land's cause until his death in
1841.[45] Despite his tremendous literary and political activity,
Niemcewicz retained his affection for America. He gave concrete
evidence of his feelings in 1810 by having Thomas Jefferson elected
to membership in the Royal Society of the Friends of Sciences
in Warsaw.

From the Revolutionary War period until 1836, there are some
traces of liberty-loving Poles emigrating to the United States.
Karol Blaszkowicz[46] and Theodore Puderowski, who served as a
drummer in the United States Navy, participated in the War of
1812.[47] Joseph Fiolkowski was one of the Polish Napoleonic soldiers, who were prisoners of the British and sent by them to Canada
to fight the United States in the War of 1812. Count Jacek Caje-
tan Francis Colonna Walewski, after Napoleon's defeat, settled in
Boston; he married the widow of David Humphreys, the noted
American author.[48] Father Thomas Praniewicz, the first Polish
resident of Philadelphia in the nineteenth century, came to Amer-

---

[43] According to Dr. A. P. Coleman, some of his descendants still live in
New Jersey.

[44] Eugene Kusielewicz, "The Jefferson-Niemcewicz Correspondence," *The Polish
Review*, II (Autumn, 1957), pp. 7-22.

[45] Sigmund H. Uminski, "Julian Ursyn Niemcewicz in America," *Polish
American Studies*, II (July-December, 1945), p. 93.

[46] Kruszka, *Historja Polska w Ameryce*, I, p. 112.

[47] Edmund L. Kowalczyk, "Jottings From the Polish American Past," *Polish
American Studies*, XI (January-June, 1954), p. 37.

[48] He was born in Poland, in 1784. He began his military career in the
army of the Duchy of Warsaw in 1806. He served gallantly through the Napoleonic
Campaigns, rising to the rank of Captain. In 1814, he was adjutant to Marshal
Francis Christopher Kellerman. He died in Paris on April 2, 1948. Edmund L.
Kowalczyk, "Polonica-Americana From the Past," *Polish American Journal*, (June
7, 1958), p. 2.

ica in 1819.[49] He was followed by Father Boniface Krukowski, S. J., who came in 1822 and was associated with the Jesuit Mission at Goshenhoppen.[50] The records of St. John Evangelist Church for the year 1835 mention occasional visits from Father Alexander Niewiadrowski, an exiled Polish priest.[51] In the thirties, several Polish Franciscan Fathers were laboring in the United States, among them was Father Anthony Rossadowski, former chaplain in the Polish army in the 1830 Insurrection. Father Gaspar Matoga, who came to the United States in 1848 and completed his studies at Fordham University, was the first Polish priest to be ordained in the United States. Father Lipowski is mentioned in Bishop J. P. Neuman's notebook.[52]

At the solicitation of Bishop Carroll, a number of Polish priests, all former members of the disbanded Society of Jesus, came to America. One of the most prominent was Father Francis Dzierozynski. The Jesuit Father arrived at Philadelphia on November 7, 1821. On August 12, 1823, Father Dzierozynski became Superior of the Jesuits in America, then organized under the title of the Mission of Maryland. According to the testimony of a distinguished Maryland Jesuit of the day, Father James Ryder, Father Dzierozynski saved the Maryland Mission from extinction, and both spiritually and morally left a decidedly salutary influence upon it.[53] Father Dzierozynski succeeded in relieving the Mission of its distressing financial burdens and in expanding its sphere of activities. He gave an impetus to higher education when he founded the College of St. John in Frederick, Maryland.[54]

It was during Father Dzierozynski's administration of the Maryland Mission that General Lafayette made his famous visit to the United States in 1824. When Georgetown University welcomed the revolutionary war hero as a guest within its walls, Father Dzierozynski greeted him with an appropriate address.[55]

---

49 Sister M. Theodosetta, C.S.F.N., "The Poles in Philadelphia to 1914," *Polish American Studies*, VIII (January-June, 1951), p. 16.

50 *Ibid.*, p. 16.

51 *Ibid.*, p. 16.

52 *Ibid.*, p. 16.

53 Sister M. Neomisia Rutkowska, H.F.N., "A Polish Pioneer Jesuit in America," *Polish American Studies*, III (July-December, 1946), p. 101.

54 *Ibid.*, p. 102.

55 *Ibid.*, p. 102.

Father Dzierozynski's superiorship of the Maryland Mission terminated in 1830, but he continued his residence at Georgetown for seven years as a Professor of Theology, assistant to the superior, spiritual director, and chaplain of the Visitation Convent. Later, as master of novices, he moved to Frederick. In 1840, he again headed the Maryland Mission, then already a province. As provincial, he accepted from Bishop Fenwick the offer of Holy Cross College in Worcester, which he staffed with capable men. He died on September 22, 1850.

It was not until the unsuccessful insurrection against Russia in 1830, that a considerable and abiding contingent of Poles, mostly soldiers and members of the lower nobility, began to migrate to the United States. Part of Napoleon's Polish Legion which was sent to San Domingo also came to the United States. The 1830 rebellion was led by the Polish nobility who, after its suppression, were forced to look to other climes. They constituted a courageous and intelligent class of people, among whom were men of letters and many in the professions.[56] These refugees from czarist Russia found a haven in imperial Austria for a short period. However, when their valuables were spent, the exiles became public charges. To rectify the unpleasant situation the Austrian government placed at the disposal of the Poles two frigates, which in 1834 transported them across the Atlantic.[57] Among Americans at that time, enthusiasm for Poland's cause ran high. The Polish National Museum in the ancient Hapsburg castle in Rappersschwyl, Switzerland, possessed many tokens of sympathy sent to the struggling Poles by their American admirers. In 1835, the "Polish National Committee in the United States," consisting of prominent Americans, was formed. The organization was headed by M. Carey, according to a pamphlet printed in Philadelphia on September 30, 1835. And at the insistence of these humanitarian citizens, Congress voted the destitute arrivals 22,040 acres of land near Rock River, Illinois.[58]

---

[56] Lubomir Gadon, *Emigracya Polska—Pierwsze Lata Po Upadku Powstania Listopadowego* (Krakow: 1901), III, p. 233.

[57] This was not the first group of Polish soldiers sent to America. In 1832, three frigates of the Royal Navy brought to America some 630 Polish soldiers released from Prussia where they were kept in internment camps after the Polish insurrection of 1830-1831. Zubrzycki, *op. cit.,* p. 195.

[58] Jerzy Jan Lerski, *A Polish Chapter in Jacksonian America,* (Madison: 1958).

Because these settlements were not reinforced by additional immigrants and because of the high mobility of the second genera' tion, the communities as such disappeared.[59] Since the men out' numbered the women, the majority of the exiles married into American families and were absorbed into American society, where they adapted themselves readily and wholeheartedly to the general culture of their environment. They mingled with their neighbors freely, and with little perceptible restraint, as fellow Americans and fellow-citizens. Eventually many of these exiles reached prominence in various fields of endeavor and thus con' tributed to the cultural growth of the young nation.

In this manner, Kazimierz Stanislaw Gzowski started his life in America.[60] He married an American from Erie, Pennsylvania; after several years they migrated to Canada, where he joined the Canadian Government's Department of Public Works as an Engi' neer in 1841; later he left this to form a private firm with important railway contracts. Eventually he became one of the foremost engineers and pioneers of the Canadian railroad system. In 1870 he built the International Bridge over the Niagara, then con' sidered a miracle of modern engineering. He was also the first president of the Canadian Society of Civil Engineers and the first chairman of the Niagara Falls Park Commission.[61] For his services to his adopted land, especially for founding the City of Toronto and for building the first international suspension bridge over the Niagara River, he was knighted by Queen Victoria in 1890.[62]

---

[59] Hardened to the conditions of the new country, these refugees refused to despair and decided to adopt an entirely different plan. Under the circumstances, there were, broadly speaking, only two roads open to Polish exiles. Either they had to adapt themselves to the rough conditions of contemporary American life, forgetting completely their pledges and patriotic allegiance to Poland, or to follow the more complicated alternative of continuing their Polish activities while adjusting to their new life in this country. To return to their own enslaved country was out of the question. Many of the 1831 exiles deliberately made the latter choice and served the cause of Poland's liberation, becoming at the same time, without any reservations, loyal, proud, and ever ardent citizens of the United States. Many exiles distinguished themselves in America by contributing to the growth of the Republic in the dynamic post-Jacksonian era. Most of the Poles finally contented themselves with assimila' tion, while preserving strong political interests in their old country of origin.

[60] Gzowski never ceased to consider himself a Pole, but his children lost all claim to Polish descent, and the Catholic Faith as well.

[61] Bochenski, op. cit., pp. 53-54.

[62] Lerski, op. cit., p. 123.

His grandson of the same name drove the celebrated Spiral Tunnels in the Kicking Horse Pass for the Canadian Pacific Railway.

Another exile who distinguished himself in Canada, after a sojourn in the United States, was Colonel Gustaw Schultz of New York. He commanded the invading army of the "patriots" who took part in the 1837 American invasion of Canada in support of William Lyon Mackenzie. For five days he repulsed all attacks by the Canadian forces in the engagement of the Upper Canadian Rebellion of 1838; finally he was captured at the Battle of Windmill Point at Prescott, Ontario, and was hung at Port Henry. Colonel Schultz was described by a contemporary as "an elegant scholar—a good military engineer." D. B. Read calls him a "victim of more designing men who led him to the course which brought him to the gallows."[63]

Jozef Truskolaski, a young exile invited by James F. Cooper to live with his family in Cooperstown, New York, took up the study of engineering, and eventually won renown as a surveyor in Louisiana and Utah.[64] Captain Alexander Bielaski made difficult surveys in Florida between 1835-1837, and was a pioneer engineer of the Illinois Central Railroad.[65] Captain Casimir Bielawski, who did nearly all the surveying of old Spanish grants in California, was considered an authority on real estate titles in that state. He was held in hight esteem for his experience and exceptional honesty; Mount Bielawski, in Santa Clara County, California, was named in his honor.[66] Strzelecki, Holynski and Schwatka were also among America's foremost explorers.[67]

Stanislaw Hernisz, who served as interpreter for the American legation in China, published in 1854 the first English-Chinese dictionary in America.[68] In 1842, Paul Sobolewski and Eustace

[63] The memory of this Polish patriot is no longer associated with the bitter feelings, indeed, the practice has been started of decorating the window of his cell at Fort Henry with red and white roses.

[64] Lerski, A Polish Chapter in Jacksonian America, p. 123.

[65] Joseph A. Wytrwal, "Lincoln's Friend—Captain A. Bielaski," Polish American Studies, XIV (July-December, 1957), pp. 66-67.

[66] Bochenski, op. cit., p. 54.

[67] Ibid., p. 54.

[68] Ibid., p. 54.

Wyszynski published in English the first Polish monthly magazine in America, *Poland—Historical, Literary, Monumental and Picturesque*.[69] Paul Sobolewski also published in 1881 an anthology, *Poets and Poetry of Poland*.[70] Martin Rosiekiewicz published in 1834 the first handbook of the English language for the Poles, entitled *Dialogues to Facilitate the Acquisition of the English Language by the Polish Emigrants*. Major Joseph Hordynski, in 1833, published at Boston, his *History of the Late Polish Revolution*. Edward Sobolewski composed *Mohega* (Flower of the Forest), the earliest opera of the Revolutionary War, with General Pulaski as its hero; he was also the organizer of the first Symphonic Orchestra in Milwaukee, in 1861. In 1846 Gaspard Tochman organized the "Polish-Slavonian Literary Association" in the State of New York. Its purpose was "to promote the diffusion of knowledge of the History, Science and Literature of the Nations of the Slavonian race."[71]

August Wegierski established in Buffalo a prosperous school of dance and fencing. Jozef Karczewski was known as a scholar and inventor in Philadelphia. Henry Ignacy Glowacki obtained satisfactory employment from a wealthy lawyer in Batavia, New York.[72] Zajaczek, an athlete, whose specialties were juggling and weight lifting, performed on the New York stage. His debut took place at Peale's Museum on February 11, 1834, where he continued his appearance for many years.[73] L. Rutkowski and E. Polkowski, members of the Polish cavalry, also gave exhibitions of military skill at Peale Museum in New York. The following Poles were also seen on the New York stage in the 1840's and 1850's: Julian Fontana, Edward Kanski, John N. Pychowski, Louise Krolikowska, Florentine Szpaczek, Matilda Korszynska, Anna Ablamowicz, Joseph K. Salamonski, Numa Lepowski, Christine Zawistowski, Emeline Zawistowski, Alice Zawistowski,

---

69 The first Polish newspaper to appear in America was the *Echo z Polski* (Echo of Poland), published in New York in 1863.

70 Bochenski, *op cit., p.* 52.

71 *Ibid.,* p. 52.

72 Lerski, *A Polish Chapter in Jacksonian America*, p. 123.

73 Edmund L. Kowalczyk, "Jottings From the Polish American Past," *Polish American Studies*, VII (July-December, 1950), p. 81.

Hugo Potocki, Rudolph Bakowicz, Zenon Polski, Sophie Dziuba, Henry Kowalski, and Joski.

The first petition for a married woman's property law in New York reached the state legislature in 1836. It was the work of Ernestine Louise S. Potowski-Rose, who was born in Piotrkow, Poland on January 13, 1810. She migrated to England in 1832, where she married William E. Rose. In 1836 they came to New York, where she became one of the outstanding women orators of her day. Called the "Queen of the Platform," she was one of the first women to try to improve the position of her sex through legislative action.[74]

> After a good deal of trouble I obtained five signatures. Some of the ladies said the gentlemen would laugh at them; others, that they had rights enough; and the men said the women had too many rights already . . . I continued sending petitions with increased numbers of signatures until 1848 and '49, when the Legislature enacted the law which granted woman the right to keep what was her own. But no sooner did it become legal when all the women said: "Oh! that is right! We ought always to have had that!"[75]

Ernestine Potowski-Rose was also active in the planning and arranging of the annual Thomas Paine birthday celebrations. The twenty-fifth celebration, held in New York on January 29, 1850, was marked by a special gala affair, a supper and a ball held at the Chinese Museum, on Broadway between Spring and Prince Streets. At this Thomas Paine celebration, whose 113th birthday it was on that day, William Allen paid Ernestine Potowski-Rose the following tribute:

> When I think of the once happy but now fallen country of Kosciuszko, Pulaski and their dauntless associates . . . a strong sympathy and respect is produced in me for all who can trace their origin to that land of sorrow, and more especially to those who inherit the spirit of Kosciuszko, whether they be male or female. I will therefore propose as a sentiment the name of Mrs. Rose—she was the morning glory of Poland; the lily of England; and she is the rose of America."[76]

---

[74] Eleanor Flexner, *Century of Struggle*, (Cambridge: 1959), p. 65.
[75] *Ibid.*, p. 65.
[76] Yuri Suhl, *Ernestine L. Rose and the Battle for Human Rights*, (New York: 1959), p. 106.

This tribute was widely applauded and Ernestine Potowski-Rose addressed the crowded assembly:

> While we assemble to honor the memory of Thomas Paine, it would be well to remember that Paine, Lafayette, Kosciuszko and many other noble minds who enlisted in the cause of right over might, were foreigners; and that, in addition to the plea of humanity, this country owes a debt of gratitude which now is the time to pay. . . . If this country wishes to deserve the name as the place of refuge for the martyrs of freedom, let them contend for the adoption of Kossuth, Bem and Mazzini. It is said that seven ancient cities contended for Homer dead; let us contend for living heroes that have done what Homer wrote . . . and in so doing we will honor the memory of Thomas Paine, of Jefferson, and of Washington.[77]

Ernestine Potowski-Rose was also very active in the abolition movement. She addressed the American Anti-Slavery Society in 1853. Ernestine spoke after Garrison, who delivered the main address. Her speech was frequently punctuated by laughter and applause as she related her experiences in Columbia, South Carolina in the winter of 1847. "What is it to be a slave?" she asked. And she answered:

> Not to be your own, bodily, mentally, or morally—that is to be a slave. Ay, even if the slaveholders treated their slaves with the utmost kindness and charity; if I were told they kept them sitting on a sofa all day, and fed them with the best of the land, it is none the less slavery. For what does slavery mean? To work hard, to fare ill, to suffer hardship, that is not slavery; for many of us white men and women have to work hard, have to fare ill, have to suffer hardship and yet we are not slaves. Slavery is, not to belong to yourself— to be robbed of yourself. . . . This is the great abomination of slavery, that it deprives a man of the common rights of humanity, stamped upon him by his maker. . . . But the great act of emancipation of 800,000 human beings has shown to the world that the African race are not only capable of taking care of themselves, but are capable of enjoying peacefully as much liberty and as much freedom as the white man.[78]

In May, 1855, she addressed the anti-slavery convention in New York and later attended the convention of the New England Anti-Slavery Society where she shared the speakers' platform with the

---

[77] *Ibid.*, pp. 280-281.
[78] *Ibid.*, p. 140.

leaders of the abolitionist movement. When she had delivered her address, Wendell Phillips, who followed her to the rostrum, said:

> The speech, ladies and gentlemen, to which we have just listened, has Waldo Emerson's attribute of eloquence—it has *a life behind it*. What we have to do at the North is, to feel our souls our own—to dare think independently of institutions and majorities, and the old associations about us. The friend who has just taken her seat has taught us that lesson by a life that, before some of us had awakened to the duty of being free, was exerting its influence upon those about her. I am glad when she comes to the anti-slavery platform to give us the benefit of her clear insight, and her long example. They are the veteran troops of reform and free thought, that form the basis of every movement for the bettering of the race.[79]

During that same year Ernestine also spoke at a convention of the Michigan Anti-Slavery Society which was held in Battle Creek, Michigan. Ernestine Potowski-Rose also lectured on religion, free schools, the science of government, and women's rights. During the Civil War, she worked with the "Women's National Loyal League." Returning to England in 1869, she continued her work until her death at Brighton on August 4, 1892.[80]

Another famous woman of Polish nationality, whose career is bound up with American life, was Dr. Marie Elizabeth Zakrzewska. Daughter of a midwife, she often accompanied her mother on her visits among patients and gained valuable lessons which she never forgot.

> During these years, I learned all of life that it was possible for a human being to learn. I saw nobleness in dens and meanness in palaces. . . . I learned to judge human nature correctly, to see good-

---

[79] *Ibid.*, p. 170.

[80] Ernestine Potowski-Rose, who once publicly referred to herself as being "a daughter of poor crushed Poland," was also very active in the cause for Polish independence. When the 1830 uprising took place, Ernestine Potowski-Rose tried to return to Poland to fight, with weapon in hand if need be, to liberate her country from Czarist oppression. She was not permitted to advance beyond the Rhine city of Coblenz where she was threatened with arrest by the Austrian police if she insisted on going farther. In her book *Heroines of Freethought*, published in 1876, Sara A. Underwood, who had attended a peace meeting where Ernestine spoke, gave the following account of Ernestine's speech when she alluded to Poland. "I remember well how she startled and electrified the members of the Universal Peace Society . . . by her description of the sort of peace she advocated . . . with eyes flashing, her pale cheeks flushing, and her voice thrilling, she declared how she longed to plunge, with her own hand, if need be, the dagger to the hearts of the enemies of her country's liberty and rights." Suhl, *op. cit.*, pp. 21, 26, 245.

ness where the world found nothing but faults. . . . The experience thus gained cost me the bloom of youth, yet I would not exchange it for a life of everlasting juvenescence.[81]

At the age of eighteen she had been admitted, after several applications, to the school of midwifery in Berlin. There her superior work gained for her not only the highest praise but also the true friendship of Dr. Joseph Schmidt, professor in the school of midwifery and chief director of the Hospital Charite. On May 15, 1852, she was appointed chief accoucheuse in the hospital and professor in the school of midwifery, the position previously held by Dr. Joseph Schmidt. Hearing that in the United States women could become full doctors of medicine, Zakrzewska[81] resigned her position and emigrated to America in 1853. Three years later she graduated from Western Reserve College of Medicine at Cleveland, Ohio. Dr. Zakrzewska became a pioneer woman physician and pathfinder in American medicine. She left permanent monuments to her unconquerable spirit in the field of social service. She was one of the founders of the New York Infirmary for Women and Children, and its first resident physician. This was the first attempt to establish a hospital exclusively for women and staffed by women. Although several medical colleges admitted women students there was no hospital where medical women could obtain practical instruction. In 1859, Dr. Zakrzewska had gone to Boston, where she organized a new hospital, known later as The New England Hospital for Women and Children. For forty years she was its director. In addition she taught obstetrics at the New England Female Medical College; helped to organize the first American school for nurses; and inaugurated the movement to establish playgrounds for children in cities, thus gaining the title of "Mother of the Playgrounds Movement."[82] She was also a pioneer of women's rights and one of the leaders of the abolitionist movement in America.

---

[81] Sister M. Liguori, C.S.F.N., "Marie Elizabeth Zakrzewska: Physician," *Polish American Studies,* IX (January-June, 1952), pp. 2-3.

[82] Haiman, *Polish Past in America 1608-1865,* p. 95. Sister M. Liguori, C.S.F.N., "Marie Elizabeth Zakrzewska: Physician," *Polish American Studies,* IX (January-June, 1952), pp. 1-10. Bochenski, *op. cit.,* p. 54. Elise S. L'Esperance, M.D., "Influence of the New York Infirmary On Women in Medicine," *Journal of the American Medical Women's Association,* IV (June, 1949), pp. 255-561.

Among the earliest Negro women to enter the field of medicine was Caroline V. Still, daughter of two famous "agents" on the Underground Railroad, William and Letitia Still of Philadelphia. Dr. Still interned at the New England Hospital for Women and Children which had been founded by Dr. Zakrzewska; it was also from the nursing school of this institution that the first Negro trained nurse, Mary Elizabeth Mahoney, graduated in 1879.[83]

When Dr. Zakrzewska died on May 12, 1902, the *Boston Evening Transcript* paid her the following tribute.

> A sound intellect and a large sympathetic heart unselfishly devoted to the service of humanity and especially to the welfare of her own sex, have made her service to Boston an incalculable blessing to the thousands of women whom she has helped to a life of health, usefulness and happiness. . . .[84]

Six months later the following observation was made in the *Boston Transcript*:

> Marie Zakrzewska, the pioneer among women physicians of the country, was the first woman doctor in New England. . . . She was so well known, and her work so widespread in its benefactions, that there was deep interest in recalling the nobility of the woman and the unselfishness with which she devoted her life to ministering to the sick and afflicted.[85]

Many Poles contributed to the cultural maturity of the rising nation. The following, who have largely been forgotten, merit rediscovery: Henry Dmochowski-Saunders, sculptor; Count Adam Gurowski, jurist and historian;[86] Leopold F. Boeck, organizer of one of the early schools of engineering in America;[87] Julian Fon-

---

83 Flexner, *Century of Struggle*, p. 129.

84 *Boston Evening Transcript*, (May 13, 1902), p. 2.

85 *Boston Transcript*, (October 30, 1902), p. 11.

86 The learned Count Adam Gurowski, one time translator to the State Department, entered so fully into the American spirit and life that his "Diary of 1861-1865" betrayed a keen insight into the politics and general conditions of our Civil War period. Count Adam Gurowski was also employed on the editorial staff of *Greeley's Tribune* and is remembered for his memorable sally against Daniel Webster's support of the First Fugitive Slave Law. Sister M. Liguori, CSFN, "The Pole Who Wrote to Lincoln," *Polish American Studies*, X, (January-June, 1953), p. 4.

87 Leopold Julian Boeck served in the Hungarian revolution under Louis Kossuth. And it was through the intervention of the United States Minister at Constantinople that the Ottoman government refused to release Dr. Boeck, then a prisoner of state at the Turkish capital, to the Russian and Austrian authorities.

tana, composer; Edward B. Bohusiewicz, professor of music;[88] Leon Rawicz-Gawronski, song writer;[89] John Joseph Lehmanow-ski, founder of many German elementary schools in the west; and Adam Kurek, a talented musician who organized itenerant bands in America. Since Kurek changed American orchestras entirely by replacing the old drums and pipes with wind instruments, he is often called the "Father of the touring brass band in America." A prolific composer, he often named his compositions after leaders of the Polish November uprising.[90] Maksymiljan Zuboff published eight compositions and a play, Polski Wygnaniec, in America. Edward Kanski published The Recollections of Childhood in New York around 1853.[91] Tadeusz Feliks Strawinski published in 1844, in Baltimore, Marsz Piechoty Polskiej; Numy Lepowski and Jozef Salomonski also had publications to their credit.[92] Colonel Artur Grabowski was commandant of the Pennsylvania Military College and of the Worcester Highland Military Academy; superintendent of the Haskell Institute at Lawrence, Kansas; resident of Defiance College, in Ohio; and principal of the Summerville Academy of Georgia.[93] Louis Szpaczak, Henryk Kallussowski, Robert Thomain, and Severin Balezowski achieved prominence as physicians.[94] The following Poles became planta-

---

After teaching higher mathematics in the Sorbonne at Paris for a few years, Professor Boeck came to the United States where he occupied chairs in the Universities of Virginia and Pennsylvania. He was also appointed American Educational Commissioner at the Universal Exposition in Vienna by President Grant, and served in a similar capacity at the Centennial Exposition in Philadelphia. At the time of his death, he was professor of languages at the University of Pennsylvania.

[88] A professor of music in Providence, Rhode Island, Bohusiewicz had twenty selections published in America. Among his compositions were the following titles: Polski Pielgrzym, Wybor Melodji Polskich, and three Mazurki. He died in Providence in 1848.

[89] Rawicz-Gawronski is the author of the song Pozegnanie uchodzcy z Polska, for guitar and piano. It was published in Baltimore in 1844, and dedicated to Prince Adam Czartoryski.

[90] The following are the titles of Kurek's compositions: Bangor Waltz; Prince Czartoryski's Quickstep; Edmund's Quickstep; General Gielgud's Quickstep; Kurek Grand March; General Lubienski's Quickstep; Marion's Quickstep; General Mala-chowski's Quickstep; National Guard's Seventh Company March; General Radziwill's Quickstep; General Rybinski's Quickstep; General Skrzynecki's Quickstep; and Winchester Quickstep.

[91] Aleksander Janta, "O Muzyce Amerykansko-Polskiej," Nowy Swiat, (April 30, 1960), pp. 1 and 8.

[92] Ibid., p. 1.

[93] Bochenski, op. cit., p. 53.

[94] Maisel, They All Chose America, p. 211.

tion owners in Louisiana: Szczepanski, Kaczanowski, Kowalski, Jurgielewicz, Kaczorowski, Chodakowski, Czarnecki, and Colonel Ignatius S. Szymanski. In addition to his plantation, which was located fifteen miles south of New Orleans, Szymanski was also an owner of a cotton press, a racing stable, and a yacht.[95]

Before vanishing completely in the American environment these emigrants succeeded in organizing the second Polish organization in the United States "Democratic Society of Polish Refugees in America" (Towarzystwo Demokratyczne Wygnancow Polskich w Ameryce).[96] Founded in 1852, the organization concerned itself not so much with the independence of Poland as with anti-slavery propaganda.[97] There are no records of its activities after 1858. According to the *Boston Transcript* (December 1, 1853) the 23rd anniversary of the Polish rebellion of 1830 was celebrated in 1853 in New York with Polish, German, and Italian speeches. Eight years earlier, according to the *New York Weekly News* of December 6, 1845, a similar celebration was held with representatives of all the important immigrant groups on the program. In 1859, to commemorate the Warsaw uprising of 1830, Polish exiles in Cincinnati arranged a banquet at which two actual participants were present as guests of honor; the *Cincinnati Enquirer,* dated November 30, 1859, printed a description of the banquet.

The Polish debacle of 1831 by no means quenched the revolutionary fervor of the oppressed Poles. In 1836, a peasant revolt in Austrian-Poland brought devastation upon the powerful Polish nobility. In 1848, a Polish nationalistic outbreak greeted the Hohenzollerns of Prussia, and in 1863 Russia was confronted with

---

[95] Edmund L. Kowalczyk, "A Polish Family in the South," *Polish American Studies,* III, (July-December, 1946), p. 106.

[96] A number of veterans of the Revolution of 1830 organized the first organization in America in 1842. It was called "Association of Poles in America" (Stowarzyszenie Polakow w Ameryce). An appeal dated New York, March 20, 1842, calls upon the Poles in America to affiliate with the organization recently effected at the home of the Rev. Louis Jezykowicz, 235 Division Street, New York. To "Die for Poland" was the watchword of the organization. According to a brochure printed in Paris, the organization elaborately commemorated the Revolution of 1830 at the Stuyvesant Institute in New York. Felix Thomas Seroczynski, "Poles in the United States," *The Catholic Encyclopedia,* (New York: 1913), XII, p. 204.

[97] Kolat, *op. cit.,* p. 6.

still another Polish rebellion. After each failure, scores of Poles were forced to flee from the land they had fought to liberate.[98]

An interesting characteristic of the Polish immigration around the beginning of the second half of the nineteenth century was its participation in the "winning of the west." Among the most famous Poles in that area was Doctor Felix Paul Wierzbicki. Because of his participation in the Polish Insurrection of 1830, he was deported to America in 1834. In the United States, Wierz-bicki, acquired an extensive education and finally became a doctor of medicine. When the Mexican War broke out, he abandoned his practice and joined a regiment of volunteers commanded by Colonel J. D. Stevenson. His activities as a soldier brought him to California, where he remained until his death in 1860. Wierz-bicki wrote a pamphlet entitled *California as it is, and as it may be, or a guide to the Gold Region.*[99] According to Haiman, it was the first English book printed at San Francisco and west of the Rockies.[100]

A notable Forty-Niner was Alexander Zakrzewski. Among the records of Clackamas County at Oregon City, Oregon, there is one of the oldest plans of San Francisco drawn by him. He is listed as a lithographer in the first city directory of San Francisco, dated 1850.[101] The following Poles were also among the Forty-Niners: Rudolph K. Piotrowski, Doctor John Stentzel, Michael Kraszewski, Paul Petrovits and William F. Zabriskies.[102] The following Poles came after 1849; Alexander J. J. Holinski, William and John Siegried Kierski, Louis Alexander Sengteller, Vincent Lutnicki, Francis Wojciechowski, Julian W. Andrzejewski, Michael Przybylowicz, and Francis Czerwinski.[103]

---

[98] Their main difficulty in keeping organized Polish life alive was their dispersion over the United States. There were small scattered groups of Poles in Albany, Boston, Providence, Richmond, Philadelphia and St. Louis; while others moved to different smaller localities in Pennsylvania, Missouri, Kentucky, Louisiana, Ohio, Illinois, Wisconsin and Texas. This dislocation prevented them from playing an important role in the global efforts and remarkable achievements of the Polish Great Emigration; however, one should not overlook or underestimate the importance of their activities in the history of American Polish relations in general.

[99] Mondello, *op. cit.*, pp. 109-110.

[100] Miecislaus Haiman, *Polish Pioneers of California*, (Chicago: 1940), p. 42.

[101] Haiman, *ibid.*, pp. 49-51.

[102] *Ibid.*, pp. 45-56.

[103] *ibid.*, pp. 57-70.

A number of Polish political exiles participated with the Texans in their struggle for independence from Mexico. Three Polish refugees, Dembrinske, Petreswich and Kortickey, fought and died under Colonel Fannin.[104] Another Pole, Felix Wardzinski, saw action in the famous battle of San Jacinto, which sealed the triumph of the Texan War of independence against Santa Anna and the Mexicans.[105] Loius Napoleon Debicki, who emigrated to the United States in 1833, was killed in the battle of Gollath on March 19, 1836. In May, 1851, the State of Texas posthumously awarded to Debicki's descendants vast tracts of land for his services.[106]

Many Poles participated in the hostilities which broke out between the United States and Mexico in 1846. Private C. W. H. Smolinski participated in the capture of Mexico City. Adolph Wengierski rendered invaluable services during the siege of Puebla. Captain Napoleon Koscialowski, of the Third Missouri Infantry took part in the Doniphan Expedition. Colonel Jacob Zabriskie of the First Illinois Regiment was killed at the Battle of Buena Vista on February 23, 1847.[107] Felix Andrew Wardzinski served in General Butler's Division, Tennessee Regiment.[108] F. Piotrowicz, an artillery commander, as well as Hypolite Oladowski and Ignace Szumowski were also among the participants. Captain Charles Radziminski, after the war, became secretary to the Commission which surveyed the new boundary between the United States and Mexico.[109]

Although the Polish immigrants have made a much more impressive imprint on the country elsewhere, yet it was in Texas, on the site of the San Antonio River, two miles north of its junction with the Cibolo, that was the location of the first considerable

---

[104] Miecislaus Haiman, *The Poles in the Early History of Texas*, (Chicago: 1936), pp. 28-29.

[105] Mondello, *op. cit.*, p. 110.

[106] Oil was subsequently discovered on his lands. Today the lands, worth over three-hundred-million dollars, are leased by eighteen American Firms. "Debates on $300 Million Debicki Estate," *Polish American Journal*, (October 26, 1957), p. 1.

[107] *Polish American Journal*, (September 29, 1956), p. 2.

[108] *Polish American Journal*, (September 29, 1956), p. 2.

[109] A military camp in Oklahoma was named after Captain Radziminski. A mountain in the southern part of Kiowa County, southwestern Oklahoma, is still called Mount Radziminski.

Polish settlement in America. Territory was the one commodity Texas had in abundance. In 1854, a sailing vessel arrived at Galveston, Texas, and a weary group of eight hundred men, women, and children disembarked. Father Leopold Moczygemba, a Franciscan monk, was their leader.[110] Carrying their ploughs and other implements, their bedding, kitchen utensils, and a large cross from their old parish church, these peasants began their long trek inland until they finally reached the site for the future colony, which they hopefully and nostalgically named Panna Maria in honor of the Virgin Mary.[111] The established small agricultural community was the location of the first Polish church in America. It was erected in 1854. The first Polish school was established by Father Bakanowski, C. R., in 1866. The first teacher was Peter Kiolbassa.[112] The hardships enforced by the wilderness that was Panna Maria in those days caused many of the original families to move on to what they thought were greener fields. Polish settlements in San Antonio, Bandera, Yorktown, and St. Hedwig followed soon after.[113] Still later came Częstochowa, Kosciuszko, Falls City, and Polonia, all in Texas.[114] By 1906 the Polish population of Texas was estimated at between 16,000 and 17,000.[115]

Wisconsin, also, was one of the earliest goals of Polish immigrants. In 1858, a Polish family from West Prussia came to Portage County, and there, among earlier German, Irish, and French communities, founded Polonia, which grew up to be an

---

[110] Father Moczygemba had preceded the group by some three years. He had sent word that brought them through the terror of an ocean crossing and the suffering of pioneer travel inland. They had come expecting the scriptural "land of milk and honey." What they found was a prairie full of rattlesnakes. According to Father Kruszka, some of them wanted to hang Father Moczygemba on the nearest tree and were so serious about the threat that he had to seek refuge in flight. But the flight if it really occured was only temporary.

[111] Mondello, op. cit., p. 111. Rev. Edward J. Dworaczyk, Church Records of Panna Maria, Texas, (Chicago, 1944).

[112] The huge oak under which a mid-night Mass of Thanksgiving was celebrated, with the winter wind high in its branches, the only accompaniment of the choir, is still standing and is one of the most revered relics of the town.

[113] "Oldest Permanent Polish Settlement in United States was Established in Panna Maria by Fr. Moczygemba," The Alamo Register, (October 7, 1949), p. 12.

[114] Ibid., p. 12.

[115] Kruszka, Historja Polska w Ameryce, I, pp. 71-90.

interesting and prosperous Polish rural community.[116] The first Polish church was opened in Milwaukee by 1865, and the Poles have ever since been important in the life and industry of that city. During the winter of 1862-63, several Polish families settled at Pine Creek in the northern part of Trempealeau Township, Wisconsin. According to local historians of Trempealeau, these included Paul and Mike Lessman, Paul Livera, Frank Meyer, Joseph Lubinski, and Joseph Wunk (or Winock). These Poles, who had originated chiefly in the provinces of Poznan and Pomerania, formed a closely knit community. By 1868, they had established a Parish, for they were generous supporters of the Roman Catholic Church. By the mid-1870's the group dominated the area, and the newly established town of Dodge was virtually a Polish township.[117] According to accounts preserved in the House of Memories, which record local tradition there, the original settlement was the second Polish settlement in Wisconsin and one of the oldest in the country.[118] What was the attitude of the old American stock, the New Englanders, the New Yorkers, and other Middle States men, and the smaller numbers of people from the old northwest, toward the newcomers from Poland? The question cannot be completely answered, but available evidence indicates that on the whole the spokesmen of the older American group welcomed the newcomers. Luce, in reporting "assault and battery cases" among the Poles of the town of Trempealeau in 1870, good-naturedly took pains to speak highly of these people who had come to "assist in cultivating our hills and valleys."[119] The Whitehall Times, describing a Fourth of July celebration, wrote of the "husky Polack from his sod hut, the study German, the honest, hard-working Norsk," and rejoiced that they had joined hands and hearts with the native Yankees in doing honor to the great national holiday.[120] Doings among the Polish immigrants also found their way into print. "Our Polander friends have had a wedding and dance at J. K. Cysewieski's on Monday evening,

---

116 Emily Balch, *Our Slavic Fellow Citizens*, (New York: 1910), p. 230.

117 Merle Curti, *The Making Of An American Community*, (Stanford: 1959), p. 95.

118 *Ibid.*, p. 95.

119 *Ibid.*, p. 98.

120 *Ibid.*, p. 98.

and all appeared to enjoy themselves well," reported the *Arcadia Leader*. And the same journal gave the names of the heads of five Polish families that arrived in one week in the spring of 1876.[121] It is noteworthy that almost all the examples of prejudice against the Poles came from the newspapers of the 1870's rather than of the 1860's; which suggests that perhaps tensions were less evident in the early frontier period. Few examples can be cited, but they give the tone. Sometimes the reference is sarcastic or disapproving. Thus an unnamed "Polander" was badly cut with a reaper, and the family thought that they did not need a doctor. When the man died, the paper in referring to the incident commented: "They certainly don't now."[122] Or another item went as follows:

> Several Polanders resisted constable Alex Lintz while securing a cow, by virtue of a chattel mortgage, Wednesday. The result was, the Polanders were badly handled. Thinking to have revenge they had the constable arrested, but found, after a trial before an Arcadia justice, that the constable was in the right and they were wrong. Now Mr. Lintz proposes to pick them up for interfering with his duties as an officer.[123]

In commenting on one Polish dance the Independence *Weekly News Bulletin* remarked that such disgraceful scenes should not be permitted on Sunday.[124] The Arcadia *Republican and Leader* reported a free for-all in which a wife and son were intent on killing the head of the family and almost succeeded in making a corpse of him. Released on bail of $300 each, wife and husband made up and went off homeward "hugging and kissing like two lovers."[125]

The first settlement in Michigan was at Parisville, near Detroit. The first church in Parisville was erected in 1857. Andrzej Kaminski, Filip Jasnowski, Antoni Leszczynski, Stanislaw Melin, and

---

121 *Ibid.*, p. 99.

122 *Independence Weekly News Bulletin*, (August 16, 1879). Quoted by Merle Curti, *The Making of An American Community*, p. 100.

123 *Independence Weekly News Bulletin*, (July 19, 1879). Quoted by Merle Curti, *The Making of An American Community*, p. 100.

124 Curti, *The Making of An American Community*, p. 101.

125 *Ibid.*, p. 119.

Jan Lemke were among the first Poles who settled in Michigan.[126]

The Polish immigrants were so deeply drawn into the inner life of the United States that they could not remain strangers in the great crisis of the nation that culminated in the Civil War. At the time of the Civil War there were some 30,000 Poles in the United States. Of this number, 4,000 fought in the ranks of the Union army and 1,000 served the Confederacy.[127]

By a queer coincidence the Poles were among the first to die on both sides in battle. According to official records, Thaddeus Strawinski, an eighteen-year old student, was the first to die in the attack of the Confederates on Fort Sumter, the first battle of the Civil War. And the first Union officer to die was Captain Constantine Blandowski, who helped save Missouri for the Union.[128] Captain Blandowski had come to the United States in 1850, after a colorful career in the French Foreign Legion, an abortive Polish revolt at Krakow, the Polish Legion with Garibaldi in Italy, and Kossuth's revolutionary army in Hungary.[129]

There were many attempts to organize Polish units during the Civil War. The Polish volunteers in the "Polish Legion," otherwise known as the "Fifty-eighth New York Infantry," exerted great efforts to form a Polish regiment as early as April 18, 1861. Their appeals, like those of other nationality groups, harked back to their history.

> Rally around our banner, under the wing of the Polish white eagle. The spirit of Pulaski and Kosciuszko will sustain us. Distinguished officers will lead us, and the sentiment to serve the holy and just cause of liberty will be our honorable recompense.[130]

At the same time, the immigrant papers observed an attempt to organize a Polish Legion in the west, but the project was soon abandoned, and the Poles consolidated into the Garibaldi Guard.[131] During this time, Polish-born Julian Allan also made an attempt

---

[126] Dr. Stefan Wloszczewski, *Historja Polska w Detroit*, (Detroit: 1951), pp. 1-27.

[127] Kolat, *op. cit.*, p. 5.

[128] Bochenski, *op. cit.*, p. 51.

[129] John Charles Bodger, Jr., *The Immigrant Press and the Union Army*, (unpublished Ph.D. dissertation, Columbia University, 1951), p. 158.

[130] Ella Lonn, *Foreigners in the Union Army and Navy*, (Baton Rouge: 1951), pp. 143-144.

[131] Bodger, *op. cit.*, p. 113.

to organize a foreign-born regiment in June, 1861.[132] An effort
to organize a Polish cavalry regiment, the United States Lancers,
was only partially successful, but helped to form the Ninth New
York Cavalry.[133]

When President Lincoln made his appeal for volunteers to
meet the challenge of the plantation-owner class and its allies,
Vladimir Krzyzanowski, first cousin of Frederick Chopin, was
among the first to respond.[134] At the outbreak of the conflict, he
was authorized by Secretary of War Cameron to recruit a regiment among all the Poles of the Union. He succeeded in organizing a militia company consisting of four hundred men, whom
he christened the "United States Rifles." The company, however,
was quickly expanded into a regiment under his command, and
Krzyzanowski eventually became a colonel. He distinguished himself in several battles, among them, those of Cross Keys and Bull
Run. President Lincoln appointed Krzyzanowski brigadier general,
but the Senate did not immediately confirm the appointment.:[135]

> One of my two commanders, Schimmelfenning has been made
> a brigadier general as he well deserved. Krzyzanowski was less for-
> tunate the Senate failed to confirm him—as was said, because there
> was nobody there who could pronounce his name.[136]

Krzyzanowski's reputation as a leader and fighter increased after
the battle of Chancellorsville and Gettysburg and in minor en-
gagements in Tennessee.[137] Consistently democratic, sharing, danger, hunger, and fatigue with his men, he was beloved by his
"legionnaires."[138]

---

132 *Ibid.*, p. 113.

133 Lonn, *op. cit.*, p. 145.

134 Vladimir Krzyzanowski, a Polish officer who had served in the Polish
insurrection of 1830, came to America in the 1850's and completed his engineering
studies in America. He assisted in the construction of three railroads in the Middle
West, then settled down as a businessman in Washington.

135 Louis Adamic, "Americans From Poland," *Women's Day*, (August, 1944),
p. 70.

136 Carl Schurz, *The Reminiscences of Carl Schurz*, (New York: 1907), II,
p. 407.

137 The markers on the battlefields of Gettysburg indicate that a number of
the units wholly or partly composed of Poles belonged to the brigade commanded
by Krzyzanowski.

138 He left the service with the rank of brigadier general. He was the only
Pole rewarded with appointment to the Civil Service. He was appointed the first

Joseph Karge was another Pole who rose to the rank of general in the Union army. He distinguished himself in operations against "Stonewall" Jackson in Virginia and in defense of Washington. Two serious wounds received in 1862 almost compelled him to retire, but he saw the war to its conclusion. Toward the end of the hostilities, he fought with distinction at the head of a New Jersey Cavalry Regiment against Southern partisans on the Lower Mississippi. After the war, he was given command of a cavalry unit in Nevada.[139]

General Albin F. Schoepf also fought with distinction in the Union armies.[140] The number of Poles who attained the rank of captain (some of them rising from the ranks) is astonishing. Research has revealed no less than twenty; and because of the failure during the war to record the nativity of commissioned officers, this number cannot be regarded as definitive.[141] Among those who organized companies at the first call to arms were the following: Captain Adelbert Morozowicz, who organized and commanded the "Ninth Independent New York Light Artillery"; Captain Lucas Soboleski, who collected men for the "Independent Company of Lancers of Missouri"; Captain Bernard J. Stampoffski (also spelled Stempowski), a veteran of the Mexican war, who responded to Lincoln's call with "Company F of the Ninth Illinois Cavalry," from Chicago; Thaddeus C. Hulanicki, who organized and commanded Battery L of the "Second Illinois Light Artillery"; and Captain Stanislaus Mlotkowski, whose Pennsylvania Battery A of heavy artillery took its name from him, but was officially the "Pennsylvania Independent Battery."[142] Mlotkowski's battery was stationed from March 1, 1862 to the end of the war at Fort Dela-

---

American administrator of Alaska, and later served meritoriously as customs inspector at Panama. Eventually he settled down in the custom office at New York where he died in 1887. In 1938, his mortal remains were transferred to Arlington Cemetery. President Roosevelt spoke at the ceremony. General Carl Schurz, with whom Krzyzanowski served, wrote favorably of his services in his memoirs.

[139] Eventually he became professor of foreign languages at Princeton University. He held the chair of professor of languages and foreign literature for twenty-two years at Princeton University.

[140] Miecislaus Haiman, "General Albin F. Schoepf," *Polish American Studies,* II (July-December, 1945), pp. 70-79.

[141] Lonn, *op. cit.,* p. 263.

[142] *Ibid.,* p. 263.

ware, the most important defense of the Port of Philadelphia.[143]

Many other Captains of Polish descent distinguished themselves in the Union armies. When Grant attacked the Confederate encampment at Belmont on November 7, 1861, General John A. McClernand's young Polish aide-de-camp, Captain Alexander Bielaski, who had dismounted because his horse had been wounded several times, was shot down as he advanced with the flag in his hand and encouraged his men to follow.[144] The example of the famous Thaddeus Kosciuszko as a military engineer was honorably followed by Captain William Kossak of Missouri, who was on General Grant's staff. General Sherman considered Kossak's map of the battlefield at Shiloh the best he had seen. At Corinth, Kossak supervised the construction of the Union fortifications which were pronounced "very excellent" by Sherman; and at Vicksburg, he erected new casements to replace some of those deemed unsatisfactory.[145] Captain Wladislaus Leski, aide to General McDowell, called forth from General McDowell the following encomium, bestowed jointly on Leski and Captain Howard Stockton. "(They were) constantly at the front, exerting themselves with a zeal and intelligence that accomplished much for the army."[146] Captain Peter Kiolbassa was one of those foreign-born Confederate soldiers whose heart was not in the Southern cause; thus, when he was captured, he promptly enlisted as a private in an Illinois regiment and rose at length to the Captaincy of the "Sixth United States Cavalry."[147] Captain Joseph Gloskowski of the "Twenty-ninth New York" rendered valuable service and won recognition in the official records. At Antietam he sent "many important messages, one of which saved General Burnside from being cut off"; at Fredericksburg, for three days, he transmitted messages by flags, "though constantly exposed to the fire of the enemy's batteries"; and at Chancellorsvill

---

[143] Sister M. Theodosette Lewandowska, H.F.N., "The Polish Immigrant in Philadelphia to 1914," *Records of the American Catholic Historical Society of Philadelphia,* LXV (June, 1954), No. 2, p. 81.

[144] Joseph A. Wytrwal, "Lincoln's Friend—Captain Alexander Bielaski," *Polish American Studies,* XIV (July-December, 1957), pp. 65-68. Lonn, op. cit., p. 263.

[145] Lonn, op. cit., p. 263.

[146] *Ibid.,* p. 263.

[147] Helen Busyn, "Peter Kiolbassa—Maker of Polish America," *Polish American Studies,* VIII (July-December, 1951), pp. 65-85. Lonn, *op. cit.,* pp. 263-264.

his signals were the only means of communication between General Joseph Hooker's staff and parts of his army.[148] Captain Frank B. M. Bonsal, an officer of Company H, recruited at Philadelphia on July 11, 1861, was wounded at Peach Tree Creek, Georgia; he was mustered out with his company on July 18, 1865.[149] Captain Robert A. Chodasiewicz, one of the founders of the Polish Society of Argentina, served as an engineer in the Union army.[150] Julius C. A. Szenowski was aide-de-camp to Major General Carl Schurz.[151] Edmund T. Hulanicki of Chicago rose from a private to the rank of Captain in the "Twelfth United States Artillery." Captain Louis Zychlinski also served with distinction.

Of the Poles who held the rank of lieutenant, Edmund L. G. Zalinski seems to be of greatest intrinsic interest. In February, 1863, as a sixteen-year-old high-school lad, Zalinski ran away from his home in Syracuse to enlist in the "Second New York Cavalry." Attracted to the daring young fellow, General Miles soon made him aide-de-camp on his staff; and for his bravery in the "Battle of Hatcher's Run" the youth received the rank of second-lieutenant with which he emerged from the war.[152] Lieutenant Rodnowski, who was killed at "Dead Man's Corner," Port Hudson, Louisiana, on May 27, 1863, was on the staff of Major General Godfrey Weitzel. Artur Wrotnowski was appointed First Lieutenant and Adjutant of the "First Louisiana Infantry" in March, 1863; on September 3, 1863, he was appointed Lieutenant Colonel, "First Volunteers Engineers Corp's d'Afrique;" and finally he became general of the "Ninety-fifth United States Colored Volunteer Infantry," which was mustered out on November 26, 1864.[153] Maps of Lieutenants C. A. Czartoryski and Joseph Gorlinski are preserved in the Atlas of the *Official War Records*.[154] Polish-born Lieutenant J. Littman served in the "Washington Rifles Com-

---

[148] Lonn, *op. cit.*, p. 264.

[149] Lewandowska, *op. cit.*, p. 81.

[150] Edmund L. Kowalczyk, "Polonica Americana," *Polish American Studies*, X, (July-December, 1953), p. 123.

[151] Edmund L. Kowalczyk, "Jottings From the Polish American Past," *Polish American Studies*, IX (July-December, 1952), p. 92.

[152] Lonn, *op. cit.*, p. 270.

[153] Edmund L. Kowalczyk, "Jottings From the Polish American Past," *Polish American Studies*, VII (July-December, 1950), p. 87,

[154] Lonn, *op. cit.*, p. 343,

pany" according to the *Illinois Staats Zeitung*.[155] Besides Lieutenants Julian Krzywoszynski, William Gracanowski, and Jerzy
Hynicki, there were many non-commissioned officers who served
in various companies of the Union army.[156] Emilia Kossuth Zulawski, the daughter of Louis Kossuth, leader of the Hungarian revolt
in 1848-49, had four sons who fought in the Union army during
the Civil War.[157] The following Poles served in the California
Regiments: Henry Baranowski, Alexander Beinkoskey, William
F. Derproskey, Edward Holski, Michael Klima, Cassimer B. Kustel, Robert Liberski, Charles Macowitzki, John Marcovitch, Joseph
Omazta, Lyon Philliporski, Kasmier Rozmoski, Paul F. H. Sabow-
leski, and James A. Zabriskie.[158] Large numbers of Poles also served
in the following New York Regiments: Polish Legion, Steuben
Guards, First German Rifles, United Turner Rifles, Astor Rifles,
De Kalb Regiment, and the Schoening Regiment.[159] Among the
younger if not the youngest soldiers in actual combat, were Edmund L. Zalinski of New York and Stanislaw Rydzewski of New
York; they volunteered at the age of sixteen. Among the elder,
if not the eldest, was Jozef Krokowski of Jones County, Iowa, who
enlisted at the age of sixty-one. According to Miecislaus Haiman
more than 5,000 Poles served in the Union Army.[160]

Kozlowski's ranch, halfway between Bernal Springs and
Glorietta Pass in Colorado, served as a Union Army Camp, hospital, and prison camp during the Civil War in the western territories. The owner of the ranch, Martin Kozlowski, a Polish refugee
and a United States Army Veteran, complimented the Union
soldiers on their behavior during the occupation of his ranch.

When they camped at my place, and while they made my tavern

---

[155] Bodger, *op. cit.*, p. 133.
[156] Lewandowska, *op. cit.*, p. 81.
[157] Born in Hungary, on November 12, 1817, she died in Brooklyn, New
York, June 29, 1860. She is buried in Greenwood Cemetery, where a thirteen foot
high obelisk of Italian marble was erected over her grave by Polish and Hungarian
exiles. Edmund L. Kowalczyk, "Polonica-Americana From the Past," *Polish American
Journal*, (September 15, 1956), p. 2.
[158] Haiman, *Polish Pioneers of California*, pp. 70-72.
[159] "Polacy w New Yorku," *Parafia Sw. Stanislawa B. i M. w New Yorku*
1874-1949, Tadeusz K. Sztybel, Editor. (No Imprint), pp. 28-32.
[160] Mieczyslaw Haiman, *Historja Udzialu Polakow w Amerykanskiej Wojnie
Domowej*, (Chicago: 1928), p. 33,

their hospital for over two months after their battles in the canyon, they never robbed me of anything, not even a chicken.[161]

Though the Poles, as a rule, did not approve of slavery, quite a number of them, who had happened to settle in the South, fought on the Confederate side in the war.[162] In the Confederate army during the Civil War many officers of Polish birth performed services, but the most prominent was Major Gaspard Tochman. On May 1, 1861, when war was a certainty, Tochman offered his services to the new government at Montgomery to raise ten or twenty companies to be composed of persons of foreign birth, enlisting for the duration, to constitute a Polish brigade.[163] In little more than a week, he received his authorization to raise ten companies, or, if practicable, twenty companies to be organized into a brigade. Such officers of the army as were necessary to enlist the men were to be detailed to such points as Tochman might direct. By June 20 in less than six weeks, Tochman had enlisted 1,415 foreigners, exclusive of 285 natives, whom he had organized into

---

[161] Ray C. Colton, *The Civil War in the Western Territories*, (Norman: 1959), p. 50.

[162] The Poles, a liberty-loving people, opposed slavery, and favored the emancipation of the Negro. Thaddeus Kosciuszko in his will of 1798 authorized Thomas Jefferson to employ his property in America in purchasing, liberating, educating, and training the slaves for worthy citizenship. The Negro found other Polish defenders. Wengierski, in 1783, sympathized with the American Negro and wrote of them with compassion. Julian Juzurkiewicz (1804-1837), the editor of *Polacy w Ameryce*, wrote of slavery. T. Lewinski edited the abolitionist paper *The True American*, begun by Cassius M. Clay in 1845, at the constant risk of his life. Holynski, Jacob Gordon (1823-1885) and Calixtus Wolski attacked the institution of slavery in their writings. Adam Gurowski, a prolific writer of the Civil War, in his Diary from March 4, 1861 to October 18, 1863, strongly defended Negro emancipation.

[163] From two quarters Tochman was made to feel the results of his espousal of the Cause of the Confederacy. About the middle of December, he received a communication from the Polish Democratic societies in France and England, which had been passed on August 26, inquiring into his motives and policy in deviating from the constitution he had "sworn to support" and censuring him for raising a brigade of troops for the seceded states. Tochman's reply from Nashville followed the traditional argument that he was a citizen of Virginia and, in consequence of her action in joining the Confederacy, a citizen of the new Confederation. He felt he had not departed from the principles of the Poles. The second repercussion, from the United States authorities, was far more serious for it brought about the imprisonment of his wife in the upper part of her own house in Washington under close surveillance for a fortnight. The Federal authorities ransacked the dwelling and seized all her correspondence. After repeated remonstrances she was released. Ella Lonn, *Foreigners in the Confederacy* (Chapel Hill: 1940), p. 162.

twenty companies and was drilling at Camp Anite, fifty miles
north of New Orleans, under four officers who had had military
training and service in European armies. When Tochman was
denied the rank of brigadier general, he halted his efforts to raise
troops and withdrew from the service.[164]

Tochman then sought monetary reparation from the Richmond
government for the sacrifices and losses he had sustained in property, reputation, abandonment of his northern legal clientele, and
separation for two and a half years from his family. He claimed
that he was entitled under an agreement, which had the nature
of a contract, to the pay of a brigadier-general for three years,
the period for which troops were raised, or his expenses, which
he estimated at $5,925 in gold, besides a loan of $1,600 in Confederate currency which he had incurred for his support.

> The Committee on Claims recommended unanimously that "where-
> as, the Congress highly appreciates said Major Gaspard Tochman's
> devotion to the cause of freedom and his active and useful exertions
> in behalf of the Cause of the Confederate States of America," the
> sum still due him to be paid.[165]

But the committee could not get action that session and so the
persistence of Major Tochman was doomed to ultimate failure,
as action was impossible after that date in the dying Confederacy.

Valerian Sulakowski served as Colonel of the "Fourteenth
Louisiana Infantry" and later as chief engineer to Major General
John Bankhead Magruder.[166] Ignatious S. Szymanski served as
Colonel of the "Chalmette Regiment" and later as agent for the
exchange of prisoners in the Trans-Mississippi Department.[167] In
1861, Leon Jastremski enlisted as a private in the 10th Infantry
of Louisiana under General Magruder. He fought at Warwick,
Williamsburg, and Richmond. At Malvern Hill he became a prison-
ner and was exchanged. In 1862, he received the rank of lieutenant and was later made a captain. Wounded at Chancellorsville, he recovered and fought at Gettysburg; captured again and

---

[164] Lonn, *Ibid.*, pp. 160-161.
[165] *Ibid.*, p. 164.
[166] Edmund L. Kowalczyk, "A Polish Family in the South," *Polish American Studies*, III (July-December, 1946), p. 106.
[167] *Ibid.*, p. 106.

returned in 1865. Colonel Arthur Grabowski, served in the "South Carolina Regiment" and took part in the assault on Fort Sum-ter.[168] Lieutenant Ladislaus Wankowicz served in one of the Louisiana Regiments; Julian Christian Sosnowski served as colonel in the Medical Corps of the Confederate army.[169] Henry Kaminski, who worked his way through high school after his arrival in America, enlisted in the "Tenth South Carolina Volunteers." Because of his executive ability he was soon singled out to become regimental commissary.[170]

The following Poles from Panna Maria, Texas, served in the Confederate Army: W. Lissy, A. Dziuk, J. Lissy, J. Brys, T. Kolodziejczyk, F. Moczygemba, and Captain Peter Kiolbassa.[171] His brother, Ignatious Kiolbassa, served in the Union army. Ella Lonn reports the following on the Poles living in the Panna Maria area.

> It is with real surprise that the researcher discovers that there were enough Poles in the vicinity of the Texan village of Panna Maria to muster a Polish company, commanded by Captain Joseph Kyrisk, which assembled with three other companies on the Cibolo River. The Polanders were regarded by the drillmaster, an old regular from the United States army, as the best-drilled of the battalion, a fact which he attributed to their military discipline in the old country and to their habit of obeying orders.[172]

One of the engravers for the Confederate States during the Civil War was a Pole, Wojciechowski. One example of his work, a $5,000 bond broadside is in the possession of Edmund L. Kowalczyk.[173]

Even the Polish women played a role in the Civil War. Sister Veronica, of the Sisters of Mercy (nee Klimkiewicz and related to Kosciuszko) worked for some time in the military hospitals.[174]

---

[168] Ibid., p. 106.

[169] Ibid., p. 105.

[170] Lonn, op. cit., pp. 252-253.

[171] Edmund L. Kowalczyk, "Jottings From the Polish American Past," Polish American Studies, XI (January-June, 1954), pp. 37-38.

[172] Lonn, op. cit., p. 128.

[173] Edmund L. Kowalczyk, "Jottings From the Polish American Past," Polish American Studies, VII (July-December, 1950), p. 79.

[174] Sister M. Liguori, H.F.N., "Polish Sisters in the Civil War," Polish American Studies, VII (January-June, 1950), pp. 1-7.

When she died in Baltimore, Maryland, in 1930, the *Baltimore Catholic Review* carried the news of her death as follows:

> A heroine in war and peace was laid to rest. . . . Millions in this land will in the years to come stand in awe before the monuments of men whose names ring down the ages and whose fame spans the ocean's vast expanse. Few will stop to kneel at the grave of this brave woman who knew not cowardice, who walked mid disease when others fled, who bathed the brows of smallpox patients and who staunched the blood which gushed from the gaping wounds of the heroes of the Blue and the Gray. . . .[175]

There was likewise a mention of her death in the *Baltimore News*.

> Sound taps for nun, war nurse. Echoes of blazing guns of Gettysburg sounded in New Cathedral Cemetery today as a rifle fired a volley over the grave of S. M. Veronica Klimkiewicz, believed one of the few women not in the service of their country ever accorded military honors at burial.[176]

The *New York Times*[177] and the *Baltimore Evening Sun*[178] also carried a brief obituary note. Her sister, Thadia Klimkiewicz, also a Sister of Mercy, worked as a nurse during the Civil War. Similar work was performed in the South by Mrs. Sosnowski of Columbia, widow of a Polish officer of the 1831 insurrection.[179]

The following Poles, who patented inventions before the end of the Civil War, should not be lost from the record of our intellectual history: Anthony Glomicki, floor cloths; Gustave A. Blitkowski, firearms; John Kulinski, railroad car collision apparatus; Gasper Zwicki, the loom; Joseph Smolinski, pottery; Seidel de Mackiewicz and Bartholomew Beniowski, printing. Anthony Pilinski, who also was a printer, reproduced many facsimilies of early rare Americana which were presented to the *Bibliothèque Polonaise* in Paris.[180] Xavier Karczewski of Philadelphia is credited with many inventions which proved useful to American in-

---

175 *Baltimore Catholic Review*, (March 28, 1930), p. 2.
176 *Baltimore News*, (March 27, 1930), p. 19.
177 *New York Times*, (March 26, 1930), p. 27.
178 *Baltimore Evening Sun*, (March 26, 1930), p. 25.
179 Lagodzinska, *op. cit.*, p. 6.
180 Edmund L. Kowalczyk, "Jottings From the Polish American Past," *Polish American Studies*, XI (January-June, 1954), p. 34.

dustry.[181] Captain Edmund L. Gray Zalinski, who taught military science at the Massachusetts Institute of Technology, was an inventor of many military devices.[182] According to Professor Bradley, specialist in aeronautical engineering at the University of Cincinatti, Thaddeus Sobieska Coulincourt Lowe had established the first air unit, composed of six balloons, and made the first flight ninety years ago from Cincinnati to South Carolina thus earning the title of "Father of the American Air Force."[183]

Thaddeus Sobieski Coulincourt Lowe organized and directed the operations of a balloon observation service during the Civil War. He had been a meteorologist and aeronaut for some years prior to the Civil War, becoming interested in balloons as a means of investigating upper air currents. His first ascent was made in 1858 from Ottawa, Canada. Next he built an airship named the "City of New York," in which he made a number of voyages. He made ascents as high as 23,000 feet. Soon after the war began Lowe interested officials in trying out balloons for observation and, after being appointed chief of an aeronautic section, built five balloons, which rendered valuable service to the Army of the Potomac. On June 18 1861, he telegraphed a message to President Lincoln from a balloon high in the air.

A native of Piotrkow, Poland, Michael Heilprin, who settled in the United States in the 1870's, is credited by Marion M. Coleman with devising the first scheme of transliteration from the Slavic into English to the published in a serious journal. The system of transliteration was prepared at the request of the American Library Association and published in the "Library Journal" for 1885. Heilprin's scheme, known at the A.I.A. system, is the standard method of transliterating Slavic names and words into English. With some improvements, it is generally followed in the United States today.[184]

According to Henry Kalussowski, an able leader, politician, and writer, the Poles occupied relatively more government offices

---

[181] Bochenski, op. cit., p. 54.

[182] He studied at the United States Artillery School at Fortress Monroe and the School of Submarine Mining at Willets' Point, New York.

[183] "Polak Ojcem Lotnictwa U.S.," Dziennik Polski (October 28, 1959), p. 8.

[184] Joseph A. Swastek, "Historical Notes and Comments," Polish American Studies, V (July-December, 1948), p. 111.

at Washington, than citizens of other nationalities. John Tyssowski, once the "Dictator of Krakow," had held several prominent
federal positions at Washington, D. C.; he occupied the post of
chief examiner at the United States Patent Office at the time of
his death. Erasmus Andrew Florian (Florian Liskowacki) was a
pioneer banker in Memphis, Tennessee. He later established the
first private bank at San Antonio, Texas. His business transactions covered a large part of the South. Stephen Remak was
an American consul at Trieste. Captain Leo Jastremski (Jastrzebski) was mayor of Baton Rouge, delegate to the Louisiana State
Convention, and United States Consul at Callao, Peru. President
Cleveland appointed him also Secretary of Agriculture. In 1907,
Captain Jastremski was nominated for Governor of Louisiana by
the Democratic Party; this was tantamount to election, because
in 1906 the state adopted a primary election law providing for
the direct nomination of all state officers. Jastremski, however,
died on November 23, 1907, in Baton Rouge before he could take
his oath of office.

# CHAPTER FOUR

# Economic Emigration 1870-1929

However important was the contribution of the Polish political immigration to America, it is to be regarded as that of individuals, not of a group. The several thousand Polish refugees who came to the United States during this period were almost exclusively revolutionists seeking escape from imprisonment or death. Up to 1870, the Polish emigration movement was still essentially sporadic, the number of emigrants comparatively small. But the quality of the Poles coming throughout this period of political emigration was such as to give them a significance out of proportion to their numbers. Many individuals of this exile period of Polish immigration possessed superior ability and were freely admitted to American society, which looked upon them as martyrs for liberty. Even if they spoke little English, they had studied Latin and French and thus foreign languages did not present an unsurmountable barrier; in fact, a large number gained prominence in the new land by their sheer individual prowess, ability, and personality. The majority of these political immigrants, however, have gone through life in the United States alone, without depending upon or seeking the support of Polish political or social organizations, which for practical purposes did not exist. Neither, for that matter, could they find aid in churches or schools erected by and intended for the Polish immigrants. None were available. Moreover, the intellectuals, who formed the majority of the political immigrants, were lukewarm towards the Catholic Faith, and preferred to be looked upon as liberals and nationalists. Their Americanization quite frequently coincided with the loss of their faith. With a few noteworthy exceptions, they exercised no influence upon the Polish immigrants of the succeeding generations.[1]

---

[1] The leading spirit of all movements among the Poles in America throughout the period of political immigration was Henry Corvinus Kalussowski, the son of one of the Chamberlains of King Stanislaus Poniatowski. Kalussowski first came to Amer-

The total number of Poles in the United States during this period did not exceed 40,000, of whom fully one-fourth lived in Chicago. There were, however, Poles in every state and territory of the Union, with the greatest number in Texas, Michigan, Wisconsin, Illinois, Indiana, Missouri, and Pennsylvania, where they had been attracted by virgin lands or coalfields. Quite a few were attracted to California by the gold-rush of 1850.[2]

After the last rebellion in the early 1860's partitioned Poland was not again aroused to revolution, but rather to expatriation. With hopes of an independent Poland sent glimmering after the defeat of France by Prussia, uncounted hundreds of Polish aristocrats, political exiles and even peasants, desirous of improving their economic condition, made their way to America. To remain in their country was to accept a future without hope for themselves or their children. Soon settlements of Poles became more frequent especially in the northern cities of Chicago, Milwaukee, Detroit, Buffalo, and Cleveland. Polish colonies also made their appearance in the States of Pennsylvania, Nebraska, and Missouri. In 1876, a little band of Polish intellectuals, including Henryk Sienkiewicz,[3] and Helena Modjeska (Modrzejewska),[4] attempted to found a kind of Brook-Farm Community in California. The attempt failed.

In 1870, there were some 50,000 Poles and ten Polish parishes in America. By 1875, the number had reached 200,000 Poles and fifty parishes in some three hundred communities. By 1889, there

---

ica in 1834. Returning to Poland, he represented a Polish constituency in the Prussian parliament, but upon his expulsion from Poland by the Prussian government he again came to the United States. During the Civil War he organized the Thirty-first New York Regiment. Later he held positions in the Department of State in Washington, D. C., and translated the official documents relating to the purchase of Alaska from Russia by the United States. Seroczynski, *op. cit.*, pp. 204-207.

[2] Gentil G. Katoski, O.F.M., *Some Aspects of Polish Immigration, 1900-1914* (unpublished Master's thesis, Catholic University of America, 1948), pp. 8-9.

[3] Henryk Sienkiewicz, the first Polish Nobel Prize Laureate and author of *Quo Vadis*, during his stay in America wrote *Letters From a Journey in America* and the tale *Sketches in Charcoal*. Also in America, he found prototypes for two of his immortal characters in Polish literature, "Old Captain" Rudolph Korwin Pietrowski for "Zagloba" and Captain Francis Wojciechowski for "Podbipienta."

[4] The following year, Helena Modrzejewska made her debut in San Francisco, and until her retirement thirty years later, was among the foremost artists on the American stage.

were approximately 800,000 Poles in the United States. The Polish communities had 132 churches, 126 priests, and 122 schools, nearly all conducted by the Felician Sisters and the School Sisters of Notre Dame. Buffalo, Detroit, Cleveland, Pittsburg, and Mil-waukee, in addition to Chicago, had become important Polish centers as early as 1880. Wisconsin had the largest number of Polish settlements, but Chicago had the largest population.

> In 1890, there were in this country 147,440 persons born in Poland; in 1900 there were 383,407. In 1890, the three Atlantic States of New York, Pennsylvania, and Massachusetts had 34.6 per cent of the natives of Poland in the country; in 1900, they had 43.8 per cent. These three States, together with three interior States of Illinois, Michigan, and Wisconsin, had 76.9 per cent in 1890, and 77.2 per cent in 1900. The three interior States had 42.1 per cent in 1890, and 33.4 per cent in 1900.[5]

The peak was reached in the year 1912-1918, when the num-ber of Polish immigrants was 174,365.[6] It dwindled to a trickle after Poland won its independence and when new immigration laws, which sharply curtailed immigration, were put into effect. By 1920, there were approximately 3,000,000 inhabitants of Polish parentage in the United States.[7] By 1930, the census figure for foreign-born Poles in the United States was 1,268,383, and the total number of Polish stock (with one or both parents Polish) was 3,343,198.[8] If we add those of Polish descent in the second and third generations and bear in mind the unavoidable gaps in statistics caused by the fact that Poland as a State did not exist before 1919, we arrive at figures between five to six million.[9] According to the 1940 population statistics, 2,416,320 persons

---

[5] Prescott F. Hall, *Immigration and Its Effects Upon the United States,* (New York: 1913), p. 92.

[6] Robert A. Schermerhorn, *These Our People: Minorities in American Culture,* (Boston: 1949), p. 265.

[7] The exact figure is very hard to determine, since the Polish nation was under the political dominance of three foreign powers and the Poles entering before 1918 came under various passports and often declared themselves by the nationality of the conquerors. Helena Znaniecka Lopata, *The Function of Voluntary Associa-tions in an Ethnic Community: Polonia* (unpublished Ph.D. dissertation, University of Chicago, 1954), p. 15.

[8] Carl Wittke, *We Who Built America,* (New York: 1940), pp. 419-425.

[9] Casimir Smogorzewski, "Unity Among the Poles in America," *Free Europe,* (June 16, 1944), p. 189.

named the Polish language as the principal tongue of their child-hood. Of this total, 801,680 were foreign born, and 1,614,640 native born.[10] Since World War II, the number has increased slightly.[11] From 1946 to 1958, according to the International Catholic Migration Commission report, 209,312 immigrants came to the United States from Poland;[12] the majority of these immi-grants were admitted as displaced persons.[13]

Highly educated and talented Poles continued to settle in America all through the remainder of the nineteenth and the first decades of the twentieth century. Thus the American arts were enriched by such great musicians and conductors as Leopold Stokowski, Artur Bojanowski, Artur Rubinstein, Jozef Hoffman, Bronislaw Huberman, Wanda Landowska, and Dr. Arthur Rod-zinski who attained fame as an "orchestra builder and repairer." In 1933, he developed the Cleveland Orchestra into one of the finest musical organizations in the United States. In 1937, he was selected by Arturo Toscanini to organize and train the NBC Symphony. In 1943, he became the conductor of the New York Philharmonic Orchestra.[14]

"I only dream of one thing—to play Bach and Mozart," wrote Wanda Landowska as a little girl and then she sealed her dream in an envelope marked: "To be opened when I am grown up." The young daughter of a Warsaw lawyer could not wait. The very next day she opened it again, and the desire became a promise. By the time she was 14, she was a graduate of the Warsaw Conservatory of Music, and a concert pianist whose

----

10 Rev. Joseph Swastek, M.A., "What is a Polish American?" Polish American Studies, I (January-December, 1944), p. 42.

11 This group had a larger number of intellectuals than the previous groups.

12 "209,312 'Poles' came to the USA in Twelve Years," Polish American Journal, (September 26, 1959), p. 6.

13 The following have enriched American culture by their skills and talents: the late Florian Znaniecki, Professor of Sociology at the University of Illinois; Dr. Hilary Koprowski, Assistant Director of Virus Research at Lederic Laboratories; Jan Karski of Georgetown University; and Henry Arctowski, arctic explorer, formerly at the astro-physical observatory of the Smithsonian Institute.

14 The son of a Polish army surgeon, Rodzinski was born in Spaleto on the coast of Dalmatia. He studied law at the University of Lwow. Severely wounded in World War I, he resumed his studies in Vienna and took his doctor's degree, which had no connection with music. Eventually, he joined the Warsaw Opera, where Leopold Stokowski met him in 1925 and offered him an assistant conductorship in Philadelphia.

greatest joy, and biggest triumph, was her rendition of Bach's intricate *English Suite in E Minor*. By the time she was 21, she was well on her way to being Bach's pianist laureate. It was not enough. She yearned to revive the instrument that Bach used as well as his work. Few more difficult instruments exist than the 18th century harpsichord, half-harp, half-piano with its double keyboard and deep, plunky tones. With her husband Henri Lew, a folklorist who died in 1919, Pianist Landowska journeyed through Europe's museums where old harpsichords were exhibited. Finally she asked Paris' famed Pleyel firm to make her a harpsichord like the one Bach played.

Under her hands, Pleyel's harpsichord took on a rare brilliance. It was, she said, "capable of greater brilliance and more tonal variety" than any other modern harpsichord. In 1907 she carried a special harpsichord, first by train to Moscow then by sleigh, to Tolstoy's country home, Yasnaya Polyana. "I played for him," she said "and he talked to me." In 1923 she shipped her harpsichord to Philadelphia for her United States debut under Conductor Leopold Stokowski. "Anyone who has heard Wanda Landowska play Bach's *Italian Concerto* on her wonderful harpsichord," wrote Albert Schweitzer, "finds it hard to understand how it could ever again be played on a piano." Schweitzer was only one of Landowska's admirers. So many music lovers made the trip to her home in the Paris suburb of Saint-Leu-la-Foret that Paris station guards called the 2 o'clock Sunday run "Mme. Landowska's train." Landowska's art led Manuel de Falla to compose his *Harpsichord Concerto* especialy for her.

World War II forced Landowska to flee Europe. She came to the United States and settled in Lakeville, Connecticut where she concentrated on recording her interpretation of the old masters. Her recording of the 48 labyrinthine preludes and fuges of Bach's *Well-Tempered Clavier* is a modern classic. Landowska called it "my last will and testament." It was far from her last. At 76, but with the spirit of a sprite, the high priestess of the harpsichord turned once again to "my first love"—the piano, and to a second master Mozart. In the intimacy of her parlor, Landowska played some of Mozart's loveliest and most deceptively simple music (Sonatas K. 282, 283, 311, 333, Rondo in

A Minor, K. 511, Country Dances, K. 606) as RCA engineers recorded her art, sometimes in five hours at a stretch. Her recordings won cheers as one of the most important contributions to the interpretations of Mozart. Still it was not enough to satisfy her youthful dream. She recorded an album of Haydn sonatas and immediately made arrangements to record Bach's *Three-Part Inventions*. But that at last, was denied. One morning in August, 1959, she suffered a stroke and died at the age of 80.

Gilda Gray, whose real name was Maryanna Michalska, was a star in the vaudeville era which produced Al Jolson, Will Rogers, Gallagher and Shean and Sophie Tucker. She was born in Krakow, Poland. When her parents were killed in a revolution, she fled to America with her foster parents. She sang and danced in Milwaukee saloons at the age of fourteen. She could scarcely speak English, but her slithering dances were a language that needed no translation. In a recent interview Miss Gray stated that she invented the shimmy in her teens when she was entertaining in Cudahy.

> They hoisted me on a table and I sang "The Star Spangled Banner." I could hardly talk English so the words came hard, so hard that I found myself wiggling my shoulders and then the rest of me. One night a customer asked me what kind of a dance I was doing. I said I was shaking my chemise only I pronounced it "shimmy." That's how the dance and the name were born.[15]

She went on from Cudahy to appear in the "Ziegfeld Follies" with Will Rogers and George White's "Scandals." She also appeared with Gallagher and Shean and other entertainment stars. Al Jolson tabbed her "Queen of the shimmy dancers." Sophie Tucker persuaded her to change her name from Mary to Gilda because she thought the name Gilda to be more glamorous.

It was, and Miss Gray's fame spread. In less than ten years, she made more than ten million dollars. Among the more successful movies she made was "Aloma of the South Seas," in which she created a mainland version of the Hawaiian hula. With the depression Miss Gray faded into obscurity. By then the shimmy was something that belonged to the past along with the speakeasies. Her death on December 22, 1959, closed another chapter of the

15 "Gilda Gray," *Polish American Historical Association Bulletin*, Dr. Joseph A. Wytrwal, Editor, Bulletin No. 184, (December, 1959), pp. 1-2.

tumultuous "Twenties," which had acclaimed F. Scott Fitzgerald, jazz, prohibition, and racoon coats and the '29 crash.

Carole Landis, also a Hollywood star, born a Ridste, comes from one of those large Polish families which has many widely scattered relatives. Richard Boleslawski directed several outstanding Hollywood films. Jan Kiepura, a tenor, appeared in 1935 opposite Gladys Swarthout in "Give Us This Night," a Paramount film, and starred in "The Merrry Widow" on Broadway in 1943-1944. The names of Marcella Sembrich-Kochanska, Pola Negri, Carole Landis, Kathy Marlowe, Bella Darvi, Edward de Reszke, Jean de Reszke, Adam Didur and Ina Burskaya are too familiar to be more than noted.[16]

Among scientists there were Bronislaus Malinowski, anthropologist[17]; Alfred Korzybski specialist in general semantics; Felix Pawlowski, Professor of Aeronautics at the University of Michigan; Dr. Joseph Jastrow, professor of Psychology at the University of Michigan[18]; Professor Louis Karpinski, mathematician and cartographer; Dr. A. J. Lotka, statistician; W. Swietoslawski, chemist; C. Funk, the discoverer of vitamins; and Dr. Ralph Modjeski, one of the best known engineers in the United States. Chairman of the Board of Engineers of the San Francisco-Oakland bridge, Dr. Modjeski served as consultant on the Manhattan bridge over the East River, New York, and Mid-Hudson bridge at Poughkeepsie.[19] Jan Rosen, W. Benda, Tade Styka, E. Kanarek, S. Kozlow, T. Roszak,

---

[16] Charles Allan Baretski, *The Polish Pantheon*, (A roster of men and women of Polish birth or ancestry who have contributed to American culture and world civilization), (Newark: 1958), pp. 1-22.

[17] Bronislaw K. Malinowski died in 1942. He was Bishop Museum visiting professor of anthropology at Yale University. Recognized as one of the great social anthropologists of modern times, he developed a new way of looking at primitive cultures. He came to anthropology in the days when the greatest emphasis was centered on recording and classifying the peculiar antics of savage peoples and attempting to reconstruct the evolutionary histories which would lead back into a pre-human animal world. Malinowski was the first to state the necessity of participating in the lives of savages. His technique was to observe primitive society from within, through its own language and the eyes and sentiments of its members. In his numerous studies he became the founder of a new approach in that field, now known as functionalism, which emphasized the functional interrelationships of all cultural phenomena in the structures of society.

[18] He wrote fourteen books and numerous articles. From 1935 to 1938 he lectured on the NBC network.

[19] He is the son of the famous Polish tragedienne, Madame Helena Modjeska, who died in 1909. A monument to her was unveiled in 1935 in Anaheim, California.

and the Makielski brothers have been notable American painters. S. Szubalski, and M. Lednicka have given American sculpture new charm.

However from 1880 to 1930 these distinguished Poles were outnumbered by a new group of immigrants: landless peasants and urban workers whose earning power in Poland was so low that it kept them on the verge of starvation. They arrived in America with little more than calluses on their hands, had no skills to offer, no learning, and no industrial experience. But they had muscle-power, the stamina of dray horses, and an intense desire to take advantage of the freedom denied them in their homeland. Starvation-thin and big-boned, they were not afraid of work. The work available in the large cities for the Polish immigrant was primarily laboring work, indeed, it was all the Polish immigrants were capable of doing. As unskilled workers they often found themselves in jobs at the bottom of the ladder, sometimes in occupations that no native, except perhaps a Negro, would accept. Furthermore, unable to speak English when they first arrived, which was not true, for instance of the Scotch or the Irish, they were more severely handicapped; but they proved themselves to be competent and conscientious workers, they gradually earned the respect of their employers, fellow-workers, and neighbors. Although they were unlearned and humble, and from the lower classes of Polish society, they were, nevertheless, intelligent people. American industrialists in the nineteenth century were as grateful for the new hands as John Smith had been three-hundred-and-fifty years earlier at Jamestown, Virginia, despite their preference for native Americans. As a result industry sought them out. By the hundreds these newcomers fell into unskilled occupations in the textile mills of New England, in the railroads and lumber mills of the West, in the mines of Pennsylvania and West Virginia, in the slaughter-houses of Chicago, and in the steel mills of Akron and Youngstown, Ohio. With the rise of the auto industry, they entered the factories and became the core of the auto industry, which they developed to a very high degree of efficiency.

In basic industries like iron and steel making, coal mining, construction work, copper mining, smelting and oil refining, as well as in many other branches of the heavy industries, according to Bishop Woznicki, they have left their imprint.

> It is not wrong, then, to say that the Polish immigrant was the backbone of these industries for many years. This was a definite contribution to the welfare and progress of their adopted country and these men with their solid virtues and accomplishments became a substantial asset in that vortex of American development we call the "Melting Pot."[20]

Not all the Poles became factory workers. At least a third of the total Polish immigration ventured into farming: some in the Middle West, some in the South, others scattered over the Northeast. American farmers in the New England area had recruited Polish farmers for work on tobacco and vegetable farms as early as 1870. An article in the *Boston Globe,* June 29, 1902, describes the first stages of recruitment.

> Charles Parsons of Northampton, who has since died, then a pushing aggressive farmer, conceived the idea of going to New York and Castle Garden and there securing enough of the strong and sturdy immigrants to meet the demand for farm and domestic labor. The business grew rapidly. Agents at New York told the incoming immigrants as pleasing stories as was necessary to make the Pole see the Connecticut Valley farms as the promised land. . . . The contract was not particularly bad for either the farmer or the laborer. The men came first, and were followed by women and children. The number must have been in the thousands.[21]

Eventually the Polish immigrants in New England took over lands that had been ruthlessly worked and abandoned by Yankees, abandoned in the belief that the soil was exhausted. Using the understanding of the land and food-growing skill bequeathed them by the old country, the immigrants made them fertile again, thus rescuing hundreds of thousands of apparently hopeless areas for high-grade agriculture. Immigrants from Poland where land is scarce, developed methods unknown to the Americans who have been accustomed to great areas of land. The New Englanders of the Connecticut Valley speak in terms of highest praise of the industry, efficiency, thrift, and prosperity of the Poles. Even Calvin

---

[20] Bishop Stephen S. Woznicki, "Polish Immigrant is Backbone of Many Industries in New Home," *Dziennik Polski,* (September 25, 1959), p. 2.

[21] Philip Davis, *Immigration and Americanization,* (New York: 1920), p. 159.

Coolidge admitted once that it took the Polish immigrants to show the Yankees how to till the soil.[22]

The Polish immigrant advances from poverty to prosperity and thrives upon lands where American farmers would starve. By re-claiming farms abandoned by the Yankees and specializing in onion and tobacco crops, the Poles made small fortunes from their farms. Since they had established themselves, a million-dollar onion crop is not uncommon in the Deerfield Valley in Massachu-setts.[23] Konrad Bercovici, in his study of the American Pole, made the following comment on the work of the Polish farmer.

> Tens of thousands of acres of cut over land, which have been lying worthless because no native farmer cared to undertake to clear it of stumps, have been bought at a very low price . . . by Poles who have saved up enough money . . . to purchase it. What they have done with their land is an amazing feat of human endeavor. For land which had been lying worthless is now fertile and productive, and the forest fires that had been decimating timberland are now slowly being eliminated by the vast stretches of cultivated areas. As far as the land is concerned, this country has benefited considerably by the work of its half-million Poles. The fact that these men had practically to make their own land, instead of buying it readymade as other populations have done, has made the land dear to them. They consider it a part of themselves, and they love it as much as they formerly loved their own dear Polish land.[24]

Today on Long Island, Polish immigrants are engaged in truck-gardening; in the Connecticut Valley, they raise tobacco, onions and asparagus; in the northern and western States they are break-ing the prairies and converting them into fields of corn and of wheat.

A few decades ago, one of the immigration inspectors paid the following tribute to the typical Polish immigrant to America.

> Next came a bookkeeper, so he says, his father gave him money and he was coming here to make his fortune. The inspector is not satis-fied and he is turned over to the "S. I. Board." But his papers, money, and statements are clear and he is admitted; they give him the benefit of the doubt as they always do. But next in line comes a well built Pole, with nothing in the world but a carpet bag, a few bundles, and small showing of money. Ambition is written all over his face

---

22 Bochenski, op. cit., p. 56.
23 Ibid., p. 56.
24 Konrad Bercovici, On New Shores, (New York: 1925), pp. 122-123.

and he is admitted. "Now," says the recorder, pausing for a moment, "see the difference between these two gents. The first duffer will look around for a job, spend time and' money to get something to suit him, and keep his job for a short time; then he will give it up, run through his money, borrow from his friends, and then give them all the cold hand. He won't wear well, and his dad knew it when he sent him over, but he was glad to get rid of him. So lots of them are. Now look at the difference between him and that Pole. He knows nothing but work. Look at his eyes, mild but good. He has been brought up next to mother earth; turn him loose from the train when he reaches his destination and' he will dig. He won't hang around looking for a job, but he will till the soil and before you or I know it he will have crops and that is what he will live on. He comes from a hard country, is tough, and when you and I are going around shivering in an overcoat, he will be going around in his shirt sleeves. That is the stuff we want here, not the first kind, with flabby hands and sapped vitality." Sure enough the bookkeeper did not wear well, and falling into the hands of the police some months later, he was deported under the three-year immigration law, and the country was better for it.[25]

Polish women went to work in hotels and restaurants. They also served as domestic servants, did laundry and cleaning.[26] Many of their daughters went into the auto factories, running sewing machines and punch presses. Together with their husbands, they worked and saved. And with an almost inbred obsession for economic security, they bought their homes, laying the foundation for the future of their children. Eventually by taking advantage of America's opportunities, these Polish families carved themselves a place in the community.

They saw to it that their children were educated; that they would have even greater opportunity. They insisted on a better education for their children; the priests in many Polish Catholic parishes encouraged them, even to the extent of privately counseling them to send their children to non-Catholic institutions for higher specialized education.[27]

As a result, out of the Polish communities, within the past

---

[25] Bochenski, op. cit., pp. 55-56.

[26] The old Polish culture demanded the cooperative effort of every member of the family. It carried over among the immigrant families.

[27] Ray Courage, "Poles Build Freedom Way to Detroit," Detroit Free Press, (September 16, 1957), p. 23.

fifty years, came an ever-increasing number of professionals, men of learning and stature. For it was in the polish communities,[28] in the midst of the filth and the suffering that parents made super-human sacrifices to send their sons on to higher education. If the slum experience gave Americans of Polish descent that urge and drive to create out of themselves something that they could not have achieved, had their parents remained in Europe, then the slum experience with all its faults, with all its misery, and with all its difficulties was a boon both for them and for America. Con-temporary Detroit attests to the fact that the immigrant's children and his children's children took advantage of the many opportu-nities and have become successful.

The metropolitan area's 400,000 to 450,000 Americans of Polish descent are a cross-section of the American scene. Whether their names end in "ski" or have been changed to shortened, Americanized forms, they now have made names for themselves in science and medicine; politics and business; education and athletics, and music and the arts.

Within the area of greater Detroit are hundreds of Polish doctors of medicine, dentistry and science serving the community. Dr. John B. Bielawski, medical director of the Michigan Heart Association, and assistant professor of clinical medicine at Wayne State University, College of Medicine, states there are well over one hundred Medical Doctors of Polish extraction in Detroit alone.[29] Of these, he states, approximately ten per cent have taken their board examinations for such specialties as surgery, internal medicine, anesthesiology, and radiology. This percentage, Dr. Bielawski reports, is approximately the same as exists for men of undifferentiated national backgrounds.[30]

---

[28] Contrary to popular belief, Michigan's Americans of Polish descent do not all live in Hamtramck, even though the city has come to be synonymous with Ameri-cans of Polish descent. The city has dropped in population from 65,000 to about 41,000. Although normally considered a Polish town, it actually has less than 20,000 Polish Americans, the majority of the remainder are Lithuanians, Ukranians, Czecho-slovakians and Negroes. Public school enrollment dropped from a peak of 12,254 in 1932 to 6,847 in 1940. Since 1945, it has remained about 4,000, recently showing a slight increase. Pilsudski High School, one of its largest was closed after World War II; today it houses the City Government.

[29] Jean Pearson, "Detroit Poles Proud of Top Scientists," Detroit Free Press, (September 21, 1957), p. 1.

[30] A number of Polish medical men, including Dr. Bielawski, hold positions

In 1938, there were fewer than eight hundred American physicians of Polish descent. Today, there are nearly three thousand: men such as Dr. Thaddeus Danowski, professor of research medicine at the University of Pittsburgh; Lt. Colonel Edwin Pulaski, formerly chief surgeon at Walter Reed Hospital; Dr. Edward H. Warszawski, clinical professor of surgery at Loyola University; Dr. John J. Blasko, Connecticut's commissioner of mental health; and Dr. Frank Bonzell, professor of radiology at the University of Pennsylvania and former speaker of the House of Delegates of the American Medical Association.[31]

In physics and engineering the torch lighted by Madame Sklodowska-Curie is still burning brightly. Many American scientists and engineers of Polish descent can be found on the staffs of American universities throughout the United States. Dr. Stanislaw Mrozowski heads the only American university department which has a laboratory and a building devoted entirely to carbon research. In fact, he is a pioneer physicist in carbon research; in 1949, he set up the laboratory. Recently, Dr. Alexander G. Karczmar of Loyola University, Chicago, has received the first installment of a five-year $130,000 grant from the United States Public Health Service to support a graduate training program in pharmacology. The name of Dr. Emil John Konopinski, co-developer of the hydrogen bomb and renowned atomic physicist, is world-famous.[32] Dr. Edward Teller, who became famous as the father of the hydrogen bomb, claims it was Dr. Konopinski who proved by calculation, that the bomb would not ignite the atmosphere of the world or the ocean.[33]

Other atomic physicists include Dr. Gerald Pawlicki of the Oak Ridge National Laboratory; Dr. Bruno Zwolinski of the National Foundation; and Dr. Roman Smoluchowski, Professor

---

of responsibility at hospitals and universities. Dr. Casimir Weiss, for example, is medical chief of staff at St. Francis Hospital in Detroit. Dr. Casimir Staniszewski is medical director of the tuberculosis division of the out-patient department at Herman Kiefer Hospital in Detroit. An outstanding specialist in tuberculosis, Dr. Edward G. Nedwicki, is chief of the TB section at Veterans Hospital in Dearborn, Michigan. Health Commissioner for Hamtramck is Dr. Walter A. Kaplita; and chief medical examiner for Wayne County, Michigan is Dr. Edward S. Zawadzki.

[31] Maisel, *They All Chose America*, p. 218.
[32] *Courage, op. cit.*, p. 1.
[33] Pearson, *op. cit.*, p. 4.

of Physics and Metallurgical Engineering at Carnegie Institute of Technology; and Dr. John Turkevich of Princeton University, consultant to the Atomic Energy Commission and the Brookhaven National Laboratory. Dr. Konopinski is in charge of research in physics at Indiana University; at present he is doing research on the complete conversion of mass into energy.[34] There are few universities that do not have Americans of Polish descent on their faculties. For every educator born in Poland, there are several second-and-third generation Americans of Polish descent.

Pulpit eloquence has always been a marked characteristic of Polish immigrants. Among the original leaders of the nineteenth century there were not a few minor Polish Konarskis. And among the descendants of the Polish pioneers, the silver tongue is fairly common. The following excel in their own parish environment and in the larger Catholic body of the Catholic Church: Bishop Stephen S. Woznicki, Bishop Alexander M. Zaleski, Msgr. Vincent V. Borkowicz, Msgr. Feliks F. Burant, Msgr. Wallace J. Filipowicz, Rev. Valerian Jasinski, Rev. Joseph Swastek, Rev. Jacek Przygoda, Rev. Bronislaus S. Rosiak, and Msgr. W. A. Losieniecki. Father John Stanislaus Zybura of the Diocese of Cleveland wrote several philosophical works, mostly interpretations of St. Thomas Acquinas. Another who has written books of great merit, mostly philosophical, is Father John Joseph Rolbiecki, of the Diocese of La Crosse, now a member of the faculty of the Catholic University of America. Father Andrew Krzesinski's and Father Stanislaus J. Grabowski's writings have also been favorably received by reviewers. Father Grabowski, formerly a professor in college, seminary, and university, is emerging as an international authority on St. Augustine. Through his articles in various periodicals both in this country and abroad, he won

---

[34] Dr. Konopinski, who at the age of twenty-seven became full professor, might have spent his life on the production line of an automobile factory if it was not for the financial support arranged by his high school principal, E. M. Conklin, a Rotary Club member. Through the Rotarians, $700 was raised to send the all "A" student to the University of Michigan. At the University he made straight A's for the next nine years, receiving scholarships for his outstanding work. Though a modest man, Dr. Konopinski has always had a high goal. On his application to the University of Michigan he was asked, "Have you any person in mind whose position you would like to fill?" His answer: "Yes. Eminent authority on matters physical and mathematical—Professor Einstein."

recognition for scholarship and Augustinian research. In the nine years spent in European universities he obtained the doctorate in theology at the University of Innsbruck and the *magister aggregatus* of the Gregorian University in Rome. His earlier work, *The All-Present God* was published in 1954. His most recent book, *The Church An Introduction to the Theology of St. Augustine* was published in 1957. The list could be greatly extended without lowering the quality of the contribution it represents.

One name will live in the history of charity: Clara Swieczkowska, a welfare worker of international scope. A native of Detroit, Clara Swieczkowska began her activities with the Polish Community by helping to raise funds for "Dom Polski" in Detroit long before Poland reappeared on world maps. Then there were Polish floods of 1914, when she helped organize relief drives in Detroit. Later, in World War I, she was an officer in the women's division of the Polish Relief Committee. It was during this time that 26 freight cars of clothing were sent from Detroit to aid the Poles. A few years later, with the blessing of the late Bishop J. Gallagher, she organized the Polish Activities League in Detroit. The League established the first professionally-conducted Polish settlement house in America, opened the first Polish summer camp for children in the United States, published the first bilingual monthly for Polish American women, and maintained a consistent program of social services conducted along professional lines. During the depression, the Polish Activities League soup kitchens, under her direction, fed as many as 800 persons a day. Since 1935, she has been executive director of the Polish Activities League. At the beginning of World War II, Clara Swieczkowska returned to work for Polish Relief, as one of the organizers of the Polish American Relief Committee. Some other highlights of her untiring service include organizing the Polish Goodfellows, aiding in the recruitment for World War I Polish Army of General Joseph Haller, helping organize the National Council of Catholic Women, and assisting the Polish Lapins, the Ravensbruck concentration camp medical experimentees. She was also the first woman elected vice-president of the Polish Roman Catholic Union, as well as the first American of Polish descent to receive the medal "Pro Ecclesia et Pontifice" from Pope Pius IX. And she is the first woman to be elected chairman of the Michigan State Welfare Commission; her term will terminate in the fall of 1961.[35]

In music and art, Americans of Polish descent have also self-lessly made lasting cultural contributions to America. The Lutnia Singing Society of Detroit, for example, has been making music in and about Detroit for over a half-century. So excellent has their art become that the Detroit Symphony Orchestra has in-vited them as guest artists for their most serious concerts.[36] The society has been also in evidence in performances of the great Polish operas. It took an imposing part in the presentation of Moniuszko's "Halka," in 1951. The memorable cast also included the Laur Dancing Society of Detroit, which has attracted many capacity crowds to the band shell area on Belle Isle in Detroit during the last thirty years. It is through Laur Society's efforts that the Polonaise, Krakowiak, Mazur, Oberek, Goralski, and Sztajerek have become familiar in America. At every public appearance of the Laur Society there is a display of needle work that is dazzling. Many of the costumes are cherished heirlooms.

Not only in music and dance do Americans of Polish descent reveal their talents. In the world of art they have produced works of genuine merit. Walter and Harriet Krawiec have won distinc-tion in painting and cartoons, as has Sister Mary Stanisia Kur-kowska in portrait painting; Leo Makielski's murals and portraits have won high praise. Stanislaus Benda has created a mask which has been given his name.

If Korczak Ziolkowski, now 50, doesn't lose his health or his ambition during the next 20 years, he will be able to complete man's greatest monument. It will be a gigantic, 563 feet high, figure of Indian Chief Crazy Horse and his pony, carved out of the solid granite of Thunderhead Mountain, a few miles north of Custer, South Dakota. During the past twelve years, Ziolkowski has moved 1,164,000 tons of rock. The Boston born sculptor

35 "Miss Clara Swieczkowska," *Polish American Historical Association Bulletin*, Dr. Joseph A. Wytrwal, Editor, Bulletin No. 183, (November, 1959), pp. 2-3. "Personalia" *Polish American Historical Association Bulletin*, Bulletin No. 187, (March, 1960), p. 3.

36 J. Dorsey Callaghan, "Rhythm Beats in American Polish Hearts," *Detroit Free Press*, (September 23, 1959), p. 1.

figures the whole mountain weighs 18 million tons. To complete the job, Ziolkowski reasons, he will have to cut off one third or a total of 6 million tons.

In a country where the juxtaposition of "czy" and "szcz" no longer seems strange, the ancient names of Poland are cherished and carried proudly unchanged for generations. They are found in the rosters of the Symphony Orchestras, where musicians of Polish descent have been long a mainstay of serious music in America.[37] One of the more known Polish American orchestras is the Hamtramck Philharmonic, which presents annual concerts of real importance at Copernicus High School in Hamtramck, Michigan.

But the performers who currently exercise the greatest influence among the juke-box set are the leaders of Polka bands, who have written many lively new lyrics based on the lively Polish Mazurkas and Polkas. Thousands of high school students are arguing the relative merits of such hits as Frank Wojnarowski's "Broke-But-Happy-Polka" and Bernie Witkowski's recording of "Wha-He Say Mambo." In Chicago, one disc jockey casually asked his listeners to name their favorite polka band. In three days he received 22,000 post cards.[38]

A good measure of Polish progress can also be found in the field of sports. Until 1915, only a few Americans of Polish descent stood out as athletes; among them, Frank Piekarski, who made the All-American Football Team in 1904, and Stanley Ketchel (Stanislaus Kiecal) who won the middleweight boxing title of 1907. Since then a steady stream of sport stars has flowed from the Polish ethnic group. Today, in baseball alone, the list of stars of Polish descent, is impressively long. Stan Musial, who signed his second straight $100,000 a year contract with the St. Louis Cardinals, has been batting champion of his league six times.[39] Ted Kluszewski hit 49 homers two years ago for Cincinnati to earn himself a $50,000 contract.[40] Then there are: Ed Lopat, Jim

[37] Hyacinth M. Glomski, "Contribution of Americans of Polish Ancestry to the Development of Music in Chicago," *Poles of Chicago,* (Chicago: 1937), pp. 55-67.

[38] Albert Q. Maisel, "The Poles Among Us," *Zgoda* (June 1, 1958), p. 11.

[39] "Personalia," *Polish American Historical Association Bulletin,* Dr. Joseph A. Wytrwal, Editor, Bulletin No. 175, (February, 1959), p. 1.

[40] Albert Q. Maisel, "The Poles Among Us," *Zgoda,* (May 15, 1958), p. 11.

Konstanty, Ray Jablonski, Hank Majeski, George Shuba, Bill Skowron, Ted Kazanski, Mike Blyzka, Bob Kuzava, Steve Gromek, Frank Szymanski, Chet Laske, Cass Michaels, Gene Malinowski, Eddie Lubanski, Ed Klewicki, Stan Lopata, Bob Babbish and Harry Szulborski. Also Halina Tomski, Dee Wroblewski, Frank Okrie, Art Macioszczyk, Forest Evashevski, Walt Roxy, Norb Schemansky, Ed Skrzycki, Johnny Lipon, Fred Kovaleski, Johnny Crimmins, and Danny Lipinsky. These are only examples. The list of Americans of Polish extraction who have gained prominence in sports is impressive both in size and quality.[41] Though Americans of Polish descent make up but three per cent of the population, they contribute more than eight per cent of the big league players.[42]

In college football, "All-American Honors" have been pinned to one or more Americans of Polish descent almost every year since 1927.[43] Americans of Polish origin began their climb up the ladder of sports, to such an extent that jokes about the unpronounceable Polish names on football teams have become standard. At one point the "Fighting Irish" of Notre Dame had so many players with Polish names on their squad that Knute Rockne was asked how he picked his players. "Its a cinch," he answered with a grin, "when I can't pronounce 'em, they're good."[44] Many with good minds took advantage of the educational system to get into professions and thus to win respect. Today, there are about three hundred Americans of Polish descent on major college teams.[45]

In recent years, Americans of Polish descent have moved to the top in other sports. In golf there are Ted Krol, Bob Toski, and Ed Furgol who several years ago won the National Open Championship. Frank Parker among the top ten in tennis for more than

[41] Marshall Dann, "Poles Dot Top Ranks of Athletes," *Detroit Free Press*, (September 22, 1957), pp. 3a-4a.

[42] Maisel, *They All Chose America*, p. 216.

[43] Albert Q. Maisel, "The Poles Among Us," *Zgoda*, (May 15, 1958), p. 11.

[44] *Ibid.*, p. 11.

[45] Also high on the all time football list were Gene Malinowski (University of Detroit, Boston Yanks), Harry Szulborski (Purdue), Art Macioszczyk (Western Michigan, Eagles), Danny Thomas (Indiana), Frank Hojnacki (Indiana), Frank Pietraskiewicz (Hamtramck), Forest Evashevski (Northwestern, Michigan, and now coach at Iowa), Cy Janowski (University of Detroit), and Walt Jaros (Indiana University).

fifteen years. Stella Walsh, one of America's greatest all-around women athletes, has captured forty-one National AAU championships and set sixty-five world and national track records.

A growing number have entered the manufacturing and banking fields. Casimir Sienkiewicz, for example, is president of Philadelphia's $115,000,000 Central-Penn National Bank. Other Americans of Polish descent hold major posts in forty-five banks in Chicago, Milwaukee, Buffalo, and in smaller Pennsylvania, New Jersey and Connecticut towns.[46] The largest industrial firm founded by Americans of Polish descent was the Piasecki Helicopter Corporation. Frank N. Piasecki, son of Nikodem and Emilia Piasecki, was the founder, former president, and Chairman of the Board of Directors of the Piasecki Helicopter Corporation, now Vertor Aircraft Corporation, a division of the Boeing Airplane Company, with an annual output of $90,000,000.[47]

Partly through bloc voting of their nationality, one of the most significant political developments of the last twenty-five years has been the spectacular rise to power and prestige of Americans of Polish descent. The third and fourth generations of Americans of Polish descent have won positions of high responsibility in the local, state, and national governments.[48] Joseph Mruc became the first American of Polish descent to be mayor of Buffalo in 1949.

---

[46] Maisel, They All Chose America, pp. 217-218.

[47] In 1940, Frank N. Piasecki founded and headed an engineering research group which was incorporated in 1943 as the P-V Engineering Forum. In the year of its incorporation, the P-V Engineering Forum completed the PV-2, the second successful helicopter to fly in America. This achievement attracted the attention of the United States Navy, which recognizing the possibilities in Piasecki's idea for a helicopter of tandem rotor design, awarded him a contract for the engineering and construction of an aircraft of this type. Early in 1945, Piasecki flew the world's first successful tandem rotor helicopter, popularly called "The Flying Banana." It was the prototype of the modern tandem rotor transport capable of carrying as many passengers as comparable fixed wing airplanes. In 1946, the P-V Engineering Forum became Piasecki Helicopter Corporation. In the years since, Piasecki has sparked further design and production of transport helicopters now in service with the United States Navy, Army, and Air Force, and the French navy. The largest helicopter placed in production was the 22 place H-21 transport and rescue helicopter. Two prototypes of the 40 passenger H-16, the world's largest transport helicopter, began flying in December, 1953. At the present time, Piasecki is president of the Piasecki Aircraft Corporation. "Frank Piasecki, Ampola Guest, Pioneered Military Helicopters," Polish American World, (April 8, 1960), p. 1.

[48] Lawrence Gebicki, from New York, was the first American of Polish descent to become a member of the House of Representatives. He was elected in 1849.

Since 1932 the membership of the United States House of Representatives has included from ten to twelve Congressmen of Polish descent. At present, in addition to Senator Edmund S. Muskie (Marciszewski), there are twelve Americans of Polish descent serving in the House of Representatives: John C. Kluczynski, Thaddeus M. Machrowicz, John D. Dingell, John Lesinski, Clement J. Zablocki, Alvin E. O'Konski, Frank Kowalski, Daniel D. Rostenkowski, Roman C. Pucinski, Edward J. Derwinski, Thaddeus J. Dulski, and Stanley A. Prokop. The Democrats have been particularly successful in winning the votes of the Polish immigrants; of the twelve, ten are Democrats and two are Republicans. In 1940, Buffalo's Polish American vote for Franklin D. Roosevelt was prodigious. Polish wards went Democrat nine to one, with some precincts reaching twenty to one, to give President Roosevelt his heaviest pluralities in the whole country. In the 1952 elections, there were widespread defections from the Democrats in the Polish wards throughout the country. At the Democratic Presidential Convention held in Chicago in 1956, Americans of Polish descent received more recognition than in the past. Over sixty served in the capacity of delegates or alternates. Heading the list were Edmund S. Muskie, Governor of Maine, Congressmen Thaddeus Machrowicz, John Lesinski and Clement Zablocki.[49] In many cases, in the last presidential election, the children

---

[49] The following have also participated in the convention: John Babiarz, Jack Przybylinski, Peter Kezon, Joseph F. Ropa, M. M. Bieszczat, Casimir Griglik, Theodore A. Swiniarski, Marion Lenski, Simon P. Jarosinski, Edward Dombrowski, Peter J. Rzeznikiewicz, Joseph Garczynski, Steven Chmura, Joseph Wisniewski, Michael Nowak, Anna Pastuszka, Anthony Bielawski, Jerome Grzegorczyk, Stuart Strachan, John A. Tutro, Joseph Kowalkowski, J. P. Stopka, Al Podgorski, Emil Urbanski, George Wozniak, D. D. Wozniak, Zygmunt Swiontkowski, Chester J. Woytycha, Helen Buczkowska, Chauncey E. Wilowski, Charles Bugeja, Leon V. Malanowski, Adam F. Ciesinski, Mayor Steven Pankow (Buffalo), Chester Gorski, Anthony A. Majka, Steven J. Kaczmarek, John J. Janiga, Mayor John C. Jaworski (Lorraine), Mayor Frank X. Kryzan (Youngstown), Vincent Znaniecki, Leona A. Ruch, John J. Malick, Henry J. Dende, Joseph Jablonski, Joseph T. Witkowski, Joseph Kumiega, Joseph Kozlowski, Edmund F. Dawicki, Robert A. Dojewski and John Sobieski.

The following Americans of Polish descent attended as delegates the 1960 National Democratic Convention in Los Angeles: Alaska—Dolores Roguszka; California—Alan Sieroty, John Sobieski; Delaware—John E. Babiarz; Indiana—Bert Liss, Casimir Pajakowski; Kansas—Dr. Joe Hajda, Marian Lenski; Maine—Senator Edmund S. Muskie; Massachusetts—Stephen T. Chmura, Joseph Garczynski, Max Koss, Raymond Rosa, Peter Rzeznikiewicz, Albert H. Zabriskie; Maryland—Joseph Mach, Albert Sklar; Michigan—Congressmen Thaddeus Machrowicz, John Dingell

and grandchildren of the immigrants changed their politics along with their mounting prosperity and living standards, despite Adlai Stevenson's injunction to "vote Democrat so that you can live like Republicans." But while the meaning of the voting shift is still under study, the majority, retained their political allegiance to the Democratic Party even in their new mode of life. There is no "Polish" party devoted to the defense or promotion of the interests of nationality. This is in part due to the dispersion of the Polish colonies and the consequent lack of a "national" majority in any important locality. It is also due to the acceptance of the distinction between cultural and political nationalism which characterizes the relationship of Polish and other national groups to American society. With rough computation, it may be safely stated that at least one million Americans of Polish descent have the right to vote—a factor of some importance in American politics.[50]

The recent generations of Americans of Polish descent are devotedly attached to the United States, and nobly respond to her

---

and John Lesinski, Theodore Pankowski, John J. Kozaren, Joseph Kurka, Anthony Bielawski, Edwin Bukowski, Joseph Kowalski, Michael Novak, Frank Golembiewski, Lucien Nedzi; Minnesota—Dr. E. A. Dubdal, Donald Wozniak; New Jersey—Chester Wojtycha; New York— Phillip Baczkowski, Alfred Bartosiewicz, Joseph Brust, Michael Kecki, Stanley Laskowski, Don Mankiewicz, Aloysius Moszydlowski, Albert Rydzynski; Ohio—John T. Belinski, Frank Dobrowski, Theodore Orlikowski, Anthony Pecyk, Walter Pestrak, Julius Pestrak, Chester Vanik; Pennsylvania—Steve Babinczak, Bernard Brominski, Henry Dende, Joseph Dobbs, Edward Janosik, Joseph Yablonski, Anthony Kleha, John Sirotniak, Martin Skapik, Joseph Witkowski, Edward Zelherowicz; Rhode Island—Ralph Matera, Harold Moskol; Texas—L. J. Salak; Vermont—Anthony Buraczynski; Washington—Alvin Ziontz; West Virginia—Frank Rybka; Wisconsin—Congressman Clement Zablocki, Alvin Chrapata, Max Barczak, John Tondryk, Jerome Lisicki, Stephen Orgish, Frank A. Rondeau; Illinois—Mateusz Bieszczat, Peter P. Kezon, Karol Bonk, Congressman Daniel Rostenkowski, Jan C. Marcin.

The following Americans of Polish descent attended as delegates the 1960 National Republican Convention in Chicago: Connecticut—Anna-Mae Switaska, Ina Vestal, John Shostak; Illinois—Benjamin S. Adamowski, Feliks F. Kucharski, John L. Waner, Edwin P. Kolski, Mathew W. Slowik; Maryland—Henry F. Cierniak; Massachusetts—Francis Gregory Szpakowski; Michigan—Frank J. Skierski, Anthony Z. Cukrowski; New York—Albert T. Hajduk; Ohio— Tony Szymanowski; Pennsylvania—Joseph Makulski South Dakota—Leo Rozum Texas—B. Kanowska; Virginia—William Cholko; Wisconsin—Edmund G. Olszyk, Blanche M. Kulik.

[50] Thinking that the Polish vote might be a vital factor in the 1944 presidential election, Pravda, the official news organ of the U.S.S.R., calmed Soviet fears by stating that the potential maximum of voters of Polish origin in the United States was less than 600,000, a percentage of .7! New York Times (Chicago), December 14, 1944.

call in time of need. In the Spanish-American War, as in the two world wars, many American citizens of Polish descent participated, but as, in most instances, they had been born in the United States or had lived long enough to become Americanized, they did not enlist or fight as Poles. Even a partial list of their names and achievements falls outside the scope of this book and yet it is worth mentioning, for instance that among Colonel Theodore Roosevelt's "Rough Riders" in the Spanish-American War were the following Americans of Polish ancestry: Frank Kania, Joseph F. Kanski, and William T. de Zychlinski.[51] When the United States entered World War I, of the first 100,000 volunteers who answered the summons of President Wilson, no fewer than 40,000 were Poles.[52] Before that conflict terminated, 300,000 Polish immigrants and Americans of Polish descent served. Although the Polish population in the United States did not exceed four per cent of the population, on the casualty lists of World War I, Americans of Polish descent accounted for twelve per cent of those who lost their lives.

In World War II more than 900,000 served in the Armed Forces.[53] According to Army and Navy records, approximately twenty per cent of the United States Armed Forces on the eve of World War II consisted of men of Polish extraction.[54] Rose Radziminski of California had eleven sons in the Armed Forces. Similarly, Frances Dyke of Chicago had eleven sons in the Armed Forces.[55] A few hours after the Japanese attack on Pearl Harbor, the War Department notified Peter Niedzwiecki of Grand Rapids, Michigan, that his son, Robert, had fallen in the attack. Partly

---

[51] Edmund L. Kowalczyk, "Jottings From the Polish American Past," *Polish American Studies*, IX (July-December, 1952), p. 87.

[52] Dyboski, *Poland in World Civilization*, p. 115. Albert Q. Maisel, "The Poles Among Us," *Zgoda*, (June 15, 1958), p. 11.

[53] Albert Q. Maisel, "The Poles Among Us," *Zgoda*, (June 15, 1958), p. 11. Sigmund H. Uminski, "Individual Polish Americans and World War II," *Polish American Studies*, III (January-June, 1946), p. 37.

[54] Sigmund H. Uminski, "Individual Polish Americans and World War II," *Polish American Studies*, III (January-June, 1946), p. 37.

[55] Americans of Polish descent were among the first to enlist in the United States Armed Forces. A recruiting officer of the United States Navy, in charge of the recruitment office at New Haven, Connecticut, reported that in 1940 and 1941 at least fifty per cent of the volunteers at his station consisted of Americans of Polish extraction. Other recruiting stations in Polish American areas had similar reports. *Ibid.*, p. 37.

owing to the Kosciuszko-Pulaski-Krzyzanowski tradition, Americans of Polish descent have long been numerous and notable in the officers' corps of the United States Army. Scores have graduated from West Point Academy.[56] The following attained the rank of general in World War II: Joseph Barzynski, John Rataj, John Wisniewski, Matyka, and Krygier.

Many gained the headlines by their heroic exploits. Staff sergeant Alexander Kaczmarczyk died at sea on the twelfth day of Captain Eddie Rickenbacker's twenty-one day saga of endurance and fortitude: Sergeant John Bartek survived this ordeal. Sergeant Tony Postula with two companions survived thirty-two days of hunger and thirst in the Pacific. Leo Lapacinski had killed thirty-six Japanese soldiers in the battle of Tulagi in the Solomons. Marine "Skee" Wilski had killed one hundred Japanese soldiers on Guadalcanal. His exploits were publicized by Corporal Barney Ross, who described them to George K. Shaffer, staff writer of King Feature Syndicate Incorporated. Sergeant John J. Zygmunt, armed with a bazooka, held up eight German Tiger tanks, knocking one of them out completely; this was the first time an American bazookaman had eliminated a Tiger Tank. Sergeant Alexander A. Drabik seized the Remagen Bridge over the Rhine River during the critical 1945 American advance on Germany. The taking of the undamaged bridge facilitated the American advance into the heartland of Germany.

William Grabiarz, who was born February 23, 1923, joined the Army in 1941 when he was only 18 as a volunteer. He participated in five great battles in the Pacific. For his bravery he received nine distinctions among them the Purple Heart and the Congressional Medal of Honor. When his commanding officer First Lieutenant John J. Gregory was wounded on the streets of Manila on February 23, 1945, Grabiarz rushed to the side of Gregory, only to be wounded in the shoulder himself. Ignoring both pain in his injured, useless arm and his comrades' shouts to seek cover, Grabiarz continued his efforts to drag Gregory out of range. Finding this impossible, he rejected the opportunity to save himself and deliberately covered Gregory with his own

---

56 In 1939, the West Point Class of 456 cadets was headed by Stanley Dziuban of Polish extraction.

body to form a human shield, calling as he did so for a tank to maneuver into position between him and the hostile emplacement. Before the tank could interpose Grabiarz was riddled with bullets —none of which struck his commander who survived. Recently the "Scajaquada Creek Expressway" in Buffalo was renamed "Grabiarz Expressway" in his memory. John J. Gregory, who still lives in Worcester, commended the Buffalo Council for honoring Grabiarz. He also stated "I will never be able to express enough thanks for what he did. I remember him daily in my prayers."

Today, the greatest concentration of Polish immigrants and Americans of Polish descent is in the region of the Great Lakes, Lower New England, New York and Pennsylvania.[57] According to the United States Census Bureau, many of the large American cities still have large populations of Polish birth or parentage. New York is in first place with 404,000 Poles followed by Chicago with 316,000 Poles. Detroit has 147,000 Poles and Cleveland has 58,000 Poles. Los Angeles has 32,000 Poles and Washington, D. C. has 8,000 Poles.[58] According to the statistical survey made by the local Polish American Congress, there are over 75,000 inhabitants of Polish descent residing in California. Of this number, 35,000 live within the city limits of Los Angeles.

On the basis of the official census of 1950, American Polonia numbered 5,532,115.[59] By the end of 1955, the number increased

---

[57] The United States Press survey lists many interesting entries. In the State of Connecticut there are 111 Poles per 1,000 inhabitants. In Illinois, there are 96 per 1,000 inhabitants. In Michigan there are 92 per 1,000 inhabitants. In New York State there are 83 per 1,000; in Pennsylvania, 75 per 1,000; in Wisconsin, 71 per 1,000.

Polish-American population is highest in the State of New York with 1,230,000 Polish Americans. Illinois is second with 836,000. Pennsylvania is third with 787,250.

[58] Polish American Historical Association Bulletin, Dr. Joseph A. Wytrwal, Editor, Bulletin No. 174, (January, 1959), p. 1.

[59] It is a known fact that thousands of Polish Americans did not properly understand the census-takers question: "Place of parents' origin?" Since the parents came to this country from Poland which was partitioned between Germany, Austria, and Russia, many listed the country under which they lived and not the ethnic group to which they belonged. Consequently many answered that their parents came from Germany, Austria, and Russia, instead of Poland. Dr. Korczynski declared that had the question been properly formulated the strength of the Polish American population would easily reach the seven million mark.

to 6,133,000. This number, however, does not include 120,000 World War II Polish exiles settled in the United States.[60] Any estimate of the number of Americans of Polish descent in the United States is at best a guess, the exact number will probably never be known.[61] The number of Americans of Polish descent absorbed by territorial parishes, the number drifting into smaller cities where there is no contact with Polonia, the changing of names, the vast number of Polish women marrying non-Poles,[62] thus losing their Polish identity, all these factors add to the confusion in trying to arrive at a fairly accurate estimate of the number of Americans of Polish descent in the United States.

Today, Americans of Polish descent have approximately 10,000 fraternal, dramatic, literary, musical, social, cultural, religious and athletic societies all over America. A good many are branches or affiliates of the Polish-American national organizations whose total membership exceeds over 800,000. Some of these organizations are quite old; the Gmina Polska (Polish Group) was started in 1866.

---

[60] "Polish-American Strength Set at 7 Million," *Polish American Journal,* (June 22, 1957), p. 1.

[61] Some Polish American statisticians approach the problem by distinguishing between the ethnological and the cultural groups of Polish Americans. The first embraces all persons in the United States related in some degree to the Polish ethnic group of Americans of Polish "blood" is estimated at about 10,000,000 persons. The stock, regardless of their present speech, sentiment, name or status. This ethnological cultural group includes only those Americans of Polish descent who are actively conscious of their origin or who live at least to some extent under the cultural influence of the Polish American community and its institutions. This group is estimated at 5,000,000 to 6,000,000 persons. Polish Americans of the cultural group are most numerous in the following states: New York (1,200,000), Illinois (750,000), Pennsylvania (740,000), Michigan (500,000), New Jersey (400,000), Ohio (250,000), Massachusetts (250,000), Wisconsin (200,000), and Connecticut (200,000). The cities in which Polish Americans of the cultural group are most numerous are: Chicago (500,000), Detroit (300,000), Buffalo (250,000), New York (200,000), Milwaukee (100,000), Cleveland (100,000), Pittsburgh (100,000), and Philadelphia (100,000). Other cities that have large Polish American populations are Newark, New Britain, Boston, Toledo, Jersey City, and Hamtramck, Michigan. Rev. Joseph V. Swastek, "Polish Americans," *One America,* Francis J. Brown and Joseph S. Roucek, Editors. (Englewood Cliffs, 1959), Third Edition. p. 146.

[62] Mixed marriages with non-Poles are averaging one out of six with non-Catholics, while marriages with non-Polish Catholics have been averaging thirty-one out of fifty-four. In a very large Pennsylvania parish for the past decade, the average of marriages with non-Poles has been 51.6 per cent while 9.3 per cent were with non-Catholics. Msgr. Felix Seroczynski, "Poles in the United States;" *The Catholic Encyclopedia,* Supplement II of Volume XVIII, 1950.

Although there has been no immigration worth noting in recent years, the number of Polish parishes has increased from 517 in 1910 to 830 parishes in 1960. An estimated 3,000,000 Americans of Polish descent are grouped in these parishes, with perhaps half of this total belonging to other non-Polonian Roman Catholic parishes. The Polonian parishes are staffed by 2,000 Polish American priests who belong either to the diocesan or secular priesthood.[63] Many hold positions of importance in the American Catholic church. Seven are members of the Catholic hierarchy: Bishop S. V. Bona, Ordinary of the Green Bay diocese in Wisconsin; Bishop T. L. Noa, Ordinary of the Marquette diocese in Michigan; Bishop R. A. Atkielski, Auxiliary of the archdiocese of Milwaukee, Wisconsin; Bishop Alexander J. Zaleski, Auxiliary of the archdiocese of Detroit, Michigan; Bishop John J. Krol, Auxiliary of the diocese of Cleveland, Ohio; and Bishop H. T. Klonowski, Auxiliary of the diocese of Scranton in Pennsylvania.[64] In addition, over seventy-five hold the rank of monsignor or domestic prelate in eight archdioceses and twenty-two dioceses.[65]

Over 500 priests of Polish descent belong to the following orders and congregations: the Conventual Franciscans, the Friars Minor, the Resurrectionists, the Vincentians, and the Marian Fathers, each of which has its own provincial organization in the United States. A number also belong to the following religious communities: the Holy Cross Fathers, the Salesians, the Jesuits, the Benedictines, the Redemptorists, the Oblates of Mary Immaculate, the Society of the Divine Savior, the Missionaries of La Salette, the Sons of Divine Providence, and the Holy Ghost Fathers.[66] The Conventual Franciscans is the largest Polish American male religious order. It has 29 parishes, 50 convents, 2 boarding high schools, and 2 seminaries. The Franciscan Order of Friars Minor has one province and approximately 150 priests. It has 7 parishes, 12 convents, 2 boarding high schools, 1 col-

---

[63] Rev. Joseph V. Swastek, "Polish Americans," *One America*, Francis J. Brown and Joseph S. Roucek, Editors, (Englewood Cliffs: 1959), pp. 147-148.

[64] At present, Michigan-born Father Rembert Kowalski, O.F.M., is the Franciscan Missionary Bishop of Wuchang, China.

[65] Swastek, *op. cit.*, p. 148.

[66] *Ibid.*, p. 148.

lege and 2 seminaries. The Congregation of the Resurrectionist Fathers has one province with over 100 priests. They service 9 parishes and maintain 14 convents, 1 high school, 1 collegiate house of studies, and 1 seminary.[67]

The Polish National Catholic Church, organized officially in September, 1904, by Rev. Francis Hodur and 147 lay and clerical representatives from five states gathered at Scranton, Pennsylvania, has 150 priests with five bishops. They serve an estimated 75,000 members. The Polish National Catholic Church also maintains Savonarola seminary in Scranton and publishes an official biweekly organ *Rola Boza*.[68]

The number of sisters teaching in the elementary schools has risen from 1,678 in 1910 to 4,594 in 1949. Polish schools totaled 303 in 1909; in 1950 their number increased to 540.[69] The growth of the Polish Sisterhoods has been remarkable. In 1910, there were 2,110 members in distinctly Polish communities. In 1950, the total number was 8,153, distributed at follows: Felician Sisters, 3,465;[70] Sisters of the Holy Family of Nazareth, 1,556; Bernadine Sisters of the Third Order of St. Francis, 1,531; Sisters of St. Joseph of the Third Order of St. Francis, 963; Sisters of the Resurrection, 405; Franciscan Sisters of Blessed Kunegunda, 502; Franciscan Sisters (St. Louis, Missouri) 290.

There are hundreds of Polish sisters in various non-Polish communities. Of these the largest number are members of the School Sisters of Notre Dame of Milwaukee; 303 sisters teach in 28 Polish schools. The Notre Dame Sisters were the first to teach in the Polish American parochial schools in the United States. They started their work in 1868 at St. Stanislaus School in Milwaukee. In other communities the number of Polish sisters

---

[67] *Ibid.*, pp. 148-149.

[68] There are very few Baptists, Methodists, Episcopalians, Congregationalists, Presbyterians, and Witnesses of Jehovah among Americans of Polish descent.

[69] Msgr. Felix Seroczynski, "Poles in the United States," *The Catholic Encyclopedia*, (Supplement II of Volume XVIII, 1950).

[70] The Felician Sisters are the oldest and the most numerous of the Polish American sisterhoods. They came to America in 1874. In America they have expanded into six provinces, completely overshadowing the original community in Poland. They are employed in 12 archdioceses and 46 dioceses of the United States. Teaching is their major pursuit. In addition to directing one-third of the Polish American parochial school system, they also maintain 2 colleges, 3 normal schools, and 3 academies.

is not known since the communities ignore the national origin of their members.

The oldest extant Polish American institution of higher learn, ing is St. Mary's College and SS. Cyril and Methodius Seminary at Orchard Lake, Michigan. Directed by Polish American dio, cesan priests, they prepare their graduates for the priesthood. The high school department, however, is open to non-divinity students as is the college. Polish Americans also maintain four other col, leges: Alliance College for lay men and women at Cambridge Springs, Pennsylvania, supported by the Polish National Al, liance; St. Francis College for men at Burlington, Wisconsin, directed by the Franciscan Fathers (O.F.M.); Madonna College for girls at Livonia, Michigan, and Immaculate Conception Junior College for girls at Lodi, New Jersey, both under the supervision of the Felician Sisters.

On the postgraduate level, in addition to SS. Cyril and Metho, dius Seminary, Polish Americans also maintain six other seminaries for students in philosophy and theology. The Conventual Fran, ciscans and the Friars Minor each support two, while the Resur, rectionists have one seminary. The Polish National Catholic Church also has a seminary. In addition, the Polish American sisterhoods maintain twenty special educational institutions: teacher training institutes, nurse training institutes, novitiates for prospective members and academies.

In 1930, there were 15 dailies and 64 Polish weeklies pub, lished in the United States.[71] Beginning in 1891, the state laws of Wisconsin and the Milwaukee city ordinances had to be printed in Polish, and the Kurjer Polski, established in Milwaukee in 1888, became a quasi-official organ for the Polish group.[72] At the present time, there are six daily newspapers published in the Polish lan, guage in the United States: Dziennik Polski in Detroit, Kurjer Polski, in Milwaukee, Dziennik Zwiazkowy and Dziennik Chicago, ski in Chicago, Wiadomosci Codzienne in Cleveland, and Nowy Swiat in New York. Recently, the Kurjer Codzienny in Boston has changed from a daily into a weekly. Some of these dailies made their appearance in the 1870's and 1880's. In addition to these

---

71 Carl Wittke, Ph.D., We Who Built America, (Ann Arbor: 1957), p. 424.
72 Ibid., p. 422.

dailies, there are over forty weeklies and an undetermined number of monthlies published in the Polish language, many of them by various national Polish organizations. *Zgoda,* published by the Polish National Alliance, had a circulation of 32,435 in 1931. At the present time, *Zgoda* is the most extensively circulated American Polish newspaper in America; more than 339,000 members of the Polish National Alliance receive it.

The presence of a large American-born element has meant a new tendency in the Polish-American press: the appearance of periodicals and newspapers in the English language. At the beginning, this innovation was condemned by the leaders of the organizations as well as by individual immigrants. Since the termination of World War 11, the transition from Polish into English has been grudgingly approved by the organizations on the ground that they will thus have a means of access to the large numbers of young people who no longer read in the Polish language. The popularity of such newspapers as *Polish-American World* and the *Polish-American Journal,* as well as such periodicals as the *Polish American Historical Association Bulletin, Polish American Studies* and *The Polish Review,* indicate that these publications may expand and that new ones may also enter the field in the near future.

# CHAPTER FIVE

# Causes for Polish Emigration to America

Historically speaking, except for political exiles, the movement of people has always been from the negative to the positive; from dissatisfaction at home to the promise of a better life elsewhere. Since such changes involve pain to those who depart, and, above all, pain to those who are left behind, prosperous individuals are reluctant to sever primary ties, abandon homes and search for utopias somewhere in distant climes. To evoke a determination for change the negative factor must be as deplorable as the positive is favorable. Only then will the current of people flow into the land of promise, from the old to the new. Dissatisfaction with conditions in the homeland, plus the attractions beyond the Atlantic Ocean, broke the old bonds, and migration of the Polish peasant resulted. Opportunities for possible self-improvement were available in France, Argentina, Brazil, and in the United States.

Authorities on Polish-American history, including Miecislaus Haiman stated that there were three reasons why the early Polish movement to America never assumed mass proportions. First, the old Polish Republic never stood in need of colonial expansion, whether for commercial consideration, or for the relief of over-population. Poland, one of the largest states in Europe, possessed large areas in the East sparsely inhabited and never completely colonized. During her early period of expansion, Poland herself attracted a large immigration of Germans, Jews, Armenians, Tartars, and Scots. Since the Poles themselves belonged either to the nobility or were peasants, this enabled an army of Scots to serve as middlemen. Danzig was their port of entry, and from Danzig the Scots overran the country as peddlers, selling such things as tinware, knives, and scissors. Fynes Morison, writing in 1598, states:

> The Scots flock in great numbers into Poland, abounding in all things for food and yielding many commodities. And in these king-

106

doms they lived at this time in great multitudes, rather for the poverty of their own kingdom than for any great traffic they exercised there.[1]

Yet some of them became rich merchants, and King Stephen Batory, who ruled Poland from 1576 to 1586, protected "the Scots who always follow our Court," and allotted to them a special district in Krakow.[2] Not only the government, but also numerous landowners offered concessions to induce settlement. At first by hundreds, then thousands, the weavers and artisans of Saxony and Prussia crossed over to take advantage of the invitation. The villages which they founded on the sandy wastes became the cities of Lodz, Zgierz, Tomaszow, and many others whose names loom large in the textile history of the nineteenth century.

Second, contemporaneously with the beginnings of colonization in America, Poland was engaged in a series of defensive wars against the Russians, Swedes, Cossacks, Tartars, and Turks. These long and bloody conflicts, which absorbed the energy of the entire nation, were not very favorable for an organized emigration. Out of the seventy-five years between 1648 and 1717, fifty-five were years of war, hunger, fire, and pestilence. Pillage by native and foreign armies had caused more damage than actual military operations. Property had been destroyed or looted, money had been stolen and grew scarce. The population shrank by roughly one-third, and with it, the area of land under cultivation.[3]

Third, and perhaps the most important cause of the comparatively small participation of Poles in the original settlement of America, was the religious and political freedom which the

---

[1] John Murray Gibbon, *Canadian Mosaic*, (New York: 1939), p. 268.

[2] With the approval of James VI, the Scots in Poland organized a Union regulating their trade. In 1603, this Scottish Brotherhood in Poland had twelve branches with their own elders and judges. William Lithgow, in 1625, estimated that there were thirty-thousand Scots families in the country and called it "A Mother and Nurse for the Youth and Younglings of Scotland, who are yearly sent hither in great numbers." Mikhail Lermontov, among the greatest of Russian poets, was the descendant of one of these Polish Scots who migrated into Russia. His name is a Russified version of Learmont. Best known of his ballads is *The Song of the Merchant Kalashnikov*. A more sentimental tie between the Scots and the Poles was added when James Stuart, the "Old Pretender," married Clementina, the beautiful granddaughter of John Sobieski. Her son, Bonnie Prince Charlie, owed much of his vivacious charm, as well as his good looks to his Polish mother. *Ibid.*, p. 268.

[3] L. R. Lewitter, "Poland Under the Saxon Kings," *The New Cambridge Modern History of Poland*, (Cambridge: 1957), VII, p. 368.

Poles enjoyed in their country. The Poles escaped the religious strifes and persecutions that ravaged western Europe during the "Reformation Period." That good fortune was due in part to the tolerance of King Sigismund Augustus, and in part to the tendency of the population to cling to a church which distinguished them from the national enemies—Orthodox Russia and increasingly Protestant Germany. The Reformation did not go deep in Poland; nor was there a violent counter-reformation. In fact, the Polish populations enjoyed freedom of conscience even in the seventeenth century, when the traditional tolerance of the Polish constitution was on the wane.

Writers of Polish-American history usually divide the movement of Poles to the United States into three major periods. The first, extending from 1608 to 1776, consisted of a substantial number of adventurers; the second period, covering the years 1776 to 1865, consisted primarily of political emigrants; and the third period, which began in the sixties of the past century and lasted to the twenties of the present century, was made up largely of emigrants seeking economic improvement of their status. These dates are not to be interpreted strictly, since the exact limit when one period ends and the other begins cannot be determined. The classification is made along general lines when one or the other element began to prevail as the cause of Polish emigration.

The arrivals in the first period were chiefly adventurers; Sadowski, Zaborowski, and Kurczewski are typical examples. The second period included men who had been soldiers in the armies of the old Polish Republic or nobles who had owned land in their own right, whose patriotic enterprises in Poland had been unsuccessful, and who were obliged for political reasons to leave the country. Thus they came to America to fight against the English in the American armies; Kosciuszko and Pulaski are famous examples of this group.[4]

---

[4] Another possible source for inspiring Poles to come to America during the Revolutionary War period, was the career of Major General Charles Lee, of the American army. He had once been in command of the Cadet School in Warsaw, founded by King Stanislaus Poniatowski. In addition to that most of the French troops who served in America had previously been on duty in western Poland supporting the Saxon claims to the Polish throne and helping the Poles oppose Russian domination. There is no way of knowing whether or not this force had re-

Polish political immigration, which started in 1776 and reach-ed its peaks in 1830 and 1863, though more numerous than the earlier movement, also never assumed mass proportions. The rea-sons for this were the distance separating America from Poland and the peculiar state of mind of the Polish exile. Each generation left Poland with the firm conviction of its resurrection; they wanted to live as near to Poland as possible in order to return in the event of a new uprising. Accordingly, the mass of Polish political emigrants preferred to live in France and other western European countries wherever they could find a measure of freedom.

During the third period of Polish emigration to America, a new type of Pole appeared—the Polish peasant. In contrast to previous Polish immigrants, he was motivated in general by eco-nomic rather than political conditions. The rapid development of American industry demanded cheap labor. Occupied, dismem-bered, and economically backward, Poland held little hope for the future except economic stagnation in an overcrowded population center. America offered the poorer Polish classes the possibility of a more accelerated pace of advancement than in the old country, by no other means than hard physical labor and thrift. Balch stresses the point, that while the grounds of emigration are in the main economic, it is a mistake to assume that poverty is its cause in the sense that the greater the poverty of a man or district, the greater the impulse to emigration. The extremely poor could not come because they could not afford it. A settled poverty to which the people had adjusted themselves by adopting a low standard of living did not induce emigration. It was when the balance of the family budget was disturbed by a decrease of income or an in-crease of wants that a sense of poverty incited to emigration. Merle Curti, in his recent study of the early Polish community in Wisconsin also confirms this point of view.

ceived Polish recruits during its term of duty in Poland. Also the services of both Pulaski and Kosciuszko, and the later return of Kosciuszko to the United States in 1797, built up considerable interest for Poland in the United States. Moreover, American newspapers of the time published long accounts of events in Europe. Thus, in 1733, John Peter Zenger included in the New York *Weekly Journal* an account of the efforts of Stanislaw Leszczynski to secure the throne of Poland. Numerous similar examples may be cited. Clarence A. Manning, *A History of Slavic Studies in the United States*, (Milwaukee: 1957), p. 5.

For example, our first general study of nativity groups in the country, based on contemporary accounts as well as later reminiscences, warranted the generalization that the Polish immigrants who arrived in the 1860's were indeed a poverty-stricken people low in economic as well as in social status. Since this evidence was in harmony with traditional views of Polish immigration to this country as expressed in published accounts, we had little doubt that the contemporary judgment was correct.

Our interest in the fortunes of low-poverty groups, however, led us to go to considerable trouble to separate the Poles from the German and from other nativity groups with whom they were listed in the census, to calculate median values of real and personal property, and the like, and to compare graphically the Polish distributions on these measures with distributions for other nativity groups. The results of this objective study led us to an almost complete reversal of our earlier judgment. These Poles were certainly nowhere near the bottom of the economic scale, and the prevailing opinion of their economic status must have been formed on the basis of other factors, such perhaps as kind of clothing worn or appearance of dwelling. If the Poles were poorer than other groups on the very first arrival, as is quite possible, then they must have made quick and phenomenal progress to be able to make the reports they did in the 1870 census.[5]

This awakening of new wants also affected the backward regions of Poland and the news that it was possible in America to earn more and to live better led thousands of Poles to flock to the promised land.

Besides the primary causes, based on political, religious, and economic factors, a number of contributory causes also stimulated Polish emigration. There is evidence, historically, that inducements from America played no small part in the tide of immigration. "In fact," asserts Commons, "had it been left to the initiative of the emigrant, the number could scarcely ever have reached one-half of its actual dimension."[6] Perhaps one of the most important of these were the letters written home by those who had ventured out first and whose accounts of the New World were eagerly awaited and devoured by those who had remained behind. In contrast to the life of poverty and hardships in the old country,

[5] Merle Curti, *The Making Of An American Community*, (Stanford: 1959), pp. 442-443.

[6] John R. Commons, *Races and Immigration in America*, (New York: 1924), p. 107.

any minor success in America meant much to the Polish immigrants and they quickly relayed the news home.

Thousands of letters, written by the recently arrived to the
local newspapers in partitioned Poland, were printed and in many
cases reprinted by other newspapers. Gradually they filled out an
image of America in which opportunity, equality, and hope for
the future were writ large. A letter to those who feared to take
the risk of emigration would put the entire Polish village in a state
of tingling excitement. Every word was received like a jewel. The
clear detailed sentences were first read and reread by the simple
credulous people to whom they were originally addressed, then
widely circulated among relatives and friends, and often through
the whole village. "I'm learning to write, as you can see," the letter
would state in laborious print with many words misspelled."
"Conventional judgments, class interests, narrow mindedness do
not hang on your coat tails, nor trample on your heels." "Schools
here are free for everyone." "Any man may speak what is on his
mind without the least fear." "If a man will work, he need never
go hungry." "Here it is not asked, what or who was your father,
but the question is, what are you?" The material satisfaction that
the immigrant often experienced in America was sometimes exag-
gerated. "Generally our animals are larger here than they were in
our village in Poland." "Our cows milk very well, and the milk
and cream are richer than they were in Poland." "No bolts are
used in our irons; we heat them by putting them on a stove lid,
and they are much better for ironing than those we had in Poland."
In almost every case, the letter expressed the hope that the ad-
dressees would be able to come to America some day.

> And now I will write you how I am getting along. I am getting
> along very well, I have worked in a factory and I am now working
> in a hotel. I receive 18 (in our money 32) dollars a month and that
> is very good. If you would like it we could bring Wladzio over some
> day. We eat here every day what we get only for Easter in our
> country. We are bringing Helena and brother now. I had $120 and
> I sent back $90.[7]

A Polish carpenter, who had met financial reverses at home, stated:

---

[7] Philip Davis, Editor, *Immigration and Americanization*, (Chicago: 1920),
p. 742.

I intend to emigrate to America where I have friends, for the most part relatives; who write that I can come to them and they will find work for me.[8]

These letters, combined with the increasingly wretched conditions in Poland, moved first hundreds, and then thousands of Poles and their families to migrate. These two attitudes: despair and hunger in Poland, hope and plenty in America, overcame any lingering doubts the Polish emigrant may have felt as to the wisdom of his course. These letters were also considered as theoretical formulae debated by many who did not plan to go beyond the boundaries of partitioned Poland.

Some emigrated as single men, intending to make a fortune within a brief time and return to their native land. This was a strong inducement. The letter of a Polish peasant makes this clear:

I am absolutely determined to go to New York or Philadelphia to earn some hundreds of rubles there within two or three years and then to come back to our country and rent a mill or buy a piece of land with the money collected in this way.[9]

Another peasant expected to purchase land that eventually would make him independent:

I intend to go to North America, work there two or three years and only then marry, go to Parana and buy a piece of land.[10]

Wladek, a baker, states it in this manner:

Perhaps there beyond the water, I shall earn enough for my own bakery. Then I will come back, and if I don't earn, I won't come.[11]

Znaniecki and Thomas state that patriotism was also an important factor.

We know an intelligent Pole, a relatively recent immigrant, who has been very successful in business and who openly says he desires to fulfill his national duty by returning to Poland with twelve children and a million dollars for each of them.[12]

---

[8] W. I. Thomas and Florian Znaniecki, *The Polish Peasant in Europe and America*, (New York: 1927), I, p. 264.
[9] *Ibid.*, II, p. 1504.
[10] *Ibid.*, II, p. 1507.
[11] *Ibid.*, I, p. 378.
[12] *Ibid.*, II, p. 1517.

Equality of social opportunity was also considered in the matter of marriage. A Polish girl was encouraged to leave her fatherland because "in America millionaires fall in love with the poorest girls. Matchmakers are out of style, and a girl can get herself married to a man without the worries of a dowry."[13] A promoter for the Dakotas particularly urged women to come to this virgin region, where its 160-acre homesteads and "other attractions will soon find you a nest and a mate."[14] Several immigrants indicated equality and opportunity as the primary motives. A Polish tailor confessed that he had come to America because he craved equal opportunity. "He wanted to be a singer. That's why he came to America. He thought everybody could learn what they wanted.'[15] Anzia Yesierska also had the same motive. "Learning flows free. . . . I saw before me free schools, free colleges, where I could learn and keep on learning."[16] Melchior Wankowicz, a journalist who came to the United States after World War II made the following observation:

> The newcomer from the disillusioned, tired, skeptical Europe feels a heartwarming glow in the sincere optimism of a nation that is on the whole contented and satisfied with its present. That form of patriotism, free from any ideological complications and histrionics, simple and straightforward, constitutes a source of moral strength that can never be overestimated.[17]

Although the promise of America, letters from friends and relatives in the new land, and the spirit of adventure served as primary motives in the immigrant scene, it is also obvious that some immigrants crossed the Atlantic Ocean without any single reason or definite plan. Thomas and Znaniecki describe a peasant, twenty-eight years of age, who has been working as a farm clerk in Poland. His circumstances were such that he had no school instructions, no means, and no time for self-education. Yet he felt

---

[13] Elinor E. Hanna, *Attitudes toward the United States as revealed in published writings of immigrants from Europe from 1900 to 1944*, (unpublished Ph.D. dissertation, New York University, 1946), p. 36.

[14] Carl Wittke, Ph.D., *We Who Built America*, (Ann Arbor: 1957), p. 107.

[15] Anzia Yezierska, *Arrogant Beggar*, (New York: 1927), p. 9.

[16] Anzia Yezierska, *Hungry Hearts*, (New York: 1920), p. 37.

[17] Bradford Smith, *Why We Behave Like Americans*, (New York: 1957), p. 277.

that he had certain assets that simply needed direction. To the
Warsaw Society he wrote, "Where can I best employ my strength
and health?"[18] This state of readiness was quite characteristic. Apparently, the Warsaw Society recommended emigration to
America.

Frequently, conditions in America were pictured as rosier than
they actually were. Many, who had been led by glowing accounts
to expect entirely too much in America, suffered bitter disillusion-
ment. For there was always a bitter period of delay between dislocation from the old home and settlement in the new. Stout
hearts as well as "healthy stout frames" were needed to survive
the third-class railway cars for some twenty to sixty hours and
the weary vigils in lodging houses along the wharves in the seaport
cities of Europe, until passage could be arranged with some
broker and the ship would finally sail. The steerage quarters, which
contained enough fleas for all, were often oversold through greed.
Shipowners usually chartered the lower decks to agents at a fixed
rate per ton of cargo, and thus neither the owner nor the agent
manifested great concern about overloading the boat with human
freight. In addition, the steerage quarters were often cold, dirty,
disease-ridden, and rat-infested. No separate cabins were available for third-class or steerage passengers; the steerage quarters,
five feet high, often had two tiers of beds. The lack of privacy
touched the self-respect of many. There were no provisions to
separate the sexes. Young and old, male and female, lived and
slept together. The space allotted to the passengers was never
adequate and ventilation was poor. The only fresh air available
came through the hatches, and these had to be closed when air was
most needed—namely, during a storm. On many of the ships, the
passengers had to provide their own food for the entire trip; if
food was offered, it was placed on the table and passengers helped
themselves.

> The American Emigrant Company, in its pamphlet issued in New
> York in 1865, carried an advertisement of a steamship company re-
> quiring steerage passengers to provide mattress, bedding, and "mess
> tins" (plate, mug, knife, fork, spoon, and water can) but furnishing
> coffee, sugar, bread, butter, and oatmeal for breakfast; beef, pork, or

---

18 Thomas and Znaniecki, op. cit., p. 1506.

fish, soup, potatoes, and bread, with plum pudding on Sunday, for one o'clock dinner; and tea, sugar, biscuits, and butter for supper. The American Steamship Company, in 1873, charged $32 for steerage passage and $40 for "first steerage."[19]

Lack of proper medical care, scanty provisions, and bad water made scurvy, dysentery, cholera, smallpox, and "ship's fever" lethal adversaries. The vessel's inner walls were generally without paint or plaster, and ships frequently began the return voyage without disinfection.

In the darkness the long nights and days differed little from each other. Many of the immigrants had left their village for the first time and for the first time had seen the ocean which terrified them even when it was calm. They were melancholy, and sat in small groups. Many of them were still in their twenties. Others were still younger—twelve, fifteen, sixteen, or seventeen years of age. If they possessed the bare rudiments of an elementary education, they were indeed fortunate. Many thoughts passed through their minds as they crossed the Atlantic Ocean. The simple, casual life of toiling in the fields, raking hay, driving wagons, stowing hay away in mows, guarding flocks in pastures, among friends and relatives, was a thing of the past. The village church, the square, and the holidays—all were memories. But probably their most frightening thought was the possibility of rejection by the immigrant authorities and empty-handed to return to partitioned Poland. If fate was unkind, the immigrants might experience one of those dreadful storms that made them curse both the day they had left their native firesides, and Columbus for having discovered America. There were also clear days and nights on shipboard, with the stars, the moon, and the glimmering waves. Then there was dancing, singing to the accompaniment of the accordion, and games on deck. It was not all a voyage of darkness and storms and rolling, pitching seas. Lasting friendships were formed on the voyage that ripened with the years in America.

It seems incredible that people whose principal occupation in life had been farming, who had never before been far from home, and had no previous knowledge of the language, customs,

---

[19] Wittke, *op. cit.*, p. 117.

and traditions of the United States, were heading for America with as little as fifteen or twenty dollars in their possession.[20] As the ship approached American waters, the prospective immigrants heard tales of those who had been accepted or rejected. Passengers were usually divided into two broad classifications: those who travelled in first and second class, and "the rest." For the first two classes, inspection was nominal at best; but the rest, those who had suffered day in and day out in the hold, or on the deck of the ship, had to undergo a kind of "Holy Confession" before they passed into the threshold of the New World, whose forms of social life the wisest did not understand.

For many decades the immigration station for New York harbor was Castle Garden, under the supervision of the State of New York. When the Federal government received jurisdiction over immigration, Ellis Island became the principal inspection depot for newcomers. To millions of immigrants the name Ellis Island became a memory of endless red tape, days, even weeks, of waiting. questioning, examining. The doctors were ever on the hunt for granuloma, trachoma and other communicable diseases. Those who were afflicted were sent back. The officials were tireless: How old are you? What is your nationality? Have you ever been arrested for a crime involving moral turpitude? Have you got a job in America? Are you an anarchist? Are you willing to live in subordination to the laws of the United States? Are you a polygamist? Have you any friends in the United States? Give me the address. How much money have you got? Show me please.

Once the arrivals had passed inspection by the immigration authorities on Ellis Island, they faced a bewildering world. Tobacco-spitting merchants, themselves perhaps recent immigrants, waited at the dock to buy either their mattresses or their old clothes. Others pressed them to buy fruit or bread, or shouted offers for housemaids or laborers as they scanned the odd-sounding names on the shop-fronts or listened to the strange tongues in the street. Banners offering farms for sale were waved in their faces,

---

[20] Princess Radziwill had only twenty-five dollars when she arrived in the United States. Princess Catherine Radziwill, *It Really Happened*, (Binghamton: 1932), p. 174.

while agents for boarding houses and railroads shouted to gain their attention.

Despite the general tendency of Polish immigrants to idolize the United States and remember its brighter aspects, a few spoke with resentment about the treatment to which they had been subjected. Some letters expressed bitter regret that they had yielded to the lure of the New World. Certain definite first impressions of America were recorded by those who wrote of their early experiences in the United States. Anzia Yezierska recalled her plight in the following words:

> Woe is me! Bitter is Me! For what is my life? Why didn't the ship go under and drown me before I came to America.[21]

And Princess Radziwill wrote:

> What would I not have given to be back in Europe, where it seemed to me it could never be so bad as in America.[22]

Edward Falkowski, a boy of fourteen at the time of his arrival, stated:

> I found America a tough land in the days when I was a "greenie," fresh from the old country.[23]

Peter Yolles, who arrived in the United States in 1921, mentions the initial disappointment of many immigrants on seeing the extravagance of the Americans.

> The new citizen see's America's dangers in a personal way. Many of them have told me that the first great disillusionment in this country came when they saw bread in the garbage pails.[24]

Anzia Yezierska also recognized the difference between the people here and those she had known in her native land. The air of superiority toward the immigrants annoyed her considerably.

> When I first came to America, the coldness of the Americans used to rouse in me the fury of the savage. Their impersonal, noncommittal air was like a personal insult to me.[25]

---

[21] Anzia Yezierska, *Hungry Hearts*, p. 40.

[22] Radziwill, *op. cit.*, p. 108.

[23] Edward Falkowski, "Polonia to America," *Common Ground*, III (Autumn, 1942), p. 31.

[24] Robert Spiers Benjamin, Editor, "Peter Yolles," *I Am An American*, (New York: 1941), p. 51.

[25] Anzia Yezierska, *Children of Loneliness*, (New York: 1923), p. 19.

Those who lived lives of toil, whose world was a dark and noisy factory and a crowded, ugly tenement, were no doubt disillusioned with America.

Although many experienced hardship, illness, and misery, still they were unwilling to make the painful admission and write home the truth. Instead they sent highly colored reports of their journey, salary, positions, and prospects of success. Many of the letters contained steamship tickets for relatives and friends. It was difficult, if not impossible, for Poles to save the requisite money for a steerage ticket to America. To the immigrant in the United States, however, such an amount was comparatively small, and their readiness to make the loan made it possible for many to emigrate.

The emigrant who returned to his native country, for one reason or another, was also a great promoter of emigration. He gave Europeans an opportunity to see and hear with their own senses what America was like. In many cases, the immigrant who came to America was not merely seeking money; he was interested in the distinction that money could secure for him. A Polish immigrant states this explicitly:

> Yes, I have succeeded in America; but success among new friends is not like success among the old. I think in a year or two I shall return to Paris and Warsaw for a while. It will not cost much. I will get myself a job on the steamship to save my passage fare. It will be sweet to have money—real American dollars—to spend over there.[26]

This immigrant wished to return to his old village to receive recognition. Had he paid his passage by first class, he would not have attracted attention; he might even be snubbed as an immigrant trying to put on airs. By saving his fare, he had more money to spend among his friends and kinsfolk, where it meant something.

In Poland, the immigrant was easy to recognize, at least during the early months of his return, for not infrequently he showed traces of his sojourn in America. Many times he left as a mere laborer and returned as a skilled laborer. Often his dress was gaudy, compared with the somber attire of the Polish peasants. He shaved oftener, had his hair cut differently, walked faster, and employed

---

[26] William Carlson Smith, *Americans in the Making*, (New York: 1939), p. 92.

a terminology that was part of the Polish-American dialect. He was conspicuous because of his fountain pens, rings, gold watch-chain, gold teeth, silk shirt, stiff collar, shoes, and the American money that he flourished. He was a living advertisement of American prosperity. As a rule the emigrant who had met with a modicum of good fortune in America tended to exaggerate rather than to minimize his accomplishments in the adopted country.[27] Not only did he intelligently answer all questions asked him about America but frequently he compared the conditions there to the disadvantage of the homeland. In his comparison, he stressed the utilitarian aspects of life in the United States as against the impractical and sentimental in the homeland. He spoke of the chances he had to go to work, save, and deposit his money in banks. If he worked long and hard, he earned livable wages. If there was unemployment, those without jobs were few in proportion to those gainfully employed. One did not have to be a political favorite or a person of social rank to obtain an ordinary government position. Sometimes he admitted shamelessly that in the United States he had worn his first new pair of shoes, bought his first new shirt, and learned to bathe regularly. And his sentiments in favor of emigration frequently crystallized in exhortations addressed to the peasants to open their eyes and seek fortune abroad, where so many of their countrymen had made theirs. The living examples of such prosperous men, scattered through the villages, induced many others to emigrate to America to try their luck. Nothing appealed to youth as much as stories of the riches awaiting those with the courage to go after them.

Together with both the letters written home and the returned emigrant, other factors induced mass emigration to the United States. President Lincoln urged Congress to enact laws to stimulate immigration in 1863. On July 4, 1864, Lincoln signed a bill authorizing the president to create a Commissioner of Immigration, under the State Department. This bill also permitted the importation of laborers from Europe under a contract which

---

[27] Many, however, returned home worn out physically and mentally, though with some money. While in America they worked harder than at home and lived little or no better. They spend themselves to the utmost under the stimulus of the "boss," the climate, or their own ambition and their desire to make enough money to return to their native country and enjoy themselves.

called for twelve months' labor to pay for the immigrant's passage
to the United States. Several companies were organized to recruit
and depict the grandeur of the new star of the West. Protests
against immigrant contract labor, however, led to the repeal of
the law in 1868.[28]

To attract desirable immigrants was the overpowering ambition of practically every state in the Union. State after state began
to enact legislation to encourage and stimulate migration to its
borders artificially. The attractions offered by favorable legislation
and the persuasiveness of the agents of state immigration com-
missions were important factors in explaining the immigrant tide.
Virginia, in 1866, passed an act to encourage immigration; Gaspard Tochman, a Polish rebel of 1830, was appointed as one of
its agents.[29] The Illinois Central Railroad carried on one of the
most vigorous colonization programs of any railroad in the United
States. Besides providing augmented facilities and lower fares for
those inclined to try a new land, it employed, in 1870, General
John Basil Zurchin, a Russian engineer, a former officer in the
Civil War, to organize the Polish Colonization Agency (Agencja
Polskiej Kolonizacji) to bring Polish immigrants into Illinois.
Zurchin was successful to an unexpected degree in developing both
Polish agricultural and mining colonies.[30]

Full of natural resources, and protected from foreign wars and
internationl competition, America's industrial potential had only
to be established and developed. And as expected, the rapid industrialization of the United States, especially in the later half of
the nineteenth century, opened old Europe as a potential market
for the new industrial giant committed to an individualistic tradition. The merchant ships, which docked in European ports laden
with American goods, soon found themselves searching for European commodities for the return voyage to help pay the overhead.
Unfortunately for the merchantmen, these goods for which there
was a demand in America were either scarce in Europe or not
bulky enough to bring in good financial returns.

---

[28] Sister Lucille, C. R., "The Causes of Polish Immigration to the United
States," Polish American Studies, VIII (July-December, 1951), p. 89.

[29] Carl Wittke, We Who Built America, (New York: 1946), p. 109.

[30] Ibid., p. 112.

In due time, however, one commodity was discovered: the countless immigrants who sought cheap passage on the returning freighters. Transporting this human cargo proved profitable. It could withstand abuse; it did not have to be insured; and it loaded itself. Thus it came to be that the Polish immigrants helped supply tonnage for freighters which might otherwise have sailed for America with their holds half empty.[31] In order to funnel this human cargo onto their ships, the companies staked out spheres of influence in all Europe where they operated to the mutual satisfaction of themselves and the eager emigrants. Steamship brokers enhanced the appeal of the New World by wide advertisement of its opportunities. Pictures of transatlantic liners, placed in village stores and coffeehouses, helped to give to emigration a realistic touch. Furthermore, representatives of shipping companies penetrated into remote areas, sounding the call to go to America. Often they spread false and irresponsible stories of the job and wealth opportunities awaiting the peasants.

Once started, Polish migrations moved at an unequal tempo, year after year, decade after decade. With the arrival of each immigrant in America, additional prospects back in Poland received information, encouragement, and perhaps a monetary loan to help them across the ocean avenue of escape. These personal connections added momentum to the entire phenomenon. If the established immigrants in America did not furnish the passage money, their homes frequently served as reception centers for the more recent arrivals. Such opportunities were bound to encourage even the hesitant.

In comparison to other national peasant groups, the Polish peasant appeared rather late on the American scene. The reasons the Polish peasants left home to go to America after 1860 instead

---

[31] This drive for third class passengers was but another scheme to win the maritime scramble. In the race for mastery of the ocean-going trade, the struggle was often desperate; and the mark, the franc, the sterling, were frequently ignored. Each merchant line proudly displayed its trim, lavishly equipped passenger lines; but those sumptuous saloons, tennis courts, dance halls, and swimming pools were also a heavy drain upon the gross receipts. Yet expensive though they may have been, no line could afford to abandon such forms of entertainment. The front had to be upheld. So in the final analysis, it was the humble human cargo in the hold of the freighters and below the palm-studded decks of the luxury lines that made profit possible.

of before, are reasonably clear. Except on rare occasions, Polish newspapers, periodicals, and publishing firms gave slight cover-age to the United States. Geography also played an important part in the slow start. Because all three segments of the divided country were removed from roads of ocean commerce, it was doubly expensive for the peasants to reach the United States. Coupled with this maritime isolation, was the low state of enlight-enment in the Polish villages, where the peasant's mental horizon was confined to a limited and changeless world.[32]

Of the partitioned kingdom, Prussian Poland, located nearest to the sea, was the first to send its surplus population into the world labor market.[33] The German government was more in-terested in the fertile Polish fields than in the Polish inhabitants.[34] Therefore, the Hohenzollerns placed no obstacles in the way of the emigrating Poles. Once the dikes of uncertainty were cracked in the 1870's, the Polish emigration continued to flow. Beginning somewhat slowly at first, the stream of Polish immigration swelled and spread to such proportions as to sweep away with it not only the natural increase of the peasant population, but also a portion of the normal population of these provinces. In West Prussia,

---

[32] Only 6.9% of the immigrants coming to America in the years from 1901 to 1904 possessed any type of higher education; 27.5% could not read or write. Dr. Leopold Caro, *Emigracya i Polityka Emigracyjna ze Szczegolnem Uwzglednieniem Stosunkow,* (Poznan: 1914), p. 95.

[33] Both Poznan and West Prussia had been annexed to Prussia during the partitions of Poland, the former in the Second Partition of 1793 and the latter in the First Partition of 1772. Silesia was lost to Poland in the middle of the four-teenth century. Prussian-Poland consisted of three provinces. The Duchy of Poznan was the westernmost, and it extended to within one hundred miles of Berlin. The other two provinces were those of East and West Prussia, which border along the Baltic. Krolewiec (Konigsberg) was the largest town in East Prussia. In West Prussia, Gdansk was the only town of importance.

[34] Until the Russian-Polish revolt of 1830-1831, the Poznan Poles shared in the administration of their province, although a Germanizing policy was carried on in West Prussia after 1816 by the provincial governor, Theodor von Schon. He built up German elementary schools, promoted German acquisitions of land, and abolished the Polish language in the courts and administration. Immediately after the 1830 revolution, under the governorship of Edward von Flottwell, a disciple of von Schon, Poznan was subjected to a Germanizing policy. Poles were removed from the administration, the Catholic Church was molested, and in general an anti-Polish program was carried out in which the Polish historian, Joseph Feldman, claims to discern seeds of the later Bismarkian program.

emigration had reached alarming dimensions; the normal population was actually reduced by 41,000.[35]

To the economic causes were added, in 1871, the linguistic
and religious persecutions resulting from Bismarck's "Kulturkampf" policy. Bismarck was known to be a furious enemy of the
Poles and of all things Polish. Since to Bismarck the Polish question was closely bound up with Prussia's security, he approached
it with the ruthlessness which always marked his policy when
security was at stake. One year before his appointment as chancellor, Bismarck described his feelings about the Poles in a letter,
written on March 26, 1861, to his sister.

> Fight the Poles until they have lost their desire to live; personally
> I feel sympathy for them in their position, but we want to exist and
> nothing is left for us but to exterminate them. The wolf is not
> responsible for God's having created it as it is, so it kills wherever
> it can.[36]

The Catholic clergy, the Polish nobility and gentry, Bismarck
regarded as enemies of the Prussian state. But he differed from his
contemporaries in the fact that he did not regard the Polish community in general as enemies of the Prussian state. Bismarck believed that the Polish peasants were loyal subjects of the Prussian
government.[37] During the Franco-Prussian War of 1870, he watched the Polish Peasants marching, fighting, and suffering; he was
deeply impressed with their courage, patience, kindness, and
manliness. As he contemplated this fecund people, he felt that the
intermixture of Polish and German stocks in Prussia was highly
valuable and resulted in a people politically superior to the purely
German Westphalians and Swabians.[38] To assimilate the Poles
completely, laws were passed which required all inhabitants of

---

[35] Paul Fox, The Poles in America, (New York: 1922), p. 58.

[36] Zygmunt Wojciechowski, Poland's Place in Europe, (Poznan: 1947), p. 294.

[37] Bismarck had seen the Polish peasants fight in the war of 1870 where the
Polish national airs were used to play regiments into battle. Zygmunt Wojciechowski,
Poland's Place in Europe, p. 294. Henryk Sienkiewicz, in his short story "Bartek
Zwyciezca," described this method of awakening Polish heroism. His hero, Bartek,
along with other soldiers of his regiment, composed of Polish peasants from the
Poznan area, felt very much afraid on the battlefield at Gravelotte until they heard
the Polish national hymn played. Henryk Sienkiewicz, Nowele, (Warszawa: 1944),
pp. 62-66. Also Sielanka and Other Stories, (Boston: 1898), pp. 285-290.

[38] Conversation with Bluntschli, April 30, 1868. Otto von Bismarck, Die
Gesammelten Werke, (Berlin: 1924-1932), VII, pp. 253-254.

Prussia to speak the German language. Laws were also enacted to give the government control of parochial schools. This was very irritating to the Catholics, especially the clergy.[39]

The actual measures taken with regard to the schools of the Prussian province were spread over the period from 1872 to 1887. They included the following. The School Inspection Law of 1872 placed all public and private educational establishments under the supervision of officials to be named by the State. A Royal Edict of October 26, 1872 made German the language of instruction in the institutions of higher education in Poznan for all the subjects, including Religion. On December 6, 1872 an order from Kultur-minister Falk limited the use of Polish as the language of instruction to only three institutions in the Polish districts of Prussia. The Edict of July 24, 1873, for the Province of Prussia, made German the language of instruction in the lower schools for all subjects except religion and church singing. Polish was used only where it was necessary to assist the children's understanding of what was being taught. The Edict of October 27, 1873, made the same provisions for the Province of Poznan.

A series of orders terminated parallel classes in all secondary schools in Prussia by October, 1874. Religion, like all other subjects, was to be taught in the official language of instruction. The law of appointment and tenure of teachers of July 15, 1886 took from local officers and magistrates, both lay and clerical, all power to nominate teachers for posts in West Prussia and Poznan, as well as for the district of Opole; the power was placed entirely in the hands of the central government. The administrative Edict of May, 1886, ordered parents in the Polish provinces on pain of punishment to see to it that their children received instruction in the German language. The law of September 7, 1887, discontinued

---

[39] The influence of the clergy was extended by their participation in the supervision of education and by their teaching in the Polish provinces, so that Catholic children of both Polish and German family background were reached by them. Bismarck always asserted that the chief reason for the "Kulturkampf" was the fact that through education and religion the Poles were "Polonizing" German Catholics. In 1884, he said that in West Prussia, especially by 1870, children whose grandparents had been of German origin and German name no longer knew that they were Germans at all, could no longer speak German, and considered themselves Poles. This he blamed on "Polonizing" by the clergy. Bismarck's Reichstag Speech of December 3, 1884. Otto von Bismarck, *Die Gesammelten Werke*, (Berlin: 1924-1932), XII, p. 552.

all instruction in the Polish language in the Volksschule of Poznan and West Prussia and transferred the teaching time thus released to instruction and practice in the German language.

All Poles were affected by the enforcement of the use of German as the sole official language in legal and administrative matters. Some found the names of their towns or villages German-ized; others found their agricultural or industrial cooperative societies or the recreational organization to which they might belong watched suspiciously by the government.

> Toleration of the Polish language came to an end. The names of the streets and towns were changed, and some two thousand Polish towns received German names. The Polish names no longer appear in the official Post Office list, and letters and telegrams addressed in Polish are either greatly delayed in transmission or are not delivered at all. Very few Poles are admitted to any of the public services, and these, it is said, have to Germanize their names.[40]

Bismarck's aversion to the Catholic Church was reflected in his "Kulturkampf" policy. The Polish clergy were harried by various church laws. Many were expelled from their positions. The Jesuits were banned from the Empire. Some, including Archbishop Ledo-chowski, were jailed.[41] As long as the "Kulturkampf" lasted, the Polish clergy was under the surveillance of the Prussian State.

Bismarck's contempt for the Polish nobility and gentry was expressed in the famous Colonization Act of 1886. Because the Polish nobility and gentry refused to be assimilated, Bismarck claimed they were "deepening the gulf between the two nations." Furthermore, Bismarck claimed, they were dangerous to the state because they possessed about 650,000 hectacres of land in Poznan (a hectacre is 2.47 acres). To provide security for the State, Bismarck made the proposal to the Reichstag to appropriate 100,000,000 marks with which to buy out or expropriate the

---

[40] Ninian Hill, *Poland and the Polish Question*, (New York: 1915), p. 141.

[41] Within Prussia and Germany the Catholicism of the Poles gave them a common outlook which partly overcame the sharp class distinctions in their society. The clergy were extremely influential with the common people, and not only Bismarck but many German deputies charged that the priests were among the strongest of Polish nationalists. Instances of their combining sermons with exhortations on behalf of language and nationality were described frequently by Germans from Polish provinces. One of the most ardent Polish nationalists in the Diet and Reich-stag was Florian Stablewski, who in 1891, became Archbishop of Poznan.

Polish nobility.[42] With an appropriation of 100,000,000 marks in 1886, Bismarck organized the Colonization Commission, which launched its drive of resettlement and repurchase.[43] All eastern lands were to be settled with German farmers married to Germans; Bismarck discovered that too many mixed marriages turned Polish after several years.

> The peaceful penetrators and German colonists instead of Germanizing the Poles, were, in many cases, themselves Polonized. They married Polish women, adopted Roman Catholicism, and their children were Poles resentful of the obligation to use German instead of their "mother tongue" in public affairs.[44]

In the first twenty-five years of its existence, through class legislation, expropriation, and colonization, the Commission has attained a certain measure of success; on 336,000 hectacres of Polish soil it had settled 150,000 Germans, summoned to the Polish provinces not only from Germany proper, but also from other European countries.[45] In addition, 450 new German villages were created and in the 300 villages already existing the German element was strengthened.[46] The 1886 settlement law, directed against the large Polish landowners, also affected the Polish peasants, since it replaced some of the large Polish estates employing Polish farm workers by small German farms operated by independent farmers. Bismarck did not stop with land purchase. He strove also to stamp out Polish nationalism and to inculcate a spirit of devotion to Prussia. To make explicit the hopeless situation of the Poles, Bismarck stated:

---

[42] Bismarck admitted that this might sound bad but said it was no different from expropriating for a railroad or other public service. In this case it was for the security of the State and to ensure peace on the eastern borders. The nobles would be well paid and could go to Austrian Poland, unless they preferred Paris or Monaco.

[43] The concept of internal colonization in Prussia was a tradition coming down from the days of Frederick William, the Great Elector in the seventeenth century. The concept of colonization as a weapon against the Poles went back at least to Frederick the Great, who instituted the system of taking over lands held by Polish magnates in West Prussia after 1772 and settling German peasants thereon. If the nobility were dispossessed the peasants would be the most loyal subjects of the Prussian king.

[44] Julia Swift Orvis, "Partitioned Poland, 1795-1914," *Poland*, Bernadotte E. Schmitt, Editor, (Los Angeles: 1945), pp. 63-64.

[45] Jan J. Kowalczyk, *Prussian Poland, A Stronghold of German Militarism*, (Copenhagen: 1917), p. 29.

[46] *Ibid.*, p. 29.

You will never realize your ambitions except as the result of a war, disastrous to Germany, when Prussia has been smashed to pieces.[47]

An additional cause of discontent among the young Polish peasants, especially in the last three decades of the nineteenth century, was the introduction of severe compulsory military service laws. Every Polish youth was obliged to serve in the German army for four years. It was not so much the service itself that drove them out of the country as the excessively harsh discipline imposed by the haughty young upper-class Prussian officers. The fact that most of these martinets were the sons of the nobility or of other owners of large estates added to the social discontent. But it was easy for the person who wanted to avoid this obligation to step over the Rhine into France, where passport formalities were more or less perfunctory; and the long newspaper lists of those who failed to respond to the call for military registration indicate the popularity of this way of escape.

Bismarck's influence led in 1894 to the formation of a society for the Germanization of the Duchy of Poznan. Three Prussians, Hennemann, Kennemann, and Tiedemann, organized this body which, in keeping with their initials, was called the "Hakata." The organization started work by fomenting German sentiment in Prussia and Poznan. Not content with the fact that the government deprived the Poles of the right to enter the civil service or even to work as a porter at a government railway station, the Hakata began to boycott artisans, doctors, and lawyers of Polish descent.

This policy was intensified as investigation revealed that the Polish populations of the eastern provinces was increasing much more rapidly than the German. Dr. Satler expressed in the Reichstag in 1898, both the Prussian creed of force and the traditional policy of "Drang nach Osten," which for so long had sought to justify the subjection of the Polish people in the interest of German security:

---

[47] Bismarck had intended to suggest the impossible, but the remark proved prophetic. Maurice Bruce, *The Shaping of the Modern World*, (New York: 1958), p. 63.

The position between us Germans and you Poles is a natural
necessity: it is not the result of ill will or the desire to harm any
Polish national, but primarily the consequence of the geographical
situation of the territories on which our two nations live. We Germans
cannot permit that another nation be the ruler of a territory which is
at a distance of only a few hours' ride from the capital. From this
point of view you (Poles) must realize that we are compelled to
eliminate this other nation . . . that it is our natural obligation to
seek not only to make loyal citizens of the Prussians of Polish
nationality, but also to transform them into real Germans.[48]

The revelation in the Prussian parliament that Polish school
children had been flogged for refusing to say the Lord's Prayer in
German led in 1902 to a lively denunciation of the method used
by the Prussian government in the attempt to Germanize the
Poles. That this attempt had failed was admitted by Count Bulow
in the speech delivered on January 13, 1903, in which he replied
to the critics of the Government's policy. But the moral he drew
was that the policy must be sharpened. In the autumn of 1906, in
consequence of the re-introduction of German as the medium of
religious instruction, some 400,000 Polish school children went
on strike. The affair created an immense sensation in Germany
and abroad. It was denounced as being wholly due to the machina-
tions of the priests; the fury of the German chauvinists was increased by the consciousness that their policy of ruthlessness had
not only failed, but had made them ridiculous, and they clamoured
that the rod should not be spared in reducing the enfant rebels
to obedience. The rod was not spared; but the little martyrs of
Polish nationalism held out for months against every sort of threat
and violence. The strike of the Polish school children had strikingly
demonstrated to all the world the wicked folly of the Prussian
system, but the zealots of the "Ostmarken-Verein" saw in it only
proof of the need for still more drastic measures. In speeches and
in pamphlets they clamored that the government should at least
adopt a really "strong policy" and wipe out every vestige of Polish-
ness from the "sacred soil of Germany."

The effect of the various laws and activities in Prussian
Poland was immediately seen upon the Polish immigration to

---

[48] *Ibid.*, p. 64.

Wisconsin. There had been a very gradual immigration since 1855. In 1872 there was a large immigration of priests. Through their influence a great impetus was given to the movement. That there was not a wholesale emigration from Prussian Poland at this time was due partly to the efforts of the government to restrain it, but more largely to the lack of funds to make the necessary journey.[49] Caprivi, who replaced Bismarck, adopted a more con-ciliatory policy towards the Poles. While in no sense contem-plating the resurrection of Poland, Caprivi hoped that if war should break out, the Poles could be induced to throw in their lot with the power that had treated them with the most kindness. In the spring and summer of 1891 Polish laborers had been re-admitted to Germany, and permission given for private instruction in Polish in the public school buildings. In November of that year Dr. von Stablewski was elected to the archiepiscopal chair of Poznan and Gniezno; the election of Stablewski was intended as a *beau geste* towards the papacy.[50]

With great strides made in the industrialization of Germany, however, the Polish emigration to America from the territory taken over by Germany during the partitions of Poland dropped considerably, since the surplus of labor population of the area was absorbed by Germany itself, especially by Westphalia and the Rhineland, which at that period experienced an acute labor shortage.[51]

The mass immigration of Poles from German Poland had no sooner been reduced, when that of Russian Poland started.[52] In

[49] Frank H. Miller, *The Polanders in Wisconsin*, (Milwaukee: 1896), p. 259.

[50] There were several other reasons for this new departure. One was that the votes of the Polish deputies in the Reichstag were necessary in order to enable the government to pass certain naval appropriations. (See also footnote 86).

[51] The rapid industrialization of Germany after 1870 drew a high proportion of Polish speaking laborers into German owned factories; this trend was stimulated by the remarkably high birth-rate of the Poles. Thus east German capital was in-creasingly supplied with cheap Polish labor. By the end of the century so many Poles had drifted across Germany to the Rhine and the Ruhr that they formed a considerable Polish colony in western Germany. Still, during the years from 1871 to 1898, the Poles constituted ten to twenty per-cent of the German immigration to America. The peak years of the German-Polish immigration were 1880-1893, after that it never exceeded 8,000 a year.

[52] Russian-Poland is divided into two administrative areas of great extent; these are the annexed provinces and the kingdom of Poland. The first consists of Lithuania and the Ruthenian provinces, which were annexed by Russia at the time

the years 1890-1892 approximately 70,000 Poles from Russian Poland arrived in America. The majority were peasants; however, in comparison with German Poland and Austrian Poland, Russian Poland furnished the largest percentage of laborers and small town-dwellers. Many forces made for this emigration from Russian Poland. Often a combination of circumstances contributed to the peasants' decision to leave. In the late seventies, Russia suffered from a succession of crop failures which virtually confronted many families with a choice between starvation and departure. Furthermore, during the two decades after the American Civil War, Russian Poland had been flooded with an ever-increasing number of pamphlets, newspaper articles, and private letters—all stressing the demand for workers in America and the opportunities for healthy and ambitious young people to become independent. Simultaneously, the unscrupulous methods of advertising seemed to open the eyes of many to the possibilities offered by emigration to the United States. Especially active in such enterprises were the agents of the North-American Lloyd and the Hamburg American lines. Both companies sent their agents scouring village after village deep in the Polish hinterland in search of third-class passengers.[53]

Life, however, was not too comfortable in Russian Poland, even before the famine and the advertising campaigns. At the Congress of Vienna, held in 1815, the diplomats of the European powers re-created a substitute for the Polish nation which they misnamed the "Kingdom of Poland." This kingdom was, in reality, a protectorate of Russia; its king was the Russian Czar Alexander I, who in the years immediately after 1815, seemed prepared to give a generous measure of home rule to the Polish provinces he

of the partitions of Poland. The second consists of the portion of the ancient Polish state which was united to Russia by the Congress of Vienna in 1815.

[53] This search for third-class passengers on the part of these companies was nothing unique. All maritime powers and all steamship companies employed similar methods. At times the steamship agents were joined by other propagandists who sang the praises of America in remote villages of Poland. In this group we find the factory agents, railroad agents, and even representatives from the western states of America. Many times such agents themselves were former emigrants in the employ of a company. These agents contrasted the rosy picture of flourishing America against the dismal, stagnated Polish background.

had gained at the Congress of Vienna. The Polish army was kept distinct from the Russian army; the Polish language was recognized; the religion of the Poles was respected; and a Polish parliament was established.

Alexander, however, early showed a tendency to regret the liberal attitude which he had adopted toward his new kingdom. At the first session of the Polish parliament in 1818, he refused to permit its members to discuss the budget, a right specifically provided for by the Constitution. In 1819, he fell into line with Metternich and ceased to sympathize with liberals; that year he imposed a censorship of the Polish press. The next year he suspended the Polish parliament; and when the Czar abolished the publication of the debates of that body by decree of February 13, 1825, it was clearly evident that he had ceased to respect the constitution he had granted the kingdom. Alexander, as Byron said, had

> . . . no objections to true liberty,
> Except that it would make nations free.
> How nobly gave he back to Poles their Diet
> Then told pugnacious Poland to be quiet.[54]

The Poles suspected that Alexander's suspension of their constitution would be followed by its abolition. The succession in 1825 of Nicholas I, who had never had an instant's patience with liberalism, convinced them of it. Nicholas, eighteen years younger than Alexander, was a true autocrat without any popular sympathies. He was crowned King of Poland at Warsaw and solemnly took the oath in public, as prescribed by law, to maintain the constitution which had been granted by his brother. Having gone through this ceremony, Nicholas proceeded to sanction every measure proposed to him by reactionary advisers for setting aside the constitution. Arbitrary arrests multiplied. Freedom of the press was abolished. Russians were appointed to positions in the civil and the military service. Taxes were levied without the consent of Parliament. Monopolies were created, and the proceeds were squandered by the government. Councils of War were

---

[54] David George Ogilvy Ayerst, M.A., *Europe In the Nineteenth Century*, (Cambridge: 1949), p. 279.

authorized to supercede the civil law. The responsibility of min-
isters to the Polish parliament was set aside. Five years were allowed to elapse since the last parliament before the next was
summoned. Practically the system of autocratic government in
Russia was extended to Poland.

As a result of all these infractions of the constitution, discontent spread throughout Poland. Secret societies multiplied in
all directions. The Poles began to prepare for a war of independence. On November 29, 1830, they acted.[55] The French revolution
of that year, which set Louis Philippe on the throne, encouraged
them to rise. The Czar's proposal to send their army to restore
Charles X of France forced them to do so. Not only did they
sympathize with the French revolution, but they knew that once
the Polish army was out of Poland the Czar would be able to
abolish the constitution without fear of opposition.

The insurrection ended finally in disaster. In crushing the
Polish rebellion, the Russian government had full sympathy of
Prussia. "Poland," said the Prussian minister, "had better be an-
nihilated, so as to have done with her once for all."[56] As an inevitable consequence of the Polish revolt, a series of punitive
measures were immediately taken against the kingdom. Military
tribunals were set up in the kingdom to try the leaders and participants in the revolt; these tribunals meted out innumerable death
sentences, banishments to the mines of Siberia, and orders con-
fiscating the property of those found guilty. When the confiscated
properties were put up for sale, Russians alone were permitted to
bid for them. A brutal Russification began, especially on the eastern borderlands of the former Polish monarchy in order to efface
the nationality, language, literature and historical souvenirs of

---

[55] The Jews of Germany generally favored the Polish cause, as did the other
German democratic elements. German Jews were among the composers of the then
fashionable "Polenlieder" and were active in the popular Polish and refugee relief.
Ludwig Boerne's article, which Wladyslaw Mickiewicz described as "the most moving
thing about our cause which appeared at the time," called for sympathy for Poland.
Heinrich Heine wrote earlier and poignantly about Poland's plight. Mickiewicz also
related that in Frankfurt the Jews collected two million franc for Poland. Z. Wertheimer of Vienna donated 200,000 gulden. Jewish ladies embroidered a Polish
flag. J. Rotschild undertook to deliver the funds and the flag to Poland. Abraham
Gordon Duker, The Polish "Great Emigration" and the Jews, (unpublished Ph.D.
dissertation, Columbia University, 1956), pp. 48-49.

[56] Lord Eversley, The Partitions of Poland, (London: 1915), p. 291.

Poland. The Ruthenian and Greek Uniat church was persecuted. Polish schools, including the University of Wilno, were closed. Many nobles, among them Prince Radziwill, were relegated to the center of the Empire. By the end of 1832, it has been calculated, 80,000 Poles were sent to Siberia.[57] To diminish further the population of Poland, 45,000 families were transported into Russia to the Caucasus and the district of the Don, while orphans and male children of rebels and refugees were sent under escort to Russia to be brought up in Russian military schools.[58] According to Brandes, not many countries could have stood such treatment as did Poland.

> After the revolt about fifty thousand Poles in all were carried' out of the country. They were either sentenced to hard labour in the salt works and mines or in the forts, or to domicile in some country village from which it would be impossible for them to escape, yet with narrowly restricted choice of occupations. Others again would be allowed to move freely within certain limits; yet even they were strictly forbidden certain occupations, as, for instance, all kinds of teaching. They were taken to their places of destination in bands of about three hundred' persons, guarded by the Cossaks and watchdogs, passing the nights in large sheds, where there were pallets for women and children, while the others slept as they could.[59]

A similar fate awaited the small autonomous kingdom of Poland, created by the Congress of Vienna in 1815. The constitution granted by Czar Alexander I to the "Congress Kingdom" was suppressed. Many confiscated Polish estates were bestowed upon Russians with the right of primogeniture, thus creating a new Russian aristocracy in Poland. The University of Warsaw was closed. The Lycee of Krzemieniec was transferred with all its collections and establishments to Kiev, there to become the nucleus of the Russian university founded in 1834. Marshal Ivan Paskevitch was named Lieutenant-Governor of the kingdom, and under his oppressive rule, from 1832 until his death in February, 1856, the kingdom was subjected to a policy of reaction and

---

[57] Major F. E. Whitton, A History of Poland From the Earliest Times to the Present Day, (New York: 1918), p. 249.

[58] Ibid., p. 249.

[59] George Brandes, Poland A Study of the Land, People and Literature, (London: 1904), p. 21.

Russification. The country was divided into Russian provinces; and the Russian system of taxation, coinage, and administration was imposed upon the Poles. Polish soldiers and officers were mustered into Russian ranks and distributed over widely different points of the Russian empire.[60] A. Jakubowski, exiled to the United States, described the Russian schools in Poland, soon after the in-surrection of 1830 as very limited and imbuing pupils with the "divine right of kings."

> Russia has established schools since the revolution in which are taught only reading and writing, with catechism of the Emperor who, according to its doctrines rules on earth as the Almighty does in Heaven.[61]

The most important and most disastrous of the Polish revolts against Russia was the second great Insurrection of 1863. The Polish provinces of Russia had not escaped the general intellectual and political agitation that followed the Crimean War. Economic distress in the cities and the countryside promoted unrest. The moderate elements among the Polish landowners hoped for poli-ical concessions from Alexander II. The Czar began to grant Poland some measures of autonomy; however, these failed to satisfy the aspirations of the more nationalistic Poles. Impatient and distrustful of Russian promises, they whipped up a fever for military action against the oppressor.

In January, 1863, the inevitable uprising broke out simultan-eously against Russian garrisons in some fifteen places in "Con-gress Poland," in the districts of Lithuania and in White Russia.[62]

---

[60] By a Ukase of October 19th, 1831, men belonging to the numerous Polish petty gentry, but unable to justify their right of belonging to the class of Russian nobility, were deprived of the privileges they had hitherto enjoyed and were sub-jected to the payment of special taxes and declared liable to military service in a proportion four times as high as that applied to other classes. The numbers of Polish gentry removed in this way from their native land in the reign of Nicholas I, attained about 18,000. Adam Zoltowski, *Border of Europe—A Study of the Polish Eastern Provinces,* (London: 1950), p. 110.

[61] Anthony Louis Kar, *The Response of the People to the use of Formal Education in the attempted denationalization of Poland,* 1795-1914 (unpublished Ph.D. dissertation, University of Michigan, 1955), p. 108.

[62] It was precipitated by the Russian government. Under a law authorizing conscription for the army, the Russians made a sudden swoop by night on 2,000 young men whom they suspected of disaffection, and sent them as conscripts to the military depots in Siberia. This had the effect of driving the Poles into frenzy and revolt.

Lacking an army, the rebels could not engage in open contest with the Russian army, but were compelled to resort to the tactics of guerilla warfare. Open struggle was carried on for a year and a half with the greatest courage, but without hope of success; sporadic guerilla warfare continued for another six months. Although the last resistance was not put down until April 1865, most of the rebellious areas were pacified by mid-1864 after the execution of some 1,500 rebels and the death in combat of 30,000 others. Conducted with great heroism and self-sacrifice by groups of badly armed "partisans," the insurrection stirred interest abroad and even some ineffective diplomatic interventions. The insurrection was followed by more determined Russification, persecution, and oppression. The reign of Russian terror was most severe in Lithuania, which was ruled by the notorious Muraviev, "the hangman." It began with mass executions of persons accused of taking part in the insurrection, and the confiscation of their property. The insurrection deprived the Poles of the last of their privileges. The Kingdom of Poland was incorporated in the Russian Empire in 1864 as the Vistula province. Crowds of Russian officials and teachers streamed into the province of the former Polish kingdom and occupied positions hitherto held by Poles. The Polish estates were burdened with a special fine. A ukase, sanctioned on December 10th, 1865, forbade persons of Polish origin to acquire manorial lands in the nine western governments of the empire: Podolia, Wolynia, Kiev, Minsk, Mohilev, Vitebsk, Wilno, Grodno, and Kowno. Persons exiled from these provinces, whose property was sequestered, were granted a term of two years in which to sell such property to purchasers of Russian origin.[63] In 1874, the vice-royalty was abolished; and in 1876, the Russian judicial system was introduced. By the 1880's almost everything Polish was prohibited. The Polish language was barred from public

---

63 This new law which went under the name of the December Ukase, brought considerable losses to the Polish community. The loss of property up to 1873 under this ukase reached a million acres. The most conspicuous case in later years was that of Werki, near Wilno, which Princess Hohenlohe was obliged to sell at short notice with other landed property to the amount of two million acres, representing the former unentailed estates of the Radziwill family from which she was descended. Numerous Poles connected in diverse ways with these estates suffered damage through their sudden break-up. Zoltowski, op. cit., pp. 127-128.

offices and schools. The famous inscriptions in Russian: "It is strictly forbidden to speak Polish" hung even in the schools of the kingdom, where education was deliberately kept at a low level. The use of the Polish language was forbidden in the newspapers, over shopdoors, and even in private conversation. A tram-car conductor was fined twenty-five roubles, more than his month's pay, for having answered a Polish question in the same language. This incident occurred at the beginning of the twentieth century.[64]

In addition to their efforts at denationalization, Russian op-pressors undertook a methodic persecution of the Catholic Church. The church was deprived of its revenues through the confiscation of ecclesiastical property. The village priests became the salaried officers of the State; the land belonging to the church was put up for sale and only Russians were allowed to bid for it. Direct communication with the Holy See was forbidden; and a number of clergymen and bishops were exiled into Siberia. Diocesan seminaries were staffed with Russian orthodox instructors. Three-fourths of the monasteries were suppressed. Since 1864, more than a hundred religious orders of men and women were sup-pressed.[65]

During the periods following the fatal insurrections of the nine-teenth century, the whole country was in mourning. Women wore black dresses and no jewelry; there were no dances and gay parties. In her memoirs, the wife of Marshall Jozef Pilsudski describes her grandmother mourning the 1863 Insurrection:

> The failure of the insurrection had been the bitterest disappoint-ment of her life. Ever after she dressed in deepest black, relieved only by a narrow white edging of lace at the neck and wrists, and on her finger she wore a mourning ring.[66]

Whatever Romanov might rule from St. Petersburg, his Polish subjects down along the rivers Bug and Vistula could expect few considerations. Nicholas I threw himself into a policy of complete assimilation of Poland by Russia. The great French

---

[64]Brandes, op. cit., p. 67.

[65] Sister Mary Tullia Doman, C.S.S.F., "Mother Mary Angela Truszkowska," Polish American Studies, X (July-December, 1953), p. 67.

[66] Alexandra Pilsudski, Memoirs of Madam Pilsudski, (London: 1940), pp. 65-66.

historian Michelet summarized explicitly that devilish attempt of national annihilation in the following passage.

> It was undertaken not only to kill Poland, her laws, her religion, her language, literature and national civilization, but to *kill the Poles*, to annihilate them as a race, to paralyze the very nerve of the population in order that if it should still continue to live, it would be nothing but a herd of human creatures whence the Polish people, as a living, potential energy, would vanish completely.[67]

Professor Konovalov also appraised severely the conditions following the Insurrection of 1863.

> The Rebellion of 1863 was crushed in blood, and the Russian reaction to it was even more severe than in 1830. Everything was regarded as tainted with "Polonism," i.e., the identifying of the Polish people with the armed propaganda of Latinism in the midst of the Slav world, was systematically attacked. There was ruthless repression by an administration that was now, as it had not hitherto been, almost purely Russian in personnel. The extreme was reached when Russian was required to be taught in village schools and religious teaching in Polish was prohibited.[68]

During the reigns of Alexander II, Alexander III, and Nicholas II, public gatherings in the Polish regions were frowned upon, the Polish language was prohibited in the higher schools, and all public functions were conducted strictly in Russian. Polish schools, Polish spirit, however, still lived. An example of Polish undying nationalism was displayed at the unveiling exercises of Mickiewicz's statue in Warsaw.

> After much solicitation Czar Nicholas II permitted the erection of the statue in memory of this Polish literary giant. However, on the eve of the unveiling, orders were issued prohibiting any speeches or demonstrations at the exercises. On the designated day a large crowd assembled on the city square; and there without speeches, without song or music, the figure of the poet was disclosed to the assembled throng of Warsaw. For a moment the crowd stood in silent admiration. Then men, women, and children broke into tears, and silently wept. No books, no schools, no papers, yet they all knew Mickiewicz. They saw before them the embodiment of Poland; they looked at each other and saw the cause of its misery. To behold this

---

[67] Jerzy Jan Lerski, *The United States and the Polish Exiles of* 1831 (unpublished Ph. D. dissertation, Georgetown University, 1953), p. 16.

[68] S. Konovalov, *Russo-Polish Relations,* (Princeton: 1945), p. 22.

scene and the people was to understand those opening lines of Poland's
National Anthem, "Poland is not yet lost, while we still are alive."[69]

During his first trip to Poland, in 1885, George Brandes made
the following observations:

> While the stage, as I have just said, is still Polish, the Polish lan-
> guage is absolutely forbidden in the University. All lectures, no
> matter whether they are delivered by men of Russian or Polish birth,
> must be in Russian. Not even the history of Polish literature may
> be taught in the language of the country. Nay, even in the corridors
> of the University the students are forbidden to speak Polish with
> each other.
>
> Even more dangerous to Polish nationality is that provision of the
> law which requires that all instruction in the schools shall be in
> Russian. Even the scanty instruction in the Polish language is given
> in Russian. And so strict is the prohibition against speaking Polish
> in playtime, or generally in the schoolgrounds, that a boy twelve years
> of age was recently shut up for twenty four hours in the dark because
> coming out of school, he said to a comrade in Polish: "Let us go
> home together." But the regime to which the schools are subjected
> with regard to the suppression of the national peculiarities is not
> confined to the domain of language. In a family which I was invited
> to visit, the following incident happened. The son of the family, a
> boy of sixteen, the only son of a widow, one evening in the theatre
> had thrown a wreath to Helena Modrzejewska on behalf of his
> comrades. A few days after, in obedience to an order from the Minister
> of Education, the principal of the school called him up, and told him
> that he must not only leave the school, but that all future admission to
> any other school whatever was forbidden him; it was the punishment
> for having been guilty of a Polish demonstration. The boy went home
> and put a bullet through his head.
>
> We may perhaps wonder what provisions which in certain cir-
> cumstances drive a half-grown lad to suicide are maintained, or that
> so innocent a thing as the throwing of a wreath is forbidden. But
> the answer is, that as a rule everything which betrays a love for the
> language is forbidden in Warsaw.[70]

Eve Curie, in the biography of her mother, Marie Sklodowska
Curie, has also given a glimpse of school conditions in Russian
Poland.[71]

---

[69] Stanley R. Pliska, *Polish Independence and the Polish Americans* (unpublished Ph.D. dissertation, Columbia University, 1955), p. 21.

[70] Brandes, *op. cit.,* pp. 16-18.

[71] Eve Curie, *Madame Curie* (Garden City: 1943), pp. 17-21.

Because of the political circumstances thousands upon thousands of subjugated Poles were to wend their way westward to
America to avoid the eastward journey to Siberia. The American
statistics of immigration record 740,438 Poles from Russian
Poland during the years 1899-1914. More probably the figures
should reach 900,000 or 28% of the Russian immigration to the
United States from 1820-1918.[72]

The mass immigration from Austrian Poland, called Galicia,
acquired momentum in 1900, and reached its highest mark in
1910 when immigration statistics recorded in that year 60,675
Polish immigrants from Austrian Poland.[73] According to Dr. Caro,
432,817 Poles emigrated from Austrian Poland from 1899 until
1910.[74] The immigration from Austrian Poland consisted of peasants, with a slight increase of common laborers, professionals,
and intellectuals in the last few years preceding World War I.

Austrian Poland was a backward agricultural country with
a surplus of landless farm workers. Although the country possessed all the conditions necessary for a vigorous economic development, under Austrian rule, Austrian Poland or Galicia,
underwent a prolonged period of economic exploitation and centralized absolutism. From the moment that Maria Theresa established a central chancellery at Vienna, a bureaucracy, essentially
"Austrian," came into being. The bureaucrats who worked the
imperial organization had no sympathy either with local patriotism or with aristocratic privilege. Their ideal was a uniform
empire based on enlightened principles. Like Joseph II, their supreme example, they were to spread enlightenment. This meant
the extension of the German language. No other language or culture existed: there were no works of literature, of philosophy,

---

[72] Dr. Mieczyslaw Szawleski, *Wychodztwo Polskie w Stanach Zjednoczonych
Ameryki,* (Lwow: 1924), pp. 15-16.

[73] Austrian-Poland, an area half as great as the State of New York, is divided
into two districts. The western district was formerly in Little Poland and included
the city of Krakow; the eastern and larger district was formerly the palatinate of
Halicz (from whence the word "Galicia") or Ruthenia, and includes the city of
Lwow. Austrian-Poland was located on the northern and north-eastern frontier of
the empire. It consisted for the most part of the wide wind-swept plains from
which Poland took its name, but the southern part is mountainous. The Carpathians
are mostly just large green hills, the only real peaks of the chain are the high Tatras.

[74] Dr. Leopold Caro, *Emigracya i Polityka Emigracyjna ze Szczegolnem
Uwzglednieniem Stosunkow,* (Poznan: 1914), p. 25.

even of agronomy, except in German; no men of learning except at German universities; no source of culture on which to draw except Germany.[75]

Monica Gardner gave the following account of the severe and arbitrary treatment meted out to Austrian Poland from 1795 to 1815.

> Under Austria the Galician Poles were treated as the victims of a brutal war rather than as a nation whose rights had been ratified in a European Congress. The policy of Metternich was to crush every Polish element underfoot. The stipulations of the Treaty of Vienna were regarded as non-existent. The offices of the national government were filled with Austrians and Czechs. Punishment by death was inflicted with appalling frequency on those who held Polish aspirations. The Polish language was abolished in the schools. It was a penal offence for the Polish students to be heard speaking Polish to each other even out of lesson hours, or to be caught reading in Polish. House to house inquisitions were made for Polish books. Those who possessed them, read them or lent them, went to prison. The publication of Polish writings was attended with almost prohibitive difficulties on account of the heavy censorship.[76]

The Austrians also interfered with the home life of their subjects in Galicia.

> The war upon the Polish language is not confined to the limits of the school. Polish parents are not permitted to have Polish tutors and governesses for their children. German officials are authorized to enter a private house at any moment to ascertain if the children are being taught in Polish.[77]

The Polish magnates, who did not owe their greatness to the Hapsburgs, never forgot that they were Poles. In 1846, they broke into national revolt, a premature fragment of the revolution of 1848.[78] The insurgents, who were of very advanced democratic leanings, had immediately proclaimed full freedom for the

---

[75] A. J. P. Taylor, The Hapsburg Monarchy 1809-1918, (London: 1952), p. 23.

[76] Monica M. Gardner, Poland, A Study in National Idealism, (London: 1915), pp. 8-9.

[77] Ibid., p. 24.

[78] The reforming work of the Monarchy threatened their independence; agrarian reform challenged their economic privilege; and the growth of an imperial bureaucracy destroyed their monopoly of local administration. As a result, the nobility, in the nineteenth century, had to defend their traditional privileges against the Monarchy, although these were the creation of the Monarchy.

peasants, to whom they promised full possession of their lands. Panic-stricken at the arrival of the revolution which Austrian officials long prophesied and with inadequate Austrian forces, the Austrian government then struck back by a proceeding which, even in the tragic history of partitioned Poland, remains unique in its horror. Before the proclamations of the nobles were suffi-ciently known, Austrian officials managed to persuade the peasants in certain districts of western Galicia that the insurrection, led only by the nobility, was designed to enslave them.[79] They organ-ized well-paid bands who turned upon the nobles and through hideous massacres helped the Austrian army to stifle in blood the opening of the insurrection.

The insurrection, moreover, served Austria as a pretext to annex the Republic of Krakow, in spite of the protests of France and England. Victor Hugo's words in the French Chamber of Lords on March 19, 1846, when the fate of the Republic of Kra-kow was discussed, expressed a wide-spread feeling:

> Two nations among all other have for four centuries played a disinterested role in European civilization: these two nations are France and Poland: France dispelled darkness, Poland repelled bar-barism; France spread ideas, Poland covered frontiers. The French people had been civilization's missionary in Europe; the Polish people, its knight.[80]

However, after almost a century of Austrian rule, it became evident that the numerous German officials and military men and their families established in the country, far from making any headway toward its Germanization, were, on the contrary becom-ing more and more assimilated to their environment. This was true to such an extent that many of them threw in their lot with the Poles or at least adopted the language and customs of the

---

[79] During the previous few decades the system of Austrian government had been to demoralize the peasants and awaken in them a hatred of their landlords. The Austrian law maintained the right of landlords to labor dues. It also forced on the nobles the duty of apportioning taxes and made them select recruits for the army and act as rural police. No better means could have been employed to sap the popularity of the landed classes among the peasantry. On the other hand the bureaucracy took the peasants under their care, protecting them whenever they were prosecuted by the nobles for theft and other activities.

[80] Hans Kohn, *Pan-Slavism, Its History and Ideology,* (Notre Dame: 1953), p. 30.

country.[81] Thus the strivings in 1848 of the Poles for more autonomy for Austrian-Poland, caused consternation among the Austrians, for they feared that the nationalistic movement in Galicia
might eventually lead to independence.

> There was a mass demonstration at Lemberg (Lwow), where a
> petition was drafted demanding amnesty for political prisoners, ex-
> clusion of non-Poles from state offices, use of the Polish language as
> the official tongue, and assumption of the title of King of Poland by
> the Hapsburg Emperor.[82]

Austrians, however, insisted that Austria should never give the
Poles complete independence, arguing that the Polish peasants,
who comprised the vast majority of the population, were very
loyal to the Hapsburg emperor. Furthermore, they believed that
an independent Poland would be an easy target for Russian invasion. Others believed that an independent Poland could protect
Germany against a Russian invasion.

> The Russian Goliath is looking at us with disdain. The rising self
> consciousness among the nationalities and the fact that we are cele-
> brating the tabernacle feast of freedom are distasteful to him. He is
> already holding his weapons ready in his clumsy hand, and his tongue
> wants to shout out the call for battle. We need a David, and we
> have one. Everyone knows the new David will hurl his rock at the
> Russian giant. His foot is rooted in the north and his head is in
> Paris. The David of the nineteenth century is a free Poland. . . .Only
> through Poland can we ward off the danger hovering over us, at least
> for the present. Germany must be united before we can be a match
> for the barbarian of the northeast; but Poland can successfully open
> the glorious prelude for the big battle, for she will fight for her
> highest treasure—for freedom. What I am saying is the desire of all
> the good people of our German Fatherland. We have seen the jubila-
> tion over Austria's and Prussia's amnesty to the captured Poles. We
> can win only if what has been begun so gloriously will be consistently
> carried further. Poland is difficult. She will rise up. If she wins her

---

[81] This unforseen development came to the surface more visibly at moments
of crisis. The names of high Austrian officials are on record whose sons joined their
Polish friends and enlisted in the Polish armies in 1830-31. The names of Austrian
officers have been preserved who suffered heavy punishment after having participated
in the secret organizations which prepared the revolutionary outbreak of 1848.
Many prominent Poles with German names are descended from families who, at
this period, adopted the language and outlook of those they had been sent to hold
down. Zoltowski, op. cit., p. 106.

[82] R. John Rath, *The Viennese Revolution of 1848*, (Austin: 1957), p. 144,

freedom through revolt, we will have lost a future friend. If our part of Poland falls into the hands of the Russians, slavery and barbarism will exist in the very heart of Europe. Austria's Italy opened the eyes of all Europe when she called out: "Too late! Too late!" Let us take care that Poland will not do the same. Let us not rashly play the same game.[83]

The fear of Russia also found expression during the Polish insurrection of 1863, in the Austrian parliament. Amid the applause of the Austrians, a Polish deputy from Galicia, who had justified the national uprising, declared:

> On the day on which the Poles shall cease to wish to be Poles, or despair of the restoration of Polish independence on that day pan-Slavism will be born and come fully armed into the world. Let Europe consider if the guest would be welcome to her.[84]

For Austria Pan-Slavism was certainly not a welcome guest, and if its advent could be checked by concessions to the Poles in Galicia, the respite would be cheaply bought. Furthermore, the Austrian monarchy, defeated in Lombardy in 1859, and crushed at Sadowa in the Prussian War in 1866, needed reorganization, and strengthening by the admission of non-German speaking peoples to the Government. To prevent the disruption of his Empire, Francis Joseph granted provincial home rule to the Polish magnates of Galicia. Socially they were the closest to the Austrian nobility and they were the first and practically the only ones to be accepted on fully equal terms in Vienna.[85] Galicia, the largest

---

[83] Carl Dolde, "Ein Freies Polen," *Constitution*, No. 21, (April 14, 1848), pp. 308-309.

[84] W. Alison Phillips, M.A. *Poland*, (New York: n.d.), pp. 210-211.

[85] The most talented, influential, and representative of the Polish gentry were the conservatives of Krakow, the so-called "Stanczyks." They were named after their pamphlet *Teka Stanczyka* (The Portfolio of Stanczyk), written by Jozef Szujski, S. Tarnowski, and S. Kozmian. It was designed to combat the revolutionary democratic ideology. It was they who propagated the principle of moderation, not only in social questions but also in relation to the Vienna government, advocating hyperloyalism and a sort of "Austrian patriotism."

If the peasant movement in Galicia ever developed into a powerful political organization, this occurred in spite of the conservatives and only with a hard struggle against them. Great credit during this first phase of fighting for the rights of the peasants goes to Boleslaw and Marja Wyslouch, political leaders of unusual ideological integrity, and to Jakob Bojko, a peasant from Greboszow, who by hard work acquired a considerable intellectual and moral culture. These were the people who created the ideological basis for the peasant movement in Galicia. In the later more active phase of the struggle, Jan Stapinski and Wincenty Witos distinguished themselves.

province in the empire, now enjoyed a local Polish administration. Polish officials, by degrees, filled all positions in the administration and the judiciary; and a generation of citizens grew up who re-ceived all their education in Polish, including the public teaching of Polish history and literature in schools supported by taxes. Official careers lay as widely open to Poles under Austria as they had been closed to them under Prussia and Russia. There was hardly an Austrian Government between 1860 and 1914 which did not include a Polish minister. In 1914, at the outbreak of the war, the following Poles occupied important posts in Austria: Bilinski, Minister of Finance of the Dual Monarchy; Zaleski, Finance Minister of Austria; Tarnowski, Ambassador in Sofia; Pomiankowski, Ambassador in Constantinople; Szeptycki, Mili-tary Attache in Rome; Adamkiewicz, Chief of the Austrian In-telligence Service in Serbia. The army included generals Baczynski, Beck-Rzykowski (Chief of Staff), Grzesicki, Przyborski, Zielinski, and others.

By 1871, a special Austrian ministry for Galician affairs was created and financial arrangements were adjusted along the lines desired by Polish magnates, who were able to win some conces-sions from Austria, such as the Polonization of the administration and jurisdiction and the introduction of Polish as the language of study in schools and at the Jagiellonian University in Krakow. Other reforms and concessions followed, and already existing rights were extended. The universities in Krakow and Lwow for example, were made more exclusively Polish, a Polish Educational Council was organized as the highest educational institution in the country, the Krakow Learned Society was transformed into the Academy of Science and Arts in 1872, and the Polytechnical School in Lwow became an institution of higher learning. In 1889, Francis Joseph won the hearty applause of Poles everywhere when he elevated the archbishop of Krakow, universally esteemed as the primate of Polish Catholicism, to the rank of prince. In 1894, the centennial of the heroic rising of Kosciuszko was com-memorated at Krakow, with the representatives of the Russian and Prussian Poles in attendance. Similar all-Polish gatherings marked the burial of the national poet Mickiewicz in Krakow in 1895, and the anniversary of the ancient Jagiellonian university in Krakow. By these concessions the Austrian government helped to cement the devotion of Polish leaders to the crown and assured the ministry of the vote of Polish deputies in the imperial parlia‑ment. Whereas Poles in Russia were looked upon and treated as inferiors in Galicia they reigned supreme.[86]

Economically, however, Galicia continued to be treated as an Austrian colony, destined to furnish agricultural products and raw materials to the various provinces of Austria‑Hungary in return for manufactured goods. Thus its own industries could not be developed; to create industry in Galicia, it would have to com‑pete with the highly developed production of Silesia, Moravia, and Bohemia, which lie just to the west and in the same customs ter‑ritory.[87] Thus custom policies, tariffs, various government regula‑tions and powerful trusts were simply intended for the strangula‑tion of Galician industries.[88]

Even the agricultural system in Austria was deplorable. The abandonment of the feudal system in 1868, whereby one child

---

[86] One of the less obvious effects of the slowly developing rapproachment be‑tween France and Russia during this period was the resulting change in the orienta‑tion of the nationalist aspirations of the Poles. With the bulk of their territory enclosed in Russian territory, the Poles had traditionally pinned their hopes on liberal republican France. But by 1890 France was obviously flirting with Russia. In the future war, which was to reconstitute Poland as a nation, the Poles turned their hopes more and more toward Austria and Germany. Already in June, 1890, the Poles in the Reichstag, under the leadership of Koscielski, had voted for Caprini's "little army bill." Again in March, 1891, the Poles helped pass the naval appropria‑tions. For this service, Koscielski received from the Kaiser a picture of the fleet of the Great Elector and an expression of royal gratitude. Koscielski was also dubbed "admiralski" by his political critics. With the public display of Franco‑Russian enthus‑iasm at Cronstadt, leading Poles came out even more strongly for loyalty to Germany. At an assembly of Polish Catholics at Thorn, Father Florian von Stablewski, a former opponent of the Prussian government during the Kulturkampf, declared that the Poles could not remain neutral in the present situation. "Upon which side we should station ourselves is determined for us by our history, our education, our culture. We are sons of a people which has never denied its attachments to the West. . . ." They wanted politically to be Prussians, said Stablewski, culturally to remain Poles. J. Alden Nichols, Germany After Bismarck, (Cambridge: 1958), pp. 126‑128.

[87] Vienna's restrictions on industry and commence in this region, forced the young men graduating from the two Polish universities or the Institute of Tech‑nology to enter government service unless they could follow one of the free profes‑sions. As a result there sprang up a bureaucracy nominally Polish but permeated by Austrian spirit.

[88] There was some salt mining and some production of petroleum but these industries were largely in control of capitalists outside the province, thus these enterprises yielded little money to the inhabitants of the province.

received the family holding intact, the decreasing death-rate, and the high birth-rate, cut the peasant's acre into tiny patches. This became almost tragic. In 1820 the landed properties numbered 527,470; in 1920 when mass immigration began, it rose to 1,008,541, or almost 100%. An example of rural unemployment can be drawn from Galicia, which in 1902 numbered 440,000 households with less than five acres of land, thus guaranteeing a livelihood that was precarious at best. An additional 369,000 homesteads in Galicia produced enough to provide some sort of existence for eight months.[89]

The rural population of Galicia was very dense. In 1900 those supporting themselves by agriculture numbered 183.9 per square mile; for the rest of Austria-Hungary it was 93.2, and 88 for Germany and Denmark. In addition, the soil in Galicia is not very productive. Yet about half of the agricultural population of Galicia owned landed property which did not measure over five acres; 84% owned farms of less than 12.5 acres, not enough to provide sustenance for the family. To make matters worse, these holdings were very often scattered over wide areas in small lots, one peasant holding twenty to thirty separate lots.[90] Agricultural labor earned an average of sixteen to twenty-six cents a day in American money. Throughout the province the young people, who had no other wealth than their own labor, found it increasingly difficult to obtain a patch of arable land and a modest cabin in which to raise a family. The primitive character of agriculture among the Polish peasants is illustrated in the following letter written by a Polish peasant to a Polish immigrant in the United States who had written home describing some American agricultural machinery which he had purchased.

> Now as to machines which you bought and which are so expensive, don't they know scythes and sickles there? With these tools you can do much during the summer.[91]

The absence of industrial development, the scarcity of available agricultural land, the primitive methods of production, and the growth of a population which the land could not support, ac-

---

[89] Pliska, op. cit., pp. 23-24.
[90] Balch, op. cit., p. 138.
[91] Thomas and Znaniecki, op. cit., I, p. 368.

counted in great measure for the mass emigration movement from Galicia in the decades before World War I. According to Polish sources, a total of 852,790 Poles emigrated from Galicia between the years 1881-1910, for the most part, to the United States.[92]

It was only the enactment of restrictive legislation, after World War I, which effectively reduced the volume of Polish immigration to the United States. The quota law of May 26, 1924, limited the number to 5,982 yearly. The "Golden Door" of Emma Lazarus had swung all but shut. Whereas in 1900, the American population was 13 per cent foreign-born, in 1950 it was only 7 per cent, and in 1965 it will be negligible.

---

[92] Szawleski, op. cit., p. 17.

# CHAPTER SIX

# The Organization of Poles in America

The home we first knew on this beautiful earth,
  The friends of our childhood, the place of our birth,
In the heart's inner chamber sung always will be,
  As the shell ever sings of its home in the sea.[1]

As with all movements of history, a multiplicity of factors was responsible for Polish emigration. Foreign oppression, an overflowing population, primitive methods of agriculture, meager productivity of the soil; all were instrumental in producing the Polish exodus. In addition to land hunger, the Poles suffered from low wages, excessive taxation, and insufficient industrial development.

The year 1870 marked a period of greater Polish emigration to the United States. This exodus was the result of the unrestrained agitations of transatlantic ship agents, Russian crop failures of 1876, Bismarck's cruel policy of extermination directed against the Poles, and the German, Austrian and Russian practices of assisting the exportation of "undesirable Poles" to America.

Although the underlying cause for Polish emigration may be found in the stimulus given to this movement by Germany, Russia, and Austria, yet it may be traced fundamentally to the lack of economic well-being.[2] Modern transportation had only greased the wheels of the vast movement of peoples caused by fundamental economic changes.

There is no authority on Polish immigration to America who does not reiterate the fact that the fundamental economic changes were the real forces which were uprooting the Polish

---

[1] Stanley R. Pliska, *Polish Independence and the Polish Americans,* (unpublished Ph.D. dissertation, Columbia University, 1955), p. 38.

[2] Stanley Bruno Stefan, *The Preparation of the American Poles for Polish Independence* 1880-1918 (unpublished Master's thesis, University of Detroit, 1939), p. 2.

peasants from their stable, ordered way of life. Father Waclaw Kruszka bluntly states that the important cause driving the Polish peasant to the shores of America' was the desire to improve his material welfare. The peasants had no intention of bringing about the restoration of Poland.[3] They were not concerned with the na-tionalistic furor that moved some of the intellectuals and noblemen to labor for the restoration of the ancient state. The immigrants were preoccupied with economic problems, with the transition from labor on the soil to unskilled toil in the mills and mines. Beyond that their thoughts were concerned with the restoration of their churches, mutual assistance societies, and the preservation of village customs. Miecislaus Haiman, Sister Lucille, Emily Balch and Henryk Sienkiewicz also state that the primary factor driv-ing the Polish peasant to America was economic.[4] The Congres-sional Immigration Commission of 1911 attributed the movement of population from Europe to United States, with few exceptions, to economic causes. Emigration for political reasons, and to a less extent, from religious oppression, undoubtedly did exist, but even in provinces where these incentives were important, the emigrants came to the United States not merely to make a living, but to make a better living than was possible at home.

Prior to 1870 the Polish immigration into the United States was composed chiefly of political exiles; they usually belonged to the intellectual elite. Many of them possessed marked ability. However, the forces of Americanization proved themselves too strong to be resisted or overcome individually by these early political immigrants and they rapidly became assimilated and dis-solved in the "American Sea."[5] In fact, they melted in the common life so completely, that the later immigrants could find no point of attachment with them.[6] They left no trace, except a few docu-

    [3] Ks. Waclaw Kruszka, *Historja Polska w Ameryce,* (Milwaukee: 1905), I, p. 51.

    [4] Miecislaus Haiman, *Polish Past in America, 1608-1865,* (Chicago: 1939), p. 3. Sister Lucille, CR, "The Causes of Polish Immigration to the United States," *Polish American Studies,* VIII (July-December, 1951), p. 86. Emily Balch, *Our Slavic Fellow Citizens,* (New York: 1910), pp. 34-37, 50-55, 80. Sister M. Nobilis, S.S.N.D., "Sienkiewicz and the Poles in America," *Polish American Studies,* II (January-June, 1945), p. 35.

    [5] Karol Wachtl, *Dzieje Zjednoczenia Polskiego Rzymsko-Katolickiego w Ameryce,* (Chicago: 1913), p. 49.

    [6] Paul Fox, *The Poles in America,* (New York: 1922), p. 100.

ments referring to the first Polish association which they established in this country.[7] Their education and intellectual attainments did not prevent—in fact, they only enhanced—their complete assimilation.[8]

The positive reaction of the Polish immigrant to the American
environment occurred only when the Polish peasant had crossed
the ocean and entered the United States. According to Agaton
Giller and Oscar Handlin, the Polish immigrant peasant acquired
a consciousness of his national character mainly through his experience in the United States.[9] In Poland the peasant had been held
firm in the grip of the customary and the familiar. The old patterns
of the village community, however galling, formed a path of
stability, where the peasant knew what was expected of him, no
matter how precarious his living. His family and ancestors were
rooted to the soil and bound by customs that had been handed
down for generations. Centuries long removal from participation
in national affairs and national life and the 150 year political
subjection to foreign hostile governments prevented the masses
of peasants from developing any national consciousness or attachment to Poland as a State. Jakob Bojko gave the following description of the fate of the peasant in partitioned Poland.

> The peasant had to work, and he thought of nothing else but
> work. He did not worry about changes in government or government
> policies, for this was not his business. He was expected to carry out
> his duties with humility. These duties consisted of harvesting, plough-
> ing and harvesting in endless succession.[10]

Engrossed in the routine of labor from sun to sun, the
peasant did not possess an intimate knowledge of Poland's
past, which to Bojko was the most important prerequisite for

---

[7] William I. Thomas and Florian Znaniecki, *The Polish Peasant in Europe
and America*, (New York: 1927), II, p. 1486.

[8] It is a known fact, that in the history of Polish emigration the intellectuals
succumb first to denationalization in whatever country they change to reside permanently as immigrants. Such is the story of the Polish immigration in Russia,
whether voluntary or inforced. It consisted mainly of the educated class, soldiers,
professionals, and government officials. The Polish intellectual exiles to Russia contributed immensely to her development, but at the same time, were lost forever to
their native land. Their children simply consider themselves Russians.

[9] Oscar Handlin, *The American People in the Twentieth Century*, (Cambridge: 1954), p. 68.

[10] Jakob Bojko, *Dwie Dusze*, (Toledo: 1911), p. 63.

bringing the peasant to a higher level of moral or political maturity. Bojko's faith in the importance of culture and education became manifest in such details as, for example, his concern about the poor taste displayed by the peasant in his choice of the images of saints, with which he decorated his huts. In his published work he wrote sadly:

> Anyone who visits a peasant hut cannot fail to notice the awful pictures of saints (bohomazy) on the walls. Perhaps it would not be so bad if the awful things had at least Polish inscriptions. But no, the inscriptions are usually in German, sometimes in French, and quite often in Russian. . . . How painful it is to see and read inscriptions like: Heilige Anna, Abendmohl Christi, Herr Jesu etc. in a Polish hut.[11]

Bojko contemptuously called such pictures "German smearwork" (Szwabska babranina), but assumed a serious tone in denouncing the absence of pictures of Polish history in the peasant cottages.[12]

> Oh, what again it would be to the national cause if the portraits of Queen Jadwiga, Sobieski, Kosciuszko, or Poniatowski decorated the walls of the peasant huts. From their earliest years, the children would become acquainted with the history of our heroes and would want to learn more about their lives.[13]

Fixed in one place for centuries, the peasants thought of themselves mostly in the simple terms of their own village circle, within which they were at home and outside of which they were only strangers. Always their interests had been local, limited to the little area within the shadow of their own church tower, so that even a man from only a few miles away was distinguishable in dialect and costume. These were stabilizing influences, but they discouraged deviations from customary patterns.

---

[11] Ibid., p. 24.

[12] Jakob Bojko, whose son married the daughter of Wojciech Wytrwal, was an excellent narrator of anecdotes. He used stories mainly as a vehicle for his sarcasm and skillfully brought home to the listener or reader the point he wanted to make. He achieved this effect by keeping his story brief, telling it in terse, laconic phrases, with no superfluous explanations or deviations. We find in his writing a story about his conversation with a conservative member of the Austrian Parliament, who asked him once. "Is it true, my dear colleague, that you used to be a cowherd?" "Yes," said Bojko, "that is correct. But you may be thankful that you are not." "Why?" answered the other man. "Because if you had been a cowherd, sir, you would still be one today." Ibid., p. 15.

[13] Ibid., pp. 24-25.

The new ways of buzzing big American cities and the quickly growing farm communities were bewildering to the immigrants from the backward but secure villages. With his queer dress and language, which was either unknown or wrongly accented, as well as the retained traits of Poles, the immigrant became an object, caught within forces over which he had no mastery.[14] The immigrant who reached the United States, found himself cut adrift from the stratified rural environment, from the village where his family had lived from time out of mind, and where the comfortable shell of known custom and familiar faces safely ensphered him. Without the influence that had formerly governed his life, he found it enormously difficult to adjust to his new surroundings. He also became conscious of his Polish heritage.[15] This seems strange to those who have seen the peasant indifferent to national duties in Poland. This national consciousness and unity was formed by the huge populations and vastly extended reaches of territory; the different languages and customs; the complex and ever changing technologies; the great emphasis on specialization; the complicated literate symbol systems; the labyrinthine social structures; the self-consciousness among other alien groups, frequently hostile; the fears of social annihilation; and the realization of the differences between Poles and non-Poles.[16] In all this, the common language, common religion, and mutual recollection of old experiences were influential. This instinct for national self-preservation brought it about that the Polish peasant in America, who until this time had been indifferent toward Poland's calamity, became an heir to Mickiewicz, Kosciuszko, Słowacki, Reymont,

---

[14] Ethnic origin, recency of immigration, and religion made him seem more of an outsider than other minorities.

[15] Stanislaw Osada, *Historja Zwiazku Narodowego Polskiego*, (Chicago: 1905), p. 103.

[16] Emily Balch, in *Our Slavic Fellow Citizens*, described the process by which the Polish immigrant, who came to the United States, gained a stronger ethnic consciousness than he had ever had in his little rural village, and how, upon meeting others from the land of departure, he developed new nationalistic passions, which native and foreign-born leaders alike exploited. These emotions had become ephemeral in the second generation members of the group. "Pan-Slavic Feelings" died out, as the sons of immigrants found nearer goals more meaningful. For the children of the aliens, the real focus of life lay in how to pass the barriers which lay between native Americans and foreigners, between those who were inside and those who were just outside, unable to reach the fruits of the promised land.

Zeromski, Sienkiewicz, Joselevitch, and hundreds of others who spent their lives in the cause of Polish independence.[17] As an active patriot, the immigrant manifested a great desire, almost a need, to do something for the land of his birth, which he now idealized as the home of suffering heroes and glorious causes, and as the splendid repository of all those treasures which the social frontier in America stripped from his heritage.[18]

While to the end of their days, many peasants still referred to themselves in village terms, or continued to call themselves Germans, Austrians, or Russians, nevertheless, a cohesive Polish group steadily evolved which learned to think of itself tied to a particular nation; one not yet in existence, but characterized by common language and culture. In 1900, perhaps four-hundred-thousand thus identified themselves. By 1910, a million foreign-born and seven-hundred-thousand native-born put themselves into the category of Poles.[19]

The Polish immigrants were creatures of their environment and they found it difficult if not impossible to cut themselves entirely from their old moorings. They usually learned English and tried to adopt American ways and customs; but they never entirely shook off the influences of their early life. A great deal of this sentiment was caused by homesickness and attachment for the family and friends in the old country. The peasants, thousands of miles from native roots, never forgot their memories of a happy childhood spent among family and friends or the memories of poverty and want of their younger days. In addition, various obligations toward others in the old country made the sentiment constant. Nostalgic memories of home usually manifested themselves in a readiness to do something to alleviate the misery of those still in partitioned Poland. One of the most important kinds of material help was financial; money remittances were sent to support parents, to help discharge family debts, or to maintain, improve, or purchase additional property. They also contributed toward village improvements and subscribed to national liberation

---

[17] It is true that in many cases the immigrants, only after their coming to America learned that they were Poles.

[18] Rev. Joseph Swastek, "What is a Polish American?" *Polish American Studies,* I (January-December, 1944), p. 38.

[19] Handlin, *op. cit.,* p. 70.

projects.[20] It is therefore not surprising that even though abstract
national ideas did not appeal to the peasant masses, incidents in
the native country caused considerable excitement in the form
of meetings, collections, and protests in the United States.

Only after the initial shock of the contact with American conditions had worn off, did the bulk of the peasant immigrants,
without name or influence to help them, often with no money
save what they won by their own efforts, set about constructing
a life for themselves on the social frontier.[21] The difficulties of
adjustment during the early years were enormous. All at once,
it seems, they had to adjust to the discipline of the industrial society, become acquainted with the customs and traditions of the
land, overcome homesickness, endure nativist opposition, and ac-
climate themselves to a society composed of diverse ethnic and
religious groups. Whatever intercourse existed between the Polish
peasants and the American was of a business or political nature.[22]
It was not social. The native American population did not stay
in the neighborhoods invaded by immigrants, but moved to up-
town districts or suburbs. This naturally left the immigrant settlements solidly foreign and quite to themselves, where they lived

---

[20] The influence of American money was especially visible in Austrian Poland.
Tile replaced thatch, taxes and debts were paid, field was added to field, better
tools and more cattle were bought, phylloxera-smitten vineyards were replaced with
immune vine stocks, churches were built and adorned. Sometimes even cripples and
invalids were supported by contributions from fellow-villagers at work in America.
    Another result was that the people lived better. The price of poultry had risen
because the peasants now ate it to some extent themselves. They paid eight and ten
dollars for a suit of European clothes. Sewing machines were becoming common
and many town improvements were undertaken. Wages had risen as had the price
of land. The rise in land values was sometimes excessive. There was no chance for
investment except in land and so competition together with speculation had run
prices up from sixty dollars an acre to as high as four hundred dollars. Willard
E. Givens, *Galician Immigration*, (unpublished Master's thesis, Columbia University, 1915), p. 19.
    [21] The Polish peasants came from places where they had been a part of a
culture which possessed a set of values, customs, manners, and taboos which inter-
locked into an organic whole. In the course of settlement in American industrial
centers, this culture broke down. The loss to the Polish peasant was all the more
destructive, for, in contact with the poorest aspects of life in the United States,
they gained so little. Also the rapid process of Americanization did not enable the
peasant to salvage much that he had brought with him.
    [22] One dilemma in evaluating the effects of immigration had to be faced: how
to surmount the exploitation of the immigrant labor market. The American public
tolerated low wages in cases where "only foreigners" were involved.

in anonymity amidst but apart from the thousands around them. They were an aggregate of individuals concentrated in one area, but they were not a community. Small wonder that one Greek humorously remarked:

> We have been in America for six months. . . . We had neither heard English nor become acquainted with Americans. In the mill there worked Polish men and women and only Polish was spoken in the factory and in the streets of the small town.[23]

And his friend added.

> I believe the captain of our ship made a mistake and instead of bringing us to America brought us to Poland.[24]

In this environment, the Polish immigrants attempted to carry on as had been their custom in the old country.[25] Although sensitive to the emptiness which so often followed the great adventure of coming to America, the Polish immigrants, grappling constantly with the American environment, slowly moulded it to their needs and purposes. Eventually they formed in two chronological stages the "American Polonia" (Polonia Amerykanska), neither Polish nor American, but with features of both; a marginal society with institutions peculiar to itself. Its roots were in the soil of Poland but its structure and content were increasingly modified by adaptation to the new situations, arising out of transition from the old to the new world.[26] In the isolated and tightly knit villages of the old world, it has long been in the mores that the primary group is responsible for its own members, all of whom were expected to live up to their obligations.

An appeal to a charitable institution is considered even in Poland

---

[23] Theodore Saloutos, *They Remember America: The Story of the Repatriated Greek-Americans*, (Berkeley: 1956), p. 19.

[24] *Ibid.*

[25] Living in segregated groups, they established relationships of interdependence on a secondary level, without close contact with the dominant culture. There were few, if any direct relationships between these people and American families, schools, churches, or recreational groups. Hence during the pioneer period there was almost no difficulty in retaining their culture, and it was, indeed, even reinforced by the arrival of fellow-countrymen from partitioned Poland.

[26] The word "Polonia" is to be understood as meaning all persons of Polish extraction, living on American soil, who form an inseparable and integral part of the whole, that is of the American people, and not something apart from its milieu, a distinct, separate Polish community.

a mark of social downfall; it is even more of a disgrace in the eyes of Polish immigrants here because of the feelings of group responsibility which is imposed, or thought to be imposed, by the American milieu. The immigrant has been accustomed to see the wider social group hold every narrower social group within the limits responsible for the behavior of every member; the village praises or blames the family as a whole for the activities of an individual, the parish does the same with reference to the village group, the wider community with reference to the parish or village. The American population is supposed to do the same—and of course, in some measure actually does the same—with reference to the foreign colony in its midst. Every Pole who accepts help of American institutions is thus considered not only disgraced personally as a pauper, but as disgracing the whole Polish colony.[27]

During the early stages of the evolution of "Polonia" mutual help was exercised sporadically, from case to case, by means of collections made for the benefit of the sick or poor individual, a family in distress, a transient, or the departed who needed burial. For many years the brunt of social welfare fell on the more settled and financially solvent members of the community. However, when the vast stream of immigrants that poured in incessantly increased the need for charitable donations, the financially solvent in particular were eager to substitute for this unregulated voluntary assistance a regular system of death and sickness insurance. Thus they favored the establishment of a mutual aid society which would diminish their risks and contributions.

The mutual aid society usually took the name of a patron saint, an American Revolutionary War hero, or someone identified with the group. The first mutual aid society established in America was that of St. Stanislaus Kostka in Chicago, in 1864.[28] According to the constitution of 1866 the following were the objectives of the society: to visit and help the sick; bury the dead; help widows and orphans; and encourage peace and morality in the community. The initiation fee was between $5.00 and $10.00, and the monthly dues were $.50. In case of the death of any members, a special fee of $1.00 was charged.[29] To join a society

27 Thomas and Znaniecki, op. cit., II, p. 1519.

28 Sister M. Andrea, S.S.N.D., "The Societies of St. Stanislaus Kostka Parish, Chicago," Polish American Studies, IX (January-June, 1952), p. 28.

29 Mieczyslaw Haiman, Zjednoczenie Polskie Rzymsko-Katolickie w Ameryce 1873-1948, (Chicago: 1948), p. 24.

was to be a member of the group, and most immigrants, individualists though they were, saw that their lives were enhanced by cooperation with others. Few immigrants would have denied John Donne's "No man is an island."

In time, the "mutual aid society" became a kind of social club and community center after working hours. The center was usually a large hall filled with tables and chairs. Here Polish songs, rhythmic folk dances, lively music and stirring dramas were developed and perpetuated; gems of Polish literature were read and reread, and many episodes from Polish history were related. The walls of the center were adorned with framed lithograph pictures of Polish revolutionary heroes, of a battle in which the Poles emerged the victor and the Turk or Prussian the loser, or of a Polish castle, manor, or church. The rooms were also supplied with newspapers which could be read at leisure. In these newspapers, the immigrants might read shipping news, stories of crime and accidents, poems, moral advice, essays, and bits of curious and useful information. More important, the newspapers carried political articles on current issues in the United States and in partitioned Poland. The reading of the speeches, the poetry, the news, the stories, the jokes, and the ads that appeared in the newspapers led many immigrants to the discovery that such reading was in itself a liberal education, and one which gave them a better foundation than that they had received from the rural schools in their native land. If the immigrant was sufficiently ambitious and gifted he might even find in these newspapers a vehicle for his own thoughts, since the newspaper, by printing contributors' letters, became a kind of public forum.

The atmosphere of the center, clouded with foul cigarette or cigar smoke, was hardly inviting to the eye or nose. But this was the place to hear local gossip, who had died or was getting married, who was leaving for partitioned Poland, or returning to America; to exchange information or misinformation on the latest trend in employment or on the competence or incompetence of the officers of the club.

Later on, in addition to the "mutual aid societies," political clubs were also formed. The first political club organized in Philadelphia was the "Kosciuszko Club," founded in 1871. The

[31] Thomas and Znaniecki, *op. cit.*, II, p. 1523.

first meetings were held in the home of one of the members. Monthly dues were very small and the organization grew rapidly. Each member was required to obtain citizenship; when he received his final papers, the members of the club pre- sented him with a gift of three dollars. As the organization ex- panded, larger quarters were needed, and it was then that a large room was secured at the corner of Front and Green Streets. The club had a few books and at each meeting the members were required to visit the "library" and sign their names. Books were not plentiful in those days and the club was a haven to many newcomers to the United States, who spent many happy hours there. The members were urged to be good Amricans. The club used the following motto: "A good Pole is a good American Citizen."[30]

Gradually a yearning for the return of Poland's national freedom was beginning to develop. All of these latent yearnings and sentiments were woven into the developing pattern of the immigrant's new life in America. Eventually the "mutual aid societies" and "political clubs" assumed other functions and activ- ities. They became centers of information for newcomers, visitors, and travelers. Their leaders released to the local and national press news and information about any opportunities which the locality could offer to the Polish immigrants. They also appeared publicly at Divine Services on national and religious festivals. And they acted as the representatives of the colony in its relations with American institutions and agencies that tried to reach the Polish community for social purposes.[31] Politically conscious, they were frequently sensitive to the need to reconcile the conflicts between the immigrant group and the surrounding community.

It was quite different in the American Catholic churches. There the evidences of their foreignness crowded in upon the Polish immigrants. Catholics for the most part, the Polish immigrants found the Church already in existence in the cities to which they came. But the church was not theirs. Built by other worshippers,

---

[30] Sister M. Theodosetta, H.F.N., "'The Polish Immigrant in Philadelphia to 1914," *Records of the American Catholic Historical Society of Philadelphia*, LXV (June, 1954), No. 2, pp. 83-84.

the priests, the saints, the names, the very language were un-familiar. Eventually the leaders of the mutual aid societies and political clubs, desiring more recognition, prestige, and security, adopted as one of their objectives the establishment of Polish parishes in the image of what they had known in the Old Country. They well realized that a Polish parish, with Polish priests, would assure the permanence of the social cohesion of the colony. Furthermore, the parish would not only provide better social cooperation but it would stimulate interest in new lay activities which had little or no religious significance: musical clubs, in-surance funds, even cooperative merchandising groups.[32]

The establishment of the parish marked the second phase in the development of Polonia. As envisioned, it became the center of all social and cultural activities. Now the tendency to con-gregate grew stronger. At the turn of the twentieth century, for example, two Polish parishes alone were larger in size than many dioceses. In 1899, St. Stanislaus Kostka parish in Chicago boasted a membership of over 50,000 parishioneers and the Buffalo parish of St. Stanislaus Bishop and martyr numbered 30,000.[33]

The parish church in America took on for the peasant immi-grant the form of a "Poland in miniature."[34]

The Polish immigrant regarded his parish in America as both a religious and community center, a replica of his village, his church in Poland, and all of the activities associated with them in his native land. The parish provided the immigrant and those of his faith with a set of beliefs; it also offered the immigrant the opportunity of common religious worship and the benefit of spiritual guidance in his own language. In addition to faith and morals, the sermons were concerned with the problems of con-temporary life. The funeral sermon retailed and interpreted news

[32] Sister Mary Assumpta Pogorzelska, S.S.J., A Historical Study of Religion and Education as Underlying Influences in the Localization of the Poles of Cleveland up to 1915, (unpublished Master's thesis, Saint John's College of Cleveland, 1951), p. 44.

[33] Kruszka, op. cit., II, p. 28.

[34] The sphere of social contact for the peasant in Poland was very small, limited to the village, a nearby county-seat town, where he journeyed few times dur-ing the year on the big market days, or a town whose church was known to have a religious shrine, a miraculous image, to which he would make a pilgrimage on festive days. Such was the limited knowledge of Poland had by the peasants.

of shipwrecks and other calamities. The ordination sermon was weighted with theological learning, and the election-day sermon aimed to advance political understanding. The sermons also introduced a belief in equality of oportunity for all and a chance for everyone to rise from the lower to the higher levels of society. Each social class is open to properly qualified people below it. By applying himself, by using the talents he has, by acquiring the necessary skills, the immigrant can rise from lower to higher status and his family can rise with him. Finally, the stimulus the weekly sermon provided for household discussion enlarged the mental horizons of many immigrants who thus found an intellectual interest in Christianity, as well as comfort and support.[35]

For the Polish immigrants, the priests who had emigrated to America proved to be confessors, teachers, counselors, social directors, almsgivers, and even political leaders. They reminded their parishioners that only through the faith and language of their parents could they maintain their national identity. They warned the immigrants against succumbing to the teachings of Protestants and non-canonical priests who were capitalizing on their spiritual needs, often misleading and seducing them into acceptance of strange and idolatrous creeds. They issued endless warnings against mixed marriages and deviations from the parental path. A genuine Pole was true to his religion and to the country of his birth. The church, with its appeal to divine sanctions, was an effective weapon in the fight for cultural survival.

The parish provided the immigrant with the necessary incentive for congenial social life and a focal point about which to develop it, since activities of a wider scope, outside the parish, interested the peasant very little.[36] Of the tremendous advances made in mechanization, with the accompanying interdependence of individuals and communities, the peasant knew next to nothing.

With the establishment of the parish, emphasis was placed on establishing Polish schools where young people would be instructed in the traditional faith and language. The clergy, whose

---

[35] After the sermon, notices of meetings and society activities were read off by the priest. This practice is still kept in Polish American churches even in this age of abundant newspapers.

[36] Norman T. Lyon, *History of the Polish People of Rochester*, (Buffalo: 1935), pp. 27-28.

duties were multiple and pressing, became the leading representatives of intellectual interests. This was especially evident in the
support they gave to elementary education. They placed somewhat less emphasis on secondary education; however, they did
not neglect it.

Like the church, the parish school brought the Polish immigrants territorially together; created a bond between the old and
new generation by preserving the Polish language; encouraged
the young people to acquire the cultural traditions of their parents;
and developed familiarity with the civilization and problems of
the old land.[37]

The teaching corps, thoroughly American in thought and
speech, and thoroughly Polish in its sympathies with the incoming
immigrants, made for a healthy conservatism and precluded violent ruptures with traditions of the past.[38]

The Polish-American schools prospered in the congenial atmosphere of the Polonias, because parents frequently took the
position that children grew away from them and from the stabilizing influence of Polish customs too rapidly when they entered
public schools, where English origins and culture were most
honored.

> The Polish children who attend school here, and many of them
> who come here within school age or who are born here are attending
> public schools, learn new things which baffle them and surprise them
> indefinitely. They don't hear any more about Poland, and if it being

---

[37] The school's purpose was not only to impart Christian education but to
acquaint the child with its Polish heritage. From its first day in school the child
was taught the prayers in Polish and catechetical instruction was given in the same
language. In the higher grades, reading and writing in Polish, Polish history, and
Polish literature formed part of the grade school curriculum. To insure this religious
and national education the Poles hired the help of the Polish Sisterhoods, urged
them for that purpose to establish or transfer their homes from Poland to America
or else new religious communities of Sisters were established. Their members were
recruited among the Poles in America. In 1942, the Polish teaching sisterhood
numbered 4,822 members, in charge of 553 elementary schools. Rev. S. Targosz,
*Polonja Katolicka w Stanach Zjednoczonych w Przekroju,* (Detroit: 1943), p. 5.

[38] Fully ninety-five per-cent of the teachers in the Polish American Schools
are American by birth. The older religious communities, several of which have
reached a high degree of efficiency, cannot supply the increasing demand in the
schools already under their charge. New parishes must content themselves with such
as the more recently established communities can afford. The presence of lay teachers
in the Polish schools is evidence of the inadequacy in the number of Polish nuns.

referred to by the teachers it is usually with an air of superiority. The Polish heroes except Kosciuszko and Pulaski are not recognized, not worshipped in this country. America and not Poland is being constantly eulogized by the teachers and set as an example of national and spiritual superiority, and the Polish boy or girl soon does not know what to make of it. Has he not already a definite fatherland in Poland? Has he not learned to identify himself with Polish people which in the opinion of his father and mother is the best people in the world? How should he take the deprecatory remarks about his old country, and the light making or overlooking of his Polish heroes? Have his parents been wrong or misleading in their teachings and ideas?[39]

Sometimes the parents kept their children at home and out of school as long as possible; or they would have them taught the first elements of knowledge in Polish and in the Polish spirit. The child learned so much about Polish culture and the exalted courage of the Poles, that he attributed, especially during his early years, everything great to Poland and the Poles. Thus it was not strange that a little boy once asked his mother in the presence of Brandes: "Is it possible that Columbus was not a Pole?"[40]

The fear of losing the children haunts the older generation. It is not merely the natural desire of parent to retain influence over child. Nor is it simply the dread that the wayward offspring will mar the good name of the immigrant group by abuse of his newly found freedom. It is a vague uneasiness that a delicate network of precious traditions is being ruthlessly torn asunder, that a whole world of ideals is crashing into ruins; and amidst this desolation the fathers and mothers picture themselves wandering about lonely in vain search of their lost children.[41]

Desiring some means of cushioning the sudden cultural shock to the younger generation, parents and clergy made certain that the Polish language was taught as well as something of the history and culture of Poland.[42] The training in Polish parochial schools

---

[39] Joseph S. Schneiweis, *Certain Aspects of Polish Assimilation in the State of New York*, (unpublished Master's thesis, Columbia University, 1930), pp. 25-26.

[40] George Brandes, *Poland, A Study of the Land, People and Literature*, (London: 1903), pp. 67-68.

[41] Julius Drachsler, *Democracy and Assimilation*, (New York: 1920), p. 80.

[42] When the Polish newspaper, the *Kuryer Polski*, proposed in 1910, that the Polish language be taught in public schools of Milwaukee along with German, Catholic leaders regarded this step as a program to destroy the parochial school system and

was different from that of the public school. It was more demand-
ing and severe; it punished physical aggression but encouraged
the discharge of such energies in social achievement. Ideally, it
trained for individual responsibilitiy and autonomy. It frowned
on the free expression of impulses and rewarded restraint, fore-
sight, and the acceptance of superior, but more remote, goals.
When such training was successful, individuals were produced
who were often candidates for social mobility.

Kasimir I. Kozakiewicz, ex-president of the Polish Roman
Catholic Union, made the following observation about the Polish
school.

> I remember my grammar school days, and perhaps you do too;
> our almost entire school day was conducted in the Polish language,
> only some of the time was devoted to English reading, writing, spell-
> ing, history, and geography. If my memory serves me right we even
> studied arithmetic in both Polish and English.[43]

Anna G. Tremaine, a teacher in the Buffalo public school system,
who had the son of Health Commissioner Fronczak in her class,
made the following comment.

> The boy was very slow, no slower than his Polish companions,
> but slower than we thought he should be, judged by his father's posi-
> tion. The father could not understand his son's lack of progress. With
> a good deal of hesitation he finally confessed his difficulty to us. He
> did not understand much of what was said. Up to the time he entered
> high school he had attended Polish schools and the family talked Polish
> at home entirely, because the father feared the children would forget
> their Mother Tongue.[44]

Peter A. Speek in the early twenties visited an old and comparatively large Polish colony in Posen, Michigan. His field
notes supply the following information on the Polish school in that
area.

---

bitterly resisted it. In 1912, Archbishop Messner of the Milwaukee Archdiocese
issued a degree forbidding all Catholics to read the *Kuryer Polski*. The newspaper
rejoined with a damage suit for $100,000 which was thrown out of the courts. Since
then the Polish parochial school system has not been successfully challenged.

[43] Kasimir I. Kozakiewicz, "The President's Pad," *Narod Polski*, (May 19,
1955), p. 15.

[44] Anna G. Tremaine, *The Effect of Polish Immigration on Buffalo Politics*,
(unpublished Master's thesis, Columbia University, 1928), p. 56.

There is at the church a four-room parochial school housed in a substantial brick building, with five teachers including a priest. The school year lasts ten months. Teaching is in English, except that an hour each day is devoted to the Polish language and Polish history. The priest admitted that the teaching of religion is in Polish. The school program is the same as in the standard public schools of eight grades. The same textbooks are used. Although the law does not require examination of the children, nevertheless to appease the county officials and show the efficiency and value of their school they send the children to the county board of education for examination, and the county board' has always expressed great satisfaction with the advancement in education of the children of the Polish school. The teachers are all Poles, appointed by the bishop, candidates being presented by the priest.[45]

## The priest explained as follows the need for this school.

It Americanizes the children more quickly than the American school—that is, it is more efficient in teaching the children the American way of life and American history than the American public school, for the teachers are all Poles, know their people and their psychology better than do the teachers in the public schools. During a later discussion the priest admitted that the Church service is in the Polish language and that the Polish school exists rather for sentimental reasons of a racial character than for practical reasons. The settlers also claimed that the Polish school and' the Church service in the Polish language are needed for the reason that they like this better; they complained that the expenses are too high; they would have the county or state help them. Sometimes a few adults come to the school, but they are irregular in attendance.[46]

## In several of the rural immigrant communities, visited by Speek, there were successful bilingual churches.

In the Polish colony at Posen, Michigan, the sermon in the Catholic Church is in two languages, Polish and English. The priest explained that the Polish language is needed, as the people, especially the older people, understand it better and the priest is able to penetrate their souls more intimately in their mother tongue. The English language is needed' for two reasons: among the colonists are a few American farmers who belong to the same church and do not speak Polish; and a few of the younger generation understand English better than Polish, especially those newcomers who have been born outside of the colony among Americans.[47]

---

[45] Peter A. Speek, A Stake in the Land, (New York: 1921), pp. 168-169.
[46] Ibid., p. 169.
[47] Ibid., pp. 187-188.

Why the Poles endured so many great sacrifices to build schools where their Polish language would be perpetuated is ably expounded by Father Walery Jasinski, who gives the following reasons why Americans of Polish descent should study the Polish language and Polish culture.

You study because you love and respect your parents. Only he who values highly what is dear and sacred to his parents loves and respects them. The Polish language is the language they used—and still use—in prayers for the many graces granted to you and to themselves. It is, moreover, the reflection of the culture and the spirit of the nation. It is one of the richest languages from the point of view of grammar and expression, which is evidence of the high culture and the intelligence of your forefathers. Does one who does not care to study the language of his parents really love them? On the contrary, he who neither knows nor understands the language of his parents, does not know or understand either his parents or what is dear to them. Is one who has little interest in his parents, who are God's greatest gifts to him, a good child?—Son, you love and respect your parents; therefore do not say that you do not want to study the language of your forefathers.[48]

In his second exposition of the spirit behind the study of the Polish language and culture, Father Jasinski states:

You want to study the Polish language and the culture of Poland because you want to be a useful citizen of the United States. You are an American citizen. This privilege, from the point of view of the Decalogue, imposes upon you a responsibility. What are you willing to render to America in return for the benefits you receive as a citizen? Is he not a thief who takes but does not give? You don't want to be a parasite; you must, therefore, enrich America's culture in some way. You have much to give her. Your heritage is rich with a thousand years of Polish culture. You may draw from that treasure plentifully. A glimpse into the histories of America and Poland will convince you that the educational, religious, and pedagogical culture of Poland is older and wealthier than the American culture. The history of European culture is aware of Poland's five-hundred years of university tradition. Poland was so much in the lead in Physics that within twenty years' time two International Physics Congresses were held at War-

---

[48] Rev. Walery Jasinski, Ph.D., *Po Co Sie Uczyc Jezyka Polskiego i Kultury Polskiej w Ameryce,* (Plymouth: 1941), p. 5.

saw her achievement in the arts and other sciences—astronomy, chemistry, engineering, theology, literature, music, art and architecture—is equally praiseworthy. Is one, I ask, a useful American citizen who has such gigantic treasures, but who does not want to share them with America? How can one who does not know the treasures of Polish culture himself, because he does not care to study, enrich America with them?[49]

Thus their children as useful citizens, may contribute to the enrichment of the intricate and complex culture of America.[50]

The children in the majority of cases, become accustomed to speak and to think in English; this language becomes their daily language, while the Polish language and Polonism are the synonyms of the festal celebrations of the Polish holidays. Hence, we see children that on the platform have just sung Polish songs or declaimed Polish verses, speaking familiarly with one another in English as they are descending from the platform. These children later, when they grow up, will speak familiarly with one another likewise in English, carrying on at the same time a conversation with guests in Polish. Many of them will remain in the mob, but many of them will be graduated from the universities—in this way there arises the Polish American intelligent class.[51]

Within the limits of these parishes, national ideals grew.[47] Polish life emanated from the parish and began to assert itself socially and culturally. Social clubs for the preservation of quaint, colorful customs and old memories, singers' unions, orchestras, art clubs, athletic associations, historical societies, literary builds, political leagues, engineering societies, crafts circles and press associations came into being.[52] Political societies found their sup-

---

[49] *Ibid.*, p. 6.

[50] Rev. Walery J. Jasinski, *Teksty Dotyczace Asymilacji Polakow w Ameryce,* (Detroit: 1944), p. 1944.

[51] Louis E. Van Norman, *Poland The Knight Among Nations,* (New York: 1907), p. 334.

[52] The salient events around which Polish history centers itself, helped much to enkindle in the masses of Polish immigrants national idealism and national consciousness. Polish history for the most part reads as though it were Church history, it is almost impossible to draw the line between the one and the other.

Poland's entrance upon the historical scene of Europe dates with the introduction of Christianity within her boundaries. With the conversion of Lithuania and the ensuing union of the two nations, Poland emerged as the most powerful state on the European continent in the XV and XVI centuries. Its greatest military achievements were associated with religion, v.g., the defeat of the Knights of the Cross at Grunwald in 1492, the victory over the Swedes at Czestochowa in 1655, that of Sobieski over the Turks at Vienna in 1683, and her constant war with the

port mainly in the parish.

In Chicago, particularly, the Polish churches have fostered the development of "citizens clubs." A typical example is that of "King Casimir the Great Polish Citizens Club."

> This club was formed about six years ago. Its purposes are to naturalize the men of the church, to educate its members in political subjects, and to work for the general improvement of the district, which in this case is solidly Polish. The club has about three hundred members, and meets monthly, the active attendance being composed mainly of men not yet naturalized. Meetings are usually conducted in Polish, but two-thirds of the members can now speak English and practically all of them can catch the drift of addresses in English.
>
> To date upward of two hundred and fifty men have been naturalized, and many more than that have been assisted in taking out first papers. For the past three years, a class in English and civics, meeting twice a week, with an attendance of twenty-five to thirty, has been conducted with a paid instructor. The club also concerns itself with such local matters as garbage collection and upkeep of streets, and sends frequent delegations to the city hall.[53]

Members who gained prominence or rose in the professional ranks were referred to as products of a given parish. The amateur parish theater presented Polish plays, arranged national celebrations which commemorated the important events in the history of Poland. Problems affecting the immigrants' own interest or nationality and appeals from the native land for aid in wide-spread disasters were acted through the parish unit.

When the parish had been organized, the mutual aid societies and the political clubs ceased to be the central and only representative institutions of the community, for leadership naturally passed into the hands of the Polish clergy. Literate and more

---

Ottoman Empire merited for Poland the glorious title "The Bulwark of Christianity."

The celebration therefore and commemoration of any historical event would be incomplete without the preliminary opening with solemn church services and appropriate sermon. A certain sacredness was thus added to the history of Poland. Her glorious past was unfolded to the Polish immigrant, and with it, national idealism, national consciousness rose to unprecedented heights. To the church, the parish, its clergy and the Polish parochial school was intrusted the role not only of spiritual, moral guides, but also the preservation and propagation of Poland's history, of her greatness. They emerged as the creators of national idealism among the Polish immigrants in America.

[53] John Daniels, *America Via the Neighborhood*, (New York: 1920), p. 116.

capable of dealing with the American environment, the priests were in a position to assume the leadership of their countrymen. But the mutual aid societies and the political clubs did not surrender entirely any of their social functions; they simply shared the initiative in communal matters and representation of the community with the priests and other associations which now began to appear in rapid succession.

Before long the purely local character of Polonia no longer sufficed, and the impulse to gather all Polish-Americans in a common body appeared in the latter part of the nineteenth century. As the Polish parishes were the centers of all community activities, it was not long before a Polish pastor, Father Gieryk of Detroit, advanced the idea of uniting all of the various Polish-American social and charitable societies into one national organization. In June, 1873, Father Gieryk made known his idea in an open letter published in the few existing Polish weeklies.[54]

John Barzynski of Union, Missouri, editor of a Polish weekly newspaper, and his brother, Father Vincent Barzynski of Chicago, took up Father Gieryk's idea to form one large national organization to promote religious unity among the Poles.[55] They called a meeting of all persons interested in forming such an organization in Detroit for October 3, 1873. At this meeting, Father Gieryk was nominated chairman, and John Barzynski appointed secretary of the new organization. The name "Polish Roman Catholic Union in America" (Zjednoczenie Polskie Rzymsko-Katolickie w Ameryce) was adopted. The objectives of the new organization, as defined in 1874 at the National Congress in Chicago were: (1) to uphold the national spirit of Polish-Americans, (2) to help them persevere in the Faith of their forefathers, (3) to maintain in the youth a lively interest in things Polish, and (4) to aid in the building and improvement of parochial schools in the United States.[56]

As the number of Polish immigrants increased after the Civil

---

[54] Father Gieryk was dissatisfied with the mutual aid societies because they did not stress religion.

[55] Brigadier General Joseph W. Barzynski, a West Point graduate, is the son of John Barzynski.

[56] Dr. Karol Wachtl, *Polonja w Ameryce*, (Philadelphia: 1944), pp. 164-165.

War, Poles complained of Irish control of their church.[57] Although deeply religious, the Poles did not feel at home in what they called the "Irish-Catholic Church" of the United States.[58] Polish leaders, especially Father Kruszka, denounced the Irish influence.[59]

It is an undeniable fact that although the Irish form only about one-third of the Catholic population, of the hundred Catholic bishops in the United States, almost all are of Irish nationality, a few German bishops being only a drop in the sea. This is a fact, and against a fact there is no argument. From this fact one can easily deduct the conclusion that the Irish want a certain priest for a bishop, just because he is Irish. . . . What the Poles in their movement for a Polish bishop want, is this: to have bishops from any nationality, and not only from one exclusively, as it was practiced to this time. The Irish, as facts prove presented always and still present candidates of Irish extraction, to the exclusion of other nationalities, as if they alone had the monopoly of wisdom and sanctity and episcopal dignity. But why do the Irish mostly succeed in Rome? Simply by persuading the Roman authorities that the Irish nationality is the only American nationality—all other are "foreign" nationalities.

Since 1854, the Poles built every year churches, schools, asylums, colleges . . . paid always faithfully their church taxes, cathedraticum, seminaristicum . . . and during this long period never enjoyed any rights and privileges in the church, never had any representation in the hierarchy. This is evidently unjust and un-American! And now, when we make a just complaint, they say to us, that there was not as yet any Polish priest worthy to become a bishop but as soon as they will find one, they will make one. I need not say that this is a poor excuse, and an uncharitable one, not worthy of a true Christian. It is an open insult to the whole Polish clergy. Were so long the

---

[57] Early in the nineteenth century, when the Irish immigration was still relatively small, the Irish had championed a kind of Cahenslyism of their own in complaining to the Pope that French priests monopolized the American hierarchy. From Norfolk, Charleston, and Philadelphia came resentful protests against "foreigners" in control of local parishes, and the issue in some areas became entangled with the question of trusteeism as local parishes expressed a desire to control the temporal possessions of their churches. Ugly charges were dispatched to Rome to the effect that Frenchmen were intriguing to control the American Church. Carl Wittke, *The Irish in America*, (Baton Rouge: 1956), p. 187.

[58] By 1910, there were about six hundred Polish churches in the United States and perhaps a thousand priests.

[59] In 1853 there were protests from German Catholic groups against the practice of sending Irish priests to minister to their religious needs, and the demand for bishops and priests of their own nationality increased with the years. Carl Wittke, *We Who Built America*, (Ann Arbor: 1957), pp. 227-228.

Irish and the few Germans the only worthy, upon whom the Holy Ghost reigned to descend? One must be arrogant, to assert this. Indeed, to this privileging of one and disregarding of other nationalities we may safely ascribe the fact, that there was in the United States no gain, but a loss of millions of Catholics. The Independent Polish sect says: "If the Pope allows the organization in the United States of an Irish national hierarchy, why does he not allow the formation of a Polish national hierarchy?" An even pure Americans, I mean those of no denomination either religious or national, I have heard asking: "Where is the mark of catholicity in your church? Is it not predominantly Irish Catholic?"[60]

President Theodore Roosevelt, remarked to Father Kruszka on a certain occasion that he found his deductions logical and that he believed the Poles should have their own bishops.[61]

The PRCU supported the Polish priests who desired to preserve the integrity of the Polish parishes from absorption by the Irish-dominated Catholic hierarchy in America, which opposed the establishment of separate Polish parishes. The Irish, on the other hand, "more American than the Americans," and with a good command of English, tried to control the Polish immigrants by imposing not only Irish Bishops but also the English language on them.[62] Protests against the Irish domination and the de-

---

[60] Ks. Waclaw Kruszka, *Siedm Siedmioleci czyli Pol Wieku Zycia*, (Poznan: 1924), pp. 152-153.

[61] Right Reverend Monsignor Alexander Syski, S.T.M., "The Nestor of Polish Historians in America: Reverend Waclaw Kruszka," *Polish American Studies*, I (January-December, 1944), p. 69.

[62] The apparent apathy in respect to the promotion of Polish priests to the rank of bishops was a substantial cause for complaint in the Polish settlements. Despite their size and weight of responsibility connected with their management, these Polish ships of faith were still captained by officers of junior rank who seemed to go unnoticed in the ranks of the Catholic hierarchy here in America. It was fifty-four years after the founding of the first parish in America that the Poles were to give the Catholic Church its first Polish bishop. Bishop Paul Rhode was consecrated bishop in 1908 in Chicago. Bishop Edward Kozlowski followed him in the same rank in 1914. This alleged discrimination on the part of the Irish and German Catholics produced much discontent in Polish circles. As a matter of fact, it almost disrupted the unity of the Catholic Church among Polish Americans.

Up to 1908 not a single bishop was selected from the ranks of the Polish clergy. On the basis of an estimated twelve per-cent of the Catholic population which they comprised in the United States at the turn of the century the Polish nationalists reasoned that they should have at least two archbishops and eleven bishops selected from their number, and yet the fifteen archbishops and the ninety-four bishops in the United States as of 1900 were all non-Polish. With fortified indignation they further compared their 900 parishes to the 456 German speaking

mand for local parish control of church property finally reached such proportions that a Polish National Independent Catholic Church was organized.[63] In 1902 the Pope sent his personal representative, Archbishop A. Symons, to examine the situation.[64]

Since the original mutual aid societies had a number of systems of insurance, the PRCU decided during these early stages of organization to leave insurance alone and instead to concentrate on the ideals of the new organization. The following means were to be taken to attain the objectives of the organization: (1) establishment of educational institutions of higher learning, (2) establishment of a Polish bank for the Polish population in America, (3) establishment of a convent for women, (4) establishment of a teachers' seminary, (5) establishment of libraries, and (6) establishment of a Polish hospital. There was also discussion of the establishment of an orphanage, and of help and care for newly arrived immigrants.[65]

The convention voted that every member would pay $1.00 in dues. This revenue was to be utilized to attain the set objectives of the organization. It was also proposed that a National Congress of Polish-Americans be held the following year in Chicago. Representatives from thirty-two social and benevolent societies had participated in the 1874 Convention and had elected the following officers: President, Reverend Theodore Gieryk; General Secretary, John Barzynski; Treasurer, August Rudzinski; Chaplain, Reverend Vincent Barzynski. A Board of Controllers, composed of six priests and five laymen, was also elected as part of the Executive Board. The representatives also decided to hold annual con-

---

parishes and found that for that number of parishes the Germans gave the Catholic Church in the United States fourteen bishops and three archbishops. The Poles gave it none. To the German hating Poles this was comparable to being led to heaven by the Sultan of Turkey. Pliska, op. cit., p. 45.

63 The seceding organization has its stronghold in Pennsylvania, a seminary in Scranton, a weekly paper known as Straz, and a benefit "Union" to provide insurance. The seceders insist that they are good Catholics, although they have gradually instituted a number of changes in Church practices. John A. Hardon, S.J., "The Polish National Catholic Church," The Homiletic and Pastoral Review, LVI (April, 1956), pp. 552-561.

64 During his stay, the Archbishop visited 160 Polish parishes and delivered 350 speeches. Mieczyslaw Haiman, Zjednoczenie Polskie Rzymsko-Katolickie w Ameryce, pp. 205-213.

65 Ibid., pp. 32-33.

ventions.[66] For undetermined reasons, this Polish Roman Catholic
Union eventually became inactive.

Another leader, in 1879, who pointed out the need of uniting
all Polish-American societies then in existence in the United
States into one organization, was Agaton Giller, a Polish exile
and former member of the National Polish government during
the uprising of 1861-64, living in Switzerland. Out of his deep
concern for the future of the Poles in partitioned Poland came his
article, "The Organization of Poles in America" (O Organizacji
Polakow w Ameryce), which appeared in Polish newspapers, both
in Poland and in the United States. In this article, addressed to
the Poles living in the United States, numbering 500,000 at the
time, according to the Polish press, Giller strongly urged the
Polish immigrants to unite into one powerful organization in
order to promote the cause of Poland, especially that of the
restoration of her independence. Among the additional aims of the
proposed organization he mentioned, the revitalization of the
masses of Polish immigrants with the Polish national spirit; the
checking of the losses among the Polish immigrants who no longer
feel attachment either to their Fatherland or their native language;
the possibility of exerting greater influence on American political
life through the medium of a nation-wide union of the Poles;
greater opportunity for their economic betterment through con-
certed action; and the possibility of serving as a medium of
exchange between the Polish and American cultures.

With his acute vision, Giller gave the immigrants not only
a political purpose, but also a means to fulfill it, and first and
foremost the consciousness that the Polish immigrants, in spite
of their dispersal in the United States, were a political force, if
they would only use their strength for the redemption of Poland.
Like all great political thinkers, Giller grasped the profound yet
simple secret that the dormant Polish national spirit in the Polish
immigrants could be converted into a source of strength and
fortitude, of initiative and heroism, if there were linked to it the
idea of redemption and liberation of partitioned Poland. No

66 This practice was continued for a period of twenty-six years, after which
time, the conventions were held every three years until 1937 when the practice was
changed to a quadrennial convention.

people can be saved except by itself, and the Polish problem can be solved only by the Poles. So Giller pleaded.

In response to Giller's plea, on February 15, 1880, Julius Andrzejkowicz invited Julius Szajnert, Julius Lipinski, Vincent Domanski, John Biadynski, Antoni Wojczynski, John Nepomucyn Papielinski, John Biachowski, Theophil Kucielski, and Peter Beczkiewicz to attend a meeting in Philadelphia.[67] There they discussed not only the famine that existed at the time in the Polish province of Slask, but they also discussed and studied the political patterns of European countries so that they too, in an opportune time, might organize a "Young Poland Movement" to liberate partitioned Poland from Russia, Prussia, and Austria. They believed that the Polish immigrants would eventually become a force strong enough to exert a decisive influence in world politics, if it could be united in a common cause. Andrzejkowicz's letter, dated February 18, 1880. contained the following observation.

> What influence may be elicited upon a nation was shown by Mazzini's genius in his idea of creating a unified and independent Italy; to him more than to Garibaldi does Italy owe its independence. He awakened the desire of unity and independence, the accomplishment of which Cavour, the statesman. and Garibaldi, a man of action and hero, had realized.[68]

In a series of questions, Andrzejkowicz urged his fellow citizens, the Polish immigrants in the United States, to form national organizations.

> What is the status of the Polish immigrant in America? Isn't America far safer than England? Aren't we strong and independent? Do we not have freedom of speech, press and assembly? Why, then, couldn't we form national organizations with a strong central government endowed with unlimited confidence and power?[69]

---

[67] At that time there was a famine in the province of Slask in Poland and some of the Poles who were living in Philadelphia were raising a relief fund to send to their countrymen in Europe. While canvassing for this, some of the members became acquainted with Julius Andrzejkowicz, a prosperous business man, who was a partner in a paint and dye business.

[68] Stanislaw Osada, Historja Zwiazku Narodowego Polskiego, (Chicago: 1905), p. 111.

[69] Ibid., p. 111.

At the Philadelphia meeting, Julius Andrzejkowicz stressed the necessity for all Polish organizations in America to unite into an alliance or federation under the name of "Polish National Alliance" (Zwiazek Narodowy Polski). It was understood that each society that joined this alliance would retain its individual character. The plan of the proposed organization was patterned somewhat on the existing federal system of government; like each state, each society was to be recognized as a distinct and separate entity, with a voice and the right of representation in the central organization, so as to render possible a united effort in any particular emergency or on behalf of a common cause. In conformity with the decision, an appeal was directed to all existing organizations to express their opinions of the proposed plan, and to indicate whether they would participate. This appeal read in part.

> Compatriots, here we have found a haven of refuge; here we have freedom of association, of the press and of speech. Though we have numbers we lack strength for like the grains of dust we are scattered and isolated, we are nothing, powerless to assist ourselves or to render a service to the country. Gathered together and organized in a powerful alliance, not only shall we uplift ourselves morally and materially, but we shall create a mighty power which we shall be able to use for the good of our native land. What is more important, we shall create the power of public opinion, which today is mightier than armament or the bayonet, an opinion predicated on the precepts of liberty, equality, and fraternity.[70]

Immediately thereafter an open invitation was published in the Polish press asking all Polish-American Societies to join the proposed association. Societies from Illinois, California, Pennsylvania, Michigan, New York and Wisconsin responded immediately. After the completion of the first draft of the Constitution, Juliusz Andrzejkowicz designated September 20, 1880, as the date for the first National Convention of the Polish National Alliance. The place chosen was Chicago. The date of this appeal, which was the first official act of the organization, is established as the date of the founding of the Polish National Alliance. The platform adopted by this convention, which was incorporated into

---

[70] Casimir E. Midowicz, "The Polish National Alliance," *Poland Journal of Commerce and Industry*, VIII (August, 1927), p. 489.

the constitution of the new organization, is interesting as well as enlightening as to the purpose of the Polish National Alliance.

1. To lay the foundation of institutions for the material and moral development of the Polish element in the United States through the medium of an iron fund, which shall be permanent and undivided property of the Alliance, is hereby acknowledged as essential, to the category of institutions of this character shall belong immigration homes, schools and all institutions of general learning, libraries, homes of shelter, and commercial institutions located in acceptable places.
2. To protect the interests of Polish immigrants.
3. To promote the political establishment of Polish immigrants as citizens of the United States through the medium of the official publication of the Alliance, and through entry into relations with the American press for the purpose of protecting our interests. Every person becoming a member of the Alliance shall seek to become a citizen of the United States.
4. To provide fraternal assistance to the members of the societies comprising the Alliance, based on insurance, and obtained by means of compulsory assessment determined by the convention.
5. To sponsor the arrangement of patriotic affairs commemorating national memorial days, and to urge the discharge of duties dictated by national honor.
6. To advocate moderation and temperance in the use of alcoholic stimulants.
7. To guarantee the freedom of religious convictions, the P.N.A., adherring to the position that religious matters constitute the concern of the Holy Apostolic See, does not regard it proper to interfere there with or constitute the same as a pre-requisite to membership to its ranks.[71]

Thus was the organization founded, and its course of action mapped out. According to its charter, the PNA was created for cultural, educational and humanitarian purposes, specifically in relation to the Polish immigrants in the United States. The comparatively rapid expansion of the organization was made possible by an efficient propaganda machine, and by editors and organizers who knew how to play on the sentiments of the Polish immigrants.[72]

---

[71] The Convention adopted the policy of non-Denominationalism. This it did in order to be consistent with the Articles of the Polish Constitution of May 3, 1791, and the American Constitution, both of which respect their citizens' choice of religion. Midowicz, *op. cit.*, pp. 489-490.

[72] Leaders, various cultural organizations and the foreign language press, al-

From the objectives adopted by the convention we must
conclude that it was clear in the minds of these perceptive founders
of the Polish National Alliance that one of their aims must be
an unqualified support of education and the world of scholarship.
They fully realized that intellectual poverty would impede their
efforts at advancement on all fronts. The desire for a propitious
climate in which the children of new immigrants could be reared
found voice in the first issue of Zgoda, the official publication of
the Polish National Alliance. It posed the question: "Shall the
Poles wear the crown of American citizenship with dignity? Shall
they stand on equal footing with the Germans, the French, the
English, in the professions, in literature, in commerce, in politics,
in the crafts?" And it gave the answer: "The field is open to all.
The most able will be victorious. . . . The emigration then will
rise and be an equal in the family of Christian and enlightened
nations. It will be a credit to itself and to the nation."

The PNA in its first constitution professed "obedience to the
Roman Catholic Faith, since that is the faith of the vast majority
of the Polish nation," but further committed itself to a programme
of "toleration of all creeds in the spirit of Poland's ancient constitution."[73] Socialists were barred. All official religious services
were to be conducted according to Catholic rites. Succeeding
conventions gradually eliminated all reference to religion and the
bar to the admission of Socialists was removed. Anarchists and
criminals were still barred.

The overwhelming majority of the members of the PNA
were Catholic; however, many clerical leaders were dissatisfied
with the PNA.[74] The threat of Americanization and the threat

though trying to keep immigrants loyal to the old values, have not been conspicuously
successful in their efforts to impart its enthusiasm to the masses. We have only to
read the accounts which the leaders give in their own press of the difficulties they
are having to maintain in America the language and the traditions of the homeland,
to realize how glacial and, in the long run, wholly irresistible, under conditions of
American life, is the trend toward a common language, a common life, and a common tradition of all the peoples in the United States.

[73] Felix Thomas Seroczynski, "Poles in the United States," The Catholic
Encyclopedia, XII (New York: 1914), p. 208.

[74] The misgivings which the Catholic Clergy had of the PNA were not totally
unfounded. Among the first members of the PNA were political refugees from
Poland after the abortive insurrections and a sprinkling of the cultured Poles, the

that the rising PNA might be dangerous to the exclusive supremacy which the clergy desired to keep in its hands, pushed the
clergy into politics. A few months after the PNA was established, Father Vincent Barzynski, with several other priests, re-
vived the PRCU.[75] Following the inclination of Father Barzynski,
who after participation in the Revolution of 1863, adherred to the
Positivist School, the PRCU was not willing to permit its members
to take active interest in Poland's national struggle.

The Positivist School, prevalent in Russian Poland in the
1860's and the Krakow Historical School, which had studied and
published materials on medieval and early modern Polish history,
had maintained that the downfall of Poland was attributable to
the mistakes and faults of the Poles. Jozef Szujski, rector of the
five-hundred-year-old Jagiellonian university, author of volumes,
poet, playwright, novelist and great master of the history of
Poland held that it was not the external factors but internal
factors that determined Poland's weakness, that brought Poland
to catastrophe. The prolonged immutability of economic conditions in Poland kept Poland at a very low economic level up to
the final partition. Poland's premature parliamentarism decimated the monarchical power, thus taking away from the nation,
from the state, its guide and leader in the domain of foreign
policy and bringing it to internal disorder. Also Poland's colon-
izing mission in Lithuania and the Ukraine was an ambitious
enterprise which exceeded the strength of the nation. This Polish
"Drang nach Osten" absorbed too many forces which should
have been devoted to reforming the nation. The best, most
active and creative elements of the nation were lost, absorbed
by the immense territories united to the Republic, and the Republic was gutted. Humanism and the Reformation likewise
weakened Poland, having decimated the homogeneous force and

---

intelligentsia. These, were known for their indifferentism to the Catholic Religion, in
fact, the children of some have not only lost their Polish nationalism, but their
Faith as well.

75 Father Barzynski also founded St. Stanislaus College in Chicago, in 1891.
At one time it numbered 15 professors and 210 students. He also gave the Poles
their first Catholic paper, *Gazeta Katolicka*, their first daily paper, the *Dziennik
Chicagoski*, and he formed the first teaching corps of Polish nuns.

organization of Catholicism. In accomplishing its civilizing mission in the East, Poland gradually lost or at least attenuated its
occidental characteristics; it underwent the contagion of oriental
and Muscovite barbarity.

Where scholarship demanded it, the Krakow Historical
School, which was presided by Szujski's disciple, Michael Bobrzynski, sometime Galician governor, had no qualms about as-
signing the dismemberment of Poland to the grievous incompetence and blindness of the Polish nobility. In his book *History
of Poland* which was published after the Franco-Prussian War,
Bobrzynski accuses the Polish nobility of having produced no
men sufficiently ardent and powerful, passionate and decisive,
to have the courage to push history into drama, into great
conflicts of passions and of political ideas. Polish toleration
seemed to him a proof of weakness, not strength, and the struggle
against powerful and resolute monarchical power appeared to
him one of Poland's greatest historical sins. In an age when kings
throughout Europe boasted of reigning by Divine Right, one
could not but look down upon a king who reigned by the vote
of the nobilitiy. The civil liberties of the Polish nobility were the
source of all Polish calamities. The fact that the rights of the
individual were never sacrificed to the needs of the state led Poland
to ruin. Bobrzynski also hails the influence of Byzantium in the
orthodox Slav states where the Church was subjugated to the laic
power. Bobrzynski was the advocate of absolute power and the
admirer of great sovereigns who had had the strength to impose
their will on the nation. Under his ferociously brave and bold
pen, Polish parliamentarism was the cause of Poland's annihilation. "Our fall could come only after a whole series of faults,
after a long period of violations of the higher laws of God assigned to the life and development of nations."

In addition, both schools stressed that the romantic enthusiam
of the past decades should give way to cold logic; not armed
uprisings, not military revolutionary plots, but economic, cultural, and national uplifting of the masses of the Polish people
should be the order of the day and patriotic duty of every Pole.

Another school of history flourished at Lwow University

with Professor Xavier Liske, a scholar of vast erudition in charge.[76] Historians at Lwow extolled the constructive achievements of Poland in the past and, in contrast to their fellows at the Krakow Historical School, attributed chief responsibility for Poland's downfall in the eighteenth century to the rapacity of predatory neighbors. Intellectual warfare between the Krakow "realists" and the Lwow "romantics" enlivened Polish historical learning, enfused it with a dynamic character, and brought to light a wealth of new evidence on the antecedents of Poland's spoilation. But after 1900 the romanticizing interpreters were reluctantly obliged to acknowledge the victory of the Krakow scholars.[77] The Krakow Historical School was, however, replaced at the beginning of the 20th century by an "optimistic" approach. Warsaw historians writing at the beginning of World War I were convinced that "Poland had produced a superior type of state (compared with the European West and East), a morally superior historic type, preceding other countries in this field, and there lay the principal cause of Poland's fall.

Tadeusz Korzon in his *Listy otwarte, Mowy, Rozprawy, Rozbiory* demonstrated all the value and importance that must be attached to the federative and republican institutions of ancient Poland. Wladyslaw Smolenski in *Przewrot umyslowy w Polsce wieku XVIII* gave a detailed description of the moral revolution produced in Poland at the end of the eighteenth century, immediately before the catastrophe, which had bequeathed to the nation regenerative and renovative principles. R. Rembowski in *Konfederacja i Rozkosz* proved in a plan of comparative history that all the "anarchies" and all the risings of the *szlachta* in Poland represented nothing exceptional in Europe. Finally Szymon Askenazy devoted himself to the task of demonstrating that the Partitions had been the result of entirely exterior factors. His rich archival researches, his great knowledge of diplomatic documents and persons, his penchant for biography, and his Polish nationalistic spirit facilitated for him the execution of the enter-

---

[76] In his seminars many of the leading Polish historians of the next generation received their professional training. His brilliant colleague, Szymon Askenazy, who was educated in the Russian University of Warsaw, concerned himself with polemical researches in modern history, especially the Napoleonic period and diplomacy.

[77] Arthur J. May, *The Habsburg Monarchy*, (Cambridge: 1951), pp. 54-55.

prise. It was Russia, Prussia, and Austria who had dismembered Poland, and not Poland herself.

Positivism brought with it the so called "triple loyalty" which implied the acceptance of the existing political authorities by the conservative elements of the Polish society. Positivism also in-sisted that nationality could be divorced from statehood, and that the Polish nation should accommodate itself to foreign rule and concentrate only on the cultural development of the Polish nationality, as the only thing that mattered.[78] In the eyes of the Polish National Alliance this loyalty was servility. One side of that loyalty was expressed in some sympathy toward Slavophil-ism.[79] Positivism created also a petty materialism with its cos-mopolitanism and complete indifference toward political inde-pendence.[80]

Henryk Sienkiewicz in his youth was a follower of Positivism. However, from the nineteenth century until World War I, he played a role in Poland that can only be compared to that of Mickiewicz in the Romantic Period. Sienkiewicz, passionately enamored of Poland's past, no longer searched for a mystic ex-planation of Poland's suffering. In his writings Sienkiewicz evoked the heroic Poland of the seventeenth century and the triumphant Poland of the fifteenth century instead of exalting the persecuted Poland of the nineteenth century. His Trilogy, showed how that Poland of the past, devasted with "fire and sword" (*Ogniemi*

---

[78] Czeslaw Poznanski, *The Rights of Nations*, (New York: 1945), p. 105.

[79] A movement which has as its objective the unification of all Slavic peoples. The Pan-Slavism of this period sought the preservation and development of a Slav civilization through the union of all Slav peoples in a strongly centralized autocratic and orthodox state, ruled by the Russian Czar as the head of the largest group of Slav peoples. The Poles opposed Pan-Slavism as it would have meant giving up their nationalism and their Catholicism. Excluded from Germany by Prussia, Austria felt obliged to become a constitutional state and to rely upon the Slav subjects for the support of its Empire. This made the Poles valuable to Austria. Not only were they one of the largest Slav groups, but they were also the only ones definitely opposed to Pan-Slavism, which was a real menace to the continued control by Austria of its subject peoples.

[80] In Austria, where after 1867, the cultural rights of the Poles were respected and where the Poles had provincial self-government, the Polish conservatives were the staunchest supporters of the Dual-Monarchy. And even in Russian and Prussian Poland, the conservative class, the great landowners and industrialists proclaimed the gospel of loyalty to the State, fondly hoping that as a reward for this loyalty, they might obtain a reversal of the policy of forcible Russification and Germanization.

*Mieczem*) had successfully emerged from the "deluge" (*Potop*), through the chivalry of Polish knights (*Pan Wolodyjowski*).

These novels galvanized Poland, they mobilized her spirit of resistance, they brought her faith and hope, they brought her an internal peace, they flattered her dreams of independence and gave her confidence in herself. The novels marked a turning point in Polish thought, which passed from resignation to an optimism full of faith in the destiny of the nation. In recalling the defeat inflicted at the beginning of the fifteenth century upon the Knights of the Cross, Sienkiewicz seemed to foresee the approaching war which was to bring defeat to Germany and freedom to Poland.[81]

It marked a turning point in Polish thought, which passed from resignation to an optimism full of faith in the destiny of the nation. In recalling the defeat inflicted at the beginning of the fifteenth century upon the Knights of the Cross, Sienkiewicz seemed to foresee the approaching war which was to bring defeat to Germany and freedom to Poland.[81]

Rather than to allow the Polish-American community to lose its identity in the American milieu, the PRCU leaders instinctively threw up protective barriers. They preferred the preservation of the cultural identity of the Polish-American community for their own ends, not for the benefit of Poland. Thus they discouraged and banned activities that could serve as vehicles for American encroachment. In the struggle for ethnical separateness, the leaders were also unconsciously inclined not to encourage the participation of Poles in American institutions. To defend the autonomy of the Polish Roman Catholic Church against interference, particularly from the Irish clergy, and to preserve the integrity of the Polish parishes from absorption by the Irish-dominated Catholic Church hierarchy in America were grad-

---

[81]Stanislaw Wyspianski recreated for his generation the whole heroic history of Poland from the legendary past of Krakow to Mickiewicz' Legion of 1848. In his plays he endeavored to shake the soul of the people out of lethargy into heroism, into the fulness of an inspired life of action and strength. Unflinchingly he accepted even the certainty of renewed ruin, death, and cruel sacrifice as the road to a new birth of national freedom to the new Polish state. His two greatest plays "The Wedding" (Wesele) and "Deliverance" (Wyzwolenie) proclaimed the need of a new armed rising. Jan Matejko glorified Polish history on large-scale magnificent canvasses.

ually added as objectives of the Polish Roman Catholic Union in America.[82]

The Polish-American clergy saw very well that in order to hold a strong position in its relation with the Irish-dominated Catholic Church of which they were formally a part, they would have to show a social power based upon the will of the immigrant masses. They would have to demonstrate that they had the backing of the Polish immigrant. The PRCU, nominally a lay institution, only unofficially controlled by priests, could easily be used to promote the interests of the Polish-American clergy not only vis-a-vis the American bishops but even in Rome.

The spread of the spirit of independence occasioned the first Polish Congress, which was held in Buffalo in 1896. A second was held in the same city in 1901, and a third, in Pittsburg, in 1904. These Congresses sought to find remedies for the sad conditions then prevailing in the American Polonia communities. The efforts of the promoters were largely confined to inducing the Holy See to give the American Poles bishops of their own nationality.[83]

Thus the Polish-American clergy, many of whom were recruited in the old country, wished their people to reman quiet and devoted, and limited to their own culture. Consequently, the clergy did not approve the national propaganda promulgated by

---

[82] During the long period of Poland's subjection, scarcely any institution had been left to unite the Polish people save their church and their language. In their depressed state they came to look upon the Roman Catholic Church in Poland as the Israelites did the Tabernacle in the wilderness. It was therefore a rude shock to Poles on coming to the United States to find that their church, which they had almost identified with Poland itself, was dominated by a hierarchy and people largely Irish in background, and with a "nationalism" fully as church centered as their own. Where Irish priests and bishops were in control of parishes whose membership was largely Polish, clashes were certain to occur. Since in Poland their clergy had been usually appointed through the influence of the landed gentry, they resented seeing these appointments and the control of the church property kept wholly out of Polish hands. Thus were occasioned three defections from the Roman Catholic Church between 1890 and 1900.

[83] A fourth Congress, differing radically from the three preceding, inasmuch as its spirit was purely secular, was convened under the auspices of the Polish National Alliance on the occasion of the unveiling of the Pulaski and Kosciuszko monuments in Washington, D. C., on May 12, 1910. The Congress, which was ignored by the clergy and the Catholic organizations, declared itself in favor of educational institutions for the American youth of Polish descent which would be utterly removed from "clerical" influence.

the nationalists gathered in the Polish National Alliance, and did not condone the participation of a Polish-American parishioner in American institutions and life.[84]

The Polish-American who wanted to become identified with one or the other was often caught in a dilemma. If he joined the PRCU, the members of the PNA would say he was not a true patriot; if he joined the PNA, the members of the PRCU would accuse him of being untrue to his religion.[85] Father Kruszka describes the bitter factionalism between these two groups:

> For some time neither Catholics nor Poles existed in America, but only Unionists (PRCU) or Alliancists (PNA); who was not a member of the Alliance, him the Polish National Alliance did not regard as a Pole; while whoever was not a member of the Polish Roman Catholic Union, the PRCU did not regard as a Catholic.[86]

Father Kruszka saw certain advantages in this strife.

> This fight between the PRCU and the PNA has been called "fratricide." But we must concede that this very fight brought about a rebirth. a feeling of unity, love of the fatherland, desire for education, need of the press, libraries, celebrations, . . . among the immigrant Poles in America. . . . There is nothing so bad but what it does not result in some good.[87]

During the early years of competition between the two organizations each was disposed to duplicate the other's works, to denounce the other's ways, and to claim total support for itself. These early years of competition, however, left no visible scars. Most of the ephemeral writings reflected heat rather than light, but they accustomed the Polish immigrants to read and write on controversial issues. In few other Polish organizations has the battle raged more fiercely. Since 1898, the differences between the two organizations have bcome more blurred. In fact, the following decades witnessed their cooperation in many of the American

---

[84] Energetically and steadily the PRCU has counteracted all attempts of Americanization from whatever source they came. When Bishop Eis of Marquette, Michigan, issued in 1901, an order to the effect that religion must be taught in English in all parochial schools; the Poles in particular protested. The PRCU was one of the first to raise its voice in protest. Wachtl, op. cit., pp. 29-30.

[85] To be absolutely secure, many joined both organizations.

[86] Kruszka, op. cit., IV, p. 32.

[87] Edmund G. Olszyk, The Polish Press in America, (Milwaukee: 1940), p. 10,

Polonia projects. Furthermore, patterns of mutual support were established between the two organizations, for the members of one organization feel obligated to attend a fund-raising card party or supper of the other, since their own organization has recently held a similar event. The exchange of services and money between the two organizations may have little real value: yet they are visible emblems of social solidarity, and the act of giving evokes latent feelings of unity and interdependence. This cohesiveness between the two organizations is further cemented by the interlocking memberships.

There are many individual Polonia organizations, but no organization; innumerable institutions, but not one that is recognized and can speak for all; freedom of opinion, expression, and action, but no democratic representation either in internal or external affairs, appropriate for the Polish community living in the United States. True in times of crisis the fragments coalesce and join to take a stand against the common enemy; but even this temporary coalition that springs up gourdlike overnight, holds together with great difficulty, for the lack of a regular, central, over-all coordinating organization. Once the crisis passes, each of the organizations returns to its jealously guarded independence, and "normalcy" sets in: a state of over-organized anarchy for all organizations big and small.

During these decades of organizations Polish women also formed national societies. Patriotism was not a monopoly of the men. Around 1890, efforts were made to organize the Polish women on a countrywide scale, not through local religious circles but through one large organization comparable in strength and numbers to a Polish male society. The first such attempt was the "Grosz Polski," a society of women organized to buy land in German Poland for distribution among Polish families resident in those regions. The history of "Grosz Polski" was unusually brief. It lasted barely six months, and during its brief life it failed to raise enough money to obtain for its Chicago headquarters the necessary office supplies.

On May 22nd, 1898, several progressive Polish women in Chicago met in the residence of Stefania Chmielinska to form a woman's society for the promotion of patriotism and welfare among their own and to help the oppressed in partitioned Poland. They adopted the name "Polish Women's Alliance in America" (Zwiazek Polek w Ameryce) for their society; Stefania Chmielinska became the first president. This small group laid the foundation for one of the largest Polish women's associations not only in the United States but in the world. Membership in the organization today totals over 91,000, with assets of more than twenty million dollars.

Since its inception, the Polish Women's Alliance of America has actively participated in local and national affairs, and simultaneously maintained a program of mutual aid and assistance. War relief work, assistance to displaced persons and refugees, and orphanages have been the major concerns of the organization. The organization currently sends regular shipments of clothing, equipment, and medication to hospitals, schools, orphanages and other worthy institutions in Poland.[88] In America the members maintain a home for the aged and a private summer colony for children. The organization also supports recreational programs for young people and has sponsored three successful youth conferences during the past five years. Classes in dancing, singing, literature, as well as lectures and dramatics, foster Polish ideals and promote Polish culture among its members, enriching their lives and those about them.

A semi-monthly publication, *Glos Polek,* keeps the membership informed on organizational activities, current events and subjects of cultural, civic, and social value. Over 10,000 volumes of poetry, non-fiction and fiction, both in English and Polish, are available to the members from the lending library, which the organization maintains in its home office building in Chicago. Also located on the fourth floor of the building is the museum, where cherished mementos of its founders, historical documents, trophies, banners, works of art and handicraft and citations pre-

---

[88] In acknowledgement and gratitude for the substantial contribution made to its department of biology, the Catholic University of Lublin, Poland, has named its newly constructed lecture hall "The Polish Women's Alliance of America Hall." The organization also contributed to the "Rappersville Fund," with headquarters in Switzerland; provided scholarships for Americans of Polish descent at American Universities and colleges; prepared readings on current events and literary subjects; and raised funds for the Kosciuszko monument in Humbolt Park in Chicago.

sented to the Polish Women's Alliance of America are preserved.

The Polish Women's Alliance of America is an active member of the national fraternal congress and its national president Adela Lagodzinska has the distinction of being the first woman elected to the investment council of that Congress.

During this period two other organizations made their appearance: the "Polish Alma Mater of America" and the "Polish Falcons of America" (Sokols).The "Polish Alma Mater of America" was organized by Father Francis Gordon, C.R., who was concerned with the lack of adequate guidance and protection for youth under eighteen years of age. The organization was incorporated on May 4, 1910.[89] The Falcon gymnastic organization, founded in Poland, had also transplanted to America, and in the early days of Polish immigration was an important organization. It had two purposes: (1) the improvement of mental and physical health; and (2) the establishment of a free Poland. General Thaddeus Kosciuszko and Abraham Lincoln were selected as patrons of the organization. Interest in the independence of Poland attracted more members.[90] Furthermore, it was an important agency in the social life of the emigration.[91]

At the close of the Balkan wars in 1912, the Falcons stressed

---

[89] A fraternal life insurance society, welcoming to its ranks American citizens of Polish descent and professing the Roman Catholic Faith, not only for the purpose of writing life insurance but also to associate themselves together under the guidance of the Blessed Virgin Mary, Queen of Poland, for the following purposes: to transmit to America the cultural advantages of Ancient Poland; to keep the mother tongue of our mother country alive for the more rapid transmission of the good from the old to the new; to indoctrinate the Poles in the United States with the spirit of America; to teach thrift and self-support through fraternalism; to foster the tenets of the Roman Catholic Church; to encourage civic pride and patriotism, so as to build a better United States of America. Casimir J. B. Wronski, "The Polish Alma Mater of America," Poles of Chicago, Leon Zglenicki, Editor. (Chicago: 1937), p. 161.

[90] From 1911 to 1917, the Falcon Order in America broadened its program to include military training by establishing three military schools for officers, non-commissioned officers and first class soldiers. When President Wilson issued a call for volunteers in 1917, over seven thousand well trained Falcons responded. In the fall of the same year, over five thousand Falcons, not subject to American draft, joined the Polish military force.

[91] When Poland won her independence, the immigrant group began to decrease, and the second and third generation members speak English and participate in American activities, so that now the association is on the wane among the Americans of Polish descent. In certain communities of Michigan, Illinois, Pennsylvania, however, the Falcon Order survives, drawing its membership largely from third generation Americans of Polish descent.

strict military training and de-emphasized gymnastic drills. Thus as a military organization it provided basic training to the cadre from which later emerged the famous Polish Legion of World War I. These future Polish Lancers, who trained chiefly to be of service to Poland, were by no means devoid of American patriotism. Their patriotism was as much American as Polish, though at times it is difficult to distinguish between pure patriotism and a simple desire for excitement. When President Wilson and President Huerta of Mexico were exchanging threats in the spring of 1914, the Poles of Cleveland offered to place in the field 1,000 trained Falcons who, according to their leaders, possessed the same training as the United States National Guard. The Falcons were expert marksmen, all having qualified in arms during their regular Sunday target practices. They also had uniforms and weapons, and were willing to leave their jobs and their families at a moment's notice to fight for the American cause.[92]

The members of the Polish clergy were especially aroused to see poor Polish immigrant girls exploited economically and drifting away from their religion; in a few cases even becoming inmates of houses of prostitution. To rectify the situation, they decided to form a voluntary organization of Polish priests, which would gather funds to establish a home for the newly arrived Polish immigrant girls. As a result, all Polish priests residing in the United States were invited to attend a meeting in New York City in April, 1890. At this meeting a society was formed and named "Alliance of Polish Priests in America" (Zwiazek Polskich Ksiezy w Ameryce). The members elected a president, a general secretary, and a provincial secretary. The United States was divided into provinces which coincided with the Catholic archdioceses throughout the country. The provincial secretary was made responsible for collecting the contributions of the priests under his jurisdiction. The members of the association agreed to donate a minimum of two dollars, which the provincial secretary collected and forwarded to the general secretary of the association in New York City.

When the necessary funds were raised, the association rented

_____

[92] Pliska, op. cit., pp. 54-55.

a building and named it "St. Joseph's Charity Organization, Society for Polish Immigrants of New York." On February 19th, 1891, the Society was incorporated under the title of "St. Joseph's Home for Polish Immigrants." Rev. Jacob Wojcik, Rev. John Patrzycki, Rev. Matthew Barabasz, Rev. John Gulcz and Rev. Hieronom Klimecki were the incorporators of the home.[93] According to Murawski, the following were the objectives of the St. Joseph Home: (1) establishment of a Home in New York, to which all Polish immigrants, arriving at this country, may come; (2) giving adequate information regarding settlement and job opportunities to those who request it; (3) helping the aforementioned immigrants in every possible way to become good American citizens.

The first home, rented in Brooklyn, was followed by successive rentals of homes in New York City, first on Rector Street, then on Morris Street, and next at Greenwich Street; finally a home was purchased at 117 Broad Street in 1897. This was a five-story brick structure on a plot of one hundred by twenty-five feet. It contained twenty rooms and could accommodate sixty immigrants at one time. This site was at a good location since it was only a few blocks away from Battery Park, where the immigrants landed as they were released from Ellis Island. Consequently they had only a short distance to walk in order to reach the home, which was managed by the Sisters of the Felician Order under the supervision of the Association of the Polish clergy.

Frequently many of the immigrants were detained at Ellis Island by the authorities because of insufficient funds, incorrect addresses of relatives and friends, or in the case of a child unaccompanied by a parent or guardian. In such instances the St. Joseph representatives were of the utmost service in preventing deportation of new arrivals. If a person arrived in America without sufficient funds, he was usually taken to St. Joseph's, where he received lodging, food, and a ticket for his ultimate destination.

St. Joseph's Home also cooperated with other immigrant ethnic societies in America. Occasionally it provided care for Irish

---

[93] Ladislaus Francis Murawski, *The History and Development of St. Joseph's Home for Polish Immigrants of 425 West Forty-Fourth Street, New York,* (unpublished project, Fordham University, 1941), p. 13.

and German immigrants, when their own ethnic societies were unable to provide needed accommodations and other services. At the same time, St. Joseph's Home received aid from the German and Irish ethnic organizations when its home was filled to capacity. "Travellers Aid" also cooperated with St. Joseph Home by referring Polish immigrants to the home and giving aid to immigrants recommended by the staff of St. Joseph's.

In the St. Joseph's Home, the staff also acted as counsellors. They cautioned the immigrants not to trust strangers, including those who spoke Polish unless definite proof was furnished that the individual deserved credence. They made an effort to ascertain the immigrants' capabilities and preferences, in order to advise them where to settle if they had no definite destination. They conducted follow-up studies to confirm that the immigrants had reached their destinations. They exchanged foreign currency for American currency, accepted funds for safekeeping, and stored or transported belongings and baggage of immigrants. Not only did they hold correspondence of immigrants who had not yet arrived, but they answered inquiries about relatives and friends in transit. Securing employment for immigrants who had no friends and who desired to remain in New York was a very important service of the Home. Many unmarried Polish immigrant girls found themselves in this category. They were invited to stay at St. Joseph's home while the representatives made contacts to secure for them domestic positions. If a girl was placed in a domestic position, the family employing her was visited, the working contract scrutinized, and the environment considered to establish that it was desirable. Various employers also were contacted to secure employment for the male immigrants.

Since St. Joseph's Home was philanthropic, its main concern was to provide service to economically solvent immigrants and free lodging, meals, and aid to needy immigrants. Although some immigrants were able to make small donations, the income from this source was negligible. The bulk of the funds for the administration were secured from the Association of the Polish clergy, whose members pledged to contribute at least five dollars annually for its maintenance: from annual collections in many Polish parishes; and from contributions and bequests from generous

benefactors and immigrants who had once received aid and services. The Felician Sisters, to whom the management was intrusted,
received no salaries for their services: thus a considerable saving
was effected by this means.

St. Joseph's Home was well known throughout the Polish
settlements in the United States. Since the majority of the Polish
clergy were members of the Association, they frequently spoke
in their sermons to their parishioners of its services and its objectives. Representatives of St. Joseph's Home also addressed
various Polish organizations and acquainted the Polish communities with the services rendered. The number of immigrants admitted to the St. Joseph's Home fluctuated widely from month
to month. In 1907, during the month of November, over 2,000
immigrants were helped. And during the entire year some 20,000
immigrants received service.[94]

Eventually the Felician Sisters petitioned to be relieved of the
responsibility of managing St. Joseph's Home. They were succeeded by the Sisters of the Immaculate Conception, an order
founded by Rt. Rev. Msgr. Lucian Bojnowski of New Britain,
Connecticut. In 1911, when William Williams was Commissioner
of Immigration, several regulations were passed concerning the
immigrants and agencies interested in their welfare. As a result
of the new regulations, the functions of St. Joseph Home were
curtailed. With the decline of immigration from Poland, there was
a gradual change in the objectives of St. Joseph's Home and
eventually it became an establishment for unmarried girls.

---

[94] Murawski, *op. cit.*, p. 22.

# CHAPTER SEVEN

# Activities of the Polish National Alliance

Human beings do not change climates easily, whether they be physical or cultural. The change from rural life to urban life, from agricultural surroundings to industrial regimentation, from a familiar cultural climate and code of ethics and behavior to another which is completely unknown, place incalculable physical and mental strains upon the human capacity for adaptation. Immigrants who undergo these experiences need assistance from organizations or individuals who understand well at just what point the quantity and the quality of the unknowns become most unbearable, and at what points the human spirit may receive its deepest hurts from unaware dominant groups. Such an inter-preter between one world and another was the Polish National Alliance.

The Polish National Alliance (PNA), with a membership of 340,000 in thirty-two States of the United States, is not strict-ly a fraternal beneficiary organization. Its formation, activities, and accomplishments identify it as a service organization. Besides maintaining a vast insurance program for its members, the PNA is at the forefront of all fraternal organizations in the United States in its widespread activities in the benevolent, educational recreational, social and cultural fields.[1] On examination of the PNA activities it becomes evident that the ultimate aims of the organization were prestige, security, solidarity and prosperity for the Polish American community. Self-reliance, according to Henry Kalussowski, was also an important objective.

Alien friendship can only aid us; unity shall make us independ-

[1] "National Fraternal Congress of America Proclaims 'Fraternal Week' June 9-16," *Zgoda*, (June 1, 1957), p. 12.

191

ent and therefore suffices for everything. Let us not reject friendship let us value it, but let us rely only upon ourselves.[2]

From the inception of the organization, the PNA leaders realized that only as American citizens will the Polish immigrants be able to contribute to their own social, economic, and political well-being in the United States. Thus the PNA encouraged its members to acquire citizenship as early as October 25, 1883.[3] One of the aims of the 1880 Constitution was political orientation of the Polish immigrants in the United States.[4] The PNA convention, held in Detroit, in 1891, had passed a resolution which stated that members of the PNA should encourage all Poles to become naturalized citizens of the United States, since "the constitution of the United States in no way interferes with their efforts in behalf of Poland or their love for the fatherland."[5] Many other conventions had echoed the same idea.[6]

However, many factors hindered this naturalization process. The greatest single difficulty that the Polish immigrants encountered was the language barrier. After their arrival in the United States, the Polish immigrants had discovered that all relations of life, including the most practical, were expressed in a strange tongue. Frequently, they failed to grasp the baffling syntax of English and were perplexed by the subtle facility of the Americans in conversation. With all the poignant force of a new experience, they realized that they were isolated in a strange world. To add to their inferiority complex, they possessed, as a rule, names unpronounceable to the Anglo-Saxon tongue, names to

---

[2] "Polish Organizations of Chicago," *Poles of Chicago*, Leon Zglenicki, Editor, (Chicago: 1937), p. 149.

[3] Stanislaw Osada, *Historja Zwiazku Narodowego Polskiego*, (Chicago: 1905), p. 15.

[4] *Ibid.*, p. 151.

[5] Piotr P. Yolles, "Historja Polonji w Zwierciadle Zwiazku Narodowego," *Nowy Swiat*, (September 24, 1951), p. 3. Osada, *op. cit.*, p. 334.

[6] In connection with the naturalization procedure, the PNA convention gathered in 1897, reminded the Poles never to give their nationality as Germans, Russians, or Austrians, but simply Poles. For by doing so, they unwittingly approve the dismemberment of Poland. No doubt, one of the reasons for urging the Poles to become citizens of the United States was the thought of exercising greater influence on public and political life in America and adding weight to their demands and protests in behalf of Poland. They would have to be reckoned with as citizens of the United States and not as aliens without political rights, thus, in the case of the Polish Americans, hyphenism seemed to work in favor of their Americanization.

which they clung tenaciously, because they loved their nationality, and because these names meant so much to them;[7] this was done even if it worked to a disadvantage in business and politics.[8]

During these years, the melting-pot theory gave comfort to Americans who feared the enormous infiltration of people from eastern and southern Europe. It gave assurance that time, the ability to find employment, and the beneficent forces of America would slowly bring about the adoption of standardized American conduct and conversion to American ways, within and without.

> If he gets on, if he is able to realize here in America some of the fundamental wishes that were denied him in his mother country, he will eventually become an American in every sense that we desire to give to that title.[9]

Thus, no large investments were made for education or for social aid. The few haphazard attempts made to assimilate the immigrant groups were based on the following assumptions:

> We could crystallize millions of aliens of all nations, habits, and languages, flocking to us from every quarter of the globe into a new homogeneous race, better and finer than the world had ever known.[10]

Franklin Lane presented a good summary of this Americanization theory.[11]

---

[7] A Detroit attorney, Stanley L. Hoyle, who legally changed his name ten years ago, died before he could realize his wish to have it changed back. His petition to have his original name, Stanley A. Hojnacki, restored to him was dismissed by Probate Judge James H. Sexton after the judge was notified that Hoyle died. In his request to the court, the lawyer said his decision a decade ago to take the name of Hoyle had "weighed on his peace of mind." "Death Prevents Name Restoration," *Detroit News,* (March 6, 1956), p. 27. The University of Toledo, in Toledo, Ohio, recently accepted a bequest to the university of $9,000 from the estate of Irene J. Paryski, the late publisher and editor of the Polish weekly, *Ameryka-Echo,* Toledo, Ohio. Stipulation on the use of the bequest are that it be used to assist American students of Polish descent, who have not changed their Polish surnames and who speak the Polish language. *Polish American Journal,* (December 6, 1958), p. 2.

[8] Bishop Stephen S. Woznicki, "Poles' Presence in the United States Traced to Early Days in Our Nation," *Dziennik Polski,* (September 24, 1958), p. 2.

[9] William Carlson Smith, *Americans in the Making.* (New York: 1939), p. 168.

[10] Robert Ezra Park and Herbert A. Miller, *Old World Traits Transplanted,* (New York: 1921), p. 114.

[11] Everett Hale in 1852 advised that the Irishmen must be surrounded by Americans. He believed the proper ratio would be eight Irish for every hundred native-born. This would speed Americanization. Carl Wittke, *The Irish in America,* (Baton Rouge: 1956), p. 115.

One part Declaration of Independence; one part the Constitution; one part love for apple pie; one part desire and willingness to wear American shoes and another part pride in American plumbing will make an American out of anyone.[12]

Immigrants criticized the naive assumption that American clothes, practices, and customs were superior to all others, and this American spirit of condescension and coercion aroused a feeling of resentment.

What is really meant by assimilation is only the acceptance and imitation of Anglo-American civilization, of Anglo-Saxon modes of life, of Anglo-Saxon business methods, of Anglo-Saxon dress and the Anglo-Saxon language. People are considered assimilated or assimilable to that degree with which they are capable of imitating the existing order of things. Such appraisal of assimilatory abilities is false. Only those people assimilate rapidly whose own culture is not very steep, whose culture is not very valuable. It is comparatively easy for an uncultured individual or group of individuals, whose range of emotion is expressed in their own language in three or four hundred words, to learn these three or four hundred words in any language for the purpose of daily transactions and expression of emotions. But it is difficult for a spiritually higher-minded individual or group of individuals, whose culture is far deeper, needing thousands of words to express more vivid emotions, to learn these thousands of words in another language. The emotionally and culturally low individual does not leave as much behind him, over which to ruminate and think as the emotionally highly developed individual who is continually wondering whether the new is worth as much as what he has left behind him. The baser metals melt first. They melt at straw-heat.[13]

The PNA was one of the first Polish-American organizations to realize that the Polish immigrants were handicapped in their participation in the political, economic, and cultural life of America by their lack of citizenship and of knowledge of the English language and laws and customs of the United States.[14] To raise

---

[12] Smith, *op. cit.*, p. 116.

[13] Konrad Bercovici, *On New Shores*, (New York: 1925), p. 16.

[14] The acculturation of the immigrant, his adaptation to American customs, ways and thought, depend to a marked degree upon his ability to read and speak the English language. Nearly every disadvantage which the Polish immigrant encountered

the intellectual and cultural level of their countrymen, the PNA laid specific emphasis on the American "night school" as the one organization through which contact and participation in American life could be made. PNA members and non-members were encouraged continually through the PNA press and direct verbal appeals of the officials to take advantage of the American privilege of free education.[15]

The response to the appeals of the PNA was magical. Thousands of Polish immigrants flocked to American "night school" in keen anticipation of learning the English language. After a few weeks, they became discouraged and eventually dropped out. These evening schools did not meet their needs. The immigrants were interested only so long as they could use each day what they had learned the night before. Stories about beautiful posies and pretty birds did not stimulate or retain their interest.[16]

> Some Americans think that we immigrants can comprehend only such things as "I see a cat; the cat is black"—as the teachers in the evening schools make grown men repeat. But the minds of most immigrants are not quite so feeble as that. For the poor man, America is all work—work—work. We believe in work all right, but we want thought and education to go along with it.[17]

As a result, evening school attendance in many schools showed a continual decrease.[18]

To overcome this difficulty of the American evening school, the PNA organized in its local lodges, throughout the United States, Americanization and naturalization classes to convey

---

in this country can be traced in the last analysis to his ignorance of the English language.

[15] They also persuaded employers that it would be greatly to their advantage to have the Polish workers learn the English language. There would be fewer accidents if workmen could understand foremen's orders, and quite possibly a greater willingness to remain on the job if they were learning English along with it and could speak with fellow workers of other nationalities.

[16] Another weakness of the American adult evening school was the tendency to place too much attention on the externals of naturalization such as reading English and knowing the Constitution. Another weakness was the acceptance of an underlying false assumption that American culture is already a complete thing and easy to assimilate. There was also a tendency to use coercion and force.

[17] John Daniels, America Via the Neighborhood, (New York: 1920), p. 138.

[18] Herbert Adolphus Miller, The School and the Immigrant, (Philadelphia: 1916), p. 99.

civic information in the Polish language. Thus hundreds of thousands of Polish immigrants travelled on their way to citizenship
over the strong bridge constructed by the PNA which utilized the
Polish language as the indispensable means of communication until
the immigrants mastered the rudiments of English.

After World War I, PNA naturalization and Americanization classes were especially popular. When women were granted
suffrage, the PNA women's division expanded its activities to
include naturalization and Americanization classes.[19] Buffalo had
eight citizens' clubs, one with a membership of 2,000 citizens
in 1923.[20] The PNA spent more than $20,000 a year on the
naturalization activities of the Poles.[21] The naturalization classes
remained the main function of the local lodges for many years.[22]

Besides providing trained instructors, the PNA prepared a
booklet containing fifty questions and answers dealing with American citizenship.[23] The booklet also contained information about
the legislative, judicial and executive branches of the national and
state governments in the United States. Municipal government
was also considered. Questions in the handbook were in English
and Polish. Every annual PNA almanac had reprinted these
questions and answers.[24]

Since 1899, the PNA had printed at its own expense the
Constitution of the United States both in English and Polish.
Copies were distributed periodically to all the PNA lodges for the
benefit of the members. To acquaint Americans with the significance of the Polish national holidays, the PNA had printed thou-

---

[19] Karol Piatkiewicz, *Pamietnik Jubileuszowy ZNP, 1880-1940,* (Chicago:
1940), p. 120.

[20] These clubs are an important media in the political education and Americanization of immigrants. They prepare the members for citizenship and at the same
time instill in them veneration and affection for the laws and institutions of America.
"Poles Promote Citizenship," *The Interpreter,* II (June, 1923), pp. 12-13.

[21] "When the Immigrant Goes to School. A Study of Adult Education Among
the Poles in America." *The Interpreter,* V (December, 1926), p. 11.

[22] They still exist in many communities. In 1950, many of 3,793 Poles who
became citizens, utilized these classes to prepare themselves for naturalization. "3,793
Poles become U.S. Citizens in 1950," *Polish American Journal,* (October 10, 1951),
p. 4.

[23] The naturalization booklet may be obtained from the PNA for thirty-five
cents.

[24] Karol Piatkiewicz, *Illustrowany Kalendarz Zwiazkowy Rok* 1949, (Chicago:
1949), pp. 24-27.

sands of copies of the "Outline and Significance of the Third of May" and had mailed them to United States Congressmen, university libraries and public libraries.

The PNA also published annual calendars, which were as vital to the Polish immigrants of the nineteenth century as the early American almanacs had been to the pioneer Americans. The calendars were a source of intellectual stimulus to the immigrants. Read and reread, enjoyed for the jokes and humor and the engraved embellishments as well as the information their pages contained, the calendars were frequently saved for many years and provided a wide variety of reading material. Probably few immigrants had questioned the accuracy of the almost encyclopedic information found in the calendars. Yet if these popular pamphlets did not do much to foster a critical attitude toward what was contained in their pages, the best calendars had introduced to many for the first time, the writings of Sienkiewicz, Slowacki, Mickiewicz and others.

From the calendars the immigrants also received practical advice on immigration rights and citizenship, household arts and lore, bankruptcy procedures, political information, and the more pertinent laws of the United States. In the calendars there was much sprightly and homely wisdom; and from these proverbial expressions it is possible to guess at the social attitudes and general values that the immigrants held, or that the editors of these pamphlets desired them to hold. Filled with the most varied conglomeration of advertisements, these calendars sold anywhere from twenty-five cents to one dollar.

The PNA was concerned also with the national interests of the Polish immigrants. It was instrumental in sponsoring the movement for the construction of the Kosciuszko and Pulaski monuments in Washington, D. C.[25] Monuments to Polish and

---

[25] The history of these two erections and dedications can be traced to the early days of the Republic. A few years after the death of General Casimir Pulaski, the United States Congress passed a motion for the erection of a monument to Pulaski. This was forgotten. The Polish immigrants recalled it at the beginning of the twentieth century. In 1902, Congress, due mostly to the appeal of Representative A. Brick from South Bend, Indiana, assigned $50,000 and appointed a committee for that purpose. In reply to this appropriation, the PNA erected, for $76,836.86, the Kosciuszko monument and dedicated it to the United States. The act of presentation

non-Polish heroes were also erected in other large American cities through the efforts of the PNA.[26]

In 1893, the PNA was active in the restoration and preservation of the Liberty Bell. As a result of this activity, the Liberty Bell was sounded in memory of many historical anniversaries of the Polish nation. There is no doubt that the PNA helped preserve the Polish heritage and stimulate a consciousness of Polish nationalism.[27] Nevertheless, the PNA provided an environment in which Polish immigrants learned of democracy and the democratic way of life.

The PNA was always concerned with the immigration problem, and it was convinced that restriction of immigration was not the proper solution. Rather, it believed that the industrious though impecunious immigrants could help develop the natural wealth and resources of the United States, if only measures were taken to direct them into the unexploited agricultural areas of the country. At a special PNA Convention held at Chicago on February 24, 1884, the question of financial aid to the immigrants to

of the Kosciuszko Monument stated that the monument is "an expression of our loyalty and devotion to our adopted country, for the liberty of which Thaddeus Kosciuszko, nobly and gallantly fought, and for the welfare and safety of which we, the Poles in America, are at any time ready to shed our blood, as those two illustrious Poles and our predecessors, Kosciuszko and Pulaski did." Romuald Piatkowski, *Pamietnik Kongresu Polskiego w Waszyngtonie,* (Chicago: 1911), pp. 45-70.

[26] A monument to Woodrow Wilson was erected at Alliance College. Kosciuszko monuments were also erected in Milwaukee and Cudahy, Wisconsin. Recently, members of the PNA in Detroit, Michigan, contributed $1,094 for the Pulaski monument to be erected in Detroit. *Nowy Swiat,* (January 16, 1960), p. 8.

[27] The speeches and addresses during the many Polish American national celebrations; the many appeals and protest to the world against the injustice perpetrated on Poland; and the many resolutions to that effect enacted by the national PNA Conventions, did not produce the desired results with these for whom they were intended. The Poles in America during this period were not considered as a group wielding influence or political power. Nevertheless, these appeals, resolutions and protests served their limited purpose. They were highly educational in acquainting the Poles not only with their glorious past, but also with their present national tragedy. They stirred the Polish national spirit and knitted firmly the Polish ranks.

Action generally followed or accompanied the appeals, resolutions, and demands. And here immediately comes to the fore, very plainly the cleavage, the different course followed by the organizations holding sway over the Polish immigrants in the United States: the nationalistic PNA and the conservative clergy dominated PRCU.

The PNA was the more ideal, extreme, daring and nationalistic. The PRCU together with the Catholic clergy was often criticized for being too conservative, more realistic and less patriotic.

enable them to establish thriving farm settlements was discussed. The PNA Convention, held in 1887, concerned itself with Polish immigration and formed the "Colonization Commission." The "Trade and Commerce Commission," for the procurement of data and information affecting those branches of industry which con- cerned Polish immigrants, was also established; it was similar in many respects to the present American Chamber of Commerce.

In 1902, the PNA protested to the United States Senators from Pennsylvania against the ungenerous and often inhuman treatment of immigrants at the Ellis Island center of immigration in New York Harbor. The PNA also took part in 1906 with other groups in the agitation for an improved immigration depot for the port of Philadelphia, a move that bore fruit in 1912 when the modern immigration station was opened at Gloucester, New Jer- sey. As a strictly social service, the PNA had established and maintained reception homes for immigrants in New York, Boston and Baltimore in 1910. These immigration homes provided tem- porary shelter for the immigrant at a minimum cost; furnished information on American conditions; and protected the new ar- rivals from unscrupulous exploiters. At these homes, earlier immi- grants also assisted the recent  arrivals by lectures and informal talks to prevent mistakes and failures which could bring the Polish community into disrepute.

In 1910, the PNA purchased the immigration reception house in New York City for $33,000.[28] After its purchase, the four-story building was remodeled at considerable expense for its new function. This immigration house was established not for profit but for service. Polish and English speaking workers, who were paid $75.00 a month, were attached to the house. These workers visited Ellis Island where they served as interpreters, protecting the Polish immigrants from misinterpretation of the law and from the abuse of discretionary powers vested in the Board of Special Inquiry. Polish immigrants were taken in charge by the PNA workers until they had been safely settled with relatives and friends; where friends or relatives could not be located, the PNA

---

[28] This immigration house was located at 180 Second Avenue in New York City. The house was maintained by the PNA from 1911 until 1951 when it was sold to three PNA councils in the New York area.

workers inserted advertisements in the Polish dailies in an effort to find them. In addition, the PNA conducted an employment agency in its immigrant house in New York City.[29] Without the help of the PNA workers, many of the Polish immigrants would have been deported to Europe.[30] The PNA continues to facilitate immigration into the United States to the present day.

As early as 1895, the PNA had initiated a "Wydzial Oswiaty" (Department of Education), whose early efforts were channeled into three fields of endeavor: (1) the initiating of circulating libraries,[31] (2) the engagement of Professors Siemieradzki and Kurcjusz of Poland to deliver a series of free lectures on Polish culture in all the PNA lodges and (3) the creation of education societies in various cities throughout the United States for the promotion of culture and education at the local level.

"Wydzial Oswiaty" promoted intellectual and cultural activities in Polonia as widely as possible. During the first two years of its existence, it appropriated $725 for scholarships.[32] During the following years, between $12,000 to $21,000 was loaned annually, without interest, to deserving students who were not required to repay the loan until ten years later, when after the completion of their education they were gainfully employed.

---

[29] From two to five thousand immigrants per day passed through immigration inspection. History has never recorded and doubtless never will record the very great service to thousands of bewildered persons, which was rendered by those faithful and devoted PNA workers. In the years to come the problem was less acute, for by then the majority of Polish immigrants were on the way to join relatives and were assisted by them.

[30] Joseph Mierzynski, *Polacy w New York.* (No imprint, 1910).

[31] As a result of the efforts of the Department of Education, circulating libraries were established in the following cities: Perth Amboy, New Jersey; New Haven, Connecticut; Ashland, Wisconsin; Dunkirk, New York; Grand Rapids, Michigan; McKeesport, Pennsylvania; Toledo, Ohio; Newark, New Jersey; and Durea, Pennsylvania. Today, the number of these circulating libraries exceeds two hundred scattered among the respective societies in the United States.

The efforts of the department were limited by the extent of the means which the young organization could divert for educational purposes. Certain efforts received a stimulus through donations of philanthropic individuals, while others had to keep pace with the growth of the organization. Among the philanthropic donations deserving mention in this connection is that of Dr. Henry Kalussowski of Washington, D. C., who gave his private library, valued in excess of $70,000, together with his collection of documents. They were given with the understanding that the PNA would maintain and enlarge the collection. The offer was accepted by the delegates of the ninth PNA Convention held in Detroit, in 1891. This donation formed the cornerstone of the present PNA library.

[32] Osada, *op. cit.,* pp. 437-468.

In communities where no parochial schools existed, or where a sizeable number of Polish-American children attended the public school, the "Wydzial Oswiaty" organized supplementary schools to teach Polish to the children of PNA members. The well-trained instructors often varied the two hours of language study with folk songs and stories. Children willingly forfeited part of their weekend vacations to learn the language of their parents. Mary Sakowska, a prominent PNA leader and welfare worker, was the sponsor of this movement. In the year 1908, six schools were organized at Kosciuszko Park, Davis Square, Eckhardt Park, Sherman, Mark White and Russell Community Centers in Chicago.[33] Over 1000 students were enrolled annually in these schools.[34] There were 195 supplementary schools conducted by the PNA, with 14,000 children benefiting annually from these instructions by 1940. With the introduction of modern languages into the high school curriculum, the "Wydzial Oswiaty" urged members to use their influence to incorporate the teaching of Polish on the same basis as French, Spanish and German in the regular school and college curriculums.

The PNA "Wydzial Oswiaty," assisted by the other American Polish organizations, also had been instrumental in introducing Polish language, literature, and history courses in American colleges and universities. If Sluszka's facts are reliable, in 1953 48 colleges and universities, and 32 public high schools were teaching Polish; in addition, there were 63 Polish parochial elementary grammar schools where Polish language courses were always part of the regular curriculum.[35]

The lack of adequate Polish language textbooks was a serious problem for the Polish supplementary schools. The available Polish language textbooks were aimed at a level intended for use in Poland. The PNA "Wydzial Oswiaty" prepared and published special textbooks for the Polish language supplementary

---

[33] Janina Dunin and Jadwiga Krasowska-Stopowa were also pioneer teachers in this movement.

[34] A. M. Skibinska, "Polish Language Supplementary Schools," *Poles of Chicago*, Leon Zglenicki, Editor, (Chicago: 1937), p. 135.

[35] Sigismund J. Sluszka, "Polish Language Teaching in the USA," (Paper presented at Rutgers University, March 28, 1953).

schools. On the basis of these textbooks, high schools have been organizing Polish language courses.

To prepare adequately trained teachers for the Polish language supplementary schools, the PNA contributed generously to the University of Wisconsin, Northwestern University, De Paul University and others for the establishment of Polish language courses. In addition beginning in 1938, concentrated courses in the Polish language have been held intermittently at Alliance College for teachers, lawyers, doctors and other professional people. By January 1, 1940, the PNA "Wydzial Oswiaty," had expended $553,286.21 for scholarships, Americanization classes, and supplementary schools.[36]

During World War II, the PNA had taken an active part in helping the United States. As of September, 1944, the PNA United States War Bond purchases amounted to $14,500,000, and its contributions to the American Red Cross totalled $160,000.[37] The facilities of Alliance College were placed at the disposal of the U.S. Government, which utilized them as a army training school and rehabilitation center. The Welfare Association, under the guidance of Vice-President Frances Dymek, expanded its sphere of activity during World War II to render aid to hundreds of thousands of Polish refugees in all parts of the world. The appeals of the Red Cross had met with a prompt response in generous monetary and material donations in the form of woolen underclothing, sweaters and socks. Millions of bandages were made for the American armed forces by the PNA women. In addition, PNA women participated in the government's drive for waste paper, fats, and scrap metal; they prepared packages containing food and other delicacies for the American armed forces, and cooperated in the food saving campaign. In the American Defense Bond Drives they canvassed the American communities with good results.[38]

---

[36] Piatkiewicz, op. cit., p. 141.

[37] These figures do not include purchases of bonds and contributions for relief purposes made by the individual PNA members in their local lodges and councils. Miecislaus Haiman, "The Polish American Contribution to World War II," Polish American Studies, III (January-June, 1946), pp. 36-37.

[38] "Women Contributed Effectively to the development of the Polish National Alliance," Zgoda, (February 7, 1955), p. 6.

According to statistics released in Washington, D. C., in 1941, aproximately one million Americans of Polish descent served in the Armed Forces during World War II.[39] Of this number, 34,819 men and 938 women carried PNA membership cards. One of very few insurance organizations which did not insert a war clause in its certificates at the outbreak of hostilities was the PNA.[40] As a result, families of 1,017 PNA members who were killed in action received $621,776.70 in full death benefits.[41]

In addition to taking an active part in all national and local war activities, the PNA also supported the Polish cause; $1,621,785.41 was contributed for the "National Fund For Poland," the "Silesian Plebiscite," the "Ten Million Dollar Fund For Poland," and the "National Treasury at Rappersville." During World War II, the PNA and its members provided clothing and medical supplies for Polish war victims and helped substantially in the collection of $30,000,000 for the American War Relief for Poland which was directed by Francis Swietlik.[42] The PNA also supported financially the Catholic League for religious aid to Poland and the Polish-American Congress, the coordinator of all political activities in the United States.

The crowning PNA achievement was the establishment of Alliance College in Cambridge Springs, Pennsylvania. The idea of a PNA institution for higher learning was initiated at the PNA Convention in Wilkes Barre, Pennsylvania, in 1903, when members were assessed a penny a month for the creation of a school fund which would give Americans of Polish and non-Polish descent the opportunity to learn Polish history and literature, Polish traditions, and the Polish language.[43] Eventually, after much discussion of sites, the choice fell on Cambridge Springs, Pennsylvania, when Father Seweryn Niedbalski of Erie, Pennsylvania, brought to the attention of Censor Anthony Schreiber the fact

---

[39] "One Million Polish-Americans Served in World War II," *Polish American Journal*, (July 21, 1951), p. 2.

[40] "War Activities of PNA," *Fraternal World*, (September, 1947), pp. 9-11.

[41] Report of the Executive Board of Directors at PNA Convention, August 29, 1947, in Cleveland, Ohio.

[42] "$30,000,000 Wynosila Pomoc Rady Polonji Amerykanskiej Dla Uchodzcow Polskich,"*Dziennik Dla Wszytskich*, (November 24, 1951), p. 2.

[43] In 1905, this penny a month obligation was raised to two cents a month per person. In 1951, it was raised to four cents a month.

that the magnificent "Vanadium Hotel," with several hundred rooms, situated atop a hill overlooking Cambridge Springs, was available for the reasonable sum of $175,000. The colossal hotel was purchased on December 4, 1911.[44] The PNA president, Marian Steczynski, resigned from his office to direct personally the physical changes and renovations that were necessary to convert the hotel to an educational institution.[45] The first faculty included Professors Piwowarski, Dolewczynski, Fijalkowski, Janusz Ostrowski and others who were under the supervision of Romuald Piatkowski.

When the PNA entered the field of formal education on September 7, 1912, a chronicler had written:

> There is one thing extremely important for us, that the existing schools (in America) have not given, do not give and will not be able to give our youth, namely an understanding and an intelligent love of Poland's history, Polish traditions and all of Poland's rich culture, past and present.[46]

And Alliance College came into being to satisfy this perforce inadequacy.

Classes were first held on September 7, 1912; nineteen days later, on September 26, in the presence of President William Howard Taft, the school was formally dedicated.[47] The opening of the Polish-American Academy, where 326 students were enrolled, caused a great sensation in the United States and in partitioned Poland.

The work of the academy was augmented in 1915 by the foundation of a Technical Institute; that same year, the PNA Convention held in Schenectady, New York, approved the Act of Incorporation of the PNA College. Its published aims were to offer the best education at as little cost as possible to all who desired to achieve something in life; to acquaint the students with the history of the land of their forefathers; and to prepare the

---

[44] The purchase price included not only the hotel, but a campus of 160 acres of woodlands, pine forests, several ponds, and all of the hotel furnishings.

[45] K. Piatkiewicz, *Illustrowany Kalendarz na Rok* 1953, (Chicago: 1953), p. 41.

[46] *Dziennik Polski*, (April 7, 1957), p. 2.

[47] Dr. M. Dusza, "Historia Kolegium Zwiazkowego," *Pamietnik 75ta Rocznica Istnienia ZNP*, (Chicago: 1955), p. 71.

youth to be worthy members of their communities.[48]

During World War I, the school enrollment decreased rapidly. However, the establishment of a pre-officers' school increased its enrollment to 500 students. The young students were prepared for officer positions in the army, and with the departure of the Polish pre-officer groups for Europe two-hundred American soldiers arrived for training as technical experts in the Student Army Training Corps.

According to the letter sent to the Director of the school in 1921, the United States Army authorities had appreciated the efforts expended on training American recruits:

> This is to certify that the Polish National Alliance Academy in a spirit of patriotism and devotion to our country rendered efficient and loyal service in connection with the World War through the establishment and operation at that institution of a unit of the Student's Training Corps.
>
> The Adjutant General's Office
> J. W. Wainright
> The Assistant Secretary of War
> P. C. Harris
> The Adjutant General[49]

When 48 Polish orphans arrived in the United States from Siberia in 1921, the PNA Academy facilities were made available for their education and training. In 1924, the PNA Academy high school program and Trade School program was supplemented with a Junior College Curriculum. During the same year, the State Labor Department of Pennsylvania accepted PNA College as an accredited Junior College. In 1926, the Polish Ministry of Education conferred on the alumni of PNA College the privilege of admission, without examination, to the Jagiellonian University in Krakow and the University of Warsaw. A gymnasium was constructed for athletic activities and physical education in 1924. New chemical and biological laboratories were added and the library book collection was expanded in 1927.

On January 20, 1931, a sudden and uncontrollable fire destroyed the large main building containing laboratories, library

---

[48] Arthur Prudden Coleman, "Alliance College American Cradle of Polish Heritage," Zgoda, (August 15, 1957), p. 11.

[49] Dusza, op. cit., p. 73.

and classrooms.[50] Instead of being discouraged, the PNA administrators directed that plans be hastily drawn for a new fire-proof dormitory. In the meantime, temporary classrooms and living quarters were erected until the completion of the new dormitory. While the construction was in progress new electrical and radio-electrical courses were introduced; the college purchased new motors and perfected a system for operating them with alternating power. In 1931, Kosciuszko Hall, a fireproof, three-story dormitory, to accommodate 150 students, was completed.[51] It contained quarters for students, a library, a large recreation room, a billiard room, and a physician's and dentist's office.

Alliance Hall, containing lecture halls, laboratories, administrative and faculty offices, was started and completed in 1934. The hall, constructed of red brick in colonial style, with a high picturesque tower, is adorned with a clock and a colorful PNA seal. That same year, a spacious athletic field was completed. In 1942, Washington Hall was completed. It contains an auditorium, kitchen, library, music room, browsing room and a Polish room.[52] The building is constructed in colonial style with a beautiful facade of white stone. The lobby contains full-length portraits of George Washington and Woodrow Wilson.

When the PNA College became a co-educational institution, Bartlett Hotel, located in the downtown section of Cambridge Springs, was purchased in 1948. The same year, the two-year Junior College was succeeded by a four-year Senior College with the right to grant Bachelor of Arts and Bachelor of Science Degress. In 1952, Alliance College became accredited as a senior

---

[50] The extensive college library which on the eve of the fire contained more than 12,000 volumes and valuable historical documents, among which were some original letters written by George Washington, came to an untimely end. It was completely destroyed by the conflagration that reduced the large building to ashes.

[51] Dr. Stephen Mierzwa, currently associated with the Kosciuszko Foundation, was president of Alliance Junior College during the program of expansion. He was followed by E. Kuberski, the first alumnus of the college to assume directorship of the school.

[52] Over 23,000 well selected volumes, reinforced by a comprehensive reference collection, constitute the library's basic resources. Receipt of over one-hundred-and-fifty magazines and of leading American and Polish newspapers, contribute to the rapid growth of the periodical files. Professional librarians help to direct reading and research for the Alliance students. The Polish Room contains one of the largest special collections of Polish books in the United States. Among them are many rare books.

college by the Middle States Association of Colleges with the same privileges as other accredited colleges in the United States. Graduates from Alliance College became eligible for admission to the nation's leading medical, dental, engineering and law schools.

Tuition fees are $500 a year plus $500 for room and board. The fees do not meet the necessary expenditure for the education of each student.[53] Since the purpose in founding Alliance College was to offer a well-rounded education to children of PNA members at the lowest possible cost, PNA members, through a four-cent assessment per month, per member, add several hundred dollars annually for the education of each Alliance student.[54] By 1929, the PNA contribution to Alliance College amounted to $1,595,190.53.[55] The annual contributions since 1930 are as follows:

| | |
|---|---|
| 1930 | $119,985.78 |
| 1931 | 124,496.28 |
| 1932 | 124,337.04 |
| 1933 | 116,149.70 |
| 1934 | 116,995.60 |
| 1935 | 110,946.34 |
| 1936 | 133,449.21 |
| 1937 | 126,229.58 |
| 1938 | 129,032.77 |
| 1939 | 122,814.03 |
| 1940 | 82,240.37 |
| 1941 | 76,497.72 |
| 1942 | 76,143.68 |
| 1943 | 80,511.33 |

[53] Students who are members of the PNA for one full year, are allowed a reduction of $125 per semester on their bill if they take an approved course in Polish and pass it with a grade of C — or above. This reduction is also allowed to students whose parents or guardians are PNA members for three or more years; students however, must join the PNA before registration and take an approved course in Polish, passing it with a grade of C — or above. Students who meet the above membership requirements receive a further reduction of $75 per semester if they take a course in Polish literature or culture in the English language and pass it with a grade of C— or above. Schedule of Fees for the Academic Year 1957-1958. Office of the President, Alliance College, Cambridge Springs, Pennsylvania.

[54] Stephen Mierzwa, "Schools for Democracy," *The Kosciuszko Foundation Monthly News Letter*, VI (November, 1951), p. 2.

[55] *United States Congressional Record*, First Session, (July 27, 1955), pp. 353552-55349.

| | |
|---|---|
| 1944 | 81,486.93 |
| 1945 | 83.894.03 |
| 1946 | 85,588.14 |
| 1947 | 83,816.43 |
| 1948 | 135,208.75 |
| 1949 | 78,650.07 |
| 1950 | 80,515.73 |
| 1951 | 92,249.03 |
| 1952 | 123,079.46 |
| 1953 | 119,069.70 |
| 1954 | 119,161.12 |
| 1955 | 115,732.92 |
| 1956 | 164,026.69 |
| 1957 | 113,713.40 |
| 1958 | 108,363.24 |

The total from 1912 through June 30, 1958, was $4,719,615.75.[56]

Students who have maintained good scholastic records but who need financial assistance to undertake or continue their college program are eligible for financial assistance through a scholarship loan amounting up to $800. Approximately $55,000 worth of student-aid was authorized for the school year 1953-1954.[57]

Recently the PNA has been recognized with a *Who's Who in America* Citation for corporate educational philanthropy, which appeared in the Thirty-First Biennial Edition of *Who's Who in America* published in March, 1960. The Citation is as follows.

### POLISH NATIONAL ALLIANCE

The Polish National Alliance is a fraternal corporation doing business in 32 States and the District of Columbia. In the past three decades this corporation's gifts to Alliance College of Cambridge Springs, Pennsylvania, have averaged well over $100,000 per year. A total of nearly five million dollars has been given the school since contributions started in 1912.

When 363 Polish orphans, part of a group of Polish refugees evacuated from Russia in 1942, under an English-Russian agreement were sent to the Polish refugee camp in Santa Rosa Province, Mexico, the PNA brought 50 boys and 50 girls from this

---

[56] *United States Congressional Record*, (Proceedings and debates of the 86th Congress, First Session), pp. 498435-69547.

[57] A. P. Coleman, "Student Aid at Alliance College," Office of the President, (July 14, 1955)

group under student permits to the United States. The boys were sent to the PNA College in Cambridge Springs and the girls were placed in Catholic boarding schools in the Chicago area. During their eight year stay in the United States, under student permits, the PNA provided for their maintenance and education.[58]

With immigration curtailed after 1929, the PNA realized that it must depend on its youth to replace the old guard in the thinning ranks of adult members. Alliance College stimulated interest in a few hundred young people each year by offering them a splendid opportunity for a liberal arts education or a skilled trade in its technical institute, but the need for interest in the PNA was more far-reaching. It was necessary to initiate a program which would reach not hundreds, but thousands of Americans of Polish descent.

To attain this objective, the PNA, in 1931, initiated the "Harcerstwo" (Boy Scout Organization), a youth training program to foster Polish consciousness and loyalty to the PNA. Folk dancing groups, choral societies, and amateur dramatic circles were also established.[59] In the folk dancing groups, children had learned to share their parents' love for the dances of Poland.[60]

The PNA Youth Commission had supported the sports clubs and leagues by issuing complete sets of uniforms, (once every two years), for the following sports: baseball, softball, basketball and volleyball. It also presented handsome trophies to the champions and second-place teams in each PNA league. Tournament champions, second-place and third-place teams, also received trophies.

The youth program was a success from the very beginning.

---

[58] P. Kozlowski, "Refugees From Reds Cheer U.S.," *Promien,* (June, 1946), p. 26.

[59] Frank S. Barc, "The Polish National Alliance," *The Polish Review,* VI (April 11, 1946).

[60] For two hours each Monday evening some sixty-five children dance to the music of a lusty piano in the PNA hall in Hamtramck, Michigan. On Tuesday evenings there is a similar class for more advanced pupils including many teenagers. Their teacher, is Mrs. Anna Szczepkowska, who once taught dancing in a Warsaw Conservatory. The dances include the Polonaise, the Kujawiak, the Oberek, and most popular of all the polka. There are many other groups similar to this one throughout the Polish communities in the United States. "Tots Go For Polish Hop," *The Detroit News Sunday Pictorial,* (January 10, 1960), pp. 12-13.

American youth of Polish descent crowded to the PNA lodges for their weekly lessons in singing, dancing, first aid, Morse and sema-phore code, Polish literature and history. Each meeting was organ-ized and planned well in advance by the chairman of the Youth Department in the Chicago headquarters. Realizing the benefits that would come from an organized and well disciplined youth movement, the PNA appropriated $939,599.45 from 1932 to 1951.[61] The results were visible at the 1947 and 1951 Conven-tions; many former youth leaders were now taking an active part in the leadership of the PNA.

To maintain high interest among PNA members beyond the teen-age and boy-scout age, the PNA inaugurated in 1931 a sports program. Through the sports program, the PNA had continually supported such athletic activities as baseball, basketball, bowling, softball, tennis, volleyball and track. Over four-hundred PNA lodges now conduct sports programs for their members in one or several of the mentioned sports.[62]

PNA sports are planned on the city, state, and national levels. Bowling is the most popular sport activity for PNA men and women today. A total of 128 teams and over 1,000 bowlers had participated in the 1952 national PNA bowling tournament at Buffalo, New York. Currently, over 100 bowling leagues, 12 in Chicago alone, are in existence involving over 5,000 PNA mem-bers. All together, 20,000 PNA members are active participants in the bowling game. The 1957 national PNA mixed bowling tournament, held in May, at the Olympic Lanes in Milwaukee, Wisconsin, attracted approximately 800 bowlers, all PNA mem-bers, from Pennsylvania, Illinois, Michigan, Minnesota, Indiana, Ohio, and Wisconsin.

Over 125 PNA teams are engaged in softball throughout the United States. This activity has shown a rapid growth, particu-larly in the sixteen-inch, slow pitching division. The last national PNA basketball tournament, staged at Duquesne University in Pittsburg, in the winter of 1942, attracted 22 teams from 7 states

---

[61] Albin Szczerbowski, "Analiza Wydzialu Maloletnich," Zgoda, (September 8, 1951), p. 4.

[62] "National Fraternal Congress of America Proclaims 'Fraternal Week' June 9-16," Zgoda, (June 1, 1957), p. 12.

and 18 cities. The annual Chicagoland PNA basketball tournaments, inaugurated in 1943, has attracted an average of 12 teams per year.

Over 50,000 PNA members are active in one sport or another, sponsored by the PNA, for which the PNA contributes between $20,000 to $25,000 a year. All PNA sports clubs and leagues submit their results of games and tourneys to the Sports Department of the PNA Polish daily, Zgoda, for publication in the English-language columns. Zgoda devotes one full page daily to news of PNA and Polish American independent sports clubs and leagues.

The PNA has also established a welfare department through which donations of food, clothing, and other aids are distributed to families affected by industrial calamity or other misfortunes. Annually, the PNA welfare department expends approximately $16,000, which is raised by a nominal assessment of each PNA member. This PNA humanitarian activity is well known. Even though the funds in the treasury of the welfare department cannot be considered large, the PNA contributed $54,000 for the alleviation of suffering and hardship among the coal miners in America during their industrial strife. Also through this department, the PNA contributed $1,500,000 to the Hoover Mission, organized at the end of World War I, and hundreds of thousands of dollars to the American Red Cross.[63]

Since its inception, in addition to carrying on all these educational, welfare, recreational and cultural activities, while maintaining and improving the fraternal benefit system, the PNA has been also in the forefront of the struggle for justice for Poland.

---

[63] "Censor-Judge Gunther Presents Interesting History of the Polish National Alliance," Zgoda, (February 7, 1955), p. 3.

# CHAPTER EIGHT

# Activities of the Polish Roman Catholic Union

The Polish Roman Catholic Union (PRCU) was from the very beginning more than a fraternal insurance organization. According to Zygmunt Stefanowicz, editor of *Narod Polski*, the PRCU is a fraternal organization with the following specific objectives: (1) to uphold and spread the Catholic Faith, (2) to maintain and spread the Polish language, Polish traditions, and the Polish spirit, (3) to aid Poland, (4) to help members attain higher positions in the civil and religious fields, and (5) to raise the children in the Polish and Catholic spirit.[1] In accordance with these objectives, the PRCU not only provides insurance but renders material assistance to its members in commercial, political, and educational endeavors.

The PRCU movement, to improve and widen education among the Polish immigrants, assumed many forms. From the very beginning, the PRCU contributed funds to the founding, building, and expansion of the Polish-American school system. Various schools throughout the United States were recipients of this aid. St. Stanislaus Kostka College in Chicago, St. John Cantious College in Erie, Pennsylvania, and the Polish Seminary at Orchard Lake, Michigan, were also supported by special donations.[2] This activity never terminated, for as late as 1955, the PRCU presented to Archbishop Cushing of Boston $1,000 for the building of a new Polish school in Boston.[3]

---

[1] "O Celach i Zadaniah Zjednoczenia PRK," *Narod Polski*, (March 7, 1957), p. 4.

[2] Mieczyslaw Haiman, *Zjednoczenie Polskie Rzymsko-Katolickie w Ameryce*, (Chicago: 1948), pp. 553-563.

[3] Vincent M. Versen, "About the Plenary Meeting of the PRCU Directorate," *Narod Polski*, (May 19, 1955), p. 15.

On January 14, 1879, Father Moczygemba, PRCU president, presented to Pope Leo XIII, a petition for the establishment of a college in the United States. He claimed that there were 200,000 Polish immigrants living in America, and that they needed a college to prepare candidates for seminary studies. On February 6, 1879, Pope Leo XIII gave his approval.[4] In answer to the original letter of request, Pope Leo XIII subscribed on the original letter the words: "Annuimus in omnibus juxta petita" (We assent to everything as petitioned).

The third PRCU convention assessed each PRCU member one dollar which was eventually to be used for the construction of the proposed college. In accordance with the decision reached at the PRCU convention, Father Moczygemba purchased four-hundred acres for the new college on the Elba River in Nebraska, where Polish immigrants had first settled in 1877. At this time, there was a great need for Polish priests; thus the idea to organize a Polish school for the training of Polish priests developed. In 1880, it was decided to establish the college in Chicago. Eventually, Father Dabrowski assumed the leadership in the project and the foundation for the Polish seminary was established in Detroit. The PRCU was not only instrumental in establishing the Seminary, but was also responsible for its material growth.[5] From June 30, 1937 to June 30, 1950, the PRCU donated $76,101.05 for the Polish Seminary, which was eventually moved to its present site in Orchard Lake, Michigan.[6] During the past few years, the PRCU has donated annually $5000 for the Seminary.[7]

Interest in education was maintained at every convention. Delegates to the seventeenth convention, held in Milwaukee, in 1890, adopted the following resolution.

> After God we value most our nationality and our language: but this does not mean that we are careless about the English language. On the contrary, we will take all possible steps to give our children

---

[4] Haiman, *op. cit.,* pp. 51-52.

[5] *Ibid.,* p. 199.

[6] Official Minutes of the 45th Convention of the PRCU held in Syracuse, New York, in 1950, p. 5.

[7] Vincent M. Versen, "About the Plenary Meeting of the PRCU Directorate," *Narod Polski,* (May 19, 1955), p. 15.

a good foundation and knowledge of the English language and the laws of this country.[8]

Thus the delegates encouraged PRCU members to support Polish elementary and secondary schools. They also urged parents to send their children for advanced studies. These appeals did not go unheeded. In 1900, the PRCU, pointing to the large number of children attending the Polish parochial schools, stated, "Youth, School, and the Church, these are our national treasures."[9] The parish and the school system became a unique monument to the piety and good citizenship of these early pioneers.

In addition to giving material aid to the Polish-American school system, the PRCU was instrumental in introducing improvements in the school curriculums. As a result of discussions held at the third PRCU Convention, American History and Civics courses had been introduced into the curriculums of the Polish-American Schools as early as 1875.[10] The PRCU also urged its members to retain thet best elements of the Polish culture and to blend them with American virtues and traditions. It also encouraged PRCU members to be good citizens of their adopted country.[11]

The PRCU was the first Polish-American organization to conceive the idea of establishing orphanages and other charitable institutions in Polish-American communities.[12] The fifth PRCU Convention, held in Chicago in 1877 devoted its time to the problem of the Polish orphans. As a result, in 1885, a Polish orphanage was established in Chicago, under the direction of the Sisters of the Holy Family of Nazareth.[13] After taking the initia-tive in establishing the orphanage, the PRCU continued to sup-port the efforts of the clergy and sisters of the various orders engaged in this humanitarian endeavor.

---

8 Haiman, *op. cit.,* p. 109.

9 A. Kowalski, "Mlodziez, Szkola i Kosciol, to nasz skarb narodowy," *Narod Polski,* (October 3, 1900), p. 4.

10 The third convention of the PRCU was held in Milwaukee, on June 8 and 9 of 1875; more than eighty delegates attended.

11 A typical early Polish American leader was Peter Kiolbassa, for many years president of the PRCU. Elected city treasurer of Chicago, he refused to appropriate public money for his personal use, as did his predecessors. "Honest Pete" as he was nicknamed, he also filled other public offices with credit. In his day, he played a prominent part in all religious and civic affairs of Chicago and Illinois.

12 Haiman, *op. cit.,* p. 49.

13 *Ibid.,* p. 51.

In 1886, the PRCU adopted for all members a system of fraternal insurance.[14] With the demise of a PRCU member, six hundred dollars was paid to his widow by the organization. The death benefit to a widower amounted to $300.[15] In 1891, the PRCU contributed to the establishment of the "Polish Emigration House of St. Joseph" in New York City; and in 1894, the PRCU participated actively in the "Polish National Exposition" held in Lwow, Poland, by helping to construct a Polish-American Pavilion. In 1901 and 1903, at Pittsburgh, the PRCU played a leading role in the second and third Polish Catholic Congresses, where the thought ultimately crystallized that Polish-Americans should be accorded a representation in the American Catholic hierarchy. The PRCU believed that bishops of Polish ancestry would greatly minimize disrupting anti-Catholic influences among Polish immigrants. A delegation, partly financed by the PRCU, was sent to Rome to present this matter to the Holy See.[16] The PRCU also made an effort to bind all Polish-American parishes in the Polish Catholic Federation which supported the action of Polish Catholic Congresses and worked for the improvement of teaching methods in the Polish parochial schools located in the United States. The PRCU also contributed to the erection of the General Thaddeus Kosciuszko monument, which was unveiled in Chicago, in 1904, with a great display of oratory and a colorful parade.

The PRCU Educational Aid Department was established in 1905.[17] To meet the needs of this department, all PRCU members were assessed a small amount annually for an endowment fund, intended for poor and worthy students.[18] Within twenty years, $160,00 was made available.[19] From 1922 to 1925, the

---

[14] *Ibid.*, p. 76.

[15] During its long existence, the PRCU never defaulted in any payments. Since 1886, it has paid out over $30,000,000 in death benefits alone.

[16] In 1908 the entreaties of Polish Americans for a representation in the American Catholic hierarchy were granted. Rev. Paul F. Rhode, a member of the PRCU, was appointed auxiliary bishop of Chicago, and thus became the first bishop of Polish extraction in the United States.

[17] The Sixteenth Convention of the PRCU was held in Bay City, in 1899. At this convention, it was decided to establish a fund for the education of talented but poor youths. To establish this fund it was proposed that each member be assessed an additional dollar; the proposition did not go through.

[18] Haiman, *op. cit.*, p. 215.

[19] Official minutes of the thirty-eighth convention of the PRCU held in St. Louis, Missouri, in 1925. p. 10.

PRCU Educational Aid Department awarded $19,500 to university students; $4,530 to students residing in the State of Illinois, and $14,970 to students living in other States.[20]

Dr. Badzmierowski, who had received financial aid from the department, stated, that in its time the aid which he received was worth $50,000.[21] Since its inception, the department has granted more than $320,000 to students. Many of the students have attained prominent and important positions in American society. From June, 1950 to June, 1954, $9,643.25 was returned to the PRCU Educational Aid Department. During the same period 39 students received grants amounting to $10,001.85. As of June, 1954, the PRCU Aid Department had $225,010.45 loaned out to students.[22]

The PRCU Educational Aid Department also helped the PRCU Museum to save the Kosciuszko Collection of the late Dr. Alexander Kahanowicz, and the late Father Joseph Wachowski. The collection contained 73 original letters of General Kosciuszko, in addition to letters he received from General Greene, Thomas Jefferson, Robert Morris, Joel Barlow, James F. Cooper, Samuel F. B. Morse, John Quincy Adams and others. The collection also contained prints, books, and other relics pertaining to Kosciuszko.

During World War I, the PRCU played a significant role. The PRCU Convention, held in 1918, voted a special assessment for Polish relief which was distributed through the Polish Central Relief Committee. Over five hundred PRCU members joined the ranks of the Polish Army. The largest recruiting station for the Polish Army was maintained in the PRCU building in Chicago. At the same time, the building housed a recruiting station for the United States Army. Over two thousand PRCU members served in the American forces.

The 1907 PRCU Convention inaugurated the General Aid Department which provides relief to PRCU members incapacitated by sickness or other disabilities. To date the expenditures

[20] Ibid., p. 11.
[21] Ibid., p. 13.
[22] Official Minutes of the forty-sixth PRCU Convention, held in Pittsburgh, Pennsylvania, in 1954. p. 34.

for the department totalled aproximately $350,000. During the depression years, the PRCU granted a moratorium to societies that had incurred debts by overdue assessment payments. The PRCU also adopted measures to save from foreclosure real-estate properties of members with PRCU mortages.

In 1918, the PRCU Juvenile Department was established. Its primary purpose was to insure not only the future growth of the organization, but also the character training of the youth born in the United States. In 1925, the PRCU sports department was officially formed. Emil Banasik was designated as sports editor and director of the department. By 1928, the department had organized 37 baseball teams and 15 bowling teams.

In 1929, PRCU President, John J. Olejniczak, appointed the first sports committee. Under the direction of this committee, 39 baseball teams, 8 softball teams and 46 basketball teams were organized. By 1933, the PRCU sports department sponsored nation-wide tournaments. In 1934, the committee supported with equipment and uniforms 135 softball teams, 56 basketball teams and 10 women's basketball teams established throughout the United States. The PRCU sent a delegation to the Olympics, held in Los Angeles, California.[23] In October, 1934, the PRCU organized and provided uniforms for new teams in New York, Pennsylvania, Illinois, Ohio, Michigan, New Hampshire, Missouri, Connecticut, and Massachusetts. In 1936, 73 basketball teams, 52 softball teams, 37 baseball teams and 6 bowling teams were in existence. In 1937, upon the recommendation of PRCU President, Joseph L. Kania, the sports committee was dissolved; in its place the Youth Department was established. Youth activities and sports were combined in this department. The scout movement, to activate the children's interest in the PRCU, was also inaugurated.[24]

The PRCU Library, a nationally known institution, was established in 1908. This library, which possesses the largest existing collection of Polonica in the English language, is of great

---

[23] Andzia Stefanowicz, "Sports and Youth in the PRCU," *Ksiega Diamentowa* ZPRK 1873-1948, (Chicago: 1948), p. 101.

[24] The scout movement in the PRCU was first started by Nikodem Piotrowski, president of the PRCU in 1918. These movements were active unofficially within the PRCU societies from 1918 to 1933.

help to scholars throughout the United States conducting research on subjects pertaining to Poland and the American Polonia. To make the library more accessible and useful to scholars, the PRCU had published several catalogues listing the various books and materials in the PRCU library. Many of the books listed in these catalogues may be borrowed through local libraries on the usual inter-library loans.[25]

The PRCU has also published a series of books dealing with the history of the American Polonia. To disseminate information on this subject, the PRCU subsidized many lectures and seminars. At the second convention of the Polish Society of History and Museum, held in Chicago, in 1939, Alphonse S. Wolanin, archivists of the PRCU Museum, read a paper in the methods of collecting historical material. A series of lectures on Polish history and culture was organized during the winter of 1941-1942; the lecturers included Dr. Wladimir Sokalski of Loyola University, Dr. Wladimir Sklodowski of DePaul University, Rev. Boniface Slawik of Katowice, Poland, Mieczyslaw Niedzwiecki of the Chicago, *Polish Daily News* and Szczesny Lesniewicz, custodian of the PRCU Museum. On September 8, 1944, Dr. Thaddeus Mitana, secretary, Polish Institute of Arts and Sciences in America, delivered a lecture on "Educational Work in Poland"; Eric P. Kelly, of Dartmouth College, on November 5, 1944, lectured on "My Polish Interests'"; and Captain Alexander Janta, on June 22, 1945, lectured on "Poland's Part in World War II."

The *Annals* came into being in 1936. Dealing with the history and culture of the Poles in the United States, the *Annals* serve as a source of information on early American Polish history to scholars interested in the achievements and accomplishments of the Polish immigrants and their descendants. The *Annals,* official publication of the PRCU Archives and Museum were distributed gratis to university and public libraries located in Poland and the United States.[26] The following *Annals* were published from 1936 to 1947.

25 Alphonse S. Wolanin, *Polonica in English,* (Chicago: 1945), p. 6.

26 In addition to distributing the *Annals* gratis, the PRCU has also distributed other books dealing with the history of the American Polonia. For example, in 1932, the PRCU distributed gratis Mieczyslaw Haiman's *Poland and the American Revolu-*

(1) Haiman, Miecislaus, *Poles in the Early History of Texas,* 1936.

(2) Haiman, Miecislaus, *Polish Pioneers of Virginia and Kentucky,* 1937.

(3) Haiman, Miecislaus, *Poles in New York in the 17th and 18th Centuries,* 1938.

(4) Coleman, Arthur P., *A New England City and the November Uprising,* 1939.

(5) Haiman, Miecislaus, *Polish Pioneers of California,* 1940.

(6) Haiman, Miecislaus, *Polish Pioneers of Pennsylvania,* 1941.

(7) Kozlowski, Ladislaus M., *Washington and Kosciuszko,* 1942.

(8) Rutkowska, Sr. M. Neomisia, *John Tyssowski,* 1943.

(9) Dworaczyk, Rev. Edward J., *Church Records of Panna Maria, Texas,* 1944.

(10) Napolska, Sr. M. Remigia, O.S.F., *The Polish Immigrant in Detroit,* 1945-1946.

(11) Konopczynski, Wladyslaw, *Casimir Pulaski,* translated by Irena Makarewicz, 1947.

To acquaint American youth of Polish descent with the traditions and culture of the country of their forefathers, the PRCU arranged an excursion to Poland in 1932. It was the first excursion of its kind in the United States. When the scouts, daughters, and sports departments were combined in 1937, the sports section of the youth department continued to hold its yearly tournaments of baseball, basket-ball, bowling, golf, swimming, and track. During World War II, efforts were concentrated on the scout and daughter departments, since the young men were in the service of the United States. However, bowling tournaments were held yearly and basketball and baseball teams were maintained. Camp activities were encouraged and organized throughout the United States. Over 1000 scouts and daughters had attended camps in Connecticut, Massachusetts, Wisconsin, Michigan, New York and Illinois, while their older brothers and sisters were in the service of the United States.

During the diamond jubilee year (1948), the PRCU spon-

tionary *War* to the presidents of the United States and Poland, ninety-six United States Senators, forty-two Archbishops, twenty-nine Congressmen, forty-three newspapers, eighteen libraries in Poland, one-hundred-thirty university libraries in the United States and thirty-two state libraries. Many other books dealing with American Polonia has similar distribution. The services of the PRCU in this regard are unique.

sored four successful sports events: a basketball tournament with
an entry of eleven teams from Illinois, Indiana, Wisconsin,
Pennsylvania, Michigan, and Ohio; a bowling tournament with
1,148 bowlers participating from Kansas, Illinois, Indiana, Michigan, Ohio, and West Virginia; and 12 softball teams from Missouri, Ohio, Illinois, Michigan, Pennsylvania, Indiana, and Kansas.
A duck pin bowling tournament was held in Pittsburgh, with
teams participating from Ohio, Pennsylvania, and West Virginia.
Also in 1948, four ten-day periods of camping were held for
PRCU scouts and daughters at Camp Gieryk, in Custer Park,
Illinois.[27]

Narod Polski, the official organ of the PRCU, was established
in 1897. Issued on the first and third Monday of every month,
it is bi-lingual with Polish predominating. It has a circulation of
87,000 and is sent to the members gratis; non-members may subscribe for one dollar a year. Narod Polski promotes the interests
of the PRCU. It keeps the PRCU members informed of the
catalogue of events and accomplishments of the fraternal order.
It fights for justice for Poland and it fosters the cultural and
religious welfare of the American Polonia. The following practical articles have appeared in Narod Polski: "Material Value of
An Education"[28]; "Let's join the beautiful with the practical"[29];
"How to Understand Education"[30]; "How to Use your Time
Wisely"[31]; "Why Polish Women Should Study English"[32]; and
"Let's Defend Poland but Only as Intelligent Americans."[33] The
official organ Narod Polski also encouraged its members to use
the public libraries available in their communities. It called to the
attention of PRCU members the services which the public libraries
render.[34] In 1921, the PRCU initiated the publication of Dziennik

27 Stefanowicz, op. cit., p. 103.

28 "Materyalna Wartosc Oswiaty," Narod Polski, (October 5, 1910), p. 4.

29 "Laczmy Piekne z praktycznem," Narod Polski, (October 5, 1910), p. 4.

30 "Jak Rozumiec Oswiate," Narod Polski, (November 16, 1910), p. 4.

31 "O Dobrym Uzytku Czasu," Narod Polski, (November 16, 1910), p. 4.

32 "Dlaczego Polki Powinni Uczyc Angielskiego," Narod Polski, (July 28,
1920), p. 4.

33 Ks. A. Narloch, "Bronmy Polski ale Umiejetnie Jak Amerykanie," Narod
Polski (December 7, 1932), p. 4.

34 "W celu dania moznosci swiezo przybywajacem obcokrajowcom poznania
jezyka i urzadzen przybranej ojczyzny znajduja sie w bibliotece ksiazki tlomac-

*Zjednoczenia* (Polish Daily News) and continued to publish it till 1939. Like the PRCU official organ, *Narod Polski,* the new publication always endeavored to promote American, Catholic, and Polish ideals among the immigrants and their descendants.[35]

In 1935, through the efforts of Joseph L. Kania and Mieczyslaw Haiman, the PRCU Archives and Museum was established and officially opened in 1937. Devoted primarily to the preservation of the history and culture of Americans of Polish descent, the PRCU Archives and Museum, merged with the PRCU Library, has grown into an institution of national importance. Since its establishment, the institution has expanded considerably; today it occupies four floors, three of which are devoted exclusively to permanent exhibits, in the spacious PRCU building located in Chicago. During the twenty-four years of its existence, the PRCU Archives and Museum has received more than ten thousand gifts. In obtaining objects of Polish-American interest, the PRCU Museum also acquired the treasures which many Polish immigrants had brought with them to the United States from Poland. Over 100,000 Americans, individually and in groups, visited the Museum to view the permanent and special exhibits for which there is no charge. The Polish Society of History and Museum was also established; in 1947, it numbered 157 perpetual members, 165 sustaining members and 380 regular members. By 1947, the Endowment Fund of the PRCU Museum rose to $7,650.[36]

The purely Polish-American items in the Museum constitute an amazingly complete record of the American Poles. There are reports, medals set on scarlet and white ribbons, and uniforms of almost every early Polish American society displayed on life-sized manikins. Many of these, attired in colorful and picturesque costumes representing the various regions of Poland, are also on

---

zone na inne jezyki pod ogolnym tytulem 'Ksiazki dla wszystklich.' " *Narod Polski,* (July 28, 1920), p. 4.

[35] *Narod Polski* and *Dziennik Zjednoczenia* made it clear to its readers that the United States was their permanent home. They also encouraged the readers to become citizens of the United States and they urged them to take an active part in community affairs.

[36] "Time Marches On—A Need for a Living Museum," *Polish American Historical Association Bulletin,* Dr. Joseph A. Wytrwal, Editor, Bulletin No. 183 (November, 1959), p. 1.

display. Stations of the first Polish church in America, numerous original Pulaski and Kosciuszko letters, Modjeska and Marcella Sembrich costumes, General Krzyzanowski and General Karge mementos, and memorials of prominent Polish-Americans are also included in the collection.

The history and culture of Poland are also well represented. There is a beautiful and massive shrine in the center of the main hall which contains the soil from Grunwald, Czestochowa, Ostroleka, and other famous battlefields of Poland. There are portraits of all the Polish kings from Mieczyslaw I to Stanislaw August Pontiatowski. There is an Envoy's Room containing examples of Polish furniture and objects d'art. There are also magnificent tapestries on display. Specimens from Polish folklore, costumes from various parts of Poland, wood carvings, utensils, dolls, and an Easter egg collection are also included. The art gallery numbers over two hundred original paintings. Works of A. Grottger, J. Suchodolski, St. Wyspianski, W. Czachorski, J. Falat, A. Kedzierski, J. Malczewski, Juliusz and Wojciech Kossak, S. Batowski, and J. H. Rosen are on display. Sculptures by Polish and American artists are also included. The PRCU has also ten thousand reproductions of Polish art and posters on Polish subjects.

A large section of the PRCU Museum has been set aside as the Paderewski Memorial Museum. There the New York hotel room in which Paderewski died has been completely restored. All of the furnishings of the room are there, including his bed, the chair which he occupied during his piano playing while touring the world, and his piano, with a composition of Chopin opened just as it was on his last day. Many of his personal objects, including the familiar fur-collared overcoat and the black hat, in addition to hundreds of other items, such as musical scores, photographs, and concert programs are also on display.

Another interesting exhibit of the PRCU Museum is the General Kosciuszko collection. The entire memorial exhibit which was shown at the Anderson Galleries in New York was purchased by the Museum and is on display along with many other historical items pertaining to Kosciuszko. Original letters and manuscripts, paintings and medals, currency and books, comprise the General Kosciuszko collection. The Madame Modjeska Collection includes two of Modjeska's costumes worn as Mary Stuart (from act I and IV), with the original masks made by W. Benda, and many of her letters, play bills, costume sketches, and photographs. The General Pulaski collection consists of many of his letters, documents, lithographs, and an official report written five days before his death on October 6, 1779.

Even though the PRCU Museum has been established for less than a quarter of a century, it might take the best part of that time to absorb the significance of its contents. The Archives alone has a collection of thousands of daily newspapers, weeklies, monthlies, and quarterlies published in the United States and abroad. In many instances, the collections are complete from the beginning of the twentieth century.[37] In addition, the Archives contain biographies of 12,000 Americans of Polish descent; 3,000 periodicals containing articles about Poland or the Poles; 4,000 books dealing with the activities of the American Polonia; uncounted number of photographs, maps, and newspaper clippings; and a general library possessing 25,000 volumes in English and Polish relating to Poland or to writers born in Poland or America of Polish extraction.[38] The Archives of the Polish National Committee of Chicago contain approximately 30,000 letters, documents, pictures, and pamphlets dealing with the work of the Polish Americans during World War I in enlisting volunteers for the Polish army in France and in working for an independent Poland. These were also turned over to the PRCU Museum and Archives for safekeeping and cataloguing.

Over 5,428 scholars have used these collections for their special studies.[39] Many students at colleges and universities have made use of them through inter-library loans. Currently, a large number of Polish newspapers published in the United States, Canada, Mexico, Poland, Brazil, Argentina, and the Union of South Africa are received by the PRCU Archives and Museum. The present value of the collection is about $400,000.[40]

---

[37] Jerzy Walter, "Rzut Oka na 20-Letnia Dzialalnosc Museum i Archiwum Zjednoczenia," *Narod Polski*, (February 7, 1957), p. 13.

[38] Artur L. Waldo, "Trzynascie Lat Museum Polonji," *Ksiega Diamentowa ZPRK 1873-1948*, (Chicago: 1948), p. 120.

[39] *Ibid.*, p. 123.

[40] Since the demise of Miecislaus Haiman and President Kania, the activities

Since 1955, the PRCU has prepared plans to collect a quarter of a million dollars for the construction of a special building to house the Museum and Archives of the PRCU.[41] On May 1, 1956, members of the Polish Society of History and Museum proposed that a Polish-American Museum Foundation be established to raise funds for the erection of a museum building on land to be secured from the City of Chicago. The museum would contain one great exhibit hall for all general collections and smaller halls for the collections of other American Polish national organizations. The museum would be maintained by all the American-Polish national organizations.

The PRCU took an active part in the war effort during World War II. More than five thousand PRCU members served in the armed forces.[42] The PRCU purchased United States War Bonds for $9,417,495.42; this does include bonds purchased by the lodges and individual members.[43] The youth and women's departments gave their time and facilities to charity and relief work; in fact, the women's contribution to charitable work of the organization was greater than that of the men. The headquarters of tht PRCU became the logical place for organization meetings and deliberations that led to a number of large scale humanitarian enterprises. The "American Relief for Poland Organization," which was organized in 1939 to render effective relief to Polish refugees in different parts of the world, established its

---

of the Archives and Museum have been greatly curtailed. Not one publication has been published; the Annals have been suspended. General interest in the Polish Society of History and Museum lagged with resulting loss of membership. For the last fifteen years, the institution has been suffering from an acute lack of space and funds. Leadership and professional personnel, specialists in library science and museum maintenance have been conspicuously absent from the staff of the PRCU Archives and Museum. Attendance at the library became infrequent due to shortage of personnel, irregular hours, frequent suspension of activities, and unprofessional cataloging of material. Recently Jerzy C. Walter has been appointed curator of the PRCU Museum. "A Sound Selection;" Polish American Historical Association Bulletin, Dr. Joseph A. Wytrwal, Editor, Bulletin No. 186, (February, 1960), p. 1. "The Polish Roman Catholic Union Archives and Museum," Polish American Historical Association Bulletin, Bulletin No. 191 (July, 1960), p. 1.

[41] Vincent M. Versen, "About the Plenary Meeting of the PRCU Directorate," Narod Polski, (May 19, 1955), p. 15.

[42] Mieczyslaw Haiman, "The Polish American Contribution to World War II," Polish American Studies, III (January-June, 1946), p. 36.

[43] Ibid., p. 36.

main office in the PRCU building in Chicago. There were many weeks and months when the halls in the PRCU building resembled a large warehouse into which gifts of clothing poured from individuals and various organizations. Similarly the PRCU building became the headquarters for the "Catholic League" for postwar religious aid to Poland.[44]

With the cessation of hostilities, the PRCU donated $50,000 to the "American Relief for Poland Organization."[45] In 1955, the PRCU appropriated $500 for work among Polish exiles and refugees; and an additional $500 for the "Polish American Congress" for its work in liberating Poland from Soviet occupation.[46] The PRCU established plans for a nation wide appeal for Polish Relief among its 180,000 members in 1957. "American Relief for Poland" was the PRCU response to the Polish people in their plea for American aid to help themselves. The PRCU program was to aid all the destitute and crippled repatriates who were in need of assistance in their efforts to be self-supporting.[47]

On the American scene, the PRCU had donated $707.60 for the American Museum of Immigration which was to be established at the foot of the Statue of Liberty in New York to tell for all time the epic story of immigration in the building of America.[48] The Museum would memorialize the contributions, the cultures, and the traditions of the many races and nationalities that had gone into the American fabric.[49]

Since its inception in 1873, the PRCU expended millions of dollars to attain the objectives of the organization. The following sums were spent during the first fifty years of the PRCU's existence:

---

[44] In 1956, the PRCU donated $1,000 to facilitate the work of this organization. "Tysiac Dolarow od Zjednoczenia PRK na Lige Katolicka," *Narod Polski,* (November 8, 1956), p. 5.

[45] "PRCU wil help ARP," *Polish American Journal.* (August 3, 1957), p. 1.

[46] Vincent M. Versen, "About the Plenary Meeting of the PRCU Directorate," *Narod Polski,* (May 19, 1955), p. 15.

[47] "PRCU will help ARP," *Polish American Journal,* (August 3, 1957), p. 1.

[48] Jozef T. Pranica, "Ofiary Zlozone na Museum Immigracyjne w New Yorku," *Narod Polski,* (November 8, 1956), p. 3.

[49] The PRCU is trying to raise $5000 so that it may become a "Group Founder" of this museum. It's name will then be inscribed on a plaque in the Hall of Record of the Museum. Organizations representing every nationality in American life have joined in the movement to establish the museum.

Aid to needy students in colleges ...................................$ 150,000.00
Aid to crippled members .................................... 180,000.00
Death Benefits ...................................................... 7,000,000.00
Aid to Poland (Red Cross Work) .................... 350,000.00
Parochial Schools ................................................ 25,000.00
Orphanages ............................................................ 15,000.00
American War Bonds............................................ 500,000.00
Polish Bonds ........................................................ 50,000.00
Miscellaneous ...................................................... 30,000.00

Total $8,300,000.00[50]

From 1873 to 1948, the PRCU allocated $34,265,828 for the following objectives:

Death Benefits ...................................................... $28,859.374.37
Dividends to members........................................ 1,500,000.00
Aid to students.................................................... 322,375.63
For promotion of sports and scouting............ 238,447.61
For library and museum.................................... 184,199.84
For religious, humanitarian and patriotic purposes . 815,745.09
Publications .......................................................... 2,000,000.00

Total $34,265,828.04[51]

---

[50] *Zlota Ksiega Pamiatkowa 1873-1923 z okazi piedziesieciolocia Zjednoczenia Polskiego Rymsko-Katolickiego w Ameryce,* (Chicago: 1923), p. 46.

[51] Haiman, *op. cit.,* p. 568.

# CHAPTER NINE

# The PNA and PRCU Compared

The comparison between the PNA and PRCU have absorbed many Polonia leaders. There are some striking parallels. Historically, PNA and PRCU have followed identical paths of development; both came into being with the tide of Polish immigration in the late decades of the nineteenth century. Both the PNA and the PRCU desired to obtain a hegemony over the Polish immigrant group.[1] Both claimed priority of origin. Both tended to unify Polish immigrants and their descendants under their particular ideology.[2] Both felt impelled on several occasions to address Congress in petitions and to protest against impracticable bills, born of a narrow-minded nativistic spirit, that would have unduly restricted the flow of immigration to our shores at a time when an economic justification for such measures was not apparent. Both created from the raw materials of Polish immigrant stock an articulate citizenry. Both offered a practical and humane program of personal development in harmony with existing conditions. Both rely on some form of mutual insurance for stability and social cohesion.[3] Both have a core of dedicated leaders who

---

[1] The PRCU was organized in 1873 by the clergy as an effort to keep the Polish immigrant close to the clergy and the church; the PNA was organized in the 1880's by exiles of the unsuccessful 1863 insurrection in an effort to rally the Polish immigrants to work for the eventual liberation of Poland. The PNA was a lay organization and controlled by people of all creeds and faiths of Polish ancestry.

[2] Naturally each organization placed the blame on the other, stating that for the interference of the second organization, it would have achieved its aim.

[3] The insurance principle does not constitute the main power of the organization, but serves only as its formative principle. Mutual insurance is not the basis of association but rather a system of organization because it gives a minimum of rational order. Insurance introduces regularity and continuity into the successive meetings: it gives a definite purpose for each meeting; and it calls for a division of duties. Of most importance is the fact that it prevents personal disagreements from destroying the organization and counteracts very efficiently individual indifferences since a member cannot cease to participate even temporarily without losing his rights to benefits

227

have shown an organizing capacity and a skill in amassing wealth. Both organizations enjoy considerable prestige; their voice and counsel is heeded by statesmen, judges, and legislators. Governors of various states, mayors, councilmen, senators, and congressmen honor them by their presence at important functions of these organizations. Both are conscious of their responsibilities, and employ their resources for the benefit of their members, the community and the nation. The contribution of the PNA and the PRCU to philanthropic efforts on behalf of European and American Poles and to the upbuilding of the State of Poland is one of the brightest chapters in Polish-American history and in that of humanitarian enterprise in general. In charitable endeavor and social service, the Poles in the United States have been able to call upon a long tradition of philanthropy, together with a truly modern aptitude for social organization. As a result, both the PNA and the PRCU have served as models for many American public and private social welfare and philanthropic institutions.

The two organizations maintain official organs, the PNA, *Zgoda* and the PRCU, *Narod Polski*.[4] These organs serve the interest of the organization by explaining and defending its objectives and policies.[5] They also contain official information and accounts of the meetings held by the Board of Directors and the Supervisory Council; news of the various district, council, and lodge meetings; and official organizational information, such as the register of assessments paid by the different societies, death

---

and privileges as well as to the contributions which he has already paid to the organization. The fact that the mutual insurance has come to perform a social function among the American Poles out of all proportion to its economic significance is probably due to its simplicity and the small risks it involves on the part of the individual. The risks become even smaller as the organization increases its membership. This induces the members to recruit new adherents.

[4] At one time both organizations had daily organs. In 1939, the PRCU suspended its daily newspaper. The PNA maintains its daily newspaper to the present time.

[5] What distinguishes the PNA *Zgoda* from the PRCU *Narod Polski*? *Zgoda* is a propagandist press with a definite political and cultural message which dominate all other themes. *Narod Polski* has more of a religious theme. In *Narod Polski* space is rarely devoted to literary contributions or political articles. The biographies and large size photographs which appear on the front page usually include a priest of Polish descent. *Zgoda* has more pages in the English language. Also it has more information on the Youth Department and Alliance College. During the past five years, amount of space devoted to Alliance College was unusually large.

benefits paid out, notice of forthcoming meetings, accounts of local lodge celebrations and commemorative observances, lists of contributions made to national relief or other charitable causes, and information the members cannot receive from other publications.[6]

The PNA and the PRCU are superstructures; membership is granted not to individuals, but to groups or societies. The PNA and the PRCU are affiliations of local groups.[7] The PRCU organizes its groups along parish lines; the PNA organizes its groups along local or community lines.[8] When applying for membership the local lodge is given a number; in turn, it may join

---

[6] *Zgoda* and *Narod Polski* have assisted in the process of economic adjustment. Thousands of Polish immigrants would have felt completely lost without the services of information on employment opportunities, advice on legal problems, and information on the work of the various Polish organizations and welfare agencies. These organs also performed a valuable service in that they offered space for advertisements to Polish traders and establishments. Many Polish establishments were thus able to expand and prosper. These organs were also links between societies. They brought news from one community to another and facilitated the growth of the parent organization. Accounts of social events in other associations of the same organization offered a challenge to other communities to emulate the same kind of activity. Seeing one's name in print for participating in some particular lodge activity had a satisfaction of its own. Thus within a medium of these organs the widely scattered community had a contact and communication which enabled it to preserve its national organizations and its comon traditions. Not only were they potent organs in the cultural sub-system, but they also served to introduce newcomers to a wider world which they first discovered in the pages of the Polish newspaper which informed immigrants of the duties to the United States. *Zgoda*, especially, urged the immigrants to learn the English language and American ways. *Zgoda* also assisted in the transition which fitted the immigrants for a larger place in the surrounding American civilization. The Polish language newspaper was an indispensable avenue of communication through which, immigrants who had not yet mastered the English language could be reached most effectively, as well as those who were able to understand American ideals and views more clearly only by reading the Polish newspapers.

[7] Each lodge or society selects its own name, writes its own constitution, elects its own officers, and is free in the management of its own lodge affairs, but its constitution and by-laws are subordinate to the by-laws of the PNA or PRCU constitution. The local association is never entirely absorbed economically into the superterritorial system but preserves some independent functions. It handles the matter of assistance in sickness, aid to poor or unfortunate members, and other purely local matters which the highly centralized organization cannot efficiently attend. In case of death, the lodge president is immediately notified and he in turn assigns available lodge members to be of assistance to the bereaved family. If the family requests it, lodge members serve as pallbearers also. The local lodge gives immediate financial assistance, if necessary, for funeral expenses. This aid is appreciated since there is some delay before the beneficiary can receive payment of the life insurance.

[8] Karol Piatkiewicz, "Co Kazdy Zwiazkowiec ZNP Wiedziec Powinien," *Dziennik Zwiazkowy*, (October 9, 1948), p. 1.

with other groups to form districts called "Osada" by the PRCU and "Gmina" by the PNA. The "Convention" or "Sejm" is the supreme governing body, where laws are enacted, resolutions adopted, and administrative officers elected. At each convention or sejm elected officers give an account of their administration. The convention or sejm is also the tribunal of last appeal. In the interim, between the assembly of the general conventions, the administrative officers are: the president, vice-president, secretary, treasurer and board of directors. In addition, the PNA has its censor; the PRCU, its chaplain.

The PNA and the PRCU may be termed large insurance associations; however, both were established as ideological organ-izations. The PNA in its very initial stages appeared with a plan of life insurance for its members; the PRCU adopted the in-surance plan in 1886, thirteen years after its establishment. De-pending upon the events of national importance or the lack of them, the one or the other element, ideological or material, pre-vailed in these organizations.

The early Polish-American organizations that preceded the PRCU and the PNA, with only ideological aims, found no favor with the Polish immigrants.[9] This is not surprising. From 1865 to the enactment of the quota Bill, in 1924, the mass migration of Poles to America was prompted by economic conditions in Poland. Intent on improving their economic status, these immi-grants responded favorably only to organizations which promised improvement of their fate in America. Any appeal to the mass of Polish immigrants to form organizations and establish lodges, had to offer economic advantages if it was to prove successful. Even early local parish societies offered some small prospects of material security to their members or their families in case of death or accident. Thus, large national organizations, especially the PNA and the PRCU, found the ground prepared for the inauguration of life-insurance plans, which eventually brought millions of dol-lars to their treasuries and enabled them to put into effect various programs.

The following similar or identical activities were sponsored

---

[9] Sister M. Accursia Bern, O.S.F., "Polish Miners in Luzerne County, Pennsylvania," Polish American Studies, III (January-June, 1946), p. 9.

by the PRCU and the PNA. Each organization, the PNA and PRCU, provided care for the newly arrived immigrants and also maintained reception homes in New York City for their adjust- ment.[10] Each organization established libraries in their main ad- ministrative buildings in Chicago; in additon, both have instituted and subsidized circulating libraries among the various lodges. Both have generously awarded scholarships to young Americans of Polish descent in American colleges and universities.[11] Both en- thusiastically established museums for the preservation of past Polish contributions to America.[12] Both maintain youth programs for their members.[13] Both recommended and sponsored official excursions of their organizations to Poland.[14] Although these excursions have been expensive to the organizations, both highly recommended these tours to Poland for children of PRCU and PNA members.[15]

Every activity and undertaking initiated by the PRCU has been duplicated by the PNA and vice-versa. There is, however, one element that sharply defines the PRCU from the PNA. The PRCU consists of societies or associations, religious in character, with the parish as its mainstay and nucleus. Membership in the PRCU is open to all Polish immigrants or Americans of Polish

[10] Stanislaw Osada, Historja Zwiazku Narodowego Polskiego, (Chicago: 1905), pp. 153, 156, 162. 167, 196, 219, 331. Karol Wachtl, Dzieje Zjednoczenia Polskiego Rzymsko-Katolickiego w Ameryce, (Chicago: 1913), pp. 87, 129, 152.

[11] Osada, op. cit., p. 524. Mieczyslaw Haiman, Zjednoczenie Polskie Rzymsko Katolickie w Ameryce, (Chicago: 1948), p. 215.

[12] Osada, op. cit., pp. 332-333. Wachtl, op. cit., p. 231.

[13] Karol Piatkiewicz, "Historja Zwiazku Narodowego w streszczeniu," 75ta Rocznica Istnienia ZNP, Pamietnik 1880-1955, (Chicago: 1955), p. 42. Andzia Stefanowicz, "Sports and Youth in the P.R.C.U.," Ksiega Diamentowa ZPRK w Ameryce 1873-1948, (Chicago: 1948), pp. 100-104.

[14] Zwiazek Narodowy Polski, Urzedowy Protokol Sejmu XXV w Chicago Illinois, 1927-1928, (Chicago: 1927), p. 144. Zjednoczenie Polskie Rzymsko- Katolickie w Ameryce, Sprawozdanie Zarzadu Glownego na Sejm XL, Detroit, Michigan, 1931, (No imprint), pp. 33-39. Zjednoczenie Polskie Rzymsko-Katolickie w Ameryce, Protokol Urzedowy Sejmu XLI, Springfield Massachusetts, 1934, (No imprint), p. 144. Franciszek Barc, 65 Lat Zjednoczenia Polskiego-Rzymsko Kato- lickiego w Ameryce, (Chicago: 1938), p. 52.

[15] Zwiazek Narodowy Polski, Urzedowy Protokol Sejmu XXVI, 1931. Scranton, Pennsylvania, (Chicago: 1931), p. 43. Zjednoczenie Polskie Rzymsko-Katolickie w Ameryce, Sprawozdanie na Sejm XL, Detroit, Michigan 1931, (No imprint), p. 46. Zwiazek Narodowy Polski, Sprawozdanie Na Sejm XXVII, Baltimore, Mary- land, 1935, (Chicago: 1935), pp. 63,217.

descent, who, in addition must profess the Roman Catholic Faith. The PRCU, therefore, is a Polish-Catholic organization which finds its purpose well symbolized in the motto: "For God and Country." The PNA has dispensed with the prerequisite that its members belong to the Roman Catholic Church. All Slavs or Americans of Slavic descent may become members, irrespective of religious denominational affiliations.[16] Poles of Jewish, Lithuanian, Ruthenian, Russian and German descent may and did become members. From its inception, the PNA has insisted on tolerance in religious matters.

The relations of the PNA and PRCU towards Poland were not identical. The PNA was created originally as an integral, although autonomous, part of the Polish nation, by means of a super-territorial organization in the form of a federation of local groups. PNA leaders wanted the PNA to play the role of a "fourth province of Poland"; the first three being the Austrian, German, and Russian parts.[17] For almost twenty-five years, the PNA enjoyed the privilege of bearing this title.

To attract the attention of the American public to Poland's past services, culture, and present condition, the PNA, more strenuously than the PRCU, encouraged the immigrant Poles to participate in American social life.[18] It endorsed in the form of social recognition the attainments of members and non-members in the economic, political, or intellectual life of America. The PNA was especially proud of the participation and contribution of PNA members to American life and society.

In the early period of its existence ,the PRCU did not endorse the national propaganda promulgated by the PNA; it preferred to work not for the restoration of Poland but for the preservation

---

[16] The PNA always asserted to be the only national, political Polish organization in the United States; all others are denominational. Accordingly, it claimed for itself the exclusive leadership in all matters of political nature and importance affecting the Poles in America, a claim which the PNA has not relinquished to this day. Osada, op. cit., p. 479.

[17] The idea of the "fourth province" lost its value before 1910 due to insufficient and sporadic contact with non-existing Poland, and because of the absorption of the people in local affairs, when the Polish American communities began to feel secure. Only during World War I, did the PNA try to play the role of "representative of Poland."

[18] Encouragement to participate in American society is strikingly evident in PNA publications.

of the cultural integrity of the Polish-American community. Thus it discouraged participation of Polish immigrants in political organizations which worked for the restoration of Poland or in American institutions which tended to draw the Polish immigrant away from the Polish-American community.

In general the PNA and the PRCU were not in agreement on all questions that affected the Polish immigrant in America. Each question, each problem, was acted upon, favorably or otherwise, depending upon the self-interest of the organizations rather than upon the good of the "American Polonia." Each problem of national importance was studied from the organization's viewpoint. For example, from the very beginning the PRCU supported the demands of the Polish-American ecclesiastical hierarchy. This issue was completely ignored by the PNA. This, probably, was one of the chief reasons for discord between the two organizations.[19] The clergy dominating the PRCU wanted all the moral, political, and material support of all Polish immigrants in America, to win their just rights from the Irish-dominated American Catholic Hierarchy.

From 1880 to the end of World War I, the PNA had one all-absorbing motive which is best expressed in the word: "Polska" (Poland). To arouse the Polish national spirit among the Polish immigrants to foster it and to direct it towards the liberation of Poland were the goals set by the PNA. The life and accident insurance established by the PNA served two purposes: it gave

---

[19] The first PNA constitution provided for monetary assistance to religious associations which requested it, upon their federation with the PNA. They could appeal to the PNA for funds needed for the erection of a church. The central administration would issue a loan for that purpose. A study of the various groups which form part of the PNA, disclose that practically all local organizations have contributed substantially to the Catholic Church. This was made possible by the clause in the PNA constitution which guarantees freedom and autonomy to the local groups and its members. The national conventions of the PNA have voted financial aid to the Polish Catholic Seminary and to other Catholic schools of higher learning. All these contributions have been made at the time when the struggle (1880-1905) for the guidance and control of the American Polish community was most bitter. Father Joseph Dabrowski was building the Polish Seminary in Detroit with such contributions, and he was overjoyed when he learned that the 1,893 members of the PNA had pledged themselves to contribute fifty cents a year for two years for his cause. This netted Father Dabrowski a sum of $3,472. It was all the more appreciated because "anti-religious" PNA was the first to assess its members for the benefit of the Seminary.

economic security to the Polish immigrants and it was the means through which the leaders of the PNA inculcated in the Polish immigrant masses the spirit of Polish nationalism and patriotism. Having convinced the masses of Polish immigrants on the benefits to be derived from life and accident insurance, the PNA proceeded systematically to present to them the ideal of working toward the liberation of Poland.

Before World War I, both the PNA and the PRCU had definite objectives. The primary objective of the PNA was the liberation of Poland; the primary objectives of the PRCU were the maintenance of the leadership of the Polonia clergy and a larger representation in the American ecclesiastical hierarchy.[20] PRCU members in the American Polonia parishes were thus enlisted in behalf of the ecclesiastical ambitions of the Polonia clergy.

As the idea of a Polonia dominated by the clergy continued to decline, the PRCU laid more emphasis on idealization of the Polonia parish system, extolling it over all other forms of community organization. Eventually, to gain more support for their objectives and more members, the PRCU was forced to adopt the liberation of Poland as one of its goals; combining nationalism with the religious ideal already included in the parochial char-

---

[20] This is not surprising. Most immigrants and their children continued to take an active interest in the political affairs of the countries of their origin. One need only remember, in this connection, the struggle that lasted more than a century, on the part of the Irish-Americans, to secure the independence of Ireland. As early as 1798, a group of Irish refugees fled to America after the failure of the revolution of that year; here in America they organized a liberation movement. Through the next half-century, the agitation continued. After the Civil War, it actually produced an "Irish Republic in the United States," which went so far as to organize an invasion against Britain's Canada.

In the same way, the German-Americans from the 1830's onward were preoccupied with the unification and with the ultimate welfare of their homeland. Comparable developments will be found among Americans of such diverse origins as the Albanians, Italians, Hungarians, and the Czechs. Actually, it did not even require the stimulus of a movement for independence to call such activities into being. Analogous movements appear among such groups as the English immigrants who had no concrete grievances of this order. They maintained societies that attempted to influence public policy on Great Britain's behalf. In a sense, the desires of the Scottish-born Andrew Carnegie and the English born E. L. Godkin to further Anglo-American unity were expressions of loyalty to the place of their birth. The struggle for Irish or Polish independence was not simply an Irish or a Polish struggle; because freedom was involved, it was also an American struggle. And Irish-Americans and Polish-Americans participated fully in those battles not as Irishmen or as Poles, but as Americans.

acter.[21] Now the process of arousing the dormant patriotism of the Polish immigrants and their attachment to the native land, carried on so successfully by the PNA, was deepened and broadened by the PRCU. The means and methods used by the PRCU were practically the same, except that the PRCU could operate on a wider scale. The PRCU could work for this ideal through the church, school, and community. The objective to "liberate Poland received greater importance and value. Nevertheless, the PRCU developed into a weak copy of the PNA as the latter continued to grow by stressing national values above all else.

Because of PNA objectives, it follows logically that the PNA would strive to prevent the Poles from denationalization. However, this was not the case. The PNA did not hinder the naturalization of their members. On the contrary, the PNA urged the Polish immigrants to apply for citizenship papers and to become loyal citizens of the United States. The inducements of the PNA leaders, that the Polish immigrants become citizens of the United States, had a political ring, namely, that only as American citizens would they be taken into account, only as American citizens could they best advance Poland's cause and work toward their own progress. But, with the change of political allegiance, the Poles were taught not to forget their national origin.

Since the termination of World War 1, the activities of the PNA and PRCU are for the most part an extension of the activities they performed before the war. These activities run parallel along many lines and continue to do so with but few exceptions. The PNA expends more funds for educational purposes than does the PRCU. Alliance College at Cambridge Springs, Pennsylvania, and the support of the supplementary schools account for the added expenditure. The PRCU officially pledged itself to give aid to the Polish Theological Seminary at Orchard Lake, Michigan, but does not conduct any supplementary schools, since members, being Roman Catholic, avail themselves of the Polish parochial schools.

---

[21] Up to this time, the PRCU with its narrow parochial orientation tended to "ignore without daring to oppose, Polish political patriotism," preferring to keep "the Polish immigrants . . . limited to their culture and isolated from the American milieu." W. I. Thomas and Florian Znaniecki, *The Polish Peasant in Europe and America*, (Boston: 1918), II, p. 1605.

# CHAPTER TEN

# Dissolution and Asseveration

The period from 1919 to 1925, for the Polish immigrants in the United States, was one of hesitancy, changing moods, and mixed patriotic emotions. The establishment of an independent Polish Republic, and the consequent official distinction between Polish and American citizenship, made it necessary for all Polish immigrants to subject their attachment to the land of their birth to a new orientation. The attachment to the ideal Poland had made it easier to reconcile one's loyalty to America. Confronted, however, with two political realities: America, the land of freedom and opportunity, and independent Poland, the process became complicated and demanded a solution.

This profound change which affected the entire ethnic group in the American Polonia became apparent even before the Armistice whistles made their first sounds. The change, precipitated by the war, affected differently the divided segments of Polonia. Immigrants with determination to make Poland strong, willingness to fight for its defense and the desire to work for its future greatness, returned to Poland.[1] The majority, however, elected to

---

[1] Considering the number of Polish immigrants residing in the United States at the time, the number of Polish re-emigrants can be considered small. According to Dr. Szawlewski, 96,237 returned to Poland during the period from 1919 to 1923. Of this number 32,561 were born in the United States. All the persons returning to Poland were not Poles by national origin.

The repatriates who returned from the United States could not help but bring to Poland some of both the material and the intangible qualities of American life. In going from an advance to a retarded social economy, they took with them money, higher standards of living, a spirit of optimism, reformist attitudes, and pronounced pro-American sentiments. They had come into contact with a different language, with different customs and attitudes. They could hardly have failed to acquire new skills and techniques; their tempo of life had quickened; they had seen people worship in different churches; for better or for worse, they were exposed to the American press, periodicals and literature; and they had sensed the pulsating effects of living in a strong and wealthy country. What they brought back often filtered down into the poverty-stricken areas of the country, and many of the services

stay in the United States, to accept American citizenship, and to remain ardently loyal to their adopted country. To indicate that they intended to bind their future and that of their children with the United States, large numbers initiated naturalization procedures. Comparisons between the United States and the realistic, not the ideal Poland, led to decisions in favor of the United States; Poland was a poor country in which to establish instantly any new system of life.

> Here were about 28,000,000 people who had for four years been ravished by four separate invasions during this one war, where battles and retreating armies had destroyed and destroyed again. In parts there had been seven invasions and seven destructive retreats. Many hundreds of thousands had died of starvation. The homes of millions had been destroyed and the people in those areas were living in hovels. Their agricultural implements were depleted, their animals had been taken by armies, their crops had been only partly planted and even then only partly harvested. Industry in the cities was dead from lack of raw materials. The people were unemployed and millions were destitute. They had been flooded with rubles and kronen, all of which were now valueless. The railroads were barely functioning. The cities were almost without food; typhus and diseases raged over whole provinces. Rats, lice, famine, pestilence—yet they were determined to build a nation.[2]

In pointing out the advantages of American citizenship, the PNA and PRCU press was almost lyrical. The press had made it clear to its readers that the United States was their permanent home, but only as residents possessing full rights of citizenship could they participate fully in community affairs. The editors also reminded them that they should consider themselves fortunate to be in a country which encouraged its immigrants to become citizens. Thus they should cooperate and not be obdurate.

To facilitate naturalization procedures for the Polish immigrants the PNA and PRCU provided teachers as well as class-

---

they rendered were of a character normally furnished by local governments in America. Even though their names failed to appear on the facades of the libraries, museums, and schools of Poland. their contributions were nevertheless genuine. Their devotion to Poland was more altruistic than that of the upper classes that remained in Poland.

[2] Herbert Hoover, *The Memoirs of Herbert Hoover,* (New York: 1951), p. 356.

rooms.[3] Naturalization papers came to have a meaning and purpose, for the Polonia leaders were convinced that in any demonstration of strength, Polonia would have to demonstrate its voting power. Immigrants who held first citizenship papers, or even better, naturalization papers, won recognition and esteem from Polonia leaders. Immigrants who did not show the intention of applying for first citizenship papers were declared failures, immigrants who possessed them but failed to apply for naturalization papers within a reasonable time were labeled dullards (cymbaly).[4] The constitutional provisions and utterances of many prominent intellectuals in the American-Polish organizations, indicate that the immigrants' first attraction was the United States. In that climate of opinion, not one member protested when, in 1924, the PNA refused full rights to members who were Polish citizens or when the PNA introduced motions that only American citizens could hold superior administrative positions in the organization.[5] In 1931 an effort was made to amend the PNA constitution whereby only American citizens would be qualified to serve as officers in the PNA organization or act as delegates to the PNA conventions.[6]

In time, the nostalgic and sentimental attachment to Poland and the wartime enthusiasm faded gradually into the background. Since the Quota Law of May 26, 1924 had reduced the number of Polish immigrants to 5,982 annually, the 1920's witnessed the arrival of a comparatively small number of immigrants. During

---

[3] To be objective about the situation, it can be stated that naturalization never was discouraged, but before the Armistice many immigrants planned to return to Poland, and then, citizenship papers were not worth the effort. Prior to 1920, Polish housekeepers asked what good would citizenship papers do them around the kitchen stove or the washtub; and during the war years, Polish editors were busy recruiting an army, made up primarily of non-citizen Poles. Encouraging naturalization at that time might have reduced the size of the sources from which that army was being drawn. However, after the war the situation changed. Polish women after 1920 could become not only citizens but also voters. They also had more opportunities to enter the business world.

[4] Stanley R. Pliska, *Polish Independence and the Polish Americans* (unpublished Ph.D. dissertation, Columbia University, 1955), p. 474.

[5] If these amendments failed adoption at the convention, it was only because the proponents were accused of using this scheme to perpetuate their hold on the organization. Exclusion of non-citizens would facilitate such control by the few chosen naturalized ones.

[6] *ZNP Konstytucja, Prawa, Reguly i Przepisy,* (Chicago: 1931). pp. 22, 73,

this decade a generation which had never seen Poland and was unable to think in Polish terms of their parents matured. Now even parents gave more thought to the land of their children than to the land of their birth. Passing years but strengthened their fiber and their love for America, while the ties of memory and affection that bound them to the Old World faded into oblivion. A study conducted among the Poles in Buffalo revealed that only seven per cent of the second generation considered themselves Poles; fifty-seven per cent stated that they were Americans; and thirty-nine per cent styled themselves as Polish-Americans or American Poles.[7] The era of the Polish-American hyphen had passed. Dreams of the past gave way to realities of the present. Group Polonia leaders were now involved in problems affecting the social, cultural, economic, and political progress of the Polish immigrant group and their children in America. The local problems and projects which absorbed their time, efforts, and interests, and the general trend of Americanization decreased their involvement in the affairs of Poland. Furthermore, during this period no event of international importance that took place in Poland could compel Polonia leaders to ignore their own problems and activities and focus their attention there. The Polish language and customs had not disappeared, but ideals had changed. The activities in Poland's behalf from 1919 to 1925 were confined largely to social relief and monetary loans to help stabilize the Polish economy. The reports of the PRCU and PNA conventions held between 1925 and 1935 contain little material bearing directly on Poland. Each "convention" or "sejm" attested to the fact that the strong links that bound Polonia to Poland no longer existed. At most preoccupied with their own local problems and projects in the United States, these organizations mention only their devotion to Poland. For some time the PNA was avowedly Polish, but since Polish patriotism was not a vital matter with the majority of Polish immigrants and their descendants, the PNA gradually became an American-Polish organization which endeavored to enhance the status of

---

[7] Niles Carpenter and Daniel Katz, "The Cultural Adjustment of the Polish Group in the City of Buffalo: an experiment in the technique of Social Investigation," *Social Forces*, (September, 1927), p. 80.

Polonia and its members by stressing the contribution of the Polish immigrants to the progress and prosperity of the United States.

Even the parishes, despite the patriotic and active priests, who were absorbed in expensive renovations and building programs, were becoming indifferent and conspicuously inactive.[8] Many Polonia pastors believed that the American-Polish Community had contributed more than its share to the new Polish State. Many pastors felt that the time had come when Poland should terminate its dependence on the American Polonia. Perhaps Father A. Ignasiak, pastor of a parish in Erie, Pennsylvania, ex-pressed their attitude when he made the following observation.

> It will be difficult to gather funds for Poland, and furthermore the Poles in Europe should begin doing something for their country. They should bring up the youth in such a way that they will appreciate their freedom and independence. There is absolutely no reason why we scattered here over the United States should help save Poland for those who never showed us any consideratoin and even made fun of us.[9]

Instances when post-war Polonia expressed the change in its orientation towards Poland were the Emigration Congresses sum-moned by the National Division (Wydzial Narodowy).[10] Over 1,000 delegates had attended the first Congress held in Detroit in 1918. In the presence of the Polish representatives, Dmowski and Paderewski, the Congress issued a statement of loyalty to the United States; expressed appreciation to France and England for their support of the Polish cause; and concluded with a promise

---

[8] Several other reasons could be advanced which cast light on the gradual disappearance of the patriotic and active priests. Exhaustion and age has overtaken the older Polish priests and the younger generation of American priests of Polish descent do not seem to share the enthusiasm of the older priests in matters of national importance. They also do not show the same interest in the national patriotic ideals which stirred the older Polish clergy. Also since the American Catholic Hierarchy frowns upon this type of activity, many of the younger American priests of Polish descent are further discouraged from participating in this type of activity.

[9] Pliska, op. cit., p. 468.

[10] These Congresses were meetings of delegates of all the existing associations with the exception of those which remained with the KON (National Defense Committee).

[11] Mieczyslaw Haiman, Zjednoczenie Polskie Rzymsko-Katolickie w Ameryce, (Chicago: 1948), p. 356.

to raise ten million dollars for Polish relief. Further withdrawal from Polish political life is indicated by the following objectives adopted by the National Division of the Emigration Congress:

1. In reaffirming the need for a central organization to educate the youth, it gives stipends only to Polish-American students as loans, not to Poles living in Poland or wanting to study here.
2. The National Division should defend Polish interests in America; a very pressing matter is the equality of Polish clergy; the commission recommends the matter be presented to the Vatican delegates in Washington; it feels the schism among Polish Americans is due to lack of proper clerical representatives.
3. Poles should defend their constitutional rights in this country.
4. The National Division should concern itself with the matter of Americanizing Poles who intend to live permanently in America, but not Americanizing which forgets faith and language, and with no forcing of citizenship.
5. The National Division, to the extent of need, should concern itself with actions of assistance and material help to needy in Poland.
6. The National Division is apolitical concerning the internal political life of Poland and will not support any party, but it will consider its duty, in case of danger to the nation and its unity, to give active support to those parties in the fatherland who stand at the defense of national interests and democratic government.

The withdrawal from Polish political affairs was accompanied by an increasing awareness of American society. Previously, Polish emigrants had been orientated only towards Poland, and had ignored American local problems and needs. The conception of the nationalistic Polonia leaders was that no Polish immigrant could possibly be interested in anything but Poland. Family, employment and the entire life of the individual, were secondary to the country of birth. Only work for Poland gave meaning to life. This philosophy, preached in the years before World War I to the Polish immigrants and their descendants, finally led to a revolt. At the third Emigration Congress, the shift of interest of the American Polonia was definitely indicated by the motto: "The Emigrant Group for the Emigrant Group" (Wychodztwo dla Wychodztwa). All who lived in America, alien-born and native-born, were resolved to become Americans. Strongly and openly, the third Congress proclaimed itself concerned only in the American scene. "We for ourselves," was a rather unusual and frank expression of self-interest. It was also in extreme contrast to the previous motto of "Everything for Poland."

The break with the past orientation of the Polish immigrants in America was made public in Warsaw, in 1934, at the second convention of the "International Alliance of Poles from abroad." PNA and PRCU delegates made the following declaration:

> We came to this convention not as Poles from abroad, but as Americans of Polish descent. We are loyal citizens of the United States, but as citizens of the United States we would like to cooperate with you only in the cultural field.[12]

The Polish immigrants love the land of their birth, but they love the land of their adoption more. Their first and last allegiance is to the country in which they have settled and raised their families, and where is centered every interest they and their children have.

> Our first and most important duty is to be good Americans, take an active part in all phases of life here, and take advantage in full of all opportunities and privileges, as are rightfully ours, not as a numerous minority, but as mutual originators and participators in the common good of the American Republic.[13]

However, they did not intend to forsake their heritage of their fathers. Bishop Rhode in his address at the 41st PRCU convention made the following observation.

> If we forget our Polish heritage we become nothing but ships in the wind without anchors.[14]

The 1938 Convention of the "Alliance of Polish Women in America" (Zwiazek Polek w Ameryce) contained the following observation.

> Our working together with Poland results from the realization that, wanting to be worthwhile citizens of the United States and to understand this new world, this new swing to life, to live in this great

---

[12] Haiman, op. cit., p. 427. Dr. Coleman, president of Alliance College, was also among the participants at this convention.

[13] F. Starzynski, "Polish Americans," Polish Medical and Dental Bulletin, (November, 1938), p. 18.

[14] Haiman, op. cit., p. 433.

family of nations, we can not be among them like leaves blown around by the wind, but we must point out our worth of descent and history; we must respect our past, if we want others to respect us.[15]

Perhaps the most clearly formulated view on the value of pre-serving one's heritage is that of Dr. Watson Kirkconnell.

> There is nothing so shallow and sterile as the man who denies his own ancestry. The "100% American or Canadian" is commonly one who has deliberately suppressed an alien origin in order to reap the material benefits of a well-advertised loyalty. There can be little hope of noble spiritual issues from such a prostituted patriotism. Unfor-tunately, it is abetted by the ignorant assumption of many an English-speaking citizen that alien origin is a natural mark of inferiority. He who thinks thus is a mental hooligan—whether he be a lawyer, militia colonel, or bishop of the church. What we sorely need, on the con-trary, is enough common intelligence to recognize both the rich diversity of racial gifts on this earth and the strength which racial roots can contribute to the individual.[16]

This view was dependent on a new and specific interpretation of American society and its culture.[17] Laur Society, a cultural group in Detroit, stated explicitly in its published program the ideal of this new ideology.

> The enrichment of American culture through preservation, cul-tivation, and propagation of Polish heritage in language, song, dance, music, drama and literature, is the ideal of the Laur Society. This ideal is possible because it is based upon the conviction that there are enormous possibilities in ordinary people.[18]

In this third stage of orientation, the Americans of Polish descent emphasize the point that they had become an integral part of the United States. However, they did not intend to disappear

---

[15] Jadwiga Karlowiczowa, *Historia Związku Polek w Ameryce*, (Chicago: 1938), p. 189.

[16] Watson Kirkconnell, *Canadian Overtones*, (Winnipeg: 1935), preface.

[17] According to this new ideology, America is a country composed entirely of sub-cultures and sub-societies. All these societies help form the composite which is America. Each culture contributed something to this composite. The function of the Polish American organizations is twofold: to find the best elements of Polish culture and "national characteristics" and impart these to the younger generation; and also to make the general American society conscious of the Polish contribution to the American composite.

[18] Joseph A. Wytrwal, "Avenue of Pageant Pathway," *Laur Souvenir Pro-gram*, (Detroit: 1951), p. 6.

without a trace as had the Polish immigrants before 1870. On the contrary, grouped around their parishes, schools, local and national organizations, they wanted to make their contributions to the creation of a common American culture; believing that out of the best elements of the diverse cultures in the United States, a superior civilization would be moulded.

In 1908, at the height of the last surge of immigration, Israel Zangwill's *The Melting Pot,* a naive and sentimental play about American immigrants captured the imagination of American theatergoers. The title has been immortalized as the classic description of the immigrant's reception and future in America. "There she lies, the great Melting Pot," exclaimed the hero David Zuexano. "East and West and North and South, the palm and the pine, the pole and equator, the crescent and the cross—how the great Alchemist melts and fuses them with his purging flames!" According to the "Melting Pot" hypothesis, America was the great melting pot into which immigrants of all origins, classes, and kinds were dumped unceremoniously, and from which they were confidently expected to emerge, after a very brief intensive purification, with the dross of foreignism completely purged away, one hundred per cent pure and unadulterated Americans.[19]

In recent years, the "Cultural Pluralists" hypothesis had evolved and found vigorous expression and wide support. A complete antithesis of the "Melting-Pot" hypothesis, it had its origin not among native Americans, but within the immigrant population of the country. Its basic principle is that the immigrants have as much to contribute to American culture as to receive from it; perhaps even more. According to this hypothesis, immigrants are encouraged to believe that they bear an ancient national culture, hoary in tradition, distinguished in achievement, and still creative in purpose and action.

---

[19] Recently Dr. Max Kapustin, an orthodox rabbi and a native of Germany, rejected the "Melting Pot" hypothesis which maintains that the United States has a plurality of cultures woven into a pattern one and indivisible. This concept of Zangwill's according to Dr. Kapustin, comprehends many others instead of the principles embodied in the American documents for two centuries. "These are respect for personality, group personality and faith in progress and improvement of society." " 'Melting Pot' Theory Criticized," *Polish American Historical Association Bulletin,* Dr. Joseph A. Wytrwal, Editor, (February, 1960), p. 2.

"The "Cultural Pluralist" hypothesis ushered in a new spirit and a new attitude on the part of many immigrants toward American culture and the Americanization process. Above all, a deep-rooted conviction developed that the immigrants owe it to themselves, to their children, to their native lands, and perhaps also to the American people and American culture to maintain their old native cultures zealously and aggressively and to resist the influence and encroachments of the American environment.

In accordance with this hypothesis, some Polonia leaders imagine the United States as a symphony orchestra composed of a variety of instruments which play different notes, but all of which blend to give the listener a masterpiece of harmonics and inspiring music. Other Polonia leaders have compared the American culture to a garden filled with beautiful flowers of many varieties, colors, and scents. Among these, the Polish flower has its opportunity to blossom forth in rich and exciting beauty.[20] Whether consciously or not, Polonia leaders were the most persistent exponents of the "Cultural Pluralist" hypothesis. According to this hypothesis, the ethnic groups cherish their own traditions and at the same time refuse to isolate themselves from the larger culture.[21] Jozefa Kudlicka expressed it in the following manner:

> I am not speaking as a Pole. I am speaking as an American. I feel I am 200 per cent American because I am 100 per cent Pole.[22]

The stress on the Polish heritage, however, does not necesarily mean identification with the Polish culture, but rather with the Polish culture as interpreted by Americans of Polish descent.[23]

> The culture of any nation cannot be simply a blend of cultures of other nations. The grafting of the fruit or products of strictly Polish culture on the foreign soil of America may enrich American culture quantitatively for a certain time but not qualitatively. Rather the emerging culture of the United States will be enriched qualitatively

[20] Jozef A. Wytrwal, "Towarzystwo Laur Zespol Tancow i Spiewu w Detroit," *Bialy Orzel*, (July, 1951), pp. 12-14.

[21] The "Cultural Pluralist" hypothesis had been set in motion by Randolph Bourne and Horace Kallen.

[22] Lola Kinel, "Jozefa Kudlicka," *Common Ground*, I (Winter, 1940), p. 35.

[23] There is a marked tendency to make more extensive use of the means and opportunities which the American community itself offers, and not to rely exclusively on the Polish ethnic group.

by the values of the Polish spirit and character in those Americans of Polish extraction who as intelligent and educated individuals will take an active and creative part in American life, contributing to the art, science and literature of this country in the way that Joseph Conrad enriched England and Marie Sklodowska-Curie enriched France.[24]

The cultural pluralist movement made the Americans more conscious of their ethnic heritage, prouder of their characteristic diversities, and more aware of the material their heritage offers for literature, art, folklore, and folkways. Wisconsin, for example, was left with a distinctive *state* culture rather than with a micro-cosm of the national culture. The various Old-World cultures were never completely submerged in Wisconsin as they were elsewhere in the nation. Even today, scattered here and there throughout the state, are little nuggets of Old-World culture: the Swiss in New Glarus, the Norwegians near Mount Horeb, the Poles in Pulaski, the Icelanders of Washington Island, the Amish, the Germans, the French, the Danes, and the Dutch. "We are not a melting pot but a beef stew," stated John Rector Barton, rural sociologist of the University of Wisconsin. "We were all thrown together in the same pot, but the beef remained the same and the carrots remained the same and the peas remained the same."[25] The general characteristics of the dish are made up of the dominant characteristics of its elements: the Poles, the Germans, and the Russians.

The "Melting Pot" hypothesis was the application to Amer-ican life and cultural evolution of the old principle of complete, passive assimilation. The "Cultural Pluralism" hypothesis was the expression of an equally old principle of cultural particularism and unchanging orthodoxy. One is as extreme as the other. One is as mischievous in its practical effects as the other. The "Melt-ing Pot" hypothesis would destroy for America all that the immigrant would give to it. The "Cultural Pluralism" hypothesis would destroy for the immigrant all that America has to give to

---

[24] Thaddeus Slesinski, "Past, Present, Future Report Given to Polish Cultural Clubs," *Dziennik Polski*, (August 7, 1959), p. 2.

[25] William Barry Furlong, "Wisconsin: State of Insurgents," *The New York Times Magazine*, (April 3, 1960), p. 119.

him. Neither the "Melting Pot" hypothesis nor the "Cultural Pluralism" hypothesis is in any way compatible with the principles óf Americanism and the true spirit and aims of American life and national existence.

There is a distinctive American people and a unique evolving American culture. Therefore the underlying premise of the "Cultural Pluralism" hypothesis is not necessarily true. Contiguous racial groups can fuse, both physically and spiritually, to form a new and distinct national and racial group, with its own particular spirit and culture. Historians had established this truth. This culture is slowly, steadily evolving and expanding in a rich variegated pattern is equally obvious. And that to this evolving American culture the immigrants of the last half-century have contributed very much, and have even more to contribute, is equally beyond question.

The correct attitude to assume and the constructive principle to follow is neither total assimilation nor total isolation. Rather it is the historic middle course. It is the process of active versus passive assimilation, of assimilating without being assimilated, of cultural giving in the same proportion as cultural receiving. It means the conscious preservation, in the midst of the American environment, of the basic and permanent values of the old cultures which must be preserved neither to maintain eternally active loyalty and affiliation with the native land, nor for the perpetuation of hyphenated Americans eternally separate from all other Americans. These values must be preserved rather to the end that the maximum of what is true and of eternal value in the old cultures may be conserved and contributed with a minimum of loss to the expanding content of the evolving American culture. The middle course must be a slow, natural, spontaneous and creative process of active assimilation and spiritual growth, and must express the true American spirit of freedom, good will, and progress.

The "Melting Pot" and "Cultural Pluralism" hypotheses, Polish independence, the "Quota Law of 1924," and the changing leisure-time activity pattern of the immigrants and their descendants were bound to create a serious and precarious situation for all the American Polish fraternals. Their membership could no longer be increased by new immigration. The amusement and recreation afforded by the lodge have been supplanted by the auto-mobile, the movie, radio, and television. The two basic needs supplied by the lodge—insurance and fellowship—have gradually become commercialized. And with the decline and disappearance of nationalism among the Polish immigrants in America, the "raison d'etre" of the PNA and PRCU would be seriously under-mined if a new program and new objectives were not to rally the Polish immigrants and their descendants around their banners. Not only were new objectives necessary, but also intensive action to hold the ranks and numbers of those already enrolled. The growth, increase, and continued existence of these organizations dictated only one program to which all the American-Polish na-tional organizations had to subscribe if they wished to survive, namely to help the Polish immigrants and their descendants, socially, culturally, and civically in the American environment.

The objectives of the PNA and PRCU were reduced to three outstanding projects: (1) education: the defense of the Polish language and Polish schools, and promotion of higher learning (2) defense of the rights of the Poles in the United States, with special emphasis on equal representation of the Polish clergy in the ranks of the Catholic Hierarchy in America; (3) American-ization, the question of Polish-American youth, to keep alive in them the consciousness of their Polish heritage.[26]

If the trend of events shortly before the war had won over the Catholic clergy and the PRCU to the orientation of the PNA for an all-out effort for Poland, so now after the war, the Polish clergy and the PRCU could equally claim the distinction of win-ning over, also by force of circumstances and events, the PNA to their own pre-war orientation, namely to give primary attention to the progress of Americans of Polish descent in America. In their activities and efforts, the PNA and PRCU have not lost or cast off all ideals; but with the change of historical events and political conditions, these ideals have been modified.

This change and modification of purpose affected the PNA

---

[26] Stanislaw Osada, *Jak Sie Kszaltowala Polska Dusza Wychodztwa w Ameryce*, (Pittsburgh: 1930), p. 43.

and the PRCU in different ways: for the PRCU, it was simply a matter of reconversion, a return to its pre-war objectives and activities which had been suspended for the duration; for the PNA, it necessitated a complete change in orientation, which was accomplished in an adroit way.

> We have fulfilled our duties toward Poland with dignity. All future efforts in that direction have to a certain degree come to an end. And now it is high time that we think of ourselves. We have much to accomplish.[27]

Acknowledging that the main purpose of the PNA, namely the restoration of Poland's sovereignty, had been achieved, the PNA considered itself released from its obligation to give organized aid to Poland, so that it could give primary attention to the economic, cultural, political, and social advancement of Americans of Polish descent.

Before 1939, the preponderant majority of Americans of Polish descent had almost forgotten their tribal origin and heritage; their very sentimentality about Polish institutions and customs was often no more than skin-deep. Most had never seen Poland and never expected to see it; born in America, they thought of Poland as a foreign country. Nevertheless, the PRCU and PNA made every effort to make them conscious of their Polish descent and heritage. Every "convention" or "sejm" emphasized the importance of sustaining the best of Polish culture in America, especially the rapidly vanishing language.[28] To preserve this language, it was

---

[27] Pliska, op. cit., p. 469. Zwiazek Narodowy Polski, Kalendarz Zwiazkowy, 1936, (Chicago: 1936), p. 46.

[28] No one will deny that a common language adds to solidarity, but in the United States English was rapidly becoming the language among second and third generation Poles, and they were the growing and dominant groups. However, the older American leaders feared the ties with Poland would be severed completely when the second and third generations were unable to express themselves in Polish. Yet of all the cultural influences the language undoubtedly was the most difficult to maintain. For this reason other aspects of the culture had to be emphasized. As demonstrated by Irish and Jewish organizations, unity can be retained without a common foreign language.

These stalwart American Polonia leaders would not hear of any substitutes. In their "Keep the Polish Language" campaign, the directors sent letters not to the national lodges but to the local pastors. The priests supported the move as best they could, but apathy of the younger generations and inadequate funds from the older generations soon ended all endeavors.

decided to organize evening schools in all Polish-American communities.

According to Karol Rozmarek, president of the PNA, no
other orientation was conceivable in the turn of events that the
war brought with the restoration of Poland's freedom.[29]

> The existence and the future of the Polish National Alliance, as
> the name indicates, rests principally on the longest maintenance of
> Polish consciousness in America.[30]

The new orientation of the PNA and PRCU also included
efforts to make secure and build up their membership not from
without but from within, probing as yet untapped sources.[31] By
means of intensive campaigns new members were drawn into
the organizations and the organizations gradually regained their
buoyancy.[32] In these campaigns the numerical strength, financial
resources, and security of the insurance policies were especially
emphasized.

But to increase the adult membership in the organization did
not necessarily imply that the future of these organizations was
made secure. The PNA as well as the PRCU placed special
emphasis on attracting the youth to their respective organizations
and on developing in them a consciousness of their Polish descent.
To prepare the youth for administrative positions in the PRCU,
John Olejniczak, PRCU president, struck a significant note in his
summons for the fortieth convention when he appealed to the
various PRCU groups to select young men and women as delegates who could learn to work for the welfare of the organization
as their fathers had done in the past.[33]

---

[29] The Americanization of the second generation, the barring of immigrant
reenforcements by legislation, decentralization among Polish American national
organizations, and the growing non-intercourse between Poland and the American
Poles were rapidly breaking down what solidarity there had been among the Polish
immigrants in the United States.

[30] Zwiazek Narodowy Polski, *Kalendarz Zwiazkowy, 1943,* (Chicago: 1943),
p. 79.

[31] Zwiazek Narodowy Polski, *Kalendarz Zwiazkowy, 1936,* (Chicago: 1936),
p. 46.

[32] Zwiazek Narodowy Polski, *Urzedowy Protokol Sejmu XXVI, 1931, Scranton,
Pennsylvania,* (Chicago: 1931), p. 119.

[33] J. Olejniczak, "Oredzie na Sejm Zjednoczenia Polskiego," *Polacy Zagranica,*
(February, 1931), p. 227.

The PNA and the PRCU carried insurance for children who thus became members of the organization; later on reaching maturity, they were transferred to the adult group membership. However, the PNA and the PRCU realized the disturbing loss and decline of membership of children and teen-agers. The extent of the decline is indicated by the fact that in the years 1931 and 1932 the PNA had lost 13,054 of its youth, while the PRCU, after reaching the peak in 1930 with 44,182 young people in its organization saw its numbers dwindle to 27,366 in 1935.[34] By December, 1955, the number in the PRCU dropped to 20,865;[35] in 1956 there was a slight gain to 21,522.[36] To hold members in the organization the PNA in 1931 and the PRCU started to form on a large scale Scout Troops.[37] This last undertaking checked the falling away of the teenagers from the PNA ranks.[38] The scout movement in the PNA was modeled on the Polish system; the PRCU followed the American system.[39] In 1935, the PNA numbered 52,106 members; the PRCU listed 7,440 members in 1937.[40]

In 1928 the PRCU and in 1931 the PNA established in their fraternals special Youth Departments which were as important as the Education Departments and the Welfare Departments.[41] By holding membership cards in the PNA or PRCU and by participation in their recreational activities, youth could not help but preserve their consciousness of its Polish origin. The PNA scout movement, which retained the Polish scout uniform, and re-

[34] Zwiazek Narodowy Polski, *Sprawozdanie na Sejm XXVII, Baltimore, Maryland, 1935,* (Chicago: 1935), p. 282. Franciszek Barc, *65 Lat Zjednoczenia Polskiego Rzymsko-Katolickiego w Ameryce,* (Chicago: 1938), p. 85.

[35] "Annual Statement for the year ended December 31, 1955 of the PRCU of America," *Narod Polski,* (April 19, 1956), p. 2.

[36] "Annual Statement for the year ended December 31, 1956 of the PRCU of America," *Narod Polski,* (April 2, 1957), p. 3.

[37] Zwiazek Narodowy Polski, *Urzedowy Protokol Sejmu XXVI, 1931,* Scranton, Pennsylvania, (Chicago: 1931), p. 229. Barc, *op. cit.,* p. 90.

[38] Zwiazek Narodowy Polski, *Sprawozdania na Sejm XXVII Baltimore, Maryland, 1935,* (Chicago: 1935), p. 282.

[39] Zwiazek Narodowy Polski, *Kalendarz Zwiazkowy, 1935,* (Chicago: 1935), pp. 62-64.

[40] Zwiazek Narodowy Polski, *Sprawozdania Na Sejm XXVII Baltimore, Maryland, 1935,* (Chicago: 1935), p. 267. Barc, *op. cit.,* p. 95.

[41] Zwiazek Narodowy Polski, *Sprawozdania Na Sejm XXVII, Baltimore, Maryland, 1935,* (Chicago: 1935), p. 258. Barc, *op. cit.,* pp. 100-103.

quired a knowledge of Polish and of the culture and history of Poland, was regarded as the most influential means of instilling in the youth of Polish descent the Polish national spirit.[42]

The task of instilling Polish consciousness in both young and old members was difficult to promote; in both organizations, the insurance element asserted itself and claimed attention more and more. The national objectives were at times, deliberately relegated to the background by the suspension of societies and members for non-payment of dues and insurance rates. Thousands were lost to the organization during the depression years.[43] The introduction and substitution of new insurance tables and rates to meet the requirements of State laws, caused an additional loss of members. During these changes the ideological element was not even considered.[44] Fraternal insurance organizations were given charters in different States not because of the services rendered to the members, but because they met the standards set by the States for insurance companies.[45] Some States did not permit or else restrict fraternal insurance organizations in their social activities. Thus the national work of the PNA and PRCU was curtailed.[46] Notwithstanding these limitations and difficulties, the PNA and the PRCU during the period under consideration had shown feverish activities centered mostly on increasing their membership and capital. In 1935, the PNA numbered 280,385 members; the PRCU 151,515.[47] The wealth of the PNA for the same year totalled $28,376,426.69; that of the PRCU $15,439,690.73.[48] It is to be noted in the history of the PNA and PRCU that whenever the membership in these organizations decreased, their wealth increased.

---

[42] Zwiazek Narodowy Polski, *Kalendarz Zwiazkowy, 1935,* (Chicago: 1935), p. 64.

[43] Zwiazek Narodowy Polski, *Sprawozdanie na Sejm XXVII, Baltimore, Maryland, 1935,* (Chicago: 1935), p. 228.

[44] Barc, *op. cit.,* p. 84.

[45] Zwiazek Narodowy Polski, *Sprawozdanie na Sejm XXVII, Baltimore, Maryland, 1935,* (Chicago: 1935), p. 59.

[46] Compare Massachusetts State Law regulating fraternal insurance organizations in Zjednoczenie Polskie-Rzymsko Katolickie, *Protokol Urzedowy Sejmu XL, Detroit, Michigan, 1931,* (No imprint), p. 66.

[47] Zwiazek Narodowy Polski, *Sprawozdania na Sejm XXVII, Baltimore, Maryland, 1935,* p. 228. Barc, *op. cit.,* pp. 84-85.

[48] Zwiazek Narodowy Polski, *Sprawozdania na Sejm XXVII, Baltimore, Maryland, 1935,* p. 109. Barc, *op. cit.,* pp. 84-85.

Since the old immigrants lived in a dual culture, and they wished their children to follow the same pattern. Thus Polish parochial schools flourished during the 1920's and at home the Polish language was utilized and some semblance of control was exercised over the young Americans of Polish birth. Late adolescence reversed this Polish indoctrination and the American environment prevailed.

When the second generation reached adulthood "Polonia" became less and less Polish. Chicago's Polish theater passed from the scene during the 1920's. The Polish papers were compelled by circumstances to print more English articles. Under the pressure of the changing times, even the Polish pastors had to deliver sermons in English if they wished the word of God to reach the hearts of the young.

The Polish-Americans had completed another chapter in their history by 1925. Having built a miniature kingdom in a friendly territory, they were now to behold their institutions blending together with the wider society around them. The change was not sudden since the first generation immigrants still numbered over one million in the 1920's; together with a small segment of the second and third generations, they managed to maintain the dual cultural pattern.

The second generation, however, adapting more easily to the new ways, caught up in the new rhythms, accepting the new life goals, and eager to merge with the new environment, left the cultural orbits of the first generation. As a result, they dispersed within the non-Polish neighborhoods of their communities. In this dispersion the third generation lost even more of its Polish consciousness. Polish customs faded, Polish history was forgotten, and the Polish language was becoming unknown. Studies have revealed that whereas thirteen per cent of the second generation spoke English in the homes they established, forty-five per cent of the third generation used it as the only means of communication with their parents.[49] The time was approaching when Polish parochial schools would have to teach Polish as a foreign language.

---

[49] Pliska, *op. cit.*, p. 489.

Occupational mobility had affected also the mooring of Polish American isolationism. In a land where it is possible to mount the ladder of opportunity, second-generation Americans with a better command of English and a better education, were able to rise economically and socially above their immigrant parents.[50] However, the professionals and intellectuals proved to be a failure from the Polonia point of view. Only three per cent of this segment had shown interest or took an active part in the national life of Polonia.[51]

Reports on the doctors and lawyers, members of the professional and intellectual class who grew out of the Polish communities, showed that having climbed the social ladder by means of their education and profession, they showed the greatest inclination to abandon the organizations which had provided them with opportunity and means to better themselves socially, economically, and culturally. Only the Polish clergy, held firm to their Polish individuality and it was due to their leadership that Polish-American communities were established with their unique social forms and institutions; and it was the small Polish businessmen who supplied financial support to these communities.

The Polish clergy had ascertained that many professionals of Polish descent very frequently settled in non-Polish communities, enrolled their children in public or non-Polish Catholic schools and joined non-Polish parishes, either because they did not desire to associate with Polish immigrants or for business reasons, in order to draw clients from other nationalities.[52] In most instances they had unlearned many of the habits acquired in childhood from their lowly-placed parents and had learned most of the values of the upper economic classes within which they had settled. Dedicated entirely to the pursuit of the dollar, with no thought of

---

[50] The large number of professionals and intellectual men and women found at this period of the Polish immigration history is due also to these two factors: (1) the skimping and saving of the parents to provide their children with higher education and profession. This they regarded as the safest and most profitable investment inasmuch as they expected the children to provide them in return with care and a living during their period of decline; (2) the scholarships granted by the large national organizations without interest to students, sons and daughters of their members.

[51] Rev. D. Szopinski, "Od Redakcji," *Przeglad Katolicki,* (January, 1926), p. 229.

[52] "Pogadanka of Ameryce"; *Przeglad Katolicki,* (March, 1928), p. 219.

cooperating with Polish-American communities, not only did they refuse to be included as members of the Polish ethnic community but indifferent to the Polish ethnic group they completely abandoned the Polish ethnic group to its fate. A large number no longer considered themselves Poles; they are merely Americans.[53] Not even old family names were left untouched. Many changed their names either for simplicity or in order to identify themselves with native-born Americans. Father Bolek did not hesitate to call the majority of the Polish-American professionals intellectuals simply business men eager for the greatest possible financial gain from their professions.[54]

F. Lenart, in his address at the Polish National Congress in Detroit in 1925, listed at that time for Chicago: 150 Polish doctors, 150 dentists, 300 lawyers, 70 druggists, 30 engineers and architects. Immediately he raised the question: How many of these professionals contributed their share and took an active part in the social work of the American Polonia? The number was so negligible that he preferred to leave the answer to the professionals and intellectuals.[55]

No one would deny them the privilege or right to accumulate wealth through their profession. No one would hold it against them that they preferred to be considered only Americans. Wider possibilities were open to the professionals through speedy acclimatization. Therefore they lost their pronounced Polish-American characteristics and made more rapid progress in their American surroundings. But, at the same time, these professionals pursued their profession not singly, "on their own," in a typical American community where ethnic differences or characteristics were not known or reduced to a minimum, but maintained their offices, plied their trade, and numbered their clientele among Poles in Polish communities.

The nationally-minded Polish immigrants regarded their pro-

---

[53] Dr. F. Lenart, "Potrzeba Zorganizowania Inteligencji Zawodowej Na Wychodztwie," *Kongres Wychodztwa Polskiego w Ameryce, Odezwy, Referaty, Rezolucje, Uchwaly oraz Urzedowy Protokol,* (Detroit: 1925), p. 46.

[54] Rev. F. Bolek, "Zycie Kulturalne Polakow w Ameryce," *Przeglad Katolicki,* (February, 1927), p. 180. Rev. S. Chichowski, Wspolpraca Inteligencji Swieckiej z Klerem," *Przeglad Katolicki,* (March, 1928), pp. 44-51.

[55] Dr. F. Lenart, *op. cit.,* pp. 49-51.

fessional and intellectual class with reproach and disappointment
for the following reasons: (1) the professionals and intellectuals
had their origin in the Polish community or ethnic group, which
they now openly ignore, (2) only through the efforts and contribution of the Polish communities have these individuals risen
to a higher professional and intellectual level, (3) only in Polish
communities did they at first exercise successfully their trade or
profession. The community therefore made them what they are.
Yet these professionals did not give anything in return to the
community from which they received everything.[56] Even though
in most cases this meant sacrifices, members of the PNA and
PRCU had contributed hard-earned money to success; thus, members of Polonia feel bitter toward their educated class, resent its
attitude, and consider it ungrateful.

The last reproach was justified in the reports on scholarships
furnished by the PNA and the PRCU. From the very beginning,
they had taxed their members a small sum of money each month,
perhaps only a few cents, which in time as the membership had
increased, amounted to a large sum of money for scholarships.
The PNA during the years 1932-1935 had expended $72,981.99
among 673 students attending higher institutions of learning.[57]
The PRCU spent $300,000.00 from 1908 to 1938 for the same
purpose.[58] These monetary sums were loaned out without interest
to students. The scholarships were not in the form of foundations,
of money invested and bringing dividends or interest from which
the organizations drew their funds. They were contributions of
PRCU and PNA members who voluntarily taxed themselves at
the national conventions in order to send promising students to
higher institutions of learning. It is self-evident that with more
members in the organization, and the imposition of greater contributions, the amount of money available for these scholarships
would be greater.

Thousands of American students of Polish descent benefited

[56] "Co Czyni i Jak Intelligencja Polska?" Przeglad Katolicki, (January, 1926),
pp. 111-112.
[57] Zwiazek Narodowy Polski, Sprawozdania na Sejm XXVII, Baltimore, Maryland, 1935, p. 215.
[58] Barc, op. cit., p. 88.

from these contributions, and both organizations were proud of their achievements and the type of educational work they had undertaken. But they could not help feeling resentful at the same time. According to the PRCU official reports, out of $300.000 expended for scholarships, only $21,200 has been refunded. Many who have benefited from these scholarships, evidently did not feel obligated to return the loans they received without interest, although they attained prominence and wealth in their profession.[59]

The PNA fared somewhat better even though its Educational Department also had a tidy sum of money loaned out and not yet returned.[60] Thus it was not surprising that the PNA and PRCU members accused the professionals and intellectuals, to whose higher education they have contributed, of dishonesty, ingratitude, and injustice; for had the loaned sums been refunded in due time, so many other students would have benefitted from these scholarships. The PRCU would have had at its disposal $275,000 for new scholarships. These professionals deprived many deserving and talented students from the opportunities of acquiring a college education.

These revelations caused considerable stir among Polish-American national organizations and intellectual groups. Why was there such a lack of cooperation between the organizations and the profesionals? This had been a topic for discussion for many years. Although the PNA and PRCU eliminated prejudices nursed by many Polish immigrants against higher education; although they had preached and stressed the necessity of a professional and educated class to insure progress and advancement for the Poles in America; although they often financed the education of promising students, today they are left to themselves to cope with the American Polonia's problems. The PNA and especially the PRCU placed the blame on the professionals for having isolated themselves from the Polonia environment and for failing to take over social and cultural work among the Americans of Polish descent. In the opinion of the PNA and PRCU, the professional group

---

[59] Zjednoczenie Polskie Rzymsko-Katolickie w Ameryce, *Sprawozdanie Zarzadu Glownego Na Sejm XL, Detroit, Michigan, 1931,* (No imprint.) pp. 418-420. Barc, *op. cit.,* p. 88.

[60] Lenart, *op. cit.,* p. 43.

had refused to share the leadership which the PNA and PRCU held successfully for the past eighty years.[61]

The professional and intellectual class refused to accept these accusations. They advanced reasons for leaving the compact and economically inferior Polish communities. Dr. Ostafin stated these reasons succintly in his study.

> It is typical of urban Polonia leaders to forsake narrow Polonia loyalties as they advance either in the Catholic hierarchy or the American political system. A judge or a district attorney of Polish extraction must serve the whole community, not just its Polish segment. A Roman Catholic bishop of Polish origin must emphasize his loyalty to Rome and to all the Catholics of his diocese—even though his fame and appointment may be due to the pressure of organized Polonia groups. There is a tragedy in the dissappointments which the exceptional sons of Polonia bring to her at the moment of her victory. Polonia develops and supports her leaders, but as they go up the ladder of American opportunity, she loses them.[62]

The controversy on the American professional and intellectual group of Polish descent had elicited many suggestions and comments. And it had some practical results. The Association of Polish Doctors and Dentists at their November, 1928 Convention held in Cleveland, set forth the following program of action.

---

[61] This feeling seems to persist, for even as late as June 1, 1958, Brother E. Stanislaw, President of La Salle College, made the following observations at the sixty-ninth commencement of the Orchard Lake Schools in Michigan. "Szkoda wielka, ze dorobek nasz w Ameryce, zapoczatkowany zreszta wspaniale, skierowal sie na ksztalcenie lekarzy i adwokatow, a zupelnie pominal intelektualistow i naukowcow. . . . Nie mamy dosc polskich intelektualistow i dlatego dzis odczuwamy wielki brak czegos. Tym czyms jest wlasnie brak zainteresowania naszym wlasnym pochodzeniem, nasza tysiacletnia kultura. A przeciez to jest obowiazkiem Polonii . . ." Stanislaw Krajewski, "W Ameryce Brak Polskich Intelektualistow-Mowil Brat E. Stanislaw, w Orchard Lake," *Dziennik Polski,* (June 3, 1958), p. 3. Alexander Janta, in his observations on Polish culture in America stated: "No conclusions were yet drawn from the striking fact that some Americans of Polish origin, who had achieved prominence in their professions here, often betrayed an embarrassing ignorance and an appalling lack of basic information on Polish matters. In other words, and this is still a valid statement, though they may have a university education, the level of their understanding of things Polish is at best that of a parochial school." Alexander Janta, "Barriers into bridges: Polish Culture in America," *The Polish Review,* II (Spring-Summer, 1957), p. 83.

[62] Peter A. Ostafin, *The Polish Peasant in Transition, A Study of Group Integration as a Function of Symbiosis and Common Definitions* (unpublished Ph.D. dissertation, University of Michigan, 1948), p. 280.

To take active part in social-national life. To contribute professional service, especially to charitable organizations.[63]

During this same period attention was focused by the *Pittsburczanin* on a strange phenomenon which became noticeable in the large Polish organizations. Presidents, delegates, directors during their tenure of office, frequently acknowledged as leaders of the American Poles, heralded as wholeheartedly devoted to their organizations, sacrificing their time, strength, and health for their brother-members, suddenly with removal from office, with the election of new officers, disappeared from the public arena and no longer took an active interest in the Polonia affairs, not even in their PNA or PRCU.

---

[63] "Ad Notam," *Przeglad Katolicki,* (March, 1928)), pp. 198-199.

# CHAPTER ELEVEN

# American Polonia During World War II

The outbreak of hostilities in Central Europe in September, 1939 interrupted the course of American Polonia life. Members of the American Polonia immediately condemned the barbaric German invasion of Poland, which deprived the Polish citizens of life, liberty, and the pursuit of happiness.[1] With the exception of the London Polish government-in-exile, the situation was identical with that of World War I. To obtain support for the Polish cause in the early stages of World War II, the Polish government-in-exile made attempts to revive the extreme Polish nationalism of World War I in the Polish immigrants and their descendants in America. The attempt, made through the *Polish Review,* a periodical published in New York by the Polish political exiles, failed.[2]

In 1941 the Polish and Canadian military authorities opened

---

[1] As early as August 29, 1939, while there was still the fervent hope that the crisis would be averted, the Polish Consulate reported that more than one million dollars was sent to Warsaw in the previous month. *New York Times,* August 29, 1939.

[2] Each issue of the *Polish Review* contained one or more articles either on the fighting which was carried on by the Poles dispersed over the various continents or on the "glorious past" of the Polish nation. Additional articles dealt with the activities of the Polish exiles in London; the activities of the Germans in Poland; and the activities of the Polish underground in Poland. There was very little discussion of the existing Polish political parties. The Russian communists were ignored; and only a few remarks were included on the Polish government in London.

Each issue also contained one article, unusually illustrated, concerning the artistic work of one or more Polish artists, writers, or composers. Artists, writers, or composers of non-Polish background were either ignored or mentioned only in reference to a Polish situation. The *Polish Review* appeals were directed toward a rather highly educated group of Americans of Polish descent. This was a departure from the publications of the earlier years. The adjustment to the higher educational and social economic level of the Americans of Polish descent and the various appeals did not produce the same type of nationalistic activity as had the earlier pre-World War I publications.

a camp at Owen Sound, Ontario for the training of Americans of Polish descent volunteering for service in the Polish army.[3] General Sikorski and other prominent Polish leaders made extensive tours in the United States and delivered numerous speeches urging Polonia residents to participate actively in World War II. The recruitment did not go well.[4] General Sikorski and the Polish government overestimated the probable response of the younger Americans of Polish descent. These young men were willing to fight, but only in the American army.

When General Sikorski made his second trip to America, he accused Polonia of not doing its part in helping Poland. His remarks antagonized Americans of Polish descent and several voices were heard which reflected the change of attitude from that of the situation in World War I. The PNA *Alliance Daily* retorted "We have our own problems."[5] Poor response to the recruitment campaigns, lack of central Polish associations, and concern with American war problems had indicated beyond doubt that Polonia's attention was no longer concentrated on Poland. Furthermore,

---

[3] During World War II, the United States Government permitted American citizens to volunteer for service in Allied armies on condition they do not swear allegiance to the Allied countries. General Sikorski made this arrangement with the United States Government.

[4] During World War I, 28,000 volunteers were recruited in America for the Polish army. When the Franco-Polish recruiting mission came to North America to enlist volunteers for a new Polish army on the side of the Allies, arrangements were made with the Canadian Government to provide a camp at Niagara-on-the-Lake. An account of this camp appeared in MacLean's Magazine: "It was, however, in unorganized music that the spirit of the Pole, that variable mingling of light-heartedness and melancholy, had its most compelling expression. Whenever and wherever Poles congregate, music in some form or other spontaneously broke forth. It was most effective in their unrehearsed mass singing. That which might well have brought "idle tears" to the eyes floated across the Niagara plain on many a soft summer night. Those who heard it will never forget the haunting charm of that song of happy youth shadowed by forebodings of sorrow to come, "Jak Szybko Mijaja Chwile" (How Fast the Moments Fly). Then there was the tripping, care-free march of the victorious legions of Dombrowski: "Jeszcze Polska Nie Zginela" (All is not over with Poland) welling up in their merriest moments, as when in great cheering train-loads they began their long journey to France—and to Poland. But from the suffering of their beloved land came the solemn, stately "Boze Cos Polske" (O God, Protector of Poland), by common consent regarded in Niagara Camp as the National Hymn of Poland. Men and women who have heard all that is most impressive in music have often stood with tear-filled eyes as thousands of Poles poured forth in this sublime hymn the pent-up emotions of a hundred and fifty years of persecution." John Murray Gibbon, *Canadian Mosaic*, (New York: 1939), p. 272.

[5] Dr. Karol Wachtl, *Polonja w Ameryce*, (Philadelphia: 1944), p. 421.

the presence of a legally accepted Polish government in London prevented members of American Polonia from undertaking any political activity or task of speaking for Poland. Not extreme nationalism, but rather a feeling of sympathy for Poland and its people was reflected in the American Polonia. The number and size of contributions and assessments for Polish Relief had been increased. In addition drives to raise funds for ambulances, surgical supplies, food, and clothing for the Polish forces were also organized.[6]

World War II, however, did stimulate Polonia's interest in international affairs and Poland. Polonia was far from "Laodicean" in its support of President Roosevelt's action on behalf of the anti-Axis powers. The Lend-Lease Policy was loudly applauded. The Polish Army Veterans of America adopted on April 3, 1941, a resolution which recommended that President Roosevelt secure the cooperation of Great Britain in developing a program which would render effective aid to Poland. Polonia also approved in November, 1941, President Roosevelt's repeal of the Neutrality Act. Council Six of the Polish Roman Catholic Union voted unanimously to assure President Roosevelt that it favored the repeal.[7] When in mid-August 1941 Winston Churchill and President Roosevelt drew up the Atlantic Charter, Polonia hailed the eight point statement of peace aims as just and equitable and as the "supreme achievement of our international political activity."[8]

When Russia began to "liberate" eastern Poland, and when Russian orientated and dominated Poles initiated procedures to create a new government under the Russian aegis at Lublin, Polonia leaders became alarmed. As a result, under PNA leadership, a "Congress" was held in Buffalo, New York, in May, 1944. Representatives of the American Polish fraternals, professional associations, cultural, educational, religious, and ideological societies

---

[6] Members of the PNA voluntarily submitted to a five cents a month assessment per member for the Polish War Relief Fund which amounted to $786,307.29 according to the PNA treasurer's report in April, 1951. M. Tomaszkiewicz, "Na Fundusz Ratunkowy," Zgoda, (April 15, 1951), p. 2.

[7] United States Congress, Congressional Record, 77th Congress Ist Session, p. A 5036.

[8] F. F. Wassell, Attitudes of the Various Polish-American Organizations Toward American Foreign Policy Affecting Poland: 1939-1945, (unpublished Master's thesis, Columbia, University, 1946), p. 42.

had attended and established the Polish American Congress. The Polish-American Congress was intended to integrate American Polonia into one super federation of fraternal, parish, and community groups to assert the coincidence of American, Polish, and Polonia interests.[9] Charles Rozmarek, PNA president, was elected president of the Polish-American Congress, Joseph L. Kania, PRCU president, became its first treasurer, and Honorata Wolowska, president of the Polish Women's Alliance, was the first secretary. The Polish-American Congress, in its declaration of organization, expressed its American orientation.

> We, the representatives of the united Americans of Polish descent, assembled in convention at Buffalo, New York, mindful of our civic duties, solemnly pledge our unqualified service, love, and affection to our country, the United States, and our active participation in its life. Desiring to give true expression to our sentiments and aims, we call into existence the Polish-American Congress and adopt thereby these by-laws for the government of this association.[10]

This was by far the strongest declaration of participation in American society from any Polish-American Association. Contrasted with the declaration of the "Komitet Obrony Narodowej," it indicated the change of orientation in the American Polonia. Working with and through United States groups and governmental bodies, the Polish American Congress had two objectives: to improve the Polish American status in America and also to fight for Polish independence.

The Polish-American Congress urged the United States government not to recognize the changes brought about in the course of fighting in Europe. The Congress also asserted Poland's claim to the eastern pre-war Polish provinces which was based on the objectives enumerated in the Atlantic Charter solemnly proclaimed and adopted by both Winston Churchill and Franklin Roosevelt. As to the ceding of any territory of Eastern Pre-War Poland, the Polish-American Congress proclaimed:

---

[9] Most of its attention was directed toward influencing the American government. Less contact was made and kept with Poland, and little with the London government. Thus, the Polish American Congress was a group working definitely in and with America.

[10] Polish American Congress, *The Story of the Polish American Congress and Poland's Case in Press Clippings,* I, 1944-1948, (Chicago: 1948), p. 1.

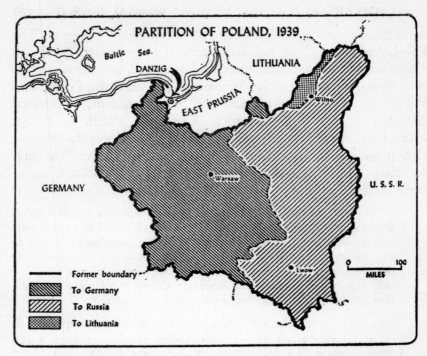

## PARTITION OF POLAND, 1939

Baltic Sea.

DANZIG

LITHUANIA

EAST PRUSSIA

• Wilno

GERMANY

• Warsaw

U. S. S. R.

• Lwow

0      100
MILES

| | |
|---|---|
| —— | Former boundary |
| ▨ | To Germany |
| ▨ | To Russia |
| ▨ | To Lithuania |

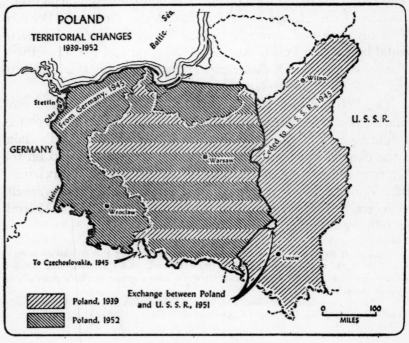

## POLAND

### TERRITORIAL CHANGES
### 1939-1952

Baltic Sea.

Stettin

From Germany, 1945

• Wilno

Oder

GERMANY

Ceded to U. S. S. R. 1945

U. S. S. R.

Neisse

• Warsaw

• Wroclaw

• Lwow

To Czechoslovakia, 1945

Exchange between Poland
and U. S. S. R., 1951

0      100
MILES

| | |
|---|---|
| ▨ | Poland, 1939 |
| ▨ | Poland, 1952 |

Poland . . . our faithful fighting ally . . . must not be shorn of one-half of her territory . . . Any compromise on the fundamental principles of the Atlantic Charter would be a repudiation of the very reasons for which our boys think they are fighting and dying . . . America must have the moral courage to face certain unpleasant realities. Russia's unpredictable change of policy, opposition to legal governments, defiance of the Atlantic Charter, are grave danger signals . . . They all confirm the mounting evidence that Stalin wants to supplant Hitler as Master of Europe.[11]

The Polish-American Congress asserted explicitly in its publications that the decisions reached at the Yalta Conference were contrary to the objectives stated in the Atlantic Charter, contrary to international law, and in violation of the fundamental principles of democracy. Furthermore the Yalta decisions deprived Poland of equal rights and destroyed her independence. The basic principle which had guided the opinion of the Polish-American Congress was strict interpretation of the Atlantic Charter and support of the Polish government-in-exile in London.

Karol Rozmarek made every effort to enlist the support of President Roosevelt for the Polish case. His requests to see the President were turned down on the basis of heavy schedules and the poor health of Roosevelt. Only when Rozmarek requested Mayor Kelly of Chicago to help him in this endeavor, did Roosevelt receive Rozmarek. Rozmarek urged Roosevelt to take a more definite stand on the Polish issue. Roosevelt replied that he could not do so because this might lead to World War II with Russia. Rozmarek did not share this view and pointed out that the President had a powerful weapon in his hand in the form of Lend-Lease. If the President told Stalin firmly that unless Stalin adopted a reasonable attitude towards the Polish Government, Lend Lease would be terminated. This, in Rozmarek's opinion, would be sufficient to convince Stalin that America would not permit a new partition of Poland. Roosevelt, fearing the loss of Polish American votes for his role in the Yalta conference, assured Rozmarek of his friendship for Poland but did

---

[11] C. Rozmarek, "Poland and the Atlantic Charter," *Polish American Congress Bulletin*, (February, 1944), p. 9.

not make any clear promise since he had already participated in a new partition of Poland.[12]

Americans of Polish and non-Polish descent also disapproved the Yalta agreements. Representatives Alvin E. O'Konski, Republican of Wisconsin, called the Polish settlement "a success for Propaganda Minister Joseph Goebbels second only to that of Munich." O 'Konski also stated:

> The selling out of Poland is a stab in the back to freedom and a stab in the back to the freedom-loving country that has done much to crush Nazism.[13]

Jan Ciechanowski, Polish ambassador to the United States during the war, also denounced the Yalta Treaty.

> As I left the House of Representatives I knew that Poland had been "sold down the river," that an illegal act had been committed, by virtue of which, contrary to international law and justice, the sovereignty of the Polish nation, vested in its legal government, had been appropriated by the Big Three Powers without giving the Polish people or their legal representatives the chance of having any say in the matter, without consulting the wishes of the Polish nation, in violation of the principles of the Polish nation, in violation of the principles of self-determination and of all the traditions for which the United States had always stood in the past.[14]

In a confidential message to his Government, Ambassador Ciechanowski reported that on October 8, 1944, during the

---

[12] According to information given to Dr. Edward J. Rozek by Professor W. W. Kulski of Syracuse University, who has done some research on the 1944 pre-election campaign, it appears that several weeks before the election Rozmarek had promised Thomas E. Dewey that the Poles would support him in his candidacy for the United States presidency. Roosevelt had not planned any tour of the country but immediately before the election was persuaded by Democratic leaders to make an appearance in the major cities. When he arrived at Chicago, various delegations were assembled on the railroad platform. Among them, somewhere in the middle, was Rozmarek with his group. When the doors of the Presidential section of the train were opened, Franklin Delano Roosevelt asked to be wheeled to Rozmarek first. Upon approaching him the President stretched forth both hands and said, "I am delighted to see you again, and I hope that you will support me so that I can see that justice is done to Poland." Rozmarek was touched by the Roosevelt gesture and replied, "Yes, Mr. President, we shall stick with you to the end." Dewey was furious that Rozmarek had broken his word. Edward J. Rozek *Allied Wartime Diplomacy A Pattern in Poland,* (New York: 1958) p. 324.

[13] New York Times, (February 14, 1945), p. 11.

[14] Jan Ciechanowski, *Defeat in Victory,* (New York: 1947), p. 360.

Pulaski Parade in New York, he spent three hours with Governor Dewey on the reviewing stand, during which Dewey told him
that Roosevelt's passive policy towards Poland revolted him and
that he, if elected, intended to take a firmer stand against the
Soviet appetites. On October 6 and October 20 Ambassador
Ciechanowski visited former President Herbert Hoover, whom
he had known for eighteen years. Hoover expressed a belief that
at Teheran President Roosevelt undertook an obligation towards Stalin to preserve a passive policy towards the Polish
question and that he had agreed to the Curzon Line with compensation for Poland in the west. According to Hoover, "Poland
was double-crossed" by Stalin and by Roosevelt. "To my question," wrote Ciechanowski, "what Poland should do," Hoover
replied:

> The only thing left for you is to appeal to public opinion. The
> President, the same way as Churchill—for their own political reasons
> and under the pretext not to spoil the relations between the Allies—
> demands from you silence and secrecy. You should, on the contrary
> bring the whole thing before the American and British public opinion.
> American public opinion will not fight for the Polish frontier if it
> will be said that an agreement was reached between you, even if
> under some pressure. But if it came out into the open that Russia is
> striving to control Poland, which she is undoubtedly doing, then you
> will get such indignation and protest from American public opinion
> between the Atlantic and Pacific Oceans that no American Govern-
> ment could conduct an appeasing policy toward the Soviet Union.[14a].

Hoover then added that in view of the danger to the United
States rising out of the pro-Soviet policy of the New Deal, such
a sobering of public opinion would be a great kindness to the
American nation.[14b]

Paul Super made the following comment on the Yalta Agreement in a letter sent to a large list of selected friends:

> Some of those who know my long connection with Poland very
> likely expect something from me regarding the Yalta decisions so far
> as they affect Poland, and regarding Poland itself, where I lived for
> 18 years, and to which land and people I have devoted 23 years of

---

[14a] Rozek, op. cit., p. 300.
[14b] Ibid.

hard work. I say nothing about politics in my Bulletin, as that publication is strictly non-political.

1. As to the Polish section of the Yalta decisions, never in a hundred years have the American people had an act committed in their name of which they have so much reason to be ashamed. As an American of long American ancestry, and proud of his country, I protest against the acceptance of this Polish arrangement by our Senate.

2. For those who know just what is happening in Poland, and who love truth and justice and righteousness and humanity, these are very sad and heavy days indeed, days of pain and sorrow, of tragedy and alarm.

3. I have spent nearly half a century trying to serve the cause of Christ in the world. To me, the fate of Poland today marks the twilight of Christianity in eastern Europe. In all those lands its sun is setting; the night will be very dark; and who knows how far the darkness will extend?

4. An Old Testament prophet stated the situation accurately in Amos 5:15, As though a man escaped from a lion, and a bear met him. This is my comment as one who has spent many years in Christian work and who knows Europe from Liverpool to Stalingrad.[15]

The National Committee of Americans of Polish Descent sent telegrams to all the United States Senators protesting the Yalta decisions affecting Poland. The telegrams urged the upper house to oppose American participation in another partition of Poland. The telegrams called the Polish Provisional Government of National Unity "a set of Soviet puppets."[16] Publishers of 41 Polish language newspapers representing approximately 6,000,000 Americans of Polish descent also petitioned the United States Senate not to ratify the Yalta plan regarding Poland.[17]

The *Catholic World* condemned the Polish settlement. It cited Russia's refusal to permit a Red Cross investigation of the story that the Red Army had murdered 10,000 Polish officers in the Katyn Forest and stated that if America allied herself with Stalin she would have the crimes of Russia on her soul. The publication further stated "to any good American or Englishman Yalta may well seem the most galling incident in history."[18] The *American*

---

15 Paul Super, *Twenty-Five Pears With the Poles,* (Trenton: 1947), p. 343.
16 *New York Times,* (February 15, 1945), p. 6.
17 *New York Times,* (February 19, 1945), p. 10.
18 *Catholic World,* (April, 1945), p. 5.

*Journal of International Law* commented on the Polish decision editorially. It also considered the legality of the transaction. L. H. Woolsey stated that the Polish decision was in some respects exactly contrary to the principles of the Atlantic Charter. He called the partition of Poland an act under "untoward circum stances of military occupation, foreign administration, movement of population, repression of sentiment, redistribution of lands and the like."[19] Herbert Wright reviewed the historic background of the boundary settlement and concluded that there was no basis for the Curzon Line.[20] He stated that the 1939 frontier had been accepted by the Soviet Union in the Treaty of Riga in 1921, and confirmed by the Treaty of Non-Aggression in 1923, and he saw no reason for changing it.

In 1947, a "Justice for Poland" group adopted a resolution calling upon President Truman to denounce the Yalta agreements and demanded the withdrawal of Russian occupation troops from Eastern and Central Europe.[21] Again in 1948, representatives of 21 Polish American groups meeting under the auspices of the Coordinating Committee of American Polish Associations de manded the abrogation of the Yalta Agreement with Russia.[22] In May, 1950, the *Saturday Evening Post* carried an editorial by Ann Su Cardwell calling for the repudiation of the Yalta agreements.

In August, 1951, the *New York Times* in editorial opinion declared:

> History will record that at Yalta the United States repudiated some of its solemn obligations, yielded to Russian imperialism and gave way to appeasement which will be regretted for decades and all for mythical reasons. The true reason for Yalta remains an inscrutable mystery. The result of Yalta remains a triumph for Communist diplomacy.[23]

General Eisenhower also attacked Yalta in his pre-convention speeches. He asserted that he had had no part in the conference

---

[19] L. H. Woolsey, "Poland at Yalta and Dumbarton Oaks," *The American Journal of International Law,* Volume XXXIV, 1945, p. 298.

[20] Herbert Wright, "'Poland and the Crimea Conference," *The American Journal of International Law,* XXXIV, 1945, pp. 305-310.

[21] *New York Times,* (June 9, 1947), p. 6.

[22] *New York Times,* (April 12, 1948), p. 7.

[23] *New York Times,* (August 20, 1951), p. 11.

himself as a military leader. Eisenhower further stated that he knew nothing about the decisions until he read them in the newspaper.[24]

A denunciation of the Yalta agreement was also written into the Republican platform.

> Teheran, Yalta, and Potsdam were the scenes of those tragic blunders with others to follow. . . . The leaders of the Administration in power acted without the knowledge or consent of Congress or of the American people. They traded our overwhelming victory for a new enemy and for new oppressions and new wars which were quick to come. The government of the United States under Republican leadership will repudiate all commitments contained in secret under-standings such as those of Yalta which aid Communist enslavement.[25]

Wassell in his study summarized the significance of the Yalta experience as follows:

> Yalta has become a symbol to those who are apprehensive about world affairs today. To say that most of the talk was mere verbage only misses the real significance of Yalta. The significance lies in the fact that Yalta was a lesson in international politics to the American people. And it is a lesson they will not soon forget.[26]

Headed by Charles Rozmarek, Polish-American Congress dele-gations had met with Presidents Roosevelt, Truman and Eisen-hower to plead the cause of a free and democratic Poland and to oppose the terms of the Yalta agreement. They also had presented the cause for an independent and integral Poland to the United Nations Conference in San Francisco in the fall of 1945. Roz-marek and three other members of the executive board of the Polish-American Congress attended the Paris Conference in 1946 and personally conferred with leaders and diplomats of Democratic countries in Paris and London where they presented the viewpoint of Americans of Polish descent.

Charles Rozmarek, speaking on behalf of the Polish-American Congress, had also testified before Congressional Committees con-sidering legislation to admit displaced persons into this country. His testimony influenced the formulation and passage of the United

---

[24] *New York Times,* (June 15, 1952), p. 50.
[25] *New York Times,* (July 11, 1952), p. 8,
[26] Wassell, *op. cit.,* p. 50,

States Displaced Persons Act of 1948 and the amended Displaced Persons Law of 1950.[27] The Polish-American Congress also worked for the creation of the Congressional Committee for the Investigation of the Katyn Massacre.

Out of the Polish American Congress came the American Committee for the resettlement of Polish displaced persons. The political situation in Poland after World War II, and the presence of large numbers of Polish citizens in western Europe who did not want to return to Poland, had influenced the American government to enact a special bill which would permit a number of displaced persons in western Europe to enter the United States; providing they possessed good health and an assurance of housing and employment. The Polish-American Congress formed in 1948 an "American Committee for the Resettlement of Polish Displaced Persons." Judge Blair F. Gunther was elected chairman of the committee which had the following objectives.

> To assist in the selection of those Displaced Persons of Political ethnic origin from European Displaced Persons Camps, who are eligible for entry into the United States; to provide them with the necessities of life, to assure them their transportation from the port of landing to their designated place of residence in the United States, to secure employment for them and a place to live in full cooperation with the Federal Displaced Persons Commissions and all related governmental, civic, and private agencies and to secure funds to successfully accomplish the above mentioned program.[28]

The program involved the cooperation of the United States Government; the Polish groups in Europe; and individual Americans of Polish descent who had signed assurances involving certain risks, as they had to be responsible for persons whom they undersigned. The whole procedure involved an effort to find employment, housing, and transportation. By the time the Displaced Persons Law had expired on December 31, 1951, the American Committee for the Resettlement of Polish Displaced Persons, had obtained 35,000 assurances.[29]

---

[27] K. Piatkiewicz, "The PNA 5th Ranking Fraternal Organization," Zgoda, (November 1, 1951), p. 2.

[28] Helena Znaniecki Lopata, The Function of Voluntary Association in an Ethnic Community: Polonia (unpublished Ph.D. dissertation, University of Chicago. 1954), p. 112.

[29] Ibid., p. 113.

The Resettlement Committee has also been instrumental in resettling 16,000 Polish displaced persons and ex-Polish soldiers from England to the United States. The Polish Immigration Committee of New York, supported by a monthly remittance from the Polish American Congress, had been successful in bringing to America more than 12,500 Polish displaced persons.[30] The Committee, assisted by Charles Rozmarek, Polish-American Congressmen, and Rt. Rev. Msgr. Felix Burant, President of the Polish Immigration Committee was also instrumental in influencing the passage in Congress of emergency immigration legislation which provided for the admission of 240,000 immigrants above the quotas to relieve the refugee problem in western Europe. A major share of the 240,000 refugees who entered the United States were from Eastern Europe.[31] The need for the Resettlement Committee, even today, is unquestionable according to Kryniewicz:

> The Committee is continuously receiving letters of complaints from Polish deportees by Hitler still in Germany, and recent escapees, asking why they cannot come to America. They have a tremendous feeling that America has unjustly treated their nation and that the United States has not fulfilled its moral obligation to these people. The Committee's job is to explain the situation to them and not excite them to become Anti-American. The Committee has attempted to create a feeling that these Polish people are not forgotten in Europe, by the people in America.[32]

The Committee has received many invitations to attend different national and local conferences concerned with the refugee problem. The executive secretary of the Committee is a member of the greater New York Welfare and Health Council, Committee on Services to New Immigrants.

Increased Americanization did not prevent many Americans of Polish descent from working for Polish Relief and Polish independence during the World War II period. However, the "All

---

[30] Report of President Charles Rozmarek at Third Convention of Polish American Congress, Atlantic City, May 30, 1952.

[31] Rt. Rev. Msgr. Felix Burant, Statement to the sub-committee on Immigration and Naturalization, (Polish Immigration Committee, 1953), pp. 1-4.

[32] Thaddeus Theodore Kryniewicz, The Polish Immigration Committee in the

for Poland" attitude was gone.[33] There was more concern with local problems, and with American general and post-war problems. A majority of the Americans of Polish descent had spent their money during the war for American Defense and War Bonds rather than on Polish Relief. After World War II, the main activity of Polish organizations in the United States involved cooperation with various agencies and governments to bring Polish Displaced Persons into the United States. It is hard to determine which factor, increased Americanization, or unwillingness to take a risk, were responsible for this situation.

A poll organized in the summer of 1943 by a United States government agency to determine the political attitudes of Americans of Polish descent toward Poland brought to light some interesting facts. Nine out of ten Americans of Polish descent believed that they should do everything to help Poland. Forty-one per cent felt that the United States should guarantee a fair territorial settlement for Poland, "even if it meant fighting Russia." One-third declared that they would be satisfied with Poland's pre-war boundaries. The majority were in favor of a "bigger Poland."[34] The poll also revealed that the Americans of Polish descent did not want to forget Poland even when they are fully integrated in the American milieu.

The Polish-American Congress had established also an "Educational and Cultural Commission." Its main contribution had been the support it gave to the Polish Arts and Science Institute (Polski Instytut Naukowy) and the Paderewski Foundation. The 1953 report of this commission enumerated a series of motions which are interesting in light of the previous inter-organizational associations and their aims.[35]

---

United States—A Historical Study of the American Committee for the Relief of Polish Immigrants: 1947-1952, (unpublished Master's thesis, Fordham University, 1953), p. 53.

[33] In June, 1942, under the leadership of Maximilian Wegrzynek, publisher of Nowy Swiat, the National Committee of Americans of Polish Descent (KNAPP) was established. It became well known and active. Its policy was to have the pre-war Poland restored and expanded at the expense of Germany.

[34] Joseph S. Roucek, "Polish Americans," One America, Francis J. Brown and Joseph Slabey Roucek, Editors, (New York: 1946), pp. 140-141.

[35] Zygmunt Dybowski, Protokol 3cej Krajowej Konwencji Kongresu Polonji Amerykanskiej, (Chicago: 1952), pp. 106-108.

1. The Commission urges that each of the thirty state divisions support, exploit, and promote the teachings of the Polish language in the public high schools and in the various colleges and universities, especially courses in the methods of teaching Polish, so as to increase the number of licensed teachers. Since 1948, Polish has been added to the curriculum of six colleges and two high schools.

2. That a "suitable national General Kosciuszko commemoration enterprise be sponsored. . . ." Also it reports that a second portrait has been added to the West Point Academy thanks to the New York Division of the Polish American Congress.

3. The Commission again recommends that the State divisions watch and protest every book, film, or news story that slants, omits, or defaces the true picture of Poland. or the Pole, or the Polish American. During the past four years, five films and fourteen books were protested.

4. That the Board compile, every six months, a list of books about any Polish subject in the English language and send the list to all state divisions and federations so that they can purchase and place them in the main public libraries; suggestions on how to publicize them were also included.

5. The central office of the Polish American Congress have complete microfilm records made of the twelve daily newspapers and donate these microfilm records to the Library of Congress, New York, Boston and Chicago Libraries.

6. All members and organizations be asked to collect and send old records, protocols, letters, clippings and other data relating to the Polish American Congress and Polish American organizations and doings to the libraries and museums of the PRCU and PNA in Chicago. Also that Paderewski data, files, signatures be sent to the Paderewski Foundation and other data, letters to the Kosciuszko Foundation. These will serve as history records for future Americans. World War I and other early day records are no longer available, lost to the present and future generations.

7. That Polish Americans show greater interest and enroll themselves in the five Polish-American colleges: Madonna College, Alliance College, St. John Kanty College, St. Mary's College in Orchard Lake and Don Bosco College in New Jersey. These colleges are urged to increase their advertising in the Polish language press.

8. That individuals who find slanted writings about Poland should communicate the Polish American Congress in Chicago for proper action.

9. That annually ten per-cent of the Polish American Funds be

utilized for educational and cultural purposes. We recommend financial support for the Polish Institute of Arts and Sciences and the Paderewski Foundation before the end of the year 1952. It is fitting that this ten per-cent be dedicated to the above out-lined cause and we recommend it be apportioned to similar in-stitutions like the Polish Singers' Alliance, Szkolki Doksztalcajace and the Polish American Encyclopaedia Commission.

10. Recommend sending a telegram to General Eisenhower then president of Columbia University.

The recommendations indicate a tremendous change of em-phasis and Americanization. The recommendations are written in English and their primary concern seems to be public opinion on Poland and Polish-Americans. Two points are made about protecting the good name of Poland. No mention is made of paro-chial schools and their problems. The recommendations also con-tain the first mention of teacher qualifications, a subject which is very much of the minds of Americans, but which has not been of serious concern to Polonia leaders. No mention is made, how-ever, of the physical maintenance of schools. Throughout the history of Polonia little discussion is made of physical facilities for parochial education or the overcrowding problem. The Polish American Congress does not mention lack of books for Polonia schools. The recommendations presume a high intellectual and educational level of Americans of Polish descent in contrast to earlier associational concerns over just literacy. Most of the work, one assumes from the recommendations of the Polish American Congress and the cultural and educational commission, lies in protests and reviewing articles on American Polonia topics which appear in the daily, monthly, and quarterly publications in the United States and abroad. The actual task, such as the collection of historical data, was performed by member associations, founda-tions, and libraries.

# CHAPTER TWELVE

# Polish-American Cultural Relationships

When Thomas and Znaniecki studied the Polish immigrants in the United States from 1914 to 1919, they were convinced that the first-generation immigrants alone had been capable of preserving Polish cultural patterns; the second generation would drift away from the heritage of their fathers, the third would abandon the Polish way of life, while the fourth would be completely assimilated.[1] However, when Znaniecki returned to the United States in 1939, he was amazed to discover that there has been an alternation, almost cyclical in nature, between the urge toward assimilation with the larger culture and the urge toward a militant assertion of the identity of the subculture. What the son of an immigrant wishes to forget, the grandson wishes to remember. Thus there was a tendency to explore and study the culture of his ethnic descent. As a result, many new varieties of Polish cultural associations had evolved which had not existed before World War I; and this in spite of the fact that nearly all members of these associations were active participants in American culture. The two factors responsible for this situation were the development of an ideology which emphasized the importance of knowledge and appreciation of Polish cultural elements and the increasingly higher educational level of Americans of Polish descent.

Most important of all American Polish cultural organizations involving cultural exchange between Poland and the United States is the Kosciuszko Foundation, founded in 1926. Its origin was the Polish Scholarship Committee which had been formed in 1923.

---

[1] Florian Znaniecki. "The Significance of Cultural Associations in the Modern World," *American Council of Polish Cultural Clubs Convention Bulletin,* (August, 1955), p. 20.

The Committee was dissolved in 1926 and in its place the Kosciuszko Foundation was established as a living memorial to General
Kosciuszko, on the eve of the one-hundred-and-fiftieth anniversary
of his enrollment in the American Revolutionary Army.[2] The
primary objective of the Foundation was to improve cultural
relations between the United States and Poland. The following
are the means through which the objectives of the Foundation are
to be realized.[3]

1. To grant voluntary financial aid to deserving Polish students desiring to study at institutions of higher learning of the United
   States of America; and to deserving American students, desiring
   to study in Poland.

2. To encourage and aid the exchange of professors, scholars, and
   lecturers between Poland and the United States of America.

3. To cultivate closer intellectual and cultural relations between
   Poland and the United States in such ways and by such means
   as may from time to time seem wise, in the judgement of the
   Board of Directors of the Corporation.

From its inception until World War II, the Kosciuszko
Foundation had exchanged between Poland and the United States
170 students, research scholars, industrial apprentices, and professors; 101 Americans studied in Poland and 69 Poles studied in
the United States. The scholarship grants totaled $125,000. Ap-
proximately ten per cent of the total number of Polish professors
and younger instructors of pre-war Poland had received aid from
the foundation.[4] The late professor Eric P. Kelly, who had received a scholarship and spent some time in Krakow, became a
prolific writer about Poland. His story of medieval Krakow, *The
Trumpeter of Krakow,* now in its twentieth printing, won the
Newberry Medal as the most distinguished contribution to American literature for school children in 1928. Eight Chopin Scholarships of $1,000 each were granted from 1952 to 1957 on the

---

[2] Dr. Henry Noble MacCracken, President of Vassar College, Samuel M.
Vauclain, President of Baldwin Locomotive Works, and Dr. Stephen Mizwa, former
president of Alliance College, were among the founders.

[3] Kosciuszko Foundation, *Annual Reports of the Executive Director,* (New
York: 1926), First Report, p. 33.

[4] Stephen P. Mizwa, "Polish-American Cultural Relationships," *Poland,* Bernadotte E. Schmitt, Editor, (Los Angeles: 1945), p. 363.

basis of national competition. The expense of auditions came to $2,020.35 and the total for Chopin Scholarships amounted to $10,020.35. Van Cliburn, pianist at the Juilliard School of Music, was awarded the Chopin Scholarship in 1952-1953. During the same period scholarships were awarded to 150 students and scholars in the total amount of $48,122.

The Kosciuszko Foundation also engaged in a variety of other activities. It was able to take many American Polish students to Poland by offering them not only free tuition but also greatly reduced rates on the Polish-American steamship line. In 1927, it distributed leaflets on General Kosciuszko to schools in large American cities. It also formed a "Peter Yolles Dissertation Fund" to purchase dissertations of students of Polish descent on Polish topics. In 1943, the Foundation organized a Copernican celebration which was held at Carnegie Hall, in New York, on May 24, 1943, under the direction of Dr. Harlow Shapley of Harvard University with the attendance of Albert Einstein and other eminent scholars and numerous representatives of educational institutions.

Through the direct and indirect influence of the Kosciuszko Foundation about twenty books have been published in America in English on Polish topics, and in Poland on American topics. In addition to *Nicholas Copernicus: A Tribute of Nations,* the Foundation had published the extensive *Great Men and Women of Poland* and a biography of *Paderewski* of which it distributed gratis the first five-hundred deluxe editions, sending the first auto-graphed copy to President Roosevelt. Over one hundred mono-graphs and pamphlets, treating some aspect of Poland and the United States, have been printed. Several hundred articles about Poland have been published in American periodicals and vice versa. To mark the millennium of 1,000 years of historical Poland, the Kosciuszko Foundation decided that whatever books the Foundation will publish or sponsor between the present and 1966, will constitute "The Poland Millennium Series of the Kosciuszko Foundation." The first book in this series, published in April, 1955, by Princeton University Press, in cooperation with the Kosciuszko Foundation, was *Czartoryski and European Unity, 1770-1861* by Marian Kukiel. Other books of the series are *A Polish Chapter in Jacksonian America* by Jerzy Lerski and *English-Polish Dictionary* by Dr. Kazimierz Bulas of the Rice Institute in Houston and Francis Whitfield of the University of California at Berkeley.

The Kosciuszko Foundation also serves as a clearinghouse of information pertaining to all phases of Polish-American cultural relations. Since 1925, thousands of inquiries have been answered on Polish culture, art, history, biography, music, folklore, costumes, and customs. The most frequent requests were for information on educational opportunities in Poland or in the United States. Publishers of books and periodicals frequently requested illustrations; American students writing papers or dissertations wrote or visited the Foundation for suggestions and information. To render service in this field, the Kosciuszko Foundation has gradually collected an extensive reference library.

The Kosciuszko Foundation established also an art gallery which contains the most representative collection of Polish masters in America: Matejko, Chelmonski, Brandt, Wierusz, Kowalski, Bacciarelli, Wyczolkowski, Jacek Malczewski, Juljusz and Wojciech Kossak, Jan Styka, Wlodzimierz Tetmajer, Falat, Aleksander Gryglewski, Czachorski, and others. The Kosciuszko Foundation Museum is in the beginning stage; nevertheless, the following items are in the collection: the first and second editions of Copernicus' *De Revolutionibus,* one of Kosciuszko's letters, and steel engravings and prints of Kosciuszko.

During World War II, the Foundation rendered aid to Polish refugee scholars. Twelve professors were brought to America and two hundred professors and younger scholars and Polish intellectuals of non-academic standing scattered in many countries on several continents were given aid. In addition, the Foundation supplied the necessary additional funds to enable eight hundred Polish students in Swiss internment camps to continue their studies in special university camp centers. For this aid to Polish professors and students, the Foundation appropriated and spent $75,000. Since the termination of World War II, the Foundation has participated in the educational reconstruction of Poland by sending books and periodicals in various fields which had been published in the United States since 1939. Through the influence of Dr. Mizwa, the American Mathematical Society, with the help of Professor J. R. Kline of Pennsylvania University, offered seven crates of mathematical publications. By February, 1947, the Kosciuszko Foundation managed to send to Poland sixty crates of books and surgical instruments. The Kosciuszko Foundation also inspired the National Books for Poland Committee under the direction of Professor Shapley of Harvard University. Through its efforts the Copernician Observatory at the University of Torun received a modern telescope from the astronomical observatory of Harvard University. The Kosciuszko Foundation also supplied medical books and journals to re-establish medical school libraries.

With the cessation of hostilities, the Foundation's main channels of activities have been scholarships, informational services, and cultural programs in the Kosciuszko Foundation House. From January 1, 1946, to June 30, 1952, there were 365 activities (meetings, conferences, lectures, concerts, art exhibits) held in the Kosciuszko House. During the following five years 494 activities were held. Since the Foundation moved to its Kosciuszko House, 859 varied activities were held in the new center. Attendance varied from 6 to 250 persons. The total Kosciuszko Foundation investments in 1957, amounted to $346,954.[5]

An important event in the annals of Polish-American relations was the establishment of "The Polish Institute of Arts and Sciences in America." The germ of the organization was the Kosciuszko Association of Polish scholars which was established on December 28, 1940. An academic association, it was composed of members of the former Polish Academy of Sciences and other Polish educational associations who had been able to escape north into Lithuania or south into Rumania during the crucial weeks of the destruction of Poland in 1939. Eventually these scholars made their way to the west. When they arrived in the United States, the Polish American organizations, working with the Polish Legation in Washington, provided funds to allow them to continue their scientific work. To furnish a center for them and keep them from being lost in the American milieu an American branch of the Polish Academy of Arts and Sciences was formed with Dr. Oscar Halecki as chairman.[6] The new institution had two ob-

---

[5] The Kosciuszko Foundation Reports 1952-1957, (New York: 1957), p. 23.
[6] Clarence A. Manning, A History of Slavic Studies in the United States, (Milwaukee: 1957), p. 64.

jectives: to work toward the development of Polish education and to widen knowledge about Poland and Polish culture in the United States in order to improve cultural relations between Poland and the United States.[7] The Kosciuszko Association, consisting of eighty members scattered throughout the United States, during its period of existence, organized two general meetings and several lecture series. It also prepared articles on various branches of knowledge for the Polish American press. Financial support for Polish emigre scholars was also provided. In 1941, members of the association had prepared a plan for a cooperative work "Republic of Poland, 1919-1939" which eventually formed the basis of a book entitled *Poland* published in 1945 by the University of California Press.

Eventually the Kosciuszko Association was reorganized and the "Institute of Polish Arts and Sciences" was formed in 1941. It became the main association not only of Polish educators and scientists, but also of Americans interested in Poland. The Institute is divided into several sections with specific areas of interest: (1) history and political studies, (2) cultural research, (3) legal, social, and economic studies, (4) history of literature and art, (5) theoretical and practical sciences. A special commission considers topics that do not fall under any of the listed areas. Since its establishment the Institute has organized formal sessions, scholarly conferences, and discussion meetings. Through its director and other members, the Institute has participated in many scholarly conventions held in the United States. The Institute has also embarked on a project to catalog all Polonica in American libraries. Also in collaboration with the Kosciuszko Foundation, the Institute has sought to encourage book-collection drives for the Polish libraries and scholars in Poland. At the Institute a library of one thousand volumes was established. In October, 1942, the Institute began to publish a quarterly *Bulletin of the Polish Arts and Sciences in America*. In addition, the Institute has published nine major monographs under the overall title of *Polish Institute*

---

[7] Its officers were, Dr. Oscar Halecki, president; Dr. Bronisiaus Malinowski, vice-president; Dr. Waclaw Lednicki and Dr. Stephen P. Mizwa, directors; and Dr. Irena Piotrowska, secretary and treasurer. Dr. Piotrowska was the only one in the administration who was American-born.

*Series.* In 1956, *The Polish Review,* a quarterly in English dedicated exclusively to Polish topics, including the analysis of events
in contemporary Poland, was inaugurated.[8]

The Joseph Pilsudski Institute of America was formed on
July 4, 1943, by Polish scholars who fled to America during World
War II. It has the following aims:

> Preservation and investigation of documents relating to Poland's
> contemporary history (since 1863); the creation of an archive of
> historical materials; the publication of books and educational period-
> icals; the patronization of scholarly works in these fields; the financing
> of scholarly research in Polish history; the organization of lecture
> series.[9]

Since its establishment it has been able to collect significant
archival and iconographical material as well as a library of about
a thousand volumes in its own specialized field. The Pilsudski
Institute had also published a series of booklets. From its publication fund, it had issued in 1944, a one volume selection of
Joseph Pilsudski writings (Wybor Pism) and two volumes of
*Poland in the British Parliament—1939-1945* by Professor Waclaw Jedrzejewicz. Also, at great expense, the Pilsudski Institute
had restored the documentary film on Pilsudski. An extensive lecture program is also maintained by the Institute.

The Polish-American Historical Association was organized
at Chicago, in 1942, as a part of the Polish Institute of Arts and
Sciences in America. It has the following objectives: to keep
some record of the history of the Polish immigrants and their
descendants; to preserve the record of their achievements; and to
promote study and research in the history and social background
of Americans of Polish descent. Consisting of Americans of Polish
descent, the Association publishes the *Polish-American Studies*

---

[8] Although many Polish scholars living in the Free Western World frequently
enjoy the hospitality of American, British and French journals, the lack of a
periodical devoted only to Polish affairs and published in a world language was pain-
fully felt. To fill this gap and to become a source of objective information and a
rallying point for study of all aspects of the Polish cultural life, past and present
is the purpose of *The Polish Review.* It opens its columns to all Polish scholars
and writers in the Free World and to scholars of all Free Nations writing on Polish
subjects.

[9] Mieczyslaw Haiman, "Polish Scholarship in the United States: 1939-1947,"
*Polish American Studies,* IV (July-December, 1947), p. 70.

which is issued twice yearly and is sent free to all members. The *Polish American Studies,* in addition to scholarly articles and important documents, contains bibliographical lists and reviews of books concerning Americans of Polish descent. It also contains news about the activities of the members of the Association. Members also receive a special mimeographed *PAHA Bulletin* which is issued each month. The Polish American Historical Association holds regular meetings in December in various parts of the country. These meetings in addition to furnishing an opportunity to read and discuss scholarly papers, enable men and women of similar interests to exchange views and ideas. Membership, which is not limited to persons of Polish descent, is secured through election by the Executive Board, upon nomination by a member, or by direct application.

The Institute of Research on Poles in America (Instytut Wiedzy o Polonii Amerykanskiej), established in 1948 at the Polish Seminary in Orchard Lake, Michigan, by Dr. Stefan Wloszczewski, sponsors lecture courses concerning the Polish community in the State of Michigan. Several pamphlets, relating to the history of the Polish immigrants and their descendants, have also been published.

The "Chicago Arts Club," which has been in existence since 1926, has been established by a group of young Americans of Polish descent. It has the following objectives:[10]

1.  To broaden our knowledge, appreciation and enjoyment of serious music, art, and literature.
2.  To render moral and material aid to promising writers, musicians, and artists.
3.  To make Polish music, art, and literature better known in the United States.

According to Clara Grabowski, the following were also enumerated as objectives of the "Chicago Polish Arts Club."[11]

1.  Let us resolve to develop heroes and heroines of our own.
2.  Let us resolve to learn just as much as we possibly can about the

---

[10] Thaddeus Slesinski, "The Development of Cultural Activities in Polish American Communities," *Polish American Studies,* V (July-December, 1948), p. 100.

[11] Helena Znaniecki Lopata, "The Function of Voluntary Association in an Ethnic Community: Polonia," (unpublished Ph.D. Dissertation, University of Chicago, 1954), p. 229.

fundamentals of literature, music and art (to be intelligent as an audience and cultural persons).

3. Let us resolve to acquire the greatest possible skill in that highest of the arts, the art of human relations.

One of the first projects sponsored by the Chicago Polish Arts Club was the lecture by Wladyslaw Benda. Other early activities of this group included: a memorial meeting for Reymont and Zeromski in Fullerton Hall of the Art Institute; Sunday afternoon concert, featuring Ina Bourskaya, at Ravinia Park; art exhibitions; debut recitals; and scholarships. In 1933, the Club arranged for a special exhibit of paintings of Polish and Polish-American artists during the Polish Week of Hospitality at the Century of Progress Exhibition. Literary contests for school children of Polish and non-Polish descent were also sponsored. By 1952, the Chicago Polish Arts Club had three sections devoted to music, plastic arts, and literature. At the regular meetings, visiting professors and musicians were presented with marked frequency. The Chicago Polish Arts Club was the first of its kind in America, but other cities soon started forming similarly directed clubs.[12]

To encourage cooperation among the various cultural organizations which came into being in the American Polonia communities, the American Council of Polish Cultural Clubs was organized. The general reasons for its existence is stated in the preamble of the Constitution.

> To perpetuate and develop the culture created by our forefathers; to encourage higher education and scholarship among people of Polish descent; to foster in Americans of Polish descent a consciousness and pride of their own heritage; to enrich the forming pattern of America's

---

[12] The first link between Americans of Polish descent interested in "culture" was formed by Professor Dybowski of Jagiellon University, who toured the United States, lecturing under the auspices of the Kosciuszko Foundation. The first cooperative effort was the sale in the various Polish communities throughout the United States of the Chicago Polish Arts Club publication *An Anthology of Polish American Poetry* in 1936. When the Chicago Polish Arts Club undertook the publication of the anthology in celebration of its tenth anniversary, news releases were mailed to all Polish language newspapers in the United States in an effort to secure material for the volume. It was due to the cooperation of these newspapers that the Chicago Polish Arts Club was successful in its undertaking. A thousand copies of this anthology, edited by Dr. Thaddeus Mitana, were sold during the next few years.

great culture by weaving into it the best from the Polish sources of inspiration, and of accomplishment, we associated ourselves together.[13]

The following are the means by which the objectives of the Council are to be attained.[14]

1. Maintaining a clearing house for the interchange of information and ideas which pertain to the promotion of Polish culture in America and should be translated into initiative and action on a national scale.

2. Proposing program material and suggesting plans for cultural activities which would stimulate interest and provide member Clubs with worthwhile guidance for the fulfillment of their objectives.

3. Encouraging the formation of new cultural clubs, particularly in such communities where they do not exist.

4. Cooperating with other Polish or Polish American organizations or activities of a similar purpose in order to maintain close contacts with the creative forces of contemporary Polish cultural life.

The annual conventions of the Council provide affiliated clubs and the general American public with answers as to the direction of the Council's development. The conventions also serve as channels for the exchange of ideas and experiences. They also furnish the opportunity to evaluate the progress of the Council and the associated clubs. The following projects were initiated by the Council. The Norwid Literary Contest was organized for the years 1952 and 1953. The Marcella Sembrich Kochanski Voice Contest was organized in 1954. Postcards with reproductions of photographs of Joseph Karsh of the Polish royal treasures stored in Canada were also prepared. The Mickiewicz Centennial was translated into action on a national scale. In addition, the Council inaugurated a quarterly bulletin for the benefit of individuals and affiliated clubs.

The development of the cultural clubs is one of the many proofs that the old cultural separation between peoples of different nationalities is nearly gone. For the most significant trend in modern times is cultural cooperation between nationalities, as

---

[13] "About the A.C.P.C.C.," *American Council of Polish Cultural Clubs Convention Bulletin*, (August, 1955), p. 16. Slesinski, *op. cit.*, p. 103.

[14] *Ibid.*, "About the A.C.P.C.C.," p. 16.

the late Florian Znaniecki stated in his most book, *Modern Nationalities*. Americans now realize that every nationality can contribute something to the creative growth of other nationalities, by what we call "cross-fertilization of cultures."

The children and especially the grandchildren of the Polish immigrants are revealing a lively interest in the history, literature and art of the land of their forefathers. Pride in these achivements has not weakened their American patriotism; but they are resolved that in the national culture of the future, the warmth and refinement of Polish civilization shall have its place alongside the solid and historic institutions contributed by the colonists and immigrants from Western Europe. Furthermore, descendants of the Polish immigrants believe that the peoples of many nationalities, functioning together, can develop creatively a world culture; and that this is the only effective way of unifying all mankind. Such cooperation requires that nationals of different cultures should understand and appreciate one another. As the first step in this direction, every individual should participate in at least two cultures and fully appreciate both; and that is what members of the Polish cultural associations in the United States are doing. As participants in American culture, Americans of Polish descent are aware that America is no longer a closed "melting pot," but the main cultural center of the modern world. American culture is of primary importance to mankind, for the American nationality is trying to promote cultural development and cooperation of all nationalities.

# CHAPTER THIRTEEN

# Jamestown Revisited

Nor for the past alone — for meaning to the future.
— *Walt Whitman*

When in 1958, Americans of Polish descent, along with their compatriots, celebrated the 350th anniversary of the landing of the Polish immigrants in Jamestown, Virginia, they could look back on the long journey that had come to an end. Individuals might remain unconscious of the epic quality of the march, but as a group, Americans of Polish descent understood its true significance. It was a time to look back along the road their forefathers and fathers had traveled, to try to get into proper perspective many things that had been out of focus while they had actually been experiencing them.

The first fact they now understood in the perspective of their history was that physical separation inevitably brings on cultural separation. The Poles in America under sixty years of age are either American-born or so firmly rooted in American soil that it would provoke a smile were one to suggest a return to Poland. Fifty years ago, the Polish orator was wont to disclaim: "We love Poland as our mother and America as our bride." Today it would be truer to say: "We love America as our mother and Poland as our grandmother of whom for a fast-growing number of us there will soon be little left but fond tradition." For reasons of mobility the Polish language lost out heavily among Americans of Polish descent. In America, there never was any undue stress upon the Polish immigrants to give up their language or their institutions. Yet these experienced nationalists, these descendants of Poles who had been able to retain the Polish language in the face of all kind of punishments, generation after generation, could not sail against the prevailing wind. They lost out in America in the course of two generations.

As an example, in Detroit, with its estimated 200,000 to 350,000 first, second, and third generation residents of Polish descent, the Polish school, has all but disappeared from the scene.

> A few years ago it was possible to study the Polish language in virtually every one of the area's forty Polish parochial schools. Now language instruction is limited to Wayne State University, the Polish SS Cyril and Methodius Seminary at Orchard Lake and small classes conducted by the organizations. This is one of the many indications of how the younger generation of Polish-Americans is being absorbed into the general life of the city.[1]

There was a long period of years when Sister Hedwig taught all first grade subjects in two languages, English and Polish, at St. Francis School in Detroit.

> Every parent in the old days wanted his children to know Polish thoroughly. That is not true today, but except for a few children in the class. I still teach them a smattering, just enough to be able to read and write simple Polish words.[2]

In varying degrees throughout the country, English is supplanting Polish in the churches. The change is more rapid in districts where the Polish group constitutes but a small minority of the entire community; but even in the large cities the transition is gaining momentum. Where there are four or more Masses on Sunday, two of these are as a rule English Masses, and attendance at these is growing as it declines at the others. The younger clergy, trained in diocesan seminaries, are becoming increasingly less proficient in the use of Polish.

Gone in many parishes are the Paschal Communion Cards, the blessing of food on Holy Saturday, and the breaking of the wafers (oplatki) at the Christmas Evening meal. The Polish greetings and partings graced with expressions redolent of the Faith are gone. The blessing of the flowers on "Lady Day"; the uniquely Polish and pathetically lovely "Bitter Lamentations" (Gorzkie Zale) of the Lenten devotions; and the chanting of the "small

---

[1] James K. Anderson, "A Polonia in Transition," *Detroit News*, (September 15, 1957), p. 8a.

[2] Harold Schachern, "Pupils Wiser, Less Ruly—Nun Compares Today's Crop of Children," *Detroit News*, (June 13, 1959), p. 14.

hours" of Our Lady's Office before the Sunday High Mass are also gone.[3]

At one time in the Detroit area, seven daily radio programs were being broadcast in the Polish language over four stations. Today only WJLB broadcasts in Polish. From 1910 to 1929, there were in Detroit five theaters where Polish plays were given exclusively. Today, the Polish theater is being kept alive by only one organization, the "Polish Artists Guild," which was organized in 1932.[4] At the beginning of the twentieth century, there were several all-Polish newspapers published in Detroit. Today there is one, the *Dziennik Polski*.[5] John Najduch, the assistant publisher, explains that the newspaper is turning to English more and more to meet the demands of younger Americans of Polish descent.[6]

The Polish immigrants who would have given their lives for the maintenance of the Polish language, could they only have stood at the end of the long road, might they have felt not merely reconciled but triumphant that things had turned out against their wishes. For an America dominated by a single nationality or race would have been culturally a poor country; that composite of cultures that has become the real America is richer, more exciting and more alive, since each dilutes and enriches the other. At the end of the long road, it is possible to see that the most remarkable fact about America is its diversity. It is from

---

[3] "The Polish-American parish is not a mere copy of the old Polish parish, but a combination, of parish, village, and commune," concluded George W. Hill associate professor of Rural Sociology at the University of Wisconsin, after a four year survey in which census reports were studied and hundreds of persons interviewed. "Customs change but the things which do not change are the ideals and values with which we look at life. They stay with us. Scratch the surface, generations later, and you will find these values." Fred L. Homes, *Old World Wisconsin: Around Europe in the Badger State* (Eau Claire: 1944), p. 352.

[4] "Polish Theater in Detroit," *Polish American Historical Association Bulletin*, Dr. Joseph A. Wytrwal, Editor, Bulletin No. 176, (March, 1959), p. 2.

[5] The process of gradual Americanization can be traced, almost measured, by the lengthening columns of American news and, in particular, by the increasing space devoted to the activities and interests of Americans of Polish descent in the United States, while Poland and Polish affairs are becoming more distant, though never wholly forgotten. *Dziennik Polski* usually runs ten pages with two to four pages published in English. Its circulation is 48,000, down from a high in the 1930s of 55,000.

[6] *Everybody's Daily*, one of the largest Polish newspapers in the United States was declared bankrupt on August 10, 1957. In recent years, it had a circulation of about 30,000.

this diversity that the greatness of the nation probably springs, and it is the triumph of America that in the midst of such diver- sity there is also unity; the mingling of traditions, temperaments, and cultures makes for health and rejuvenation.

A retrospective view helped the Polish immigrants and their descendants to gain perspective on their history and achievements for a true appreciation of things as they are. The immigrants realized that they were different from what they had been in the area of ethnic origin—each touched and changed by the alchemy of the American environment and by living and mingling with Americans of other backgrounds. The descendants of the Polish immigrants realized that the Polish immigrants had achieved a kind of biological immortality by passing into something rich and strange—Americans. And their heritage and way of life has been perpetuated in the following institutions and organizations: SS Cyril & Methodius Seminary, St. Mary's College and High School at Orchard Lake; Alliance College at Cambridge Springs, Pennsylvania; Archives and Museum of the Polish Roman Cath- olic Union; the Polish Institute of Arts and Sciences in New York; the Kosciuszko Foundation in New York; the Joseph Pilsudski Institute of America in New York; the American Coun- cil of Polish Clubs; and the American Polish national organiza- tions. The over-all outlook of these organizations and institutions is good. Their membership is thoroughly American. They have shed the chauvinism of many of their members of the years gone by. They do not seek to preserve the spirit of clanishness or the mere preservation of the Polish language but to advance the in- terests of the American Polonia materially, culturally, and spiritually.

These institutions and organizations serve a new age and are serviced by a new race of men. In perspective, what had seemed like parsimony, turned out to be something not far removed from common-sense. Where were now any of the glorious "causes" to which the immigrants had stubbornly refused to contribute? These movements had gone with the wind, but carefully conserved Polish-American funds had not gone with them. And in perspec- tive it appeared that there had been no narrow parsimony in support of churches, seminaries, schools, libraries, social centers, and cultural and national organizations.

The time had also come to place their group not against a temporary drop-curtain of parochial history but against the back-ground of America and its history themselves. Seen in that per-spective, their culture filled them with a quiet pride of national descent and with a sober sense of group achievement. They read with satisfaction Father Bolek's *Who's Who in Polish America* but they had advanced too far beyond the parochial attitude to take it with portentious seriousness. They honored those of their national descent, but they remembered that such a word as "great" is relative, and that the time has come to measure their own "great" men by the yardstick not of "Polonia" background but by the measure of the American background.

The very tendency to divisiveness that had strongly charac-terized the Polish organizations was not without its uses. To Bishop Rhode, Father Barzynski, Agaton Giller, Father Gieryk and other Polonia leaders, the Polish immigrant's centrifugal spirit seemed disastrous, but those leaders were too near to the history of their own day, and to the personal traits of the Polish immi-grants to see the picture wholly in focus. A spirit of unity is comfortable for the leaders of any group, and it is always held up as the greatest good. But destiny reveals itself in many forms, and the individualism that divided the Polish group is now begin-ning to appear as far more precious than any surface unity that might have been achieved. For an American culture that almost worships uniformity, Polish individualism served as a wholesome corrective. Looking back over three-hundred and fifty years, Amer-icans of Polish descent thought they saw in the very fanaticism of the individualism of their ancestors something that they, and America, needed.

They could understand at last that what had once seemed like religious fanaticism had in reality been destiny's means of steeling the hearts of the Polish immigrants to stay with the march of their national culture along its second stage. Pushed out as they had been like fledglings from the home nest, their flutterings would have ended in disaster and despair if they had not been sustained by their faith. They did not desert their faith, once so unpopular in America, in order to gain acceptance. At the turn of the century, the Polish clergy in America were still very much a group apart. On the part of some of the older generation was earnest agitation for a separate hierarchy or at least representation in the hierarchy. Their work precluded greater interest in the problems of the Church in America. The situation has changed vastly since 1910. The spirit of discontent has departed. Schism and heresy are dormant if not dead. American clergy of Polish descent are alert to what is transpiring. The young clerical generation is taking its rightful place in ecclesiastical affairs. The list of Polish papal chamberlains, domestic prelates, and prothonotaries is a long one. They are represented in diocesan councils, they act as rural deans in chanceries and in matrimonial courts. Their numbers in all these positions is constantly increasing. Ten Americans of Polish descent have been elevated to the episcopacy.

Also the Polish immigrants and their descendants did not forget partitioned Poland, for though they believed that freedom began with the American coastline, they saw no reason why it should also end there. They voted in the United States with an eye to the effect on the freedom of Poland, and in so doing they broadened the scope of American political thinking.

Perhaps in learning more of the long journey, these descendants of Polish immigrants realized that there was not a break in continuity between immigrants and their children, resulting in a lack of parental control and guidance. In general, the pioneers taught their children that while their nationality had certain characteristics which were a priceless heritage, the Polish nation did not by any means have a monopoly on culture and achievements. Consequently, there was much to be learned from others.

If the present showed a little of the old Polish sparkle, the past still cast a bright reflection. The Americans of Polish descent could look back upon the progress of their group in the new adopted home. Since 1870, when they had begun to arrive in large numbers, Polish immigrants were true subscribers of cultural pluralism. Maybe they could not define it, but they practiced it. They never denounced the American way of life. They hurried to become a part of that life, but at the same time they endeavored to retain as much of the old culture as seemed practical in their new environment. It is true, their press preserved the Polish language but at the same time its timely advice and explanation eased the transition into the American culture. Because they had organized themselves into some 800 local communities, the Polish immigrants and their descendants were able to give the Polish tradition a continuity which would otherwise have been shattered at the foot of the Statue of Liberty and in the labyrinthine halls of Castle Garden. "Be American but do not lose the Polish touch. Be two men of two cultures rather than one man." That could well have been the motto and the theme of Polish-American history. Their quest for identity was a voyage that had to survive shoals and rapids. They had two cultures rather than only one with which somehow they had to make their peace—identifying themselves with segments of both as they grew older, sifting both of them through their fears and insecurities, their hopes and strengths, accepting and rejecting, and out of this process having to discover who they were. Many who managed to come through this experience were perhaps the sturdier personality for having been through it, and carried with them a richer freightage of family and cultural memories.

It is true that the Polish immigrants huddled together in cities and created an aspect of clanishness. This was so because only among their own could they maintain cultural identity. Their organized communities served as a bridge spanning the gap between the countries and cultures. The organized "Polonias" provided a cushion which absorbed the shocks of acculturation; they also served as bases from which Polish immigrants and their descendants could penetrate deeper and deeper into the American culture. This was true especially of the second and third generations. Though the Polish immigrants had many common characteristics, they cannot be labeled with a collective name. Like other contemporary immigrant minorities, they found themselves subdivided into numerous social classes, disinterested groups, and conflicting factions. This was true for the foreign-born generation but it was truer for the others that were the native-born. By the time the second generation was old enough to assume responsibility in the many societies, interest groups definitely supplanted ethnic divisions and cultural pluralism found itself rapidly sur-

rendering to the dominant culture. However, the minor distur-
bances that rumbled through Polish communities during the war
years never rose to the surface. Consequently, the Polish American
propagandists were easily able to focus everybody's attention to
the Polish bloc, and externally it appeared firm and solid.

All this the Americans of Polish descent could see after their
three-hundred-fifty year march across the continent. And they
could see other things in better perspective. America had grown
at a rapid pace during this time. Covered wagons had rolled on
the deep rutted roads, ever straining westward and northward.
Acres of forest had made way for grain fields. Sawmills buzzed
and large frame buildings took the place of the lowly log cabin.
They looked to the future of their country and were content.

Although they looked back with legitimate pride on their
early beginnings in America, the anniversary served as a kind
of shadow line between what they and their fathers had been as
Poles and what they themselves now were as Americans. The
Jamestown Anniversary did mark a solid historical milestone.

# BIBLIOGRAPHY

Adamic, Louis. "Americans From Poland," *Woman's Day,* (August, 1944).

Anderson, James K. "A Polonia in Transition," *Detroit News,* (September 15, 1957).

Andrea, Sister M. "The Societies of St. Stanislaus Kostka Parish, Chicago," *Polish American Studies,* IX (January-June, 1952).

Andrews, Theodore. *The Polish National Church in America and Poland.* London: Willian Clowes & Sons Limited, 1953.

Archacki, Henry. "The Search for Clues in Sir Walter Raleigh's 'Lost Colonies,' " *Polish American Journal,* (January 31, 1959).

Ayerst, David George Ogilvy, M.A. *Europe in the Nineteenth Century.* Cambridge: Cambridge University Press, 1949.

Balch, Emily Greene. *Our Slavic Fellow Citizens.* New York: Charities Publication Committee. 1910.

Barc, Franciszek. *65 Lat Zjednoczenia Polsko Rzymsko-Katolickiego w Ameryce.* Chicago: Polish Roman Catholic Union, 1938.

Barc, Frank S. "The Polish National Alliance," *The Polish Review,* (April 11, 1946).

Baretski, Charles Allan. *The Polish Pantheon.* Newark: The Polish University Club of New Jersey, 1958.

Bercovici, Konrad. *On New Shores.* New York: D. Appleton Century Company, Inc., 1925.

Bern, Sister M. Accursia, O.S.F. "Polish Miners in Luzerne County, Pennsylvania," *Polish American Studies,* III (January-June, 1946).

Bierstedt, Robert. *The Social Order.* New York: McGraw Hill Book Company, Inc., 1957.

Bismarck, Otto von. *Die Gesammelten Werke.* Berlin: Otto Stolberg & Company, 1924-1932.

Bochenski, Rev. Antoine M., S.T.L., O.M.C. "Our Youth and Its Polish-American Heritage," *Polish American Studies,* I (January-December, 1944).

Bodger, John Charles Jr. *The Immigrant Press and the Union Army.* Unpublished Ph.D. dissertation, Columbia University, 1951.

Bojko, Jakob. *Dwie Dusze.* Toledo: A. A. Paryski, 1911.

Bolek, Rev. S. "Zycie Kulturalne Polakow w Ameryce," *Przeglad Katolicki,* II (1927).

Brandes, George. *Poland A Study of the Land, People and Literature.* London: William Hainemann, 1904.

Brown, Francis J. and Roucek, Joseph Slabey. *Our Racial and National Minorities.* New York: Prentice-Hall, 1937.

Brown, F. J. and Roucek, J. S. *One America.* New York: Prentice-Hall Inc., 1945.

Bruce, Maurice. *The Shaping of the Modern World.* New York: Random House, 1958.

Burant, Rt. Rev. Msgr. *Statement to the Subcommittee on Immigration and Naturalization.* New York: Polish Immigration Committee, 1953.

Busyn, Helen. "Peter Kiolbassa—Maker of Polish America," *Polish American Studies,* VIII (July-December, 1951).

Callaghan J. Dorsey. "Rhythm Beats in American Polish Hearts," *Detroit Free Press,* (September 23, 1959).

Caro, Dr. Leopold. *Emigracya i Polityka Emigracyjna ze Szczegolnem Uwzglednieniem stosunkow.* Poznan: Nakladem i Czcionkami Drukarni i Ksiegarni Sw. Wojciecha, 1914.

Carpenter, Niles and Katz Daniel. "The Cultural Adjustment of the Polish Group in the City of Buffalo: An experiment in the technique of social investigation," *Social Forces,* (September, 1927).

Carpenter, Niles and Katz, Daniel. "A Study of Acculturation in the Polish Group of Buffalo, 1926-1928," *University of Buffalo Studies,* VII (1928-1929).

Chandler, Alvin Duke. "The Poles at Jamestown," *The Polish Review,* II (Autumn, 1957).

Cichowski, Rev. S. "Wspolpraca Inteligencji Swieckiej z Klerem," *Przeglad Katolicki,* III (1928).

Ciechanowski, Jan. *Defeat in Victory.* New York: Doubleday & Company, Inc., 1947.

Coleman, Arthur Prudden. "Alliance College American Cradle of Polish Heritage," *Zgoda* (August 15, 1957).

Colton, Ray C. *The Civil War in the Western Territories.* Norman: University of Oklahoma Press, 1959.

Commons, John R. *Races and Immigrants in America.* New York: Fleming H. Revell Company, 1907.

Coulter, Charles. *Poles of Cleveland.* Cleveland: Americanization Committee, 1919.

Courage, Ray. "Poles Build Freedom Way to Detroit," *Detroit Free Press,* (September 16, 1957).

Curie, Eve. *Madame Curie.* Garden City: Garden City Publishing Company, Inc., 1943.

Curti, Merle. *The Making of an American Community.* Stanford: Stanford University Press, 1959.

Dabrowski, Sister Mary Adele. *A History and Survey of the Polish Community in Brooklyn.* Unpublished Master's thesis. Fordham University, 1946.

Daniels, John. *America via the Neighborhood.* New York: Harper and Brothers Publishers, 1920.

Dann, Marshall. "Poles Dot Top Ranks of Athletes," *Detroit Free Press,* (September 22, 1957).

Davis, Philip (ed.). *Immigration and Americanization.* Chicago: Ginn & Company, 1920.

Dolde, Carl. "Ein Freies Polen," *Constitution,* No. 21, (April 14, 1948).

Doman, Sister Mary Tullia, C.S.S.F. "Mother Mary Angela Truszkowska," *Polish American Studies,* X (July-December, 1953).

Drachsler, Julius. *Democracy and Assimilation.* New York: The Macmillan Company, 1920.

Duker, Abraham Gordon. *The Polish "Great Emigration" and the Jews.* Unpublished Ph.D. dissertation, Columbia University, 1956.

Dusza, Dr. M. "Historia Kolegium Zwiazkowego," *Pamietnik 75ta Rocznica Istnienia ZNP.* Chicago: Alliance Press, 1955.

Dworaczyk, Rev. Edward J. *Church Records of Panna Maria, Texas.* Chicago: Archives and Museum of the Polish Roman Catholic Union, 1944.

Dyboski, Roman. *Poland in World Civilization.* Ludwig Krzyzanowski (Ed.). New York: J. M. Barrett Corporation, 1950.

Dybowski, Zygmunt. *Protokol 3cej Krajowej Konwecji Kongressu Polonji Amerykanskiej.* Chicago: Alliance Printers, 1952.

Evans, A. W. W. *Memoir of Thaddeus Kosciuszko, Poland's Hero and Patriot.* New York: No Imprint, 1863.

Eversley, Lord. *The Partitions of Poland.* London: T. Fisher Unwin, Ltd., 1915.

Fairchild, Henry Pratt. *Immigration.* New York: The Macmillan Company, 1925.

Falkowski, Edward. "Polonia to America," *Common Ground.* III (Autumn, 1942).

Ferrell, Robert H. "The United States and East Central Europe before 1941," *The Fate of East Central Europe.* Notre Dame: University of Notre Dame Press, 1956.

Fisher. Harold H. *America and the New Poland.* New York: The Macmillan Company, 1928.

Flexner, Eleanor. *Century of Progress.* Cambridge: Harvard University Press. 1959.

Fox, Paul. *The Poles in America.* New York: George D. Doran Company, 1922.

Francis, E. K. ,'The Nature of Ethnic Groups," *The American Journal of Sociology,* (March. 1947).

Furdyna, Jacek K. "Scolvus' Discovery of Labrador," *Polish American Studies.* (July-December, 1953).

Furlong, William Barry. "Wisconsin: State of Insurgents," *The New York Times Magazine,* (April 3, 1960).

Gabriel, Ralph Henry. *The Course of American Democratic Thought*. New York: The Ronald Press Company, 1956.

Gadon, Lubomir. *Emigracya Polska—Pierwsze Lata Po Upadku Powstania Listopadowego*. Krakow: Spolka Wydawnicza Polska, 1902.

Galford, Justin B. *The Foreign Born and Urban Growth in the Great Lakes, 18550-1950: A Study of Chicago, Cleveland, Detroit, and Milwaukee*. Unpublished Ph.D. dissertation, New York University, 1957.

Gardner, Monica M. *Poland, A Study in National Idealism*. London: Burns and Oates, Ltd., 1915.

Gasiorowski, Waclaw. *Ach-Te "Chamy" w Ameryce!* Warszawa: Dom Ksiazki Polskiej Spolka Akcyjna, 1935.

Gaudentia, Sister M., Felician. "The Polish People of Passaic," *Polish American Studies*, V (July-December, 1948).

Gibbon, John Murray. *Canadian Mosaic*. New York: Dodd, Mead & Company, 1939.

Givens, Willard E. *Galician Immigration*. Unpublished Master's thesis, Columbia University, 1915.

Glomski, Hyacinth M. "Contribution of Americans of Polish Ancestry to the Development of Music in Chicago," *Poles of Chicago*. Chicago: Polish Pageant Inc., 1937.

Haiman, Miecislaus. *Poles in New York in the 17th and 18th Centuries*. Chicago: Archives and Museum of the Polish Roman Catholic Union, 1938.

Haiman, Miecislaus. *The Poles in the Early History of Texas*. Chicago: Archives and Museum of the Polish Roman Catholic Union, 1936.

Haiman, Miecislaus. *Poland and the American Revolutionary War*. Chicago: Archives and Museum of the Polish Roman Catholic Union, 1938.

Haiman, Miecislaus. *Polish Past in America, 1608-1865*. Chicago: Archives and Museum of the Polish Roman Catholic Union, 1939.

Haiman, Miecislaus. *Polish Pioneers of California*. Chicago; Archives and Museum of the Polish Roman Catholic Union, 1940.

Haiman, Miecislaus. *Polish Pioneers of Pennsylvania*. Chicago: Archives and Museum of the Polish Roman Catholic Union, 1941.

Haiman, Miecislaus. "The Debt to Men of Polish Blood," *The Polish Review*, (July, 1945).

Haiman, Miecislaus. "General Albin F. Schoepf," *Polish American Studies*, II (July-December, 1945).

Haiman, Miecislaus. "The Polish American Contribution to World War II," *Polish American Studies*, (January-June, 1945).

Haiman, Miecislaw. *Historja Udzialu Polakow w Amerykanskiej Wojnie Domowej*. Chicago: Drukiem Dziennika Zjednoczenia, 1928.

Haiman, Miecislaw. "Polish Scholarship in the United States: 1939-1947," *Polish American Studies*, IV (July-December, 1947).

Haiman, Mieczyslaw. *Zjednoczenie Polskie Rzymsko-Katolickie w Ameryce 1873-1948*. Chicago: Alliance Press, 1948.

Hall, Prescott F. *Immigration and Its Effects Upon the United States.* New York: Henry Holt & Company, 1913.

Hamilton, Arthur. *Statistics, Fraternal Societies.* Fiftieth Edition. Rochester: Fraternal Monitor, 1944.

Hanna, Elinor E. *Attitudes toward the United States as revealed in published writings of immigrants from Europe from 1900 to 1984.* Unpublished Ph.D. dissertation, New York University, 1946.

Handlin, Oscar. *The Uprooted.* Boston: Little, Brown and Company, 1951.

Handlin, Oscar. *The American People in the Twentieth Century.* Cambridge: Harvard University Press, 1954.

Hardon, John A., S. J. "The Polish National Catholic Church." *The Homiletic and Pastoral Review,* LVI (April, 1956).

Herskovits, M. J. *Acculturation.* New York: J. J. Augustin, 1938.

Hill, George M. "The Use of the Culture Area Concept in Social Research," *The American Journal of Sociology,* (July, 1941).

Hill, Ninian. *Poland and the Polish Question.* New York: F. A. Stokes Company, 1915.

Holmes, Fred L. *Old World Wisconsin: Around Europe in the Badger State.* Eau Claire: E. M. Hale and Company, 1944.

Hoover, Herbert, *The Memoirs of Herbert Hoover.* New York; The MacMillan Company. 1951.

Janta, Aleksander. "O Muzyce Amerykansko-Polskiej," *Nowy Swiat.* (April 30, 1960).

Janta, Alexander. "Barriers into bridges: Polish Culture in America," *The Polish Review,* II (Spring-Summer, 1957).

Jasinski, Rev. Walery, Ph.D. *Po Co Sie Uczyc Jezyka Polskiego i Kultury Polskiej w Ameryce.* Plymouth: Felician Sisters, 1941.

Jasinski, Walery J. *Teksty Dotyczace Asymilacji Polakow w Ameryce.* Detroit: Fireside Printing Company, 1944.

Kar, Anthony Louis. *The Response of the People to the use of Formal Education in the attempted denationalization of Poland, 1795-1914.* Unpublished Ph.D. dissertation, University of Michigan, 11955.

Karlowiczowa, Jadwiga. *Historia Zwiazku Polek w Ameryce.* Chicago: Zwiazek Polek w Ameryce, 1938.

Katoski, Gentil G., O.F.M. *Some aspects of Polish Immigration, 1900-1914.* Unpublished Master's thesis, Catholic University of America, 1948.

Kedzierska Mary B. *The Polish Family—Problems of Adjustment.* Unpublished Master's thesis, Fordham University, 1941.

Kessler, Henry H. and Rachels, Eugene. *Peter Stuyvesant and His New York.* New York: Random House, Inc., 1959.

Kinel, Lola. "Jozefa Kudlicka," *Common Ground,* I (Winter, 1940).

Kingsbury, Susan Myra. *An Introduction to the Records of the Virginia Company of London.* Washington: Government Press, 1905.

Kirkconnell, Watson. *Canadian Overtones.* Winnipeg: Columbia Press, 1935.

Kohn, Hans. *Pan-Slavism, Its History and Ideology.* Notre Dame: University of Notre Dame Press, 1953.

Kolat, Sister Mary Benedicta O.S.F. *Father Joseph Dabrowski, The Pioneer Priest and His Significant Contribution toward Catholic American School System.* Unpublished Master's thesis, Wayne State University, 1950.

Konovalov, S. *Russo-Polish Relations.* Princeton: Princeton University Press, 1945.

Kosciuszko Foundation. *Annual Reports of the Executive Director.* New York: Kosciuszko Foundation, 1926.

Kosciuszko Foundation. *The Kosciuszko Foundation Reports 1952-1957.* New York: Kosciuszko Foundation, 1957.

Kowalczyk, Edmund L. "A Polish Family in the South," *Polish American Studies,* III (July-December, 1946).

Kowalczyk, Edmund L. "Jottings From the Polish American Past," *Polish American Studies,* VII (July-December, 1950).

Kowalczyk, Edmund L. "Jottings From the Polish American Past," *Polish American Studies,* IX (July-December, 1952).

Kowalczyk, Edmund L. "Jottings From the Polish American Past," *Polish American Studies,* XI (January-June, 1954).

Kowalczyk, Edmund L. "Polonica-Americana From the Past," *Polish American Journal,* (September 15, 1956).

Kowalczyk, Edmund L. "Polonica-Americana From the Past," *Polish American Journal,* (June 7, 1958).

Kowalczyk, Edmund L. "Poles in America," *Polish American Journal,* (August 15, 1959).

Kowalczyk, Edmund L. "Poles in America," *Polish American Journal,* (September 26, 1959).

Kowalczyk, Edmund L. "Dr. Alexander Curtius," *Polish American Journal,* (October 10, 1959).

Kowalczyk, Jan J. *Prussian Poland, A Stronghold of German Militarism.* Copenhagen: Edmont R. Petersen Campany, 1917.

Kowalski, A. "Mlodziez, Szkola i Kosciol, to nasz skarb Narodowy," *Narod Polski,* (October 3. 1900).

Kozlowski, P. "Refugees From Reds Cheer U.S.," *Promien* (June, 1946).

Krajewski, Stanislaw. "W Ameryce Brak Polskich Intelektualistow—Mowil Brat E. Stanislaw, w Orchard Lake," *Dziennik Polski,* (June 3, 1958).

Kridl, Manfred. *A Survey of Polish Literature and Culture.* New York: Columbia University Press, 1956.

Kruszka, Ks. Waclaw. *Historja Polska w Ameryce*. Milwaukee: Drukiem Spolki Wydawniczej Kuryera, 1905. 13 Volumes.

Kruszka, Ks. Waclaw. *Siedm Siedmioleci Czyli Pol Wieku Zycia*. Poznan: Czcionkami Drukarni Sw. Wojciecha w Poznaniu, 1924. 2 Volumes.

Kruszka, Ks. Waclaw. *Historja Polska w Ameryce*. Milwaukee: Kuryer Publishing Comany, 1937.

Kryniewicz, Thaddeus Theodore. *The Polish Immigration Committee in the United States—A Historical Study of the American Committee for the Relief Of Polish Immigrants: 1947-1952*. Unpublished Master's thesis, Fordham University, 1953.

Kurpiewska, Florentyna Maria. *A Study of the Polish Parishes in Greenpoint, Brooklyn*. Unpublished Master's thesis, Fordham University, 1936.

Kusielewicz, Eugene. "The Jefferson-Niemcewicz Correspondence," *The Polish Review*, II (Autumn, 1957).

Kusielewicz, Eugene and Krzyzanowski, Ludwig. "Julian Ursyn Niemcewicz's American Diary," *The Polish Review*, III (Summer, 1958).

Lagodzinska, Adele. *The Polish Heritage and the Future of Chicago*. Chicago: The Polish Women's Alliance of America, 1953.

Lednicki, Waclaw. *Life and Culture of Poland*. New York: Roy Publishers, 1944.

Lenart, Dr. F. "Potrzeba Zorganizowania Inteligencji Zawodowej Na Wychodztwie," *Kongres Wychodztwa Polskiego w Ameryce, Odezwy, Mowy, Referaty, Uchwaly, oraz Urzedowy Protokol*. Detroit: No imprint, 1925.

Lerski, Jerzy Jan. *The United States and the Polish Exiles of 1831*. Unpublished Ph.D. dissertation, Georgetown University, 1953.

Lerski, Jerzy Jan. *A Polish Chapter in Jacksonian America*. Madison: The University of Wisconsin Press, 1958.

Lewandowska, Sister M. Theodosetta, H.F.N. "The Polish Immigrant in Philadelphia to 1914," *Records of the American Catholic Historical Society of Philadelphia*, LXV (June, 1954), No. 2.

Lewitter, L. R. "Poland Under the Saxon Kings," *The New Cambridge Modern History of Poland*. Cambridge: At the University Press, 1957.

Liguori, Sister M., H.F.N. "Polish Sisters in the Civil War," *Polish American Studies*, VII (January-June, 1960).

Liguori, Sister M., C.S.F.N. "Marie Elizabeth Zakrzewska: Physician," *Polish American Studies*, IX (January- June, 1952).

Liguori, Sister M., C.S.F.N. "The Pole Who Wrote to Lincoln," *Polish American Studies*, X (January-June, 1953).

Linton, Ralph. *The Study of Man*. New York: D. Appleton-Century Company, 1936.

Linton, Ralph. *Acculturation Among Seven American Indian Tribes*. New York: D. Appleton-Century Company, 1940.

Lonn, Ella. *Foreigners in the Confederacy.* Chapel Hill: The University of North Carolina Press, 1940.

Lonn, Ella. *Foreigners in the Union Army and Navy.* Baton Rouge: Louisiana State University Press, 1951.

Lopata, Helena Znaniecki. *The Function of Voluntary Asociations in an Ethnic Community: Polonia.* Unpublished Ph.D. dissertation, University of Chicago, 1954.

Lucas, Henry S. *Netherlanders in America.* Ann Arbor: University of Michigan Press, 1955.

Lucille, Sister, C. R. "The Causes of Polish Immigration to the United States," *Polish American Studies,* VIII (July-December, 1951).

Lyon, Norman T. *History of the Polish People in Rochester.* Buffalo: Polish Everybody's Daily Press, 1935.

Maisel, Albert Q. "The Poles Among Us," *Zgoda,* (May 15, 1958).

Maisel, Albert Q. "The Poles Among Us," *Zgoda,* (June 15, 1958).

Maisel, Albert Q. *They All Chose America.* New York: Thomas Nelson & Sons, 1957.

Manning, Clarence A. *A History of Slavic Studies in the United States.* Milwaukee: The Marquette University Press, 1957.

Marshall, Douglas C. "Nationality and the Emerging Culture," *Rural Sociology,* (March, 1948).

May, Arthur J. *The Habsburg Monarchy.* Cambridge: Harvard University Press, 1951.

Midowicz, Casimir E. "The Polish National Alliance," *Poland, Journal of Commerce and Industry,* (August, 1927).

Mierzwa, Stephen. "Schools for Democracy," *The Kosciuszko Foundation Monthly News Letter,* (November, 1951).

Mierzynski, Joseph. *Polacy w Nowym Yorku.* (No imprint.) 1910.

Miller, Frank H. *The Polanders in Wisconsin.* Milwaukee: Parkman Club Publications, 1896.

Miller, Herbert Adolphus. *The School and the Immigrant.* Philadelphia: Fell Company, 1916.

Mizwa, Stephen P. "Polish-American Cultural Relationships," *Poland.* Bernadotte E. Schmitt (ed.). Los Angeles: University of California Press, 1945.

Mondello, Salvatore. "America's Polish Heritage as Viewed by Miecislaus Haiman and the Periodical Press," *The Polish Review,* IV (Winter-Spring, 1959).

Murawski, Ladislaus Francis. *The History and Development of St. Joseph's Home for Polish Immigrants of 425 West Forty-Fourth Street, New York.* Unpublished Project, Fordham University, 1941.

Napolska, Sister Mary Remigia. *The Polish Immigrant in Detroit to 1914.* Chicago: Archives and Museum of the Polish Roman Catholic Union, 1946.

Narloch, Ks. A. "Bronmy Polski ale Umiejetnie Jak Amerykanie," *Narod Polski,* (December 7, 1932).

Nichols, J. Alden. *Germany After Bismarck.* Cambridge: Harvard University Press, 1958.

Niemcewicz, Julian Ursyn. *Pamietniki Czasow Moich.* Waclaw Zawadzki (ed.). Wroclaw: Panstwowy Instytut Wydawniczy, 1957.

Niemcewicz, Julian Ursyn. *Podroze Po Ameryce 1797-1807.* Emil Ripa (ed.). Wroclaw Zaklad Narodowy Imienia Ossolinskich, 1959.

Nobilis, Sister M., S.S.N.D. "Sienkiewicz and the Poles in America," *Polish American Studies,* II (January-June 1945).

Olejniczak, J. "Oredzie na Sejm Zjednoczenia Polskiego," *Polacy Zagranica,* (February, 1931).

Olszewicz, Boleslaw. *Poland and the Discovery of America.* Poznan: Rolnicze Drukarnia i Ksiegarnia Nakladowa, 1931.

Olszyk, Edmund G. *The Polish Press in America.* Milwaukee: Marquette University Press, 1940.

Orvis, Julia Swift. "Partitioned Poland, 1795-1914," *Poland.* Bernadotte E. Schmitt (ed.). Los Angeles: University of California Press, 1945.

Osada, Stanislaw. *Historja Zwiazku Narodowego Polskiego.* Chicago: Zwiazek Narodowy Polski, 1905.

Osada, Stanislaw. *Jak Sie Ksztaltowala Polska Dusza Wychodztwa w Ameryce.* Pittsburgh: Nakladem i drukiem "Sokola Polskiego," 1930.

Ostafin, Peter A. *The Polish Peasant in Transition: A Study of Group Integration as a Function of Symbiosis and Common Definitions.* Unpublished Ph.D dissertation, University of Michigan, 1948.

Park, Robert E. *The Immigrant Press and Its Control.* New York: Harper and Brothers, 1922.

Park, Robert Ezra and Miller Herbert A. *Old World Traits Transplanted.* New York: Harper & Brothers, 1921.

Pearson, Jean. "Detroit Poles Proud of Top Scientists," *Detroit Free Press,* (September 21, 1957).

Pertek, Jerzy. *Polacy Na Szlakach Morskich Swiata.* Gdansk: Zaklad Narodowy Imienia Ossolinskich w Wroclawiu, 1957.

Phillips, W. Alison, M.A. *Poland.* New York: Henry Holt and Company, n.d.

Piatkiewicz, Karol. *Pamietnik Jubileuszowy ZNP 1880-1940.* Chicago: Alliance Printers and Publishers, 1940.

Piatkiewicz, Karol. "Co Kazdy Zwiazkowiec ZNP Wiedziec Powinien," *Dziennik Zwiazkowy,* (October 9, 1948).

Piatkiewicz, Karol. *Illustrowany Kalendarz Zwiazkowy na Rok 1949.* Chicago: Alliance Press, 1949.

Piatkiewicz, Karol. "The PNA 5th Ranking Fraternal Organization." *Zgoda,* (November 1, 1951).

Piatkiewicz, Karol. *Illustrowany Kalendarz na Rok 1953.* Chicago: Alliance Press, 1953.

Piatkiewicz, Karol (Ed.). *Pamietnik 75ta Rocznica ZNP 1880-1955.* Chicago: Alliance Press, 1955.

Piatkowski, Romuald. *Pamietnik Kongresu Polskiego w Waszyngtonie.* Chicago: Alliance Press, 1911.

Pilsudski, Alexandra. *Memoirs of Madam Pilsudski.* London: Hurst & Blackett, 1940.

Pliska, Stanley H. *Polish Independence and the Polish Americans.* Unpublished Ph.D. dissertation, Teachers College, Columbia University, 1955.

Pogorzelska, Sister Mary Assumpta, S.S.J. *A Historical Study of Religion and Education as Underlying Influences in the Localization of the Poles of Cleveland up to 1915.* Unpublished Master's thesis, Saint John's College of Cleveland, 1951.

Polish American Congress, Inc. *The Story of the Polish American Congress and Poland's Case in Press Clippings 1944-1948.* Chicago: Polish American Congress, Inc., 1948.

Polish American Congress, Inc. *Sprawozdania Zarzadu Wykonawczego Poszczegolnych Komisji i Komitetow na Trzecia Konwencje Kongresu Polsko-Amerykanskiego; 30-31 Maja i Czerwca, 1952.* Chicago: Polish American Congress, Inc., 1952.

Poznanski, Czeslaw. *The Rights of Nations.* New York: Roy Publishers, 1945.

Pranica, Jozef T. "Ofiary Zlozone na Museum Immigracyjne w New Yorku," *Narod Polski,* (November 8, 1956).

Radziwill, Princess Catherine. *It Really Happened.* Binghamton: Vail-Ballou Press, Inc., 1932.

Rath, R. John. *The Viennese Revolution of 1848.* Austin: University of Texas Press, 1957.

Roosevelt, Theodore. *The Winning of the West.* New York: G. P. Putnam's Sons, 1908.

Ross, E. A. *The Old World in the New.* New York: The Century Company, 1914.

Roucek, Joseph S. "Polish Americans," *One America.* Francis J. Brown and Joseph Slabey Roucek (Eds.). New York: Prentice-Hall, Inc., 1946.

Rozek, Edward J. *Allied Wartime Diplomacy A Pattern in Poland.* New York: John Wiley & Sons, Inc., 1958.

Rozmarek, Charles. "Poland and the Atlantic Charter," *Polish American Congress Bulletin.* (February, 1944).

Rutkowska, Sister M. Neomisia, H.F.N. "A Polish Pioneer Jesuit in America," *Polish American Studies,* III (July-December, 1946).

Saloutos, Theodore. *They Remember America: The Story Of The Repatriated Greek-Americans,* Berkeley: University of California Press, 1956.

Schachern, Harold. "Pupils Wiser, Less Ruly—Nun Compares Today's Crop of Children," *Detroit News,* (June 13, 1959).

Schermerhorn, Robert S. *These Our People: Minorities in American Culture.* Boston: D. C. Heath and Company, 1949.

Schneiweis, Joseph A. *Certain Aspects of Polish Assimilation in the State of New York.* Unpublished Master's thesis, Columbia University, 1930.

Schurz, Carl. *The Reminiscences of Carl Schurz.* New York: The McClure Company, 1907. Three Volumes.

Seabrook, William. *These Foreigners.* New York: Harcourt, Brace & Company, 1938.

Seroczynski, Felix Thomas. "Poles in the United States," *The Catholic Encyclopedia.* New York: The Encyclopedia Press, Inc., 1914.

Shallna, Anthony O. "Adjudication of General Kosciuszko's Wills," *The Massachusetts Law Society Journal,* XX (December, 1949).

Sheehan, Donald. *The Making of American History.* New York: The Dryden Press, 1950.

Sienkiewicz, Henryk. *Nowele.* Warszawa: Ministerstwo W.R. i O. P., 1944.

Skibinska, A. M. "Polish Language Supplementary Schools," *Poles of Chicago 1837-1937.* Leon Zglenicki (Ed.). Chicago: Polish Pageant Inc., 1937.

Slesinski, Thaddeus. "The Development of Cultural Activities in Polish American Communities," *Polish American Studies,* V (July-December, 1948).

Slesinski, Thaddeus. "Past, Present, Future Report Given to Polish Cultural Clubs," *Dziennik Polski,* (August 7, 1959).

Sluszka, Sigismund J. "Polish Language Teaching in the U.S.A." Paper presented at Rutgers University, Brunswick, New Jersey. (March 28, 1953).

Sluszka, Sigismund J. "America Had A Slavic Language Problem Long Before the Coming of the Mayflower in 1820," *American Association of Teachers of Eastern European Languages Bulletin,* (June 4, 1953).

Smith, Branford. *Why We Behave Like Americans.* New York: J. B. Lippincott Company, 1957.

Smith, Captain John. *True Travels.* Richmond: Franklin Press, 1819.

Smith, William Carlson. *Americans in the Making.* New York. D. Appleton Century Company, 1939.

Smogorzewski, Casimir. "Unity Among the Poles in America," *Free Europe,* (June 16, 1944).

Speek, Peter A. *A Stake in the Land.* New York: Harper & Brothers Publishers, 1921.

Starzynski, F. "Polish Americans," *Polish Medical and Dental Bulletin,* (November, 1938).

Stefan, Stanley Bruno. *The Preparation of the American Poles for Polish Independence 1880-1918.* Unpublished Master's thesis, University of Detroit, 1939.

Stefanowicz, Andzia. *"Sports and Youth in the PRCU,"* *Ksiega Diamentowa ZPRK 1873-1948.* Chicago: Alliance Press, 1948.

Suhl, Yuri. *Ernestine L. Rose and the Battle for Human Rights.* New York: Reynal & Company, 1959.

Super, Paul. *Twenty-Five Years With the Poles.* Trenton: Paul Super Memorial Fund, Inc., 1947.

Swastek, Rev. Joseph. "What is a Polish American?" *Polish American Studies,* I (January-December, 1944).

Swastek, Rev. Joseph. "Poles in South Bend to 1914," *Polish American Studies,* II (July-December, 1945).

Swastek, Rev. Joseph. "Historical Notes and Comments," *Polish American Studies,* V (July-December, 1948).

Swastek, Rev. Joseph V. "Polish Americans," *One America.* Francis J. Brown and Joseph S. Roucek, Editors, Englewood Cliffs: Prentice-Hall, Inc., 1959.

Syski, Right Reverend Monsignor Alexander, S.T.M. "The Nestor of Polish Historians in America: Reverend Waclaw Kruszka," *Polish American Studies,* I (January-December, 1944).

Szawleski, Dr. Mieczyslaw. *Wychodztwo Polskie w Stanach Zjednoczonych Ameryce.* Lwow: Wydawnictwo Zakladu Narodowego Imienia Ossolinskich, 1924.

Szczerbowski, Albin. "Analiza Wydzialu Maloletnich," *Zgoda,* (September 8, 1951).

Szopinski, Rev. D. "Od Redakcji," *Przeglad Katolicki* (January, 1926).

Targosz, Rev. S. *Polonja Katolicka w Stanach Zjednoczonych w Przekroju.* Detroit: Naklad Autora, 1943.

Taylor, A. J. P. *The Hapsburg Monarchy 1809-1918.* London: Hamish Hamilton, 1952.

Theodosetta, Sister M., C.S.F.N. "The Poles in Philadelphia to 1914," *Polish American Studies,* VIII (Jnauray-June, 1951).

Thomas, W. I. and Znaniecki, Florian. *The Polish Peasant in Europe and America.* Boston: Richard C. Badger, 1918.

Thomas, W. I. and Znaniecki, Florian. *The Polish Peasant in Europe and America.* New York: Alfred A. Knopf, 1927. Two Volumes.

Tomczak, A. C. *Poles in Chicago, their contribution to the Century of Progress.* (No imprint.)

Tremaine, Anna G. *The Effect of Polish Immigration on Buffalo Politics.* Unpublished Master's thesis, Columbia University, 1928.

Uminski, Sigmund H. "Julian Ursyn Niemcewicz in America," *Polish American Studies,* II (July-December, 1945).

Uminski, Sigmund H. "Individual Polish Americans and World War II," *Polish American Studies,* III (January-June, 1946).

Van Norman, Louis E. *Poland The Knight Among Nations.* New York: Fleming H. Revell Company, 1907.

Versen, Vincent M. "About the Plenary Meeting of the PRCU Directorate," *Narod Polski,* (May 19, 1955).

Wachtl, Dr. Karol. *Dzieje Zjednoczenia P.R. Katolickiego w Ameryce.* Chicago: L. J. Winiecki, 1913.

Wachtl, Dr. Karol. *Polonja w Ameryce.* Philadelphia: Polish Star Publishing Company, 1944.

Wagner, Wienczyslaw, J. Coleman, Arthur P., Haight, Charles S. "Laurentius Grimaldus Goslicius and His Age," *The Polish Review,* III (Winter-Spring, 1958).

Waldo, Artur L. (Ed.). *Ksiega Diamentowa ZPRK w Ameryce 1873-1948.* Chicago: Alliance Press, 1948.

Waldo, Arthur L. *First Poles in America 1608-1958.* Pittsburg: Polish Falcons of America, 1956.

Waldo, Artur L. "Trzynascie Lat Museum Polonii," *Ksiega Diamentowa ZPRK 1873-1948.* Chicago: Alliance Press, 1948.

Walter, Jerzy. "Rzut Oka na 20 Letnia Dzialalnosc Museum i Archiwum Zjednoczenia," *Narod Polski,* (February 7, 1957).

Wassell, F. F. *Attitudes of the Various Polish-American Organizations Toward American Foreign Policy Affecting Poland: 1939-1945.* Unpublished Master's thesis, Columbia University, 1946.

Whitton, Major F. E. *A History of Poland From the Earliest Times to the Present Day.* New York: Charles Scribner's Sons, 1918.

Wittke, Carl. *We Who Built America.* New York: Prentice-Hall Inc., 1940.

Wittke, Carl. *The Irish in America.* Baton Rouge: Louisiana State University Press, 1956.

Wloszczewski, Stefan. *Historja Polska w Detroit.* Detroit: Nakladem Instytutu Wiedzy o Polonii Amerykanskiej, 1951.

Wojciechowski, Zygmunt. *Poland's Place in Europe.* Poznan: Instytut Zachodni, 1947.

Wolanin, Alphonse S. *Polonica in English.* Chicago: Archives and Museum of the Polish Roman Catholic Union, 1945.

Wood, Arthur Evans. *Hamtramck Then and Now.* New York: Bookman Associates, 1955.

Woolsey, L. H. "Poland at Yalta and Dumbarton Oaks," *The American Journal of International Law,* XXXIX, 1945.

Woznicki, Bishop Stephen S. "Poles' Presence in the United States Traced to Early Days in Our Nation," *Dziennik Polski,* (September 24, 1958).

Woznicki, Bishop Stephen S. "Polish Immigrant is Backbone of Many Industries in New Home," *Dziennik Polski* (September 25, 1958).

Wright, Herbert. "Poland and the Crimea Conference," *The American Journal of International Lew,* XXXIX, 1945.

Wronski, Casimir J. B. "The Polish Alma Mater of America," *Poles of Chicago 1837-1937,* Leon Zglenicki (Ed.). Chicago: Polish Pageant Inc., 1937.

Wytrwal, Joseph A. "The Polish Ballet," *Laur, Yesterday, Today, Tomorrow—Souvenir Program.* Detroit: Conventual Press, 1952.

Wytrwal, Joseph A. "Twelve Governors Issued Pulaski Proclamations," *Dziennik Zwiazkowy,* (March 12, 14, 1955).

Wytrwal, Joseph A. "General Pulaski: American Benefactor," *Congressional Record.* Volume 101. No. 74.

Wytrwal, Joseph A. "Pulaskiana in America," *Polish American Studies,* XIV (January-June, 1957).

Wytrwal, Joseph A. "Lincoln's Friend—Captain A. Bielaski," *Polish American Studies,* XIV (July-December, 1957).

Wytrwal, Joseph A. "Memorials to General Casimir Pulaski in the United States," *The Georgia Historical Quarterly,* XLIV (September, 1960).

Wytrwal, Jozef A. "Towarzystwo Laur Zespol Tancow i Spiewu w Detroit," *Bialy Orzel,* (July, 1951).

Yezierska, Anzia. *Hungry Hearts.* New York: Houghton Mifflin Company, 1920.

Yezierska, Anzia. *Children of Loneliness.* New York: Funk and Wagnalls Company, 1923.

Yezierska, Anzia. *Arrogant Beggar.* New York: Doubleday, Page and Company, 1927.

Yolles, Piotr. "Historja Polonji w Zwierciadle Zwiazku Narodowego," *Nowy Swiat,* (September 24, 1951).

*Zlota Ksiega Pamiatkowa 1873-1923 z okazji piedziesieciolecia Zjednoczenia Polskiego Rzymsko Katolickiego w Ameryce.* Chicago: Dziennik Zjednoczenia, 1923.

Zjednoczenie Polskie Rzymsko-Katolickie w Ameryce. *Urzedowy Protokol Sejmu XXXVIII ZPRK w dniach 21-25 Wrzesnia, 1925 w St. Louis, Missouri.* (No imprint.)

Zjednoczenie Polskie Rzymsko-Katolickie w Ameryce. *Urzedowy Protokol Sejmu XL ZPRK w Detroit, Michigan, 1931.* (No imprint.)

Zjednoczenie Polskie Rzymsko-Katolickie w Ameryce. *Urzedowy Protokol Sejmu XLI ZPRK w Springfield, Massachusetts w 1934.* (No imprint.)

Zjednoczenie Polskie Rzymsko-Katolickie w Ameryce. *Urzedowy Protokol Sejmu XLV ZPRK w dniach 17-21 Wrzesnia, 1950 w Syracuse, New York.* (No imprint.)

Zjednoczenie Polskie Rzymsko-Katolickie w Ameryce. *Urzedowy Protokol Sejmu XLVI w dniach 19-24 Wrzesnia, 1954 w Pittsburgh, Pennsylvania.* (No imprint.)

Znaniecki, Florian. "The Significance of Cultural Associations in the Modern World," *American Council of Polish Cultural Clubs Convention Bulletin,* (August, 1955).

Zoltowski, Adam. *Border of Europe—A Study of the Polish Eastern Provinces.* London: Hollis & Carter, 1950.

Zubrzycki, Jerzy. *Polish Immigrants in Britain.* The Hague: Martinus Nij-
hoff, 1956.

Zwiazek Narodowy Polski, *Urzedowy Protokol Sejmu XXV, 1927, Chicago,
Illinois.* Chicago: Drukiem Dziennika Zwiazkowego-Zgody, 1927.

Zwiazek Narodowy Polski, *Urzedowy Protokol Sejmu XXVI, 1931, Scranton, Pennsylvania.* Chicago: Drukiem Dziennika Zwiazkowego-Zgody,
1931.

Zwiazek Narodowy Polski. *Konstytucja, Prawa, Reguly i Przepisy.* Chicago:
Drukiem Dziennika Zwiazkowego-Zgody, 1931.

Zwiazek, Narodowy Polski. *Kalendarz Zwiazkowy, 1935.* Chicago: Alliance
Press, 1935.

Zwiazek Narodowy Polski. *Urzedowy Protokol Sejmu XXVII w Baltimore,
Maryland, 1935.* Chicago: Drukiem Dziennika Zwiazkowego-Zgody,
1935.

Zwiazek Narodowy Polski. *Kalendarz Zwiazkowy, 1936.* Chicago: Alliance
Press, 1936.

Zwiazek Narodowy Polski. *Kalendarz Zwiazkowy, 1943.* Chicago: Alliance
Press, 1943.

## TABLE I

## THE DISTRIBUTION OF POLES IN 1790[a]

| State | Heads of Families | Free White Males over 16 | Free White Males under 16 | Free White Females | Other White Persons | Total Whites | Slaves |
|---|---|---|---|---|---|---|---|
| Connecticut | 9 | 14 | 13 | 21 | | 48 | |
| Maryland | 7 | 10 | 14 | 21 | | 45 | 12 |
| Maine | 1 | 1 | 1 | 4 | | 6 | |
| Massachusetts | 9 | 10 | 10 | 22 | | 42 | |
| New Hampshire | 1 | 2 | 1 | 6 | | 9 | |
| New York | 8 | 8 | 9 | 23 | | 40 | |
| N. Carolina | 6 | 10 | 10 | 18 | | 38 | 10 |
| Pennsylvania | 32 | 37 | 39 | 83 | 2 | 159 | 8 |
| Rhode Island | ...... | ...... | ...... | ...... | ...... | ...... | ...... |
| S. Carolina | 8 | 8 | 5 | 21 | | 34 | 13 |
| Vermont | 1 | 1 | — | 2 | | 3 | |
| Virginia | 5 | (only free white persons were counted) | | | | | |
| Total | 87 | 101 | 102 | 221 | 2 | 468 | 43 |

[a] Miecislaus Haiman, Polish Past in America (Chicago: The Polish Roman Catholic Union Archives and Museum, 1939), p. 151.

## TABLE II

### NUMBER OF POLES IN THE UNITED STATES ACCORDING TO THE CENSUS OF 1860 AND 1870[a]

| State | Number of Poles 1860 | Number of Poles 1870 |
|---|---|---|
| Alabama | 94 | 38 |
| Arkansas | 4 | 32 |
| California | 730 | 804 |
| Colorado | — | 49 |
| Connecticut | 73 | 83 |
| Delaware | 5 | 4 |
| Florida | 25 | 20 |
| Georgia | 103 | 88 |
| Illinois | 341 | 1696 |
| Indiana | 91 | 523 |
| Iowa | 100 | 178 |
| Kansas | 69 | 169 |
| Kentucky | 75 | 109 |
| Louisiana | 196 | 198 |
| Maine | 8 | 6 |
| Maryland | 66 | 145 |
| Massachusetts | 81 | 272 |
| Michigan | 112 | 974 |
| Minnesota | 127 | 246 |
| Mississippi | 87 | 78 |
| Missouri | 339 | 619 |
| Nebraska | — | 57 |
| Nevada | — | 50 |
| New Hampshire | 1 | 2 |
| New Jersey | 120 | 279 |
| New York | 2296 | 4061 |
| North Carolina | 1 | 8 |
| Ohio | 326 | 526 |
| Oregon | 39 | 65 |
| Pennsylvania | 215 | 777 |
| Rhode Island | 5 | 13 |
| South Carolina | 142 | 66 |
| Tennessee | 97 | 221 |
| Texas | 783 | 448 |
| Vermont | 1 | 1 |
| West Virginia | 40 | 42 |
| Wisconsin | 417 | 1290 |
| Arizona ........ Territories | | 11 |
| Dakota | | 3 |
| District of Columbia | 30 | 49 |

## TABLE II

# NUMBER OF POLES IN THE UNITED STATES
## ACCORDING TO THE CENSUS OF
### 1860 AND 1870[a] (Continued)

| | | |
|---|---|---|
| Nebraska | 13 | |
| Idaho | | 12 |
| Montana | | 55 |
| Nevada | 9 | 12 |
| New Mexico | 13 | 12 |
| Utah | 2 | 11 |
| Washington | 11 | 25 |
| Wyoming | | 17 |
| Total: | 7298 | 14436 |

[a] Miecislaus Haiman, *Polish Past in America* (Chicago: The Polish Roman Catholic Union Archives and Museum, 1939), p. 158.

## TABLE III

## DISTRIBUTION AND DENSITY OF THE POLISH POPULATION IN THE UNITED STATES IN 1903[a]

| State | Number of Settlements | Population of State | Polish Population | Ratio | Area per Sq. Mi. | Ratio per Sq. Mi. |
|---|---|---|---|---|---|---|
| Dakotas | 20 | 349,040 | 16,600 | 22:1 | 83,365 | 1:1 |
| Illinois | 56 | 4,821,550 | 300,000 | 16:1 | 56,650 | 6:1 |
| Indiana | 39 | 2,516,463 | 33,800 | 75:1 | 36,350 | 1:1 |
| *Maryland | 10 | | | | | |
| Michigan | 73 | 2,419,782 | 140,000 | 18:1 | 58,915 | 3:1 |
| Minnesota | 60 | 1,751,395 | 80,000 | 22:1 | 83,365 | 1:1 |
| Nebraska | 29 | 1,068,901 | 29,000 | 20:1 | 70,795 | 5:1 |
| **New England | 70 | 4,142,257 | 160,000 | 21:1 | 14,555 | 11:1 |
| New Jersey | 30 | 1,883,669 | 70,000 | 27:1 | 7,815 | 9:1 |
| New York | 90 | 7,268,009 | 340,000 | 24:1 | 49,170 | 7:1 |
| Ohio | 30 | 4,157,545 | 80,000 | 50:1 | 41,060 | 2:1 |
| Pennsylvania | 112 | 6,301,360 | 350,000 | 20:1 | 45,215 | 8:1 |
| Texas | 34 | 3,048,828 | 19,700 | 160:1 | 265,780 | 1:14 |
| ***Western States | 50 | 4,032,436 | 20,000 | 200:1 | 1,778,419 | 1:100 |
| Wisconsin | 101 | 2,068,963 | 150,000 | 16:1 | 56,040 | 3:1 |
| Missouri | 12 | 3,107,117 | 28,700 | 108:1 | 69,415 | 1:2·3 |

\* Delaware, District of Columbia, West Virginia.
\*\* Massachusetts, Rhode Island, Connecticut, New Hampshire, Maine, Vermont.
\*\*\* Montana, Wyoming, Colorado, Idaho, Washington, Oregon, California, Nevada, Arizona, and New Mexico.

[a] Sister Mary Adele Dabrowska, A History of the Polish Community in Brooklyn (unpublished Master's thesis, Fordham University), p. 59.

## TABLE IV

## DISTRIBUTION OF MONEY BROUGHT BY IMMIGRANTS TO THE UNITED STATES IN 1900[a]

| Nationality | Sum Brought |
|---|---|
| Germans | $ 847,962 |
| Scandinavians | 548,969 |
| Jews | 527,163 |
| Italians | 500.037 |
| Poles | 466,939 |
| Ukrainians | 29,802 |
| | $6,271,821 |

[a] Sister Mary Adele Dabrowska, *A History of the Polish Community in Brooklyn* (unpublished Master's thesis, Fordham University), p. 59.

## TABLE V

## POLISH FOREIGN-BORN POPULATION OF THE UNITED STATES BY COUNTRY OF BIRTH 1860-1930[a]

| | |
|---|---|
| 1860 | 7,298 |
| 1870 | 14,436 |
| 1880 | 48,557 |
| 1890 | 147,440 |
| 1900 | 383,407 |
| 1910 | 937,884 |
| 1920 | 1,139,979 |
| 1930 | 1,268,583 |

[a] E. P. Hutchinson, *Immigrants and Their Children 1850-1950* (New York: John Wiley & Sons, Inc., 1956), p. 333.

TABLE VI

NINE STATES HAVING THE LARGEST POLISH POPULATION (CENSUS 1940)[a]

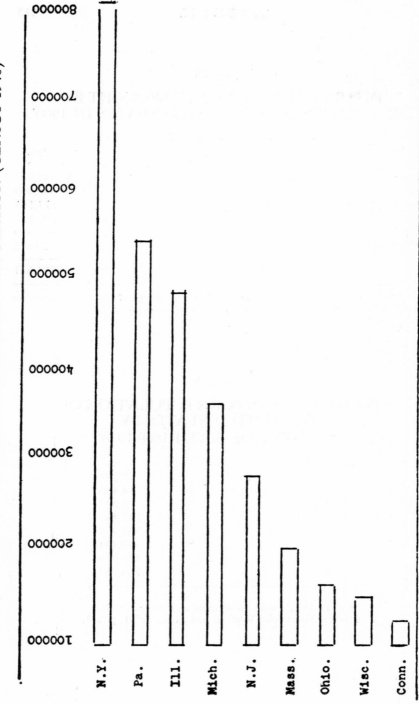

[a] Sister Mary Adele Dabrowska, A History of the Polish Community in Brooklyn (unpublished Master's thesis Fordham University), p. 75.

# TABLE VII

## NINE STATES HAVING THE SMALLEST POLISH POPULATION (CENSUS) 1940)*

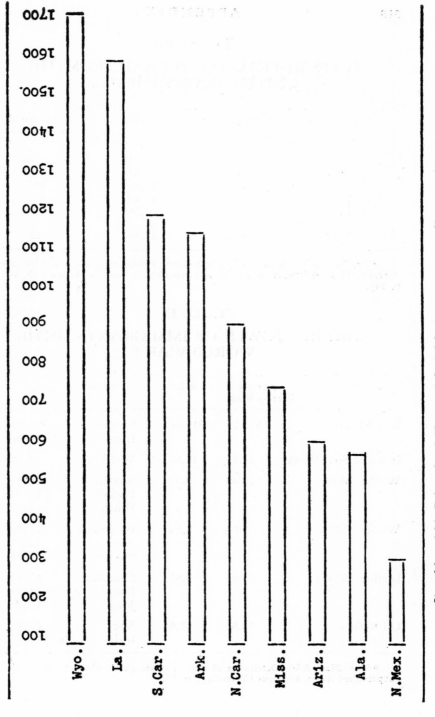

ᵃ Sister Mary Adele Dabrowska, *A History of the Polish Community in Brooklyn* (unpublished Master's thesis, Fordham University), p. 61.

## Table VIII

## POLES RE-ENTERING POLAND FROM THE UNITED STATES 1919-1923[a]

| Year | Re-Emigrants | Born in America | Naturalized in America |
|---|---|---|---|
| 1919 | 153 | 818 | 30 |
| 1920 | 17,769 | 818 | 64 |
| 1921 | 41,572 | 10,912 | 157 |
| 1922 | 31,618 | 18,062 | 406 |
| 1923 | 5,125 | 2,769 | 178 |
| Total | 96,237 | 32,561 | 835 |

[a] Dr. Mieczyslaw Szawlewski, *Wychodztwo Polskie w Stanach Zjednoczonych Ameryki*, (Lwow: Wydawnictwo Zakladu Narodowego Imienia Ossolinskich, 1924), p. 346.

## Table IX

## EARNING POWER OF IMMIGRANTS UNTIL WORLD WAR I[a]

| Industry | Average Weekly Wage | Poles | Others | |
|---|---|---|---|---|
| Iron Miners | $12.72 | $14.06 | Swedes | $15.00 |
| | | | Irish | 15.00 |
| Iron and Steel Works | 14.35 | 12.67 | Welch | 22.75 |
| Woolen Mills | 10.49 | 8.57 | Scotch | 12.00 |
| | | | English | 12.00 |
| | | | Dutch | 12.00 |
| Worsted Mills | 9.68 | 7.84 | Bulgarians | 12.00 |
| | | | Scots | 12.00 |
| | | | Swedes | 12.00 |
| Leather Works | 10.64 | 9.88 | Canadians | 12.00 |
| | | | Danes | 12.00 |
| | | | Jews | 12.00 |
| Oil Refinery | 13.81 | 12.68 | Scots | 17.00 |
| | | | Irish | 15.00 |

[a] Sister Mary Adele Dabrowska, *A History of the Polish Community in Brooklyn* (unpublished thesis, Fordham University), p. 65.

## TABLE X
## AVERAGE ANNUAL INCOME OF IMMIGRANTS
### BEFORE WORLD WAR I[a]

| Nationality | Income | Average Income |
|---|---|---|
| | | $721.00 |
| Scots | $1142 | |
| Norwegians | 1015 | |
| English | 956 | |
| Czech | 773 | |
| Polish | 595 | |

[a] Sister Mary Adele Dabrowska, *A History of the Polish Community in Brooklyn* (unpublished Master's thesis, Fordham University), p. 65.

## TABLE XI
## PER CENT OF MALES AMONG IMMIGRANTS,
### 1899-1909[a]

| | | | |
|---|---|---|---|
| Irish | 47.2 | English | 61.7 |
| Hebrew | 56.7 | Scotch | 63.6 |
| Bohemian | 56.9 | Welsh | 64.8 |
| French | 58.6 | Dutch | 65.5 |
| Portuguese | 59.0 | Finnish | 65.8 |
| German | 59.4 | Polish | 69.2 |
| Scandinavian | 61.3 | Slovak | 70.0 |

[a] Oscar Handlin, *Race and Nationality in American Life* (Boston: Little, Brown and Company, 1957), p. 111.

## Table XII

## EARLIEST FRATERNAL SOCIETIES
## IN AMERICA*

| Date of Founding | Name of the Society |
|---|---|
| 1854 | Czechoslovak Society of America |
| 1863 | L'Union St. Joseph du Canada |
| 1867 | Independent Order of St. Luke |
| 1867 | Locomotive Engineers ML & AIA |
| 1868 | Order of Railway Conductors |
| 1869 | United Workmen Anc. Order |
| 1871 | Free Sons of Israel |
| 1871 | Mutual Benefit and Aid Society |
| 1873 | Polish Roman Catholic Union |

* Arthur Hamilton, *Statistics, Fraternal Societies* (Rochester: Fraternal Monitor, 1944), p. 12.

## Table XIII

## FOURTEEN POLISH ORGANIZATIONS IN THE
## UNITED STATES*

| Name of Society | Home | Date Organized |
|---|---|---|
| 1. Polish Roman Catholic Union | Chicago | 1873 |
| 2. Polish National Alliance of U.S. of N.A. | Chicago | 1880 |
| 3. Polish Union of U.S. of N.A. | WilkesBarre | 1890 |
| 4. Polish Roman Catholic Association of N.A. | Chicago | 1894 |
| 5. Alliance of Poles | Cleveland | 1895 |
| 6. Polish Association of America | Milwaukee | 1895 |
| 7. Polish Alma Mater | Chicago | 1897 |
| 8. Polish Women's Alliance | Chicago | 1898 |
| 9. Polish Beneficial Association | Philadelphia | 1900 |
| 10. Polish National Alliance of Brooklyn | Brooklyn | 1905 |
| 11. Polish National Union | Scranton | 1908 |
| 12. Polish Union of America in New York | New York | 1917 |
| 13. Association of the Sons of Poland | Jersey City | 1903 |
| 14. Polish Falcons of America | Pittsburg | 1926 |

* Francis J. Brown and Joseph Slabey Roucek, *Our Racial and National Minorities* (New York: Prentice-Hall, 1937), p. 224.

## TABLE XIV

## DISTRIBUTION AND RELATIONSHIP OF POLISH PARISHES, CLERGY, AND ATTENDANTS TO THE TOTAL CATHOLIC SET-UP IN THE UNITED STATES IN 1903[a]

| State: | Parishes: Total | Parishes: Polish | Parishes: Ratio | Priests: Total | Priests: Polish | Priests: Ratio | Catholics: Total | Catholics: Polish | Catholics: Ratio |
|---|---|---|---|---|---|---|---|---|---|
| Dakotas | 146 | 5 | 29:1 | 75 | 3 | 25:1 | 52000 | 16600 | 4:1 |
| Illinois | 72 | 49 | 15:1 | 904 | 84 | 11:1 | 1037000 | 300000 | 4:1 |
| Indiana | 314 | 18 | 18:1 | 362 | 15 | 24:1 | 179143 | 33800 | 6:1 |
| *Maryland | Not given | | | | | | 297403 | 37500 | 8:1 |
| Michigan | 416 | 48 | 9:1 | 367 | 51 | 7:1 | 367530 | 140000 | 2·3:1 |
| Minnesota | 481 | 47 | 10:1 | 450 | 31 | 15:1 | 333000 | 80000 | 4:1 |
| Missouri | 375 | 11 | 35:1 | 565 | 14 | 40:1 | 285000 | 28700 | 10:1 |
| Nebraska | 258 | 20 | 12:1 | 180 | 12 | 15:1 | 90515 | 29000 | 3:1 |
| **New England | 630 | 30 | 21:1 | 1233 | 40 | 30:1 | 405000 | 160000 | 9:1 |
| New Jersey | 271 | 16 | 17:1 | 368 | 19 | 19:1 | 362000 | 70000 | 5:1 |
| New York | 1030 | 46 | 22:1 | 1729 | 58 | 30:1 | 249000 | 240000 | 7:1 |
| Ohio | 602 | 15 | 40:1 | 582 | 15 | 40:1 | 535000 | 80000 | 6:1 |
| Pennsylvania | 827 | 85 | 10:1 | 1174 | 90 | 13:1 | 1000000 | 350000 | 3:1 |
| ***Southern States | | | | | | | 333424 | 10200 | 33:1 |
| Texas | 264 | 30 | 9:1 | 203 | 16 | 13:1 | 202000 | 19750 | 10:1 |
| †Western States | 1093 | 8 | 137:1 | 771 | 3 | 257:1 | 688600 | 20000 | 40:1 |
| Wisconsin | 708 | 76 | 9:1 | 598 | 76 | 8:1 | 467000 | 150000 | 3:1 |

\* Maryland, Delaware, Washington, and West Virginia.

\*\* Massachusetts, Rhode Island, Connecticut, New Hampshire, Maine, Vermont

\*\*\* Virginia, Kentucky, Texas, North and South Carolina, Mississippi, Alabama, Georgia, Florida

† Montana, Wyoming, Colorado, Idaho, Utah, Washington, Oregon, California, Nevada, Arizona, New Mexico

[a] Sister Mary Adele Dabrowska, A History of the Polish Community in Brooklyn (unpublished Master's thesis Fordham University), p. 75.

TABLE XV

## POLISH IMMIGRANTS IN THE CITIES OF
## THE GREAT LAKES AREA[a]

**CHICAGO**

| | | | | | | |
|---|---|---|---|---|---|---|
| 1900 | 59,713 | 10.2% | of | foreign | born | population |
| 1910 | 125,604 | 16.0% | ” | ” | ” | ” |
| 1920 | 137,611 | 17.0% | ” | ” | ” | ” |
| 1930 | 149,622 | 17.4% | ” | ” | ” | ” |
| 1940 | 119,264 | 17.7% | ” | ” | ” | ” |
| 1950 | 94,009 | 17.9% | ” | ” | ” | ” |

**DETROIT**

| | | | | | | |
|---|---|---|---|---|---|---|
| 1900 | 13,631 | 14.1% | of | foreign | born | population |
| 1910 | 35,745 | 22.7% | ” | ” | ” | ” |
| 1920 | 56,624 | 19.5% | ” | ” | ” | ” |
| 1930 | 66,113 | 16.3% | ” | ” | ” | ” |
| 1940 | 52,235 | 16.3% | ” | ” | ” | ” |
| 1950 | 44,611 | 16.1% | ” | ” | ” | ” |

**MILWAUKEE**

| | | | | | | |
|---|---|---|---|---|---|---|
| 1900 | 17,033 | 19.1% | of | foreign | born | population |
| 1910 | 24,299 | 21.8% | ” | ” | ” | ” ...... |
| 1920 | 23,060 | 20.9% | ” | ” | ” | ” |
| 1930 | 19,593 | 17.7% | ” | ” | ” | ” ...... |
| 1940 | 14,695 | 17.5% | ” | ” | ” | ” ...... |
| 1950 | 10,989 | 17.3% | ” | ” | ” | ” ...... |

**CLEVELAND**

| | | | | | | |
|---|---|---|---|---|---|---|
| 1910 | 19,483 | 9.9% | of | foreign | born | population |
| 1920 | 35,024 | 14.6% | ” | ” | ” | ” ...... |
| 1930 | 32,668 | 14.1% | ” | ” | ” | ” ...... |
| 1940 | 24,771 | 13.8% | ” | ” | ” | ” |
| 1950 | 18,200 | 13.7% | ” | ” | ” | ” |

[a] Justin B. Galford, *The Foreign Born and Urban Growth in the Great Lakes, 1850-1950: A Study of Chicago, Cleveland, Detroit, and Milwaukee.* Unpublished Ph.D. dissertation, New York University, 1957.

## TABLE XVI

## JUVENILE MEMBERSHIP AND JUVENILE INSURANCE IN FORCE JANUARY 1st, 1944[a]

| Name of Society | Juvenile Members | Insurance Net Increase in 1943 | Juvenile Insurance in Force |
|---|---|---|---|
| 1. Alliance of Poles of America | 1,307 | 93 | $ 438,348 |
| 2. Ass'n of Sons of Poland | 1,536 | —66 | 345,715 |
| 3. Polish Alma Mater | 1,001 | —98 | 458,750 |
| 4. Polish Ass'n of America | 1,260 | —58 | 407,388 |
| 5. Polish Benefit Association | 3,020 | —280 | 1,149,445 |
| 6. Polish Falcons of America | 1,769 | 44 | 525,200 |
| 7. Polish National Alliance | 40,926 | —1366 | 21,805,751 |
| 8. Polish Nat'l Alliance of Brooklyn | 1,171 | 3 | 348,800 |
| 9. Polish National Union | 3,354 | 51 | 1,506,870 |
| 10. Polish Roman Catholic Union | 13,471 | —965 | 6,567,111 |
| 11. Polish Union of Am. of N.Y. | 3,181 | 43 | 1,709,000 |
| 12. Polish Union of U.S. of America | 8,356 | —222 | 2,462,750 |
| 13. Polish Women's Alliance | 6,274 | —25 | 3,147,000 |
| Total: | 86,626 | —2,824 | $40,862,128 |

— Indicates Decrease

[a] Arthur Hamilton, Statistics, *Fraternal Societies* (Rochester: Fraternal Monitor, 1944). p. 19.

## TABLE XVII

### CHANGES IN ADULT MEMBERSHIP AND TOTAL INSURANCE IN FORCE IN 1943[a]

| Name of Society | Increase Adult Members | Decrease Adult Members | Increase in Total Insurance in Force in 1943 |
|---|---|---|---|
| 1. Alliance of Poles | 185 | ........ | —150,921 |
| 2. Ass'n of the Sons of Poland | 99 | ........ | 44,862 |
| 3. Polish Alma Mater | ........ | 98 | — 74,659 |
| 4. Polish Association of America | ........ | 108 | — 54,272 |
| 5. Polish Benefit Association | 437 | ........ | 132,856 |
| 6. Polish Falcons of America | 464 | ........ | 260,750 |
| 7. Pol. Nat'l Alliance of America | 4891 | ........ | 4,148,702 |
| 8. Pol. Nat'l Alliance of B'klyn | 96 | ........ | 240,600 |
| 9. Pol. Nat'l Union of America | 1322 | ........ | 471,974 |
| 10. Polish Rom. Cath. Union | ........ | 460 | 686,006 |
| 11. Polish Union of Am. (N.Y.) | 16 | ........ | 50,959 |
| 12. Pol. Union of U.S. of N.Y. | ........ | 19 | — 84,900 |
| 13. Polish Women's Alliance | 492 | ........ | 410,669 |

[a] Arthur Hamilton, *Statistics, Fraternal Societies* (Rochester: Fraternal Monitor, 1944), p. 29.
— Indicates Decrease

## Table XVIII

# LODGES, MEMBERSHIP BY STATES, JANUARY, 1944[a]

| States and Lodges | Polish National Alliance | Polish Roman Catholic Union |
|---|---|---|
| Lodges: | 1815 | |
| Arkansas | 107 | 76 |
| California | 389 | 389 |
| Colorado | 514 | 514 |
| Connecticut | 10,675 | 7,932 |
| Delaware | 487 | ......... |
| Florida | 32 | ......... |
| Illinois | 63,837 | 41,154 |
| Indiana | 7,839 | 5,190 |
| Kansas | 914 | 326 |
| Maryland | 3,929 | 2,458 |
| Massachusetts | 14,129 | 7,845 |
| Michigan | 24,571 | 10,056 |
| Minnesota | 3,149 | 561 |
| Missouri | 2,424 | 2,112 |
| Nebraska | 677 | 164 |
| New Hampshire | 916 | ......... |
| New Jersey | 14,413 | 8,694 |
| New York | 34,396 | 20,462 |
| Ohio | 16,434 | 5,985 |
| Oregon | 251 | ......... |
| Pennsylvania | 62,549 | 23,497 |
| Rhode Island | 2,189 | '369 |
| Texas | 955 | 166 |
| Vermont | 45 | 536 |
| Virginia | ......... | ......... |
| Washington | ......... | |
| Washington (D.C.) | 101 | ' ......... |
| West Virginia | 2,202 | 1,362 |
| Wisconsin | 10,086 | 4,335 |
| Canada | 6 | ......... |
| Miscellaneous | ......... | ......... |

[a]Arthur Hamilton, *Statistics, Fraternal Societies* (Rochester: Fraternal Monitor, 1944), pp. 44-60.

## Table XIX

## STATISTICAL CHART OF THE POLISH NATIONAL ALLIANCE GROWTH 1880 TO DECEMBER 31, 1954[a]

|      | Membership | Assets        |
|------|------------|---------------|
| 1885 | 295        | 3,660.63      |
| 1895 | 7,515      | 28,182.71     |
| 1905 | 45,271     | 321,930.71    |
| 1915 | 110,331    | 2,937,705.55  |
| 1925 | 219,720    | 14,207,594.15 |
| 1935 | 284,289    | 29,560,771.21 |
| 1945 | 291,605    | 40,712,293.33 |
| 1954 | 337,829    | 76,290,935.72 |

[a] "Censor-Judge Gunther Presents Interesting History of the Polish National Alliance," *Zgoda*, (February 7, 1955), p. 3.

## Table XX

## IMMIGRANTS WHO DEPARTED FROM THE UNITED STATES 1908-1931[a]

| Nationality             | Number    |
|-------------------------|-----------|
| Italians                | 1,240,884 |
| Poles                   | 339,428   |
| English                 | 208,081   |
| Greeks                  | 197,088   |
| Germans                 | 161,342   |
| Magyars                 | 156,019   |
| Slovaks                 | 132,763   |
| Scandinavians           | 125,308   |
| Croations and Slovenians| 118,129   |
| Russians                | 115,188   |

[a] Annual Report of the Commissioner General of Immigration, Fiscal Year Ended June 30, 1931. U.S. Department of Labor (Washington, 1931), p. 227.

## TABLE XXI

## MEMBERSHIP IN THE LARGEST AMERICAN POLISH ORGANIZATIONS SINCE 1955

| | Membership January, 1955 | Membership January, 1956 | Membership January, 1957 | Membership January, 1958 | Membership January, 1959 |
|---|---|---|---|---|---|
| Alliance of Poles of America, Cleveland, Ohio | 15,080 | 15,280 | 15,492 | 15,720 | 15,811 |
| Association of Sons of Poland, Jersey City, N. J. | 17,159 | 17,154 | 17,171 | 17,020 | 16,882 |
| Polish Beneficial Association Philadelphia, Pennsylvania | 24,547 | 24,663 | 23,820 | 24,763 | 24,816 |
| Polish Falcons of America Pittsburg, Pennsylvania | 20,423 | 20,893 | 21,463 | 22,016 | 22,364 |
| Polish National Alliance of America, Chicago, Illinois | 337,829 | 339,401 | 339,945 | 339,295 | 337,635 |
| Polish National Alliance of Brooklyn, New York | 20,652 | 20,431 | 20,410 | 20,064 | 19,765 |
| Polish National Union of America, Scranton, Pennsylvania | 30,570 | 31,105 | 31,512 | 31,517 | 31,358 |
| Polish Roman Catholic Union of America, Chicago, Illinois | 175,502 | 174,405 | 173,246 | 171,643 | 169,652 |
| Polish Union of America, Buffalo, New York | 17,598 | 17,364 | 17,346 | ............ | ............ |
| Polish Union of the U.S. of North America, Wilkes-Barre, Pa. | 21,232 | 20,775 | 20,477 | 20,102 | 19,630 |
| Polish Women's Alliance of America, Chicago, Illinois | 85,407 | 87,528 | 88,268 | 89,143 | 89,910 |

## Table XXII

## POLISH PRESS IN AMERICA IN JANUARY 1915[a]

| Name of Newspaper | Copies Printed |
|---|---|
| Dziennik Zwiazkowy | 70,000 |
| Kuryer (Milwaukee) | 40,000 |
| Dziennik Chikagoski | 25,000 |
| Dziennik Polski | 9,000 |
| Record | 16,000 |
| Dziennik Dla Wszystkich | 12,000 |
| Telegram (New York) | 4,000 |
| Ameryka Echo | 100,000 |
| Dziennik Ludowy | 8,000 |
| Dziennik Narodowy | 25,000 |

[a] Arthur Walenty Hausner, *Emigracja Polska w Ameryce w Czasie Obecnej Wojny* (Krakow: Nakladem Biura Wydawnictw N.K.N., 1916), p. 32.

TABLE XXIII

THE SLAVS IN 1950[a]

| Nationality | Number | Religion | Citizenship |
|---|---|---|---|
| EASTERN SLAVS | | | |
| Great Russians | 95,000,000 | Greek Orthodox | USSR |
| Ukrainians | 36,000,000 | Greek Orthodox & Greek Catholic, | USSR |
| Byelo-Russians | 8,000,000 | Greek Orthodox | USSR |
| WESTERN SLAVS | | | |
| Poles | 24,000,000 | Roman Catholic | Poland |
| Czechs | 8,00,000 | Roman Catholic | Czechoslovakia |
| Slovaks | 3,000,000 | Roman Catholic | Czechoslovakia |
| Lusatians | 100,000 | Protestant and Catholic | Eastern Germany |
| SOUTHERN SLAVS | | | |
| Serbs | 7,500,000 | Greek Orthodox | Yugoslavia |
| Croats | 4,500,000 | Roman Catholic | Yugoslavia |
| Slovenes | 1,400,000 | Roman Catholic | Yugoslavia |
| Macedonians | 1,100,000 | Greek Orthodox | Yugoslavia |
| Bulgarians | 6,500,000 | Greek Orthodox | Bulgaria |

[a] Hans Kohn, *Pan-Slavism, Its History and Ideology* (Notre Dame: University of Notre Dame Press, 1953), p. 337

# INDEX

Ablamowicz, A., 52
Adamic, L., 66
Adams, J. Q., 216
'Adamkiewicz, 144
Adamkiewicz, W. 27
Adamowski, B. S. 97
Adelaida, 3
Agencja Polskiej Kolonizacji, 120
Akron, 84
Alaska 67, 96
Albanians, 234
Albany, 26, 32, 60
Albertrandi, Rev. A. 43
Alexander I, Czar of Russia, 17, 130, 131, 133
Alexander II, Czar of Russia, 134, 137
Alexander III, Czar of Russia, 137
Allan J., 65
Alleghenies, 34
Allen, W., 53
Alliance College, 104, 198, 202-209, 228, 235, 242, 274, 277, 290
Alliance Daily, 261
Alliance of Polish Priests in America, 187-190
Ameryka Echo, 193
American Anti-Slavery Society, 54
American Council of Polish Cultural Clubs, 284, 285, 291
American Emigrant Company, 114
American Journal of International Law, 268-269
American Library Association, 75
American Medical Association, 89
American Museum of Immigration, 225
American Red Cross, 202, 211
American Steamship Company, 115
Amish, 246
Amsterdam, 24, 45
Anaheim, 83
Anderson Galleries, 222
Anderson, J. K., 288
Andrea, Sister M., 156
Andrzejewski, J. W., 60
Andrzejkowicz, J. 173, 174
Antietam, 68
Arcadia Leader, 63
Arcadia Republican, 64
Archacki, H., 21

Arciszewski, C., 25
Arctowski, H., 80
Argentina, 106, 223
Arlington Cemetery, 67
Armand Legion, 41
Armenians, 106
Ashland, 200
Askenazy, S., 179
Association of Poles in America, 59
Astor, 31,
Astor Rifles, 70
Atkielski, Bishop R. A., 101
Atlantic Charter, 262, 263, 265, 269
Atomic Energy Commission, 90
August I, 12
August II, 12
Austria, 15, 49, 100, 148, 173, 180
Austrian Poland, 139-147, 154
Austrians, 139-147, 192
Ayerst, D. G. O., 131

Babbish, B., 94
Babiarz, J., 96
Babinczak, S., 97
Bacciarelli, 279
Bach, 80-82
Baczkowski, 97
Baczynski, 144
Badzmierowski, Dr., 216
Bakanowski, Rev., 62
Bakowicz, R., 53
Bakut, P., 42
Balch, E. G., 31, 63, 109, 146, 149, 152
Baldeski, Captain, 41
Baldwin Locomotive Works, 277
Balezowski, S., 58
Baltic Sea, 1, 3, 7, 23
Baltimore, 41, 58, 74, 199
Baltimore Catholic Review, 74
Baltimore Evening Sun, 74
Baltimore News, 74
Balyca, S., 42
Banasik, E., 217
Bandera, 62
Baptists, 103
Barabasz, Rev. M., 188
Barc, F. S., 209, 252
Barczak, M., 97
Bard College, 30
Baretski, C. A., 83

331

Barlin, 5
Barlow, J., 216
Barsk, J., 42
Bartek, Sgt. J., 99
Bartlett Hotel, 206
Barton, J. R., 246
Bartosiewicz, A., 97
Barzynski, J., 168, 171
Barzynski, Gen. J., 99, 168, 171
Barzynski, Rev. V., 168, 171, 177, 291
Batavia, New York, 52
Baton Rouge, 75, 76
Batory, S., 12, 107
Batowski, S., 222
Battle Creek, Michigan, 55
Battle of Buena Vista, 61
Battle of Gollath, 61
Battle of Hatcher Run, 69
Battle of Maciejowice, 38
Bay City, 215
Bayard, 31
Beck-Rzykowski, 144
Beczkowski, P., 173
Bekas, G., 42
Belinski, J. T., 97
Bethlehem, Pa., 40
Belle Isle, 92
Belmont, 68
Bem, 54
Bembo, J., 28
Bemis Heights, 36
Benda, S., 92
Benda, W., 83, 223, 284
Benedictines, 102
Beniowski, B., 74
Benjamin, R. S., 117
Bercovici, K., 86, 194
Berkeley, 279
Berlin, 5, 56
Bern, Sister M. Accursia, 230
Bernal Springs, 70
Bernadine Sisters of the Third Order of
   St. Francis, 103
Bethlehem, P., 40
Biachowski, J., 173
Biadynsky, J., 173
Bibliotheca Fratrum Polonorum, 46
Bibliotheque Polonaise, 74
Bielaski, Capt. A., 51, 68
Bielawski, A., 96, 97
Bielawski, C., 57
Bielawski, Dr. J. B., 88
Bieszczat, M., 96, 97
Bilinski, 144
Biron, Armand Louis de Gontaut, 44
Bismark, O., 123-130, 148
Black Sea, 7, 8
Blandowski, Capt. B., 65
Blaskowicz, 32, 33
Blaszkowicz, Capt. C. 32, 33
Blaszkowicz, K. 47

Blitkowski, G. A., 74
Bluntchli, 123
Bluskey, F. O., 42
Blyzka, M., 94
Bober River, 5
Bobrzynski, M., 178
Bochenski, Rev. A., 28, 32, 40, 50-52, 58,
   65, 75, 86, 87
Bodger, J. C., 65, 70
Boeck, L. F., 57, 58
Boeck, L. J. 57
Boeing Airplane Company, 95
Boerne, L., 132
Bogdan, J., 21
Bohemia, 2, 8, 145
Bohusiewicz, E. B., 58
Bojanowski, A., 80
Bojko, J., 143, 150, 151
Bojnowski, Msgr. L., 190
Bolek, Rev. F., 291
Boleslaus II, 3
Boleslaus III, 3, 5
Boleslaus IV, 5
Boleslaus Chrobry, 3
Boleslawski, R., 83
Bolich, J., 42
Bolich, P., 42
Bologna, 6
Bona, Bishop S. V., 102
Bonia, J. 42
Bonaparte, N., 15, 47
Bonita, H., 42
Bonk, K., 97
Bonnie Prince Charlie, 107
Bonsal, Capt. F. B., 69
Bonzell, Dr. F., 89
Boone, D., 32, 34
Boone, G., 32
Boone, J., 32
Borkowicz, Msgr. V. V., 90
Boston, 46, 47, 52, 92, 101, 104, 199, 212
Boston Evening Transcript, 57
Boston Globe, 85
Boston Transcript, 59
Botzen, Baron, 41
Bourskaya, I., 284
Bozec, A., 42
Bradley, Prof., 75
Brandenburg, 5
Brandes, G., 133, 136, 138, 162
Brandt, 279
Brandywine, 41
Branibor, 5
Brazil, 25, 56, 106, 223
Brick, A., 197
Brighton, 55,
Broga, A., 42
Brominski, S., 97
Brook-Farm Community, 78
Brookhaven National Laboratory, 90
Brooklyn, 70, 188

Brown, F. J., 101, 102, 273
Bruce, M., 127
Brucki, J., 32
Brust, J., 97
Brys, J., 73
Buczkowska, H., 96
Buffalo, New York, 45, 52, 78, 79, 95, 96, 100, 101, 163, 196, 210, 239, 262, 263
Bug, 136
Bugeja, C., 96
Bukowski, E., 97
Bulas, K., 279
Bull Run, 66
Bulow, Count, 128
Buraczynski, A., 97
Burant, Msgr. F. F., 90, 272
Burcky, P., 42
Burdjat, C., 42
Burlington, 104
Burnside, General, 68
Burskaya, I., 83
Busyn, H., 68
Butkiewicz, C., 27
Byron, 131
Byzantine Civilization, 2

Cadiz, 20
Cahenslyism, 169
California, 51, 60, 70, 78, 83, 96, 98, 100, 174, 217
Callaghan, J. D., 92
Gallao, Peru, 75
Cambridge Springs, Pa., 104, 203, 204 206, 209, 235
Cameron, 66
Camp Anite, 71
Canada, 33, 47, 50, 51, 223, 285
Canadian Pacific Railway, 51
Cape Elizabeth, 32,
Caprivi, 129, 145,
Cardwell, A., S., 269
Carey, M., 49
Carnegie, A., 234
Carnegie Hall, 278
Carnegie Institute of Technology, 90
Caro, Dr. L., 122, 139
Carpathian Mts., 1, 139
Carpenter, M., 239
Carroll, Bishop, 48
Casareych, H., 42
Casimir I, 3
Casimir the Great, 6
Casimir the Just, 5
Castel Rio Grande, 26
Castle Garden, 85, 116
Catholic University of America, 90
Catholic University of Lublin, 185
Catholic World, 268
Caucasus, 133
Cavour, 173
Cazenovia, 45

Celtes, 7
Centennial Exposition, 58
Central-Penn National Bank, 95
Century of Progress Exposition, 284
Chancellersville, 66, 68, 72
Chandler, A. D., 21
Charapata, A., 97
Charles X of France, 132
Charlestown, 41, 43
Chalupetzky, J., 42
Chelmonski, 279
Chicago, 42, 67, 69, 78, 79, 84, 93, 95, 96, 98, 100, 101, 104, 167, 168, 170, 184, 185, 198, 201, 209, 210, 212-215, 218, 224, 225, 231, 253, 266, 282
Chicago Arts Club, 283, 284
China, 51, 102
Chmielinska, S., 184, 185
Chmura, S., 96
Chodakowski, 59
Chodasiewicz, Capt. R. A., 69
Chojnice, Poland, 35
Cholko, W., 97
Chopin, F., 30, 66, 222
Chopin Scholarships, 278
Chrobry, B., 3
Christian, King of Denmark, 20
Churchill, W., 262, 263, 267
Cibolo River, 61, 73
Ciechanowski, J., 266, 267
Cierniak, H. F., 97
Ciesinski, A. F., 96
Cincinnati 59, 93
Cincinnatti Enquirer, 59
Cisko, T., 42
Cistercians, 2
Civil War in America, 65
Clackamas County, 60
Clay, C. M., 71
Cleveland, GG., 75
Cleveland, Ohio, 56, 78, 79, 80, 90, 100, 101, 102, 104, 187
Cleveland Orchestra, 80
Coblenz, 55
Coleman, A. P., 40, 47, 205, 208, 219,
Coleman, M. M., 75
College of St. John, 48
Collosha, P., 32
Colorado, 70
Colton, R. C., 71
Columbia, S. C., 54
Columbia University, 275
Columbus, C., 20, 115, 162
Commons, J. R., 110
Congregation of the Resurrectionist Fathers, 103
Congregationalists, 103
Congress of Vienna of 1815, 15, 130, 131, 133
Congress Poland, 133-139
Conklin, E, M., 90

Connecticut, 35, 42, 81, 95, 97, 98, 100, 101, 190, 199, 217, 219
Connecticut Valley, 85, 86
Conrad, J., 246
Constantinople, 57
Conventual Franciscans, 102, 104
Coolidge, C., 85, 86
Cooper, J. F., 51, 216
Cooperstown, 51
Copera, F., 42
Copernicus, N., 7, 278
Copernicus High School, 93
Corinth, 68
Cossacks, 12, 107, 133
Courage, R., 87, 89
Crimean War, 134
Crimmins, J. 94
Cross Keys, 66
Cudahy, 82, 198
Cukrowski, A. Z., 97
Cultural Pluralist Hypothesis, 244-248
Cumberland River, 34
Curie, E., 138
Curie, M., Sklodowska, 89, 138, 246
Curti, M., 63, 64, 109, 110
Curtiss, A., 27, 28
Curtius, 27
Curzon Line, 267, 269
Cushing, Archbishop, 212
Czachorski, W., 222
Czar Paul, 39
Czarnecki, 13, 59
Czartoryski, Lieut. C. A., 69
Czartoryski, Prince A., 58, 278
Czechoslovakia, 1
Czechs, 3, 88, 140, 234
Czerwinski, F. 60
Czestochowa, 166, 222
Czestochowa, Texas, 62
Cysewieski, J. K., 63

Dabrowka, 2
Dabrowski, Rev. J., 35, 213, 233
Dalmatia, 80
Danes, 246
Daniels, J., 167, 195
Dann, M. 94
Danowski, Dr. T., 89
Danube River, 3
Danzig, 6, 8, 106, 122
Dartmouth College, 218
Darvi, B., 83
Davis, P. 85,, 111
Dead Man's Corner, 69
Dearborn, Michigan, 89
Deaskey, L., 42
Debicki, L. N., 61
Deerfield Valley, 86
De Falls, M., 81
Defiance College, 58
De Kalb Regiment, 70

Delaware, 96
Delaware Indians, 35
Delaware River, 20, 25, 42
Delwicz, C. 42
Dembrinske, 61
Democratic Society of Polish Refugees in America, 59
Denmark, 3, 146
Dende, H. J., 96, 97
De Paul University, 202, 218
De Reszke, E., 83
De Reszke, J., 83
Derproskey, W. F., 70
Derwinski, E. J., 96
Deskey, J., 42
Desko, S., 42
Detroit, 42, 64, 78, 79, 88, 89, 91, 92, 100-102, 104, 168, 192, 198, 200, 233, 241, 243, 288, 289
Detroit Free Press, 87, 88, 92, 94
Detroit News, 288
Detroit Symphony Orchestra, 92
Dewey, T. E., 266, 267
Dewicki, E. F., 96
De Zychlinski, W. T., 98
Didur, A. 83
Dingell, J. D., 96
Diocese of Cleveland, 90
Diocese of La Crosse, 90
Displaced Persons Act, 271, 273
Dlugosz, J., 7
Dmochowski-Saunders, H., 57
Dmowski, R., 17, 240
Dnester River, 2
Dnieper River, 2
Dobbs, J., 97
Dodge, Wisconsin, 63
Dobrowski, F., 97
Dojewski, R. A., 96
Dolde, C., 143
Dolewczynski, Prof., 204
Dolo, J., 42
Dom Polski, in Detroit, 91
Doman, J., 42
Doman, M., 42
Doman, Sister Mary Tullia, 136
Domanski. V., 173
Dombrowski, E., 96
Don, 133
Don Bosco College, 274
Donne, J., 157
Donich, H., 42
Doniphan Expedition. 61
Drabik, Sgt. A. A., 99
Drachsler, J., 162
Dubdal, Dr. E. A., 97
Duchy of Moscow, 10, 13
Duchy of Poznan, 122-130
Duke Jacob of Courland,19
Duke of Anjou, 12
Duke of Lauzun, 44

Duke of Lorraine, 12
Duker, A. B., 132
Dulski, T. J., 96
Dunin. J., 201
Dunkirk, 200
Duquesne University, 210
Durea, 200
Dusky. J., 42
Duszak. Dr. M., 204, 205
Dutchmen, 22, 246
Dworaczyk, Rev. E., 62, 219
Dyboski, R., 41, 45, 98
Dybowski, Prof., 284
Dybowski, Z., 273
Dyke, F., 98
Dymek, F., 202
Dziennik Chicagoski, 104, 177
Dziennik Polski, 75, 85, 104, 204, 289
Dziennik Zjednoczenia, 220, 221
Dziennik Zwiazkowy, 104
Dzierozynski, Rev. F., 48, 49
Dziuba, S., 53
Dziuban, S., 99
Dziuk, A., 73

Easco Bay, 31
East Baltic Slavs, 24
East Prussia, 8
Echo z Polski, 52
Edict of Nantes, 31
Einstein, A., 90, 278
Eis, Bishop, 183
Eisenhower, D. D., 269, 270, 275
Elba River, 213
Elbe River, 3, 5
Elbingh, 25
Ellis Island, 116, 188, 199
Elizabeth, N. J., 47
Elster, 3
Emerson, W., 55
Emigration Congresses, 240, 241
England, 3, 10, 43, 173, 246
English, 176, 234
Episcopalians, 103
Erie, Pennsylvania, 50, 203, 212, 240
Estonia, 23
Evans, A. W. W., 39
Evashevski, F., 94
Eversley, L., 132
Everybody's Daily, 289

Fabricius, J. C., 42
Falat, J., 222, 279
Falk, 124
Falkowski, E., 117
Falls City, Texas, 62
Fannin, Col., 61
Feldman, J., 122
Felician Sisters, 79, 103, 104, 188, 190
Fenwick, Bishop, 49

Fernandez, F., 20
Ferrell, R. H., 22
Fijalkowski, Prof., 204
Filipowicz, Msgr. W., 90
Finns, 24
Fiolkowski, J., 47
First Fugitive Slave Law, 57
First German Rifles Regiment, 70
Fisher, H. H., 41
Fitzgerald, F. S., 83
Flanders, 10
Flexner, E., 53, 57
Florian, E. A., 75
Florida, 51
Folger Shakespeare Library, 21
Fontana, J., 52, 57
Fordham University, 48
Fort Casimir, 24, 26, 28
Fort Christina, 24
Fort Delaware, 67
Fort Duquesne, 35
Fort Henry, 51
Fort Nassau, 26
Fort Orange, 24
Fort Sumter, 65, 73
Fort Trinity, 26
Fortress Monroe, 75
Fox, P., 123, 149
France, 1, 15, 31, 78, 109, 127, 141, 145, 246
Francis Joseph of Austria, 143, 144
Franciscan Order of Friars Minor, 104
Franciscan Sisters of Blessed Kunegunda, 103
Franciscan Sisters (St. Louis), 103
Franco-Prussian War, 123
Fronczak, Health Commissioner, 163
Frankfurt, 132
Franklin, B., 47
Franko, M., 42
Fratres Poloni, 24
Frederick Chopin Institute, 30
Frederick, Maryland, 48
Frederick the Great, 126
Frederick William, the Great Elector, 126
Fredericksburg, 68
French, 10, 62, 176, 246
French And Indian War, 32
Friars Minor, 102
Funk, C., 83
Furdyna, J. K., 20
Furgol, E., 94
Furlong, W. B., 246

Gabriel, J., 41
Gadon, L., 49
Galicia, 139-147
Galik, J., 32
Gallagher, 82
Gallagher, Bishop J., 91
Gallus Anonymus, 2

Galveston, 62
Garczynski, J., 96
Gardner, M., 140
Garibaldi, 65, 173
Garney, A., 42
Garrison, 54
Gaski, C., 32
Gates, General, 36
Gaudentia, Sister M., 30
*Gazeta Katolicka*, 177
Gdansk see Danzig,
Gebicki, L. 95
Georgetown University, 48, 49, 80
Georgia, 42, 43, 58, 69
Germany, 99, 100, 142, 145, 146, 148, 181
Germans, 3, 6, 24, 62, 106, 176, 189, 192, 246, 260
German-Americans, 169-170, 234
Germantown, Pa., 35
Gettysburg, 66, 72, 74
Gibbon, J. M., 12, 261
Gibbon, M., 107
Gielgud, General, 58
Gieryk, Rev. T., 168, 171, 291
Giller, A., 150, 172, 173, 291
Girardot, Baron, 38
Givens, W. E., 154
Glomicki, A., 74
Glomski, H. M., 93
Glorietta Pass, 70
Gloskowski, Capt. J., 68
*Glos Polek*, 185
Gloucester, 199
Glowacki, H. I., 52
Glogow, 3
Gmina Polska, 101
Gniezno, 2, 3, 129
Godkin, E. L., 234
Goebbels, J., 266
Goerck, C. T., 33, 34
Goerck, E., 34
Goerck, H., 34
Goerck, T., 34
Golembiewski, F., 97
Golkowski, G. W., 32
Gordon, J., 71
Gordon, Rev. F., 186
Gorlinski, J., 69
Gorski, C., 96
Goslicki, W., 40
Grabiarz, W., 99, 100
Grabiarz Expressway, 100
Grabowski, Col. A., 58, 73
Grabowski, C., 283
Grabowski, J., 44
Grabowski, Count M., 44, 45
Grabowski, Rev. S., 90
Gracanowski, W., 70
Gramza, M., 21
Grand Duchy of Warsaw, 47

Grand Duke Constantine, 15
Grand Rapids, 98, 200
Grant, J., 32
Grant, U., 58, 67
Gray, G., 31
Gray, Gilda, 82
Gravelotte, 123
Great Britain, 262
Great Poland, 5
Greboszow, 143
*Greeley's Tribune*, 57
Greeks, 155
Greene, General, 36, 37, 216
Gregorian University, 91
Greenwood Cemetery, 70
Gregory, J. J., 99, 100
Griglik, C., 96
Grodno, 135
Gromek, S., 94
Grosz Polski Society, 184
Grottger, A., 222
Grunwald, 8, 166, 222
Gregorczyk, J., 96
Gryglewski, A., 279
Grzesicki, General, 144
Guadalcanal, 99
Gulcz, Rev. J., 188
Gunther, Judge B. F., 211, 271
Gurowski, A., 71
Gurowski, Count A., 57
Gzowski, K. S., 50

Hackensack, 29
Hackensack River, 28
Haight, C. S., 40
Haiman, M., 20, 28, 29, 32-34, 37, 38, 41-43, 45, 46, 56, 60, 61, 67, 70, 106, 149, 156, 171, 202, 212-215, 218, 219, 221, 223, 224, 226, 231, 240, 242, 282
Hajda, Dr. J., 96
Hajduk, A. T., 97
Hakata, 127
Hale, E., 193
Halecki, O., 280, 281
Halicz, 5
Halka Opera, 92
Hall, P. F., 79
Haller, Gen. J., 91
Hallicia, J., 42
Hamburg American Line, 130
Hamtramck, Michigan, 88, 89, 93, 101, 209
Hamtramck Philharmonic, 93
Hand, see Hanouw
Handlin, O., 150, 153
Hanna, E. E., 113
Hanouw, J., 28
Hanseatic League, 7
Hapsburgs, 49, 140, 142
Hardon, Rev. J. A., 171

Harris, P. C., 205
Harrodsburg, 34
Harvard University, 27, 30, 31, 46, 278, 280
Haskell Institute, 58
Haydn, 82
Heine, H., 132
Heilprin, M., 75
Helvetius, 40
Hendricksen, H., 25
Hennemann, 127,
Hernisz, S., 51
Henry II, Emperor, 3
Henry III, King of France, 12
Henry of Valois, 12
Henry IV of Wroclaw, 6
Herman Kiefer Hospital, 89
Hill, G. W., 289
Hill, N., 125
Hispaniola, 20
Hitler, 265
Hodur, Rev. F., 103
Hoffman, J., 80
Hohenlohe, Princess, 135
Hohenzollerns, 59, 122
Hojnacki, F., 94
Hojnacki, S. L., 193
Hojnacki, A. J., 60
Holland, 19, 24
Holland Land Company, 45
Holland, S., 32
Hollywood, 83
Holski, E., 70
Holy Cross College, 49
Holy Cross Fathers, 102
Holynski, 51, 71
Homer, 54
Homes, F. L., 289
Hooker, General J., 69
Hoover, H., 237, 267
Hoover Mission, 211
Hordynski, Major J., 52
Hospital Charite, 56
House of Burgesses, 22
House of Vasa, 12
Houston, 279,
Hoyle, S. L. 193
Huberman, B., 80
Hudson River, 28
Huerta, President of Mexico, 187
Hulanicki, Capt. J. C., 67
Hulanicki, E. T., 69
Hull, Agrippa, 38
Humanism, 177
Humbolt Park, 185
Humphreys, D., 47
Hungarians, 6, 234
Hungary, 8, 13, 65
Hussite Movement, 10
Hynicki, J., 70
Icaisky, J., 42

Icelanders, 246
Ignasiak, Rev. A., 240
Illinois, 49, 60, 78, 79, 97, 100, 101, 174, 186, 210, 217, 219, 220
Illinois Staats Zeitung, 70
Immaculate Conception Junior College, 104
Independence Weekly News Bulletin, 64
India, 7
Indiana, 78, 96, 197, 210, 220
Indiana University, 90
Indians, 20
Inflanty, 10
Institute of Research on Poles in America, 283
Instytut Wiedzy of Polonii, Amerykan-skiej, 283
International Alliance of Poles Abroad, 242
International Catholic Migration Commis-sion, 80
Iowa, 70
Ireland, 2, 234
Irish, 62, 84, 169, 189, 234
Irish-Americans, 169-170, 193, 234
Irish-Catholic Church, 169
Irish Clergy, 181
Isaki, A., 42
Israelites, 182
Italians, 234,
Italy, 2, 143, 173
Ivan the Terrible, 12

Jablonowski, Prince A., 39
Jablonski, R., 94, 96
Jackson, Stonewall, 67
Jadwiga, Queen of Poland, 7, 151
Jagiello, W., 8
Jagiellonian Dynasty, 7, 8
Jagiellonian University, 6, 144, 177, 205, 284
Jakubowski, A., 134
Janta, A., 258
James VI, 107
Jamestown, Va., 21-23, 84, 287
Janiga, J. J., 96
Janosik, E., 97
Janowski, C., 94
Janta, A., 58, 218
Japanese, 99
Jaros, 94
Jarosinski, S. P., 96
Jasinski, Rev. V., 90
Jasinski, Rev. W., 165, 166
Jastremski, L., 72, 75, 76
Jastrow, Dr. J., 83
Jastrzebski see Jastremski
Jaworski, J, C., 96
Jay, 31
Jedrzejewicz, W., 282
Jeefe, C. R., 42

Jefferson, T., 37, 45, 47, 54, 71, 215
Jersey City, 101
Jerzmanowski, 41
Jesuit Mission at Goshenhoppen, 48
Jesuits, 102, 125
Jews, 6, 106
Jews of Germany, 132
Jezykowicz, Rev. L., 59
John of Kolno, 20
Jolson, A., 82
Jones County, 70
Joselevitch, 153
Joseph II of Austria, 139
Joseph Pilsudski Institute, 282, 291
Joski, 53
Juillard School of Music, 278
Jurgielewicz, 59, 71

Kaczanowski, 59
Kaczmarczyk, A., 99
Kaczmarek, S. J., 96
Kaczorowski, 59
Kaekglosco, J. H., 32
Kaghaatsko, N., 42
Kahanowicz, Dr. A., 216
Kalussowski, H., 58, 75, 77, 191, 200
Kaminski, A., 64
Kaminski, H., 73
Kanarek, E., 83
Kania, F., 98, 223
Kania, J. L., 217, 221, 263
Kanowska, B., 97
Kansas, 58, 96, 220
Kanski, E., 58
Kanski, J. F., 98
Kaplita, D. W. A., 89
Kapustin, Dr. S. 244
Kar, A. L., 134
Karczew, 44
Karczewski, J., 52
Karczmar, Dr. A. C., 89
Karge, J., 67, 222
Karlowiczowa, J., 243
Karpinski, Prof. L., 83
Karski, J., 80
Karsh, J. 285
Katoski, G. G., 78
Katowice, 218
Katyn Forest, 268
Katyn Massacre, 239
Katz, D., 239
Kazanski, T., 94
Kean, S., 47
Kecki, M., 97
Kedzierski, A., 222
Kellerman, F. C., 47
Kelly, Mayor of Chicago, 265
Kelly, E. P. 218, 277
Kennemann, 127
Kentucky, 34, 60
Kertesz, S. D., 22

Kessler, H. H., 27
Ketchel, S., 93
Kezon, P., 96, 97
Kicking Horse Pass, 51
Kiecal, S., 93
Kiepura, J., 83
Kierski, J. S., 60
Kierski, W. 60
Kiev, 3, 133, 135
    Club, 167
King Casimir the Great, Polish Citizens
    Club, 167
Kinel, L., 245
King Feature Syndicate Inc., 99
King Louis XV of France, 12
Kingsbury, S. M., 23
Kiolbassa, I., 73
Kiolbassa, Capt. P., 62, 68, 73, 214
Kiowa County, 61
Kipa, E., 46
Kirkconnell, Dr. W., 243
Kleha, A., 97
Klewicki, E., 94
Klimecki, Rev. H., 188
Klimkiewicz, T., 73, 74
Kline, J. R., 280
Klonowski, Bishop H. T., 102
Kluczynski, J. C., 96
Kluszewski, T., 93
Knias, J., 42
Knights of the Cross, 166, 181
Kochanska, M., Sembrich, 83, 285
Kohn, H., 141
Kokogai, S., 42
Kolat, Sister M. B., 35, 40, 59, 65
Kolno, 20
Kolodziejczyk, T., 73
Kolomyja, 21
Kolski, E. P., 97
Konarski, 90
Konigsberg, 122
Konovalov, S., 137
Konopczynski, W., 219
Konopinski, Dr. E. J., 89, 90
Konstanty, J., 94
Koprowski, Dr. H., 80
Korczewski, M., 21
Korczynski, Dr., 100
Korszynska, M., 52
Kortickey, 61
Korzon, T., 179
Korzybski, A., 83
Koscialowski, Capt. N., 61
Koscielski, J., 145
Kosciuszko Association, 281
Kosciuszko Club, 157
Kosciuszko Foundation, 274, 276-280,
    291
Kosciuszko, T., 15, 36-39, 45, 53, 54, 65,
    68, 71, 99, 108, 109, 144, 151, 162,
    182, 185, 186, 197, 198, 206, 215, 216,

274, 279, 284
Kosciuszko, Texas, 62
Koslow, J., 42
Koss, M., 96
Kossak, J., 222, 279
Kossak, Capt. W., 68
Kossak, W., 222, 279
Kossuth, 54, 57, 65, 70
Kotkowski, 41
Kovaleski, F., 94
Kowalczyk, E. L., 28, 35, 43, 47, 52, 59, 69, 72, 73, 74, 98
Kowalczyk, J. J., 126
Kowalkowski, G., 96
Kowalski, 59, 279
Kowalski, A., 214
Kowalski, F., 96
Kowalski, H., 53
Kowalski, J., 97
Kowalski, Bishop R., 102
Kowan, J., 42
Kowno, 135
Kozakiewicz, K. I., 163
Kozaks, 24
Kozaren, J. J., 97
Kozlow, S., 83
Kozlowski, Bishop E., 170
Kozlowski, J., 96
Kozlowski, L. M., 219
Kozlowski, M., 70
Kozlowski, P., 209
Kozmian, S., 143
Kracolo, H., 42
Krajewski, S., 258
Krak, G., 42
Krakow, 2, 5, 7, 8, 10, 39, 82, 107, 139, 143, 144, 179, 181, 205, 277
Krakow Historical School, 177, 178, 179
Krakow Learned Society, 144
Krasoska-Stopowa, J., 201
Kraszewski, M., 60
Krawiec, H., 92
Krawiec, W., 92
Kridl, M., 12, 13
Krokowski, J., 70
Krol, T., 94, 102
Krolewiec, 122
Krolikowska, L., 52
Kromka, H., 21
Krukowski, B. S. J., 48
Kruszka, W., 20, 21, 27, 47, 62, 149, 159, 169, 170, 183
Krygier, Capt. M., 28, 99
Kryniewicz, T. T., 272
Kryzan, F. X., 96
Krzesinski, Rev. A., 90
Krzywoszynski, J., 70
Krzyzanowski, L., 46
Krzyzanowski, V., 66, 67, 99
Kuberski, E., 206
Kucharski, F. F., 97

Kucielski, T., 173
Kudlicka, J., 245
Kukiel, M., 278
Kulawy, J., 21
Kulik, B. M., 97
Kulinski, J., 74
Kulski, W. W., 266
Kulturkampf, 123, 145
Kumiega, J., 96
Kuraw, G., 422
Kurcjusz, 199
Kurczewski, Dr. A. K., 27, 28, 108
Kurek, A., 58
Kurjer Codzienny, 104
Kurjer Polski, 104, 162, 163
Kurka, J., 97
Kurkowska, Sister M. Stanislaus, 92
Kushel, J., 42
Kusielewicz, E., 46, 47
Kusky, B., 42
Kustel, C. B., 70
Kuzawa, A. B., 94
Kyrisk, Capt. J., 73


Labrador, 20
Ladislaus Herman, 3
Ladislaus the Short, 6
Lafayette, General, 48, 54
Lagodzinska, A., 21, 27, 28, 74, 186
Lakeville, 81
La Legion Royale, 45
Landis, C., 83
Landowska, W., 80-82
Lane, F., 193
Lapacinski, L., 99
Laske, C., 94
Laskey, James, 42
Laskey, John, 42
Laski, 43
Laskowski, S., 97
Latzcho, J., 32
Latzcho, M., 32
Laur Dancing Society, 92, 243, 245
Lawrence, Kansas, 58
Lazarus, E., 147
Learmont, 107
Lednicka, M., 84
Lednicka, Dr., W., 281
Ledochowski, Archibishop, 125
Lee, Major General C., 108
Lee, H., 41
Lee Legion, 41
Lee, R. E., 41
Lehmanowski, J. J., 58
Legion of Lauzun, 44, 45
Lemberg see Lwow
Lemke, J., 65
Lenart, Dr. F., 257
Lenczyca, 5
Lend Lease, 265

Lenski, M., 96
Lepowski, N., 52, 58
Lermontov, M., 107
Lerski, J. J., 49, 50, 51, 52, 137, 279
Leshinskey, S., 42
Lesinski, J., 96, 97
Leski, Capt. W., 68
Lesniewicz, S., 218
Lessman, M., 63
Lessman, P., 63
Leszczynska, M., 12
Leszczynski, A., 64
Leszczynski, S., 12, 109
Leszek, Prince, 5
Levasvick, G., 42
Lew, H., 81
Lewandowska, Sister M. Theodosette, 68, 69, 70
Lewinski, T., 71
Lewitter, L. R., 107
Liberski, R., 70
Liberty Bell, 198
Liberum Veto, 13
Liguori, Sister, HFN, 73
Ligouri, Sister M., CSFN, 56, 57
Lincoln, A., 57, 66, 67, 119, 186
Lintz, A., 64
Lipinski, J., 173
Lipinsky, D., 94
Lipon, J., 94
Lipowski, Rev., 48
Lisicki, J., 97
Liske, Prof. X., 179
Liskowacki, F., see Florian, E. A.,
Liss, B., 96
Lissy, J., 73
Lissy, W., 73
Lithgow, W., 107
Lithuania, 8, 129, 134, 135, 166, 177
Lithuanians, 6, 88
Litowski, 41
Litscho, A., 25, 26, 27
Litscho, D., 25, 26
Littman, Lieut. J., 69
Livera, P., 63
Livonia, 12, 23, 104
Locke, 40
Lodi, 104
Lodz, 107
Lombardy, 143
London Company, 23
Long Island, 86
Longfellow, H. W., 40
Lonn, E., 65-69, 71, 72, 73
Lopat, E., 93
Lopata, H. Z., 79, 271, 283
Lopata, S., 94
Los Angeles, 100, 217
Losieniecki, Msgr. W. A., 90
Lotka, Dr. A. J., 83
Louis XVI of France, 44

Louis Philippe, 132
Louisiana, 51, 60, 69
Louvre, 12
Lovick, M., 42
Lowe, T. S. C., 75
Lowicki, M., 21
Loyalists, 33
Loyola University, 89, 218
Lubanski, E., 94
Lubienski, General, 58
Lubinski, J., 63
Lublin, 10
Lucas, H. S., 45
Luce, 63
Lucille, Sister M., 120, 149
Lusatians, 3
Luske, S., 42
Lutnia Singing Society, 92
Lutnicki, V., 60
Lwow, 3, 8, 139, 142, 144, 179
Lwow University, 178
Lycee of Krzemieniec, 133
Lyon, N. E., 160

MacCracken, Dr. H. N., 227
Mach, J., 96
Machowski, I., 21
Machrowicz, T. M., 96
Maciejowice, 39
Macioszczyk, A., 94
Mackenzie, W. L., 51
Mackiewicz Seidel de, 74
MacLean's Magazine, 261
Macowitzki, C., 70
Madonna College, 104, 274
Magruder, Major General, J., 72
Mahoney, M. E., 57
Maine, 96
Maisel, A. Q., 21, 58, 89, 93, 94, 95, 98
Majeski, H., 94
Majka, A. A., 96
Makarewicz, I., 219
Makielski, Brothers, 84
Makielski, L., 92
Makulski, J., 97
Malachowski, General, 58
Malanowski, L. V., 966
Malaszko, J., 21
Malczewski, J., 222, 279
Malich, J. J., 96
Malich, P., 24
Malick, A., 42
Malick, J., 42
Malinowski, B. K., 83, 281
Malinowski, G., 94
Malvern Hill, 72
Manhattan Island, 25
Mankiewicz, D., 97
Manning, C. S., 24, 46, 109, 280
Marblehead, 43
Marcin, J. C., 97

Marciszewski, 96
Marcovitch, J., 70
Maria Theresa, 139
Marian Fathers, 102
Marion, 58
Marlowe, K., 83
Marquette, 102, 183
Maryland, 42, 96, 97
Maryland Historical Society, 41
Masney, T., 42
Masovia, 5
Masovians, 2
Massachusetts, 32, 42, 43, 79, 86, 96, 97, 101, 217, 219
Massachusetts Institute of Technology, 75
Mata, J., 221
Matejko, J., 181, 279
Matera, R., 97
Matoga, Rev. G., 48
Matyka, General, 99
May, A. J., 179
Mayflower, 27
Mazzini, 54, 173
McClernand, General J. A., 68
McDowell, General, 68
McGinnis Company, 32
McKeesport, 200
Mediterranean, 7
Melin, S., 64
Melting Pot Hypothesis, 244-248
Memphis, 75
Messner, Archbishop, 163
Methodists, 103
Metternich, 131, 140
Mexican War, 60, 67
Mexico, 187, 208, 223
Mexico City, 61
Meyer, F., 63
Michaels, C., 94
Michalska, M., see Gilda Gray
Michelet, 137
Michigan, 55, 64, 65, 78, 79, 88, 89, 96, 97, 98, 100, 101, 102, 104, 174, 183, 186, 195, 200, 209, 210, 212, 213, 217, 219, 220, 235, 283
Michigan Anti-Slavery Society, 55
Michigan Heart Association, 88
Michigan State Welfare Commission, 92
Micinski, E., 21
Mickiewicz, A., 137, 144, 152, 180
Mickiewicz Centennial, 285
Mickiewicz, W., 132
Midera, S., 42
Midowicz, C. E., 174, 175
Mierzwa, S., 206, 207
Mierzynski, J., 200
Mieszko, I, 2, 3, 222
Mieszko, II, 3
Mieszkowski, J. K., 44
Mietus, T., 21
Miklaszewicz, F., 43

Miles, General, 69
Miller, F. H., 129
Miller, H. A., 193, 195
Milwaukee, 52, 63, 78, 79, 82, 95, 101, 102, 103, 104, 162, 198, 210, 213
Minnesota, 97, 210
Minsk, 8, 135
Missionaries of La Salatte, 102
Mississippi, 34
Missouri, 60, 65, 78, 168, 217, 220
Mitana, Dr. T., 218, 284
Mitchell, H., 33
Mitsco, C., 42
Mizwa, Dr. S., 277, 279, 281
Moczygemba, F., 73
Moczygemba, Rev. L., 62, 213
Modjeska, H., 78, 83, 222, 223
Modjeski, Dr. R., 83
Modrzejewska, H., 78, 138
Modrzewski, F., 40
Mohega, 52
Mohilev, 135
Mlotkowski, Capt. S., 67
Monaco, 126
Mondello, 34, 60, 61, 62
Moniuszko, 92
Montesquieu, 40
Moravian Nuns, 40
Morison, F., 106
Morozowicz, A., 67
Morris, A. E., 30
Morris, Gouverneur, 30, 31
Morris, R., 216
Morrison, 31
Morse, S. F. B., 216
Moscow, 81
Moskol, H., 97
Mostowski, P., 35
Moszydlowski, A., 97
Mount Bielaski, 51
Mount Horeb, 246
Mount Independence, 36
Mount Radziminski, 61
Mount Vernon, Virginia, 46
Mozart, 80-82
Mrozowski, Dr. S., 89
Mruc, J., 95
Munich, 266
Muravieu, 135
Murawski, L. F., 188, 190
Musial, S., 93
Muskie, E. S., 96
Muzelius, F., 42

Najduch, J., 289
Napoleon's Polish Legion, 49
Napolska, Sister M. Remigia, 27, 219
Narloch, Rev. A., 220
Narod Polski, 163, 212, 200, 221, 228
Narragansett Bay, 33
National Council of Catholic Women, 91

Nazareth, 32
Nazism, 266
Nebraska, 78, 213
Nedwicki, Dr. E. G., 89
Nedzi, L., 97
Negri, P., 83
Negroes, 37, 38, 54, 57, 71, 88
Neomisia, see Rutkowska
Neuman, Bishop J. P., 48
Nevada, 67
Netherlanders, 45
Newark, 101, 200
Newport, Capt. C., 21
New Amstel, 26
New Amsterdam, 25, 26, 27, 28
New Amsterdam on Lake Erie, 45
Newberry Medal, 277
New Britain, 101, 190
Newcastle, 26
New Cathedral Cemetery, 74
New Deal, 267
New England, 23
New England Anti-Slavery Society, 54
New England Female Medical College, 56
New England Hospital for Women and
   Children, 56, 57
New Glarus, 246
New Hampshire, 42, 217
New Haven, 98, 200
New Holland, 23, 25, 26
New Jersey, 28, 42, 47, 95, 97, 101, 104,
   199, 200, 274
New Orleans, 34, 59, 71
New Poland, 23, 35
New Sweden, 23, 24, 28
New York, 38, 42, 45, 51-54, 58, 79, 97,
   100, 101, 104, 116, 139, 174, 200, 204,
   210, 217, 219, 222, 262
New York City, 27, 52, 67, 83, 85, 101,
   112, 187, 188, 199, 200, 231, 260, 263,
   278
New York Infirmary For Women and
   Children, 56
New York Philharmonic Orchestra, 80
New York Times, 74, 97, 260, 265, 268,
   269, 270
New York Weekly News, 59
Niagara Falls, 46
Niagara Falls Park Commission, 50
Niagara River, 50
Niagara-on-the-Lake, 261
Nicholas I, Czar of Russia, 17, 131, 134,
   136
Nicholas II, Czar of Russia, 137
Nichols, J. A., 145
Niedbalski, S., 203
Niedzwiecki, M., 218
Niedzwiecki, P., 98
Niemcewicz, J. U., 45-47
Niemerich, G., 42
Niemirycz, G. 41

Niewiadrowski, Rev. A., 48
Noa, Bishop, T. L., 102
North American Lloyd Line, 130
North Carolina, 21, 42
Northampton, 85
Northwestern University, 202
Norway, 3
Norwegians, 246
Norwid Literary Contest, 285
Notre Dame University, 94
Nowak, M., 96, 97
Nowy Swiat, 58, 104

Oak Ridge National Laboratory, 89
Oblates of Mary Immaculate, 102
Obleffsikie, F., 42
O'Callaghan, 26
Oder River, 2, 5
Ohio, 34, 35, 56, 58, 60, 84, 97, 101,
   102, 193, 200, 210, 217, 220
Oklahoma, 61
O'Konski, A. E., 96, 266
Okrie, F., 94
Oladowski, H., 61
Olejniczak, J., 250
Olejniczak, J. J., 217
Olszewicz, B., 28
Olszyk, E. G., 97, 183
Omazta, J., 70
Ontario, 51, 261
Orchard Lake, 104, 212, 213, 235, 258
Oregon, 60
Oregon City, 60
Orgish, S., 97
Orlikowski, T., 97
Orvis, J. S., 126
Osada, S., 152, 173, 192, 200, 231, 248
Ostafin, Dr. P., 258
Ostmarken-Verein, 128
Ostroleka, 222
Ostrowski, Prof. J., 204
Ottoman Empire, 167
Owen Sound, 261

Pacta Conventa, 11, 12,
Paderewski, 222, 240, 278
Paderewski Foundation, 273, 274, 275
Paine, T., 53, 54
Pajakowski, C., 96
Palatinate of Halicz, 139
Palczowski, P., 28
Pankow, S., 96
Pankowski, T., 97
Panna Maria, Texas, 62, 73
Pan-Slavism, 143, 180
Papielinski, J. N., 173
Parana, 112
Paris, 6, 12, 39, 58, 81, 126
Parisville, 64
Park, R. E., 193
Parker, F., 94

Parsons, C., 85
Paryski, I. J., 193
Paschke, F., 41
Paskevitch, Marshal I., 133
Pasko, J., 42
Passaic, 30
Passaic River, 30
Passasky, C., 32
Pastuszka, A., 96
Patrzycki, Rev. J., 188
Patterson, General J., 38
Pawlowski, F., 83
Peach Tree Creek, 69
Peale's Museum, 52
Pearl Habor, 98
Peartree, W., 27
Pearson, J., 88, 89
Pecyk, A., 97
Penn, W., 31
Pennsylvania, 31, 32, 35, 42-45, 50, 60, 67, 78, 79, 84, 95, 97, 100, 101-104, 171, 174, 186, 200, 203, 210, 212, 217, 220, 235, 240
Pennsylvania Military Academy, 58
Pennsylvania University, 280
Penobscot Bay, 32
People's Republic of Poland, 1
Percy, Lord, 33
Pereyaslav Treaty of 1654, 13
Pertek, J., 20
Perth Amboy, 200
Peru, 75
Pesko, R., 42
Pestrak, W., 97
Petreswich, 61
Philadelphia, 34, 36, 47, 48, 49, 57, 58, 60, 68, 69, 80, 81, 95, 101, 112, 157, 173, 174, 199
Philliporski, L., 70
Phillips, W. A., 143
Piasecki, E., 95
Piasecki, F. N., 95
Piasecki Helicopter Corporation, 95
Piast, 2
Piast Dynasty, 2, 5
Piatkiewicz, K. 196, 202, 204, 229, 231, 271
Piatkowski, R., 198, 204
Piekarski, F., 93
Pietraskiewicz, F., 94
Pietrowski, R. K., 78
Pilinski, A., 74
Pilsudski, A., 136
Pilsudski, J., 17, 136, 282
Pilsudski High School, 88
Piotrkow, Poland, 53, 75
Piotrowicz, F. 61
Piotrowska, Dr., I., 281
Piotrowski, N., 217
Piotrowski, R. K., 60
Pittsburg, 79, 101, 182, 210, 215, 220

Piwowarski, Prof., 204
Pleyel, 81,
Pliny, 1
Pliska, S. R., 138, 146, 148, 171, 187, 238, 240, 249, 253
Plymouth, 32
Plymouth Harbor, 33
Podgorski, A., 96
Podlasia, 2,
Podolia, 135
Pogorzelska, Sister M., Assumpta, SSJ, 159
Poland, 1-18, 55, 79, 80, 161, 166, 167, 173, 176, 177-181, 182, 186, 204, 223, 227, 232, 236, 239, 242, 249, 260, 271
Polaski, P., 42
Polaskie, A., 42
Polish Activities League, 91
Polish Alma Mater of America, 186
Polish American Congress, 100, 203, 225, 263, 270-275
*Polish American Historical Association Bulletin,* 82, 92, 93, 100, 105, 224, 270, 282, 283
*Polish American Journal,* 35, 61, 70, 80, 101, 105
Polish American Museum Foundation, 224
*Polish American Studies,* 28, 30, 47, 48, 51, 52, 56, 57, 59, 67, 68, 69, 72-75, 80, 98, 136, 149, 153, 156, 202, 224, 230, 282, 283
*Polish American World,* 95, 105,
Polish Arians, 24
Polish Army Veterans of America, 262
Polish Artists Guild, 289,
Polish Arts and Science Institute, 273
Polish Catholic Congress, 215
Polish Colonization Agency, 120
*Polish Daily News,* 218
Polish Falcons of America, 186, 187
Polish Franciscan Fathers, 48
Polish Goodfellows, 91
Polish Hussars, 7
Polish Immigration Committee, 272
Polish Institute of Arts and Sciences, 218, 275, 281, 282, 290
Polish Insurrection of 1830, 17, 133-135
Polish Insurrection of 1863, 17, 133-137
Polish Lapins, 91
Polish Legion, 70
Polish-Lithuanian Commonwealth, 8
Polish Moravian Church, 35
Polish National Alliance, 104, 105, 174, 175, 176, 177, 180. 182, 183, 191-211, 227-235, 237, 238, 242, 248-259, 261, 274
Polish National Catholic Church, 103, 104, 171
Polish National Exposition, 215
Polish National Museum in Krakow, 38

Polish National Museum in Warsaw, 38
Polish National Museum in Rappers-schwyl, 49
Polish Relief Committee, 91
Polish Republic, 236
*Polish Review*, 46, 47, 105, 258, 260, 282
Polish Roman Catholic Union, 91, 168-171, 177, 181-183, 198, 212-215, 237, 242, 248-259, 274
Polish Seminary at Orchard Lake, 212, 283
Polish Sisterhoods, 103
Polish-Slavonian Literary Association, 52
Polish Society of Argentina, 69
Polish Society of History and Museum, 221, 224
Polish-Turkish War, 13
Polish Women's Alliance in America, 185, 186, 242, 263
Polish Unitarian Library, 46
Poliskie see Polaski
Polkowski, E., 52
Polonia, Texas, 62
Poloske, E., 42
Poloske see Polaski,
Polotsk, 12
Polski, Instytut Naukowy, 273
Polski, Z., 53
Pomerania, 22, 6, 8, 63
Pomiankowski, 144
Poniatowski, Prince J., 39, 151
Poniatowski, King S. A., 12, 15, 43, 45, 75, 108, 122
Pope IX, 92
Pope Leo XIII, 213
Port Henry, 51
Port Hudson, 69
Portage County, 62
Posen, Michigan, 163, 164
Positivist School, 177-180
Post, Rev., 35
Postula, T., 99
Potocki, H., 53
Potowski-Rose, E. S., 53-55
Potsdam, 270
Poughkeepsie, 83
Pozkowski, General, 39
Poznan, 8, 63, 122-125, 129
Poznanski, C., 180
Prague, 6
Prague University, 6
Pranica, J. T., 225
Praniewicz, Rev. T., 47
*Pravda*, 97
Presbyterians, 103
Princeton University, 67, 90
Prokop, S. A., 96
Providence, 58, 60
PRCU Archives and Museum 221, 224
Prussia, 13, 49, 59, 78, 107, 173, 180
Prussians, 6, 17

Prussian Poland, 122-130
Przemysl II, 6
Przyborski, General, 144
Przybylinski, J., 96
Przybylowicz, M., 60
Przygoda, Rev. J., 90
Ptolemy, 2
Puebla, 61
Pulaski, Count C., 36, 40-42, 52, 53, 65, 99, 108, 109, 162, 182, 197, 198, 222, 223, 246, 267
Pulaski Legion, 41
Pulaski, Lt. Col. E., 89
Pucinski, R. C., 96
P. V. Engineering Forum, 95
Pychowski, J. N., 47, 52

Queen Victoria, 50
Quels River, 5

Rachels, E., 27
Radziminski, Capt. C., 61
Radziminski, R., 98
Radziwill Family, 135
Radziwill, General, 58
Radziwill, Prince, 133
Radziwill, Princess C., 116, 117
Raleigh, Sir Walter, 21
Rappersschwyl, 49
Rapersschwyl Fund, 185
Rataj, General J., 99
Rath, R. J., 142
Ravensbruck Concentration Camp, 91
Rawicz-Gawronski, L., 58
Read, D. B., 51
Red Ruthenia, 3
Regiment de Conflans, 44
Regiment of Royal Dragons, 45
Remagen Bridge, 99
Remak, S., 75
Rembowski, R., 179
Rensselaerswych, 25
Republic of Kakow, 141
Resettlement Committee, 272
Resurrectionists, 104
Rey, A., 42
Reymont, 152, 284
Rhineland, 129
Rhine River, 99, 127
Rhode Island, 58, 97
Rhode, Bishop P., 170, 215, 242, 291
Ridste, 83
Rice Institute, 279
Richmond, 60, 72
Rickenbacker, Capt. A., 99
Riga, 8
Rising, Governor, 24
Roanoke, 21
Rodzinski, Dr. A., 80
Rodnowski, Lieut., 69
Rochambeau's Army, 45

Rock River, 49
Rockne, K., 94
Rogers, W., 82
Rogowski, M., 41
Roguszka, D., 96
Rola Boza, 103
Rolbiecki, Rev. J. J., 90
Roman Civilization, 2
Romanov, 136
Rome, 91
Rondeau, F. A., 97
Roosevelt, C., 34
Roosevelt, C. C., 42
Roosevelt, E., 34
Roosevelt, F. D., 67, 96, 262, 263, 265, 266, 267, 270, 278
Roosevelt, T., 34, 98, 170
Ropa, J. F., 96
Rosa, R., 96
Rose, E., see Potowski-Rose,
Rose, W. B., 53
Rosen, J., 83
Rosen, J. H., 222
Ross, B., 99
Rossadowski, R. V. A., 48
Rosseau, 40
Rosiak, Rev. B. S., 90
Rosiekiewicz, M., 52
Rosonoschy, D., 42
Rostenkowski, D., 96, 97
Roszak, T., 83
Rotarians, 90
Rotschild, J., 132
Roucek, J. S., 101, 102, 273
Royal Newfoundland Fencibles, 33
Roxy, W., 94
Rozek, E. J., 266, 267
Rozmarek, K., 250, 263, 265, 266, 270, 272
Rozmoski, K., 70
Rozum, 97
Rubinstein, A., 80
Ruch, L. A., 96
Ruhr, 129
Russell Family, 32
Russia, 15, 49, 100, 129, 142, 148, 173, 180, 262, 265, 268
Russian Poland, 130-139
Russians, 17, 107, 192, 246,
Ruthenia, 8, 129, 139
Rutkowska, Sister M. Neomisia, 48, 219
Rutkowski, J., 27
Rutkowski, L., 52
Rybinski, General, 58
Rybka, F., 97
Rydzewski, S., 70
Rydzynski, A., 97
Ryder, Rev. J., 48
Rzeznikiewicz, P. J., 96

Saboleski, P. F. R., 70

Sadowa, 143
Sadowski, 108
Sadowski, A., 31, 34
Sadowski, Jacob, 34
Sadowski, James, 34
Sadowski, Jonathan, 41
Sadowski, S., 21
Sadowsky, J., 43
Saint-Leu-la-Foret, 81
Sakowska, M., 201
Salak, L. J., 97
Salamonski, J., 58
Salamonski, J. K., 52
Salem, 43
Salesians, 102
Salomon, Haym, 42
Saloutos, T., 155
San Antonio, 62, 75
San Antonio River, 61
Sandomierz, 5
San Domingo, 49
Sanduskie, J., 43
Sandusky, 34
Sandusky, A., 31, 43
San Francisco, 60, 78, 270
San Jacinto, 61
Santa Anna, 61
Santa Clara County, 51
Santa Rosa Province, 208
Saratoga, 36
Satler, Dr., 127
Saturday Evening Post, 269
Saunders, H. Dmochowski see Dmochowski
Savannah, 41, 42
Saxon Kings, 13
Saxony, 107
Savonarola, 103
Scajaquada Creek Expressway, 100
Schachern, H., 288
Schemansky, N., 94
Schenectady, 204
Schermerhorn, R. S., 79
Schimmelfenning, 66
Schimmelpenninck, 45
Schmidt, Dr. J., 56
Schmitt, B. E., 126, 277
Schneiweis, J. S., 162
Schoening Regiment, 70
Schoepf, General A. F., 67
School Sisters of Notre Dame, 79, 103
Schreiber, A., 203
Schultz, G., 51
Schurz, C., 66, 67, 69
Schuyler Company, 32
Schwatka, 51
Schweitzer, 81
Scotch, 84
Scotch Trick, 43
Scots, 10, 106, 107
Scottish Brotherhood in Poland, 107

Scranton, 102, 103, 171
Seabrook, W., 22
Seduskey, J., 43
Sembrich, M., 222
Sengteller, L. A., 60
Seroczynski, F. T., 59, 78, 101, 103, 176
Sexton, J. H., 193
Shaffer, G. K., 99
Shallna, A. O., 38
Shapley, Dr. H., 278, 280
Shawnee Indians, 35
Sheehan, D., 82
Sherman, General, 68
Shuba, G., 94
Siberia, 132, 133, 134
Siemieradzki, 200
Sienkiewicz, C., 95
Sienkiewicz, H., 78, 123, 149, 153, 180
Sieroty, A., 96
Sigismund III, 13
Sigismund August, 10, 108
Sikorski, General, 261
Silesia, 3, 5, 122, 145
Silesians, 2, 6
Sirotniak, J., 97
Sister Hedwig, 288
Sister Veronica, 73
Sister of the Holy Family of Nazareth, 103, 214
Sisters of the Immaculate Conception, 190
Sisters of the Resurrection, 103
Sisters of St. Joseph of the Third Order of St. Francis, 103
Skapik, M., 97
Skibinska, A. M., 201
Skierski, F. J., 97
Sklar, J., 96
Sklodowski, Dr. W., 218
Skowron, B., 94
Skrzycki, E., 94
Skrzynecki, General, 58
Slask, 173
Slavery, 54
Slawik, Rev. B., 218
Slesinski, T., 246, 283
Slovaks, 3
Slowacki, 152
Slowik, M. W., 97
Sluszka, S. J., 27, 201
Smith, B., 113
Smith, Captain J., 21, 22, 84
Smith, W. C., 118, 193
Smith, W. P., 27
Smogorzewski, C., 79
Smolensk, 8
Smolenski, W., 179
Smolinski, C. W. H., 61
Smolinski, J., 74
Smoluchowski, Dr. B., 89
Sobieski, C., 107
Sobieski, J., 96, 107

Sobieski, King John, 12, 28, 39, 166
Soboleski, Capt. L., 67
Sobolewski, E., 52
Sobolewski, P., 51, 52
Society of the Divine Saviour, 102
Society of Jesus, 48
Sohake, J., 42
Sokalski, Dr. W., 218
Soleure, 39
Solomons, 99
Sons of the Divine Providence, 102
Sorbonne University, 8, 58
Sosnowski, J. C., 73
Sosnowski, Mrs., 74
South Africa, 223
South Bend, 197
South Carolina, 41, 43, 54
South Carolina Regiment, 73
South Company, 24
South Dakota, 97
Soviet Union, 1, 267, 269
Spain, 1, 2
Spaleto, 88
Spanish-American War, 98
Speek, P. A., 164
Sproule, G., 32
SS Cyril and Methodius Seminary, 104, 288, 290
Stablewski, F., 125, 129, 145
Stach, R., 42
Stadnicki, P., 45
Stalin, J., 265, 267
St. Andrew Island, 19
St. Augustine, 90, 91
St. Francis College, 104
St. Francis Hospital, 89
St. Hedwig, Texas, 62
St. John Cantius College, 212, 274
St. Joseph's Home for Polish Immigrants, 188-190, 215
St. Louis, 60, 215
St. Louis Cardinals, 93
St. Mary's College, 104, 274, 290
St. Stanislaus Bishop and Martyr Parish, 159
St. Stanislaus College, 177
St. Stanislaus Kostka College, 212
St. Stanislaus Kostka Parish, 159
St. Stanislaus Kostka Society, 156
St. Stanislaus School, 103
St. Thomas Acquinas, 90
Stampoffski, Capt. B. J., 67
Stanislaw, Brother E., 258
Staniszewski, Dr. C., 89
Stapinski, J., 143
Starzynski, F., 242
Steczynski, M., 204
Stefan, S. B., 148
Stefanowicz, A., 217, 220, 231
Stefanski, Z. 21, 212

Stempowski see Stampoffski
Stentzel, Dr. J., 60
Steuben, Baron, 29
Steuben Guards, 70
Stevenson, A., 97
Stevenson, J. D., 60
Still, C. V., 57
Still, L., 57
Still, W., 57
Stockbridge, Mass., 38
Stockton, Capt. H., 68
Stojka, 21
Stokowski, L., 80, 81
Stopka, J. P., 96
Stowarzyszenie Polakow Ameryce, 59
St. Petersburg, 46, 136
Strachan, S., 96
Strawinski, T., 65
Strawinski, T. F., 58
Strzelecki, 51
Stuart, J., 107
Stuart, M., 223
Stuyvesant, G., 24-28
Stuyvesant Institute, 59
Styka, J., 83
Suchodolski, J., 222
Suhl, Y., 53, 55
Sulakowski, V., 72
Summerville Academy, 58
Super, P., 267, 268
Susti, 45
Sven, 3
Swarthout, G., 83
Swaartvegar, H. J., 25
Swaartvegar, J. J., 26
Swabians, 123
Swastek, J., 75, 80, 90, 101, 102, 153
Sweden, 1, 10, 13, 23
Swedes, 25, 107, 166
Swieczkowska, C., 91, 92
Swietlik, F., 203
Swietoslawski, W., 83
Swiniarski, T. A., 96
Swiontkowski, Z., 96
Swiss, 6, 246
Switzerland, 39, 49, 172, 185
Switaska, A. M., 97
Sydney, 40
Symons, Archbishop A., 171
Syracuse University, 266
Syrotjack, J., 32
Syrynski, M., 21
Syski, Msgr. A., 170
Szajnert, J., 173
Szawleski, Dr. M., 139, 147
Szczepkowska, A., 209, 210
Szczepanski, 59
Szenowski, J. C. A., 69
Szeptycki, 144
Sznayder, T., 41
Szpaczak, L., 58

Szpaczek, F., 52
Szpakowski, F. G., 97
Szubalski, S., 84
Szujski, J., 143, 177, 178
Szulborski, H., 94
Sztybel, T. K., 70
Szumowski, I., 61
Szymanowski, T., 97
Szymanski, Col. I. S., 59, 72
Szymanski, F., 94

Taft, W. H., 204
Targosh, Rev. S., 161
Targotsky, P., 28
Tarnowski, 144
Tarnowski, S., 143
Tartars, 5, 6, 13, 106, 107
Tatras, 139
Taylor, A. J. P., 140
Teheran, 267, 270
Teller, Dr. E., 29
Tennessee, 34, 66, 75
Theodosette, Sister M., 48, 158
Terlecki, W., 21
Tetmajer, W., 279
Teutonic Knights, 6, 8
Teutons, 5
Texas, 60-62, 75, 77, 97
Texas War of Independence, 61
The Alamo Register, 62
The True American, 71
The Whitehall Times, 63
Thomain, R., 58
Thomas, D., 94
Thomas, W. I., 112-114, 146, 150, 156,
    158, 235, 276
Thompson, C., 35
Ticonderoga, 36
Tiedemann, 127
Tilliskey, J., 42
Tobago Island, 19
Tolstoy, 81
Toscanini, A., 80
Tochman, Major G., 52, 71, 72, 120
Toledo, 101, 193, 200
Tomaszkiewicz, M., 262
Tomaszow, 107
Tomski, H., 94
Toronto, 50
Tondryk, J., 97
Toski, B., 94
Towarzystwo Demokratyczne Wygnancow
    Polskich w Ameryce, 59
Transylvania, 13
Treaty of Riga, 269
Treaty of Versailles, 17
Tremaine, A. G., 163
Trempealeau Township, 63
Trieste, 75
Truman, H. S., 269, 270
Truskolaski, J., 51

Truszkowska, Mother Mary Angela, 136
Tucker, S., 82
Tulagi, 99
Turkevich, Dr. J., 90
Turkey, 7, 171
Turks, 13, 107, 166
Tutro, J. A., 96
Tyssowski, J., 75

Ukraine, 13, 177
Ukrainians, 88
Ukrainian-Turkish Alliance, 13
Uminski, S. H., 47, 98
Underground Railroad, 57
Underwood, S. A., 55
Union, 168
United States Military Academy, 30
United States Navy, 95
United Turner Rifles, 70
Universal Exposition, 58
Universal Peace Society, 55
University of Bologna, 6
University of California, 279
University of Cincinnati, 75
University of Detroit, 94
University of Innsbruck, 91
University of Illinois, 80
University of Lwow, 80, 178
University of  Michigan, 83, 90
University of Padua, 6, 28
University of Pennsylvania, 58, 89
University of Pittsburg, 89
University of Toledo, 193
University of Torun, 280
University of Virginia, 58
University of Warsaw, 133, 205
University of Wilno, 123
University of Wisconsin, 202, 246, 289
Upper Canadian Rebellion, 51
Urbanski, E., 96
Usselinx, W., 24
Utah, 51
Uzdowski, G., 44, 45

Vanadium Hotel, 204
Van Cliburn, 278
Van Danstick, W. J., 25
Van der Donck, 26
Van der Lindern, M., 28
Van Houten, Z. A., 30
Vanik, C., 97
Van, Norman, L. E., 31, 166
Van Slechtenhorst, 25, 26
Van Staphorst, 45
Vasa Dynasty, 12
Vassar College, 277
Vauclain, S. M., 277
Vermont, 97
Vertor Aircraft Corporation, 95
Versen, V. M., 212, 213, 224, 225
Vestal, I., 97

Vicksburg, 68
Vienna, 13, 39, 58, 80, 132, 139, 140,
    143, 166
Vincentians, 102
Vitebsk, 135
Vistula Province, 135
Vistula River, 2, 136
Virginia, 21, 23, 31, 42, 67, 84, 97, 120,
    287
Virginia County Court Book, 23
Vollenhoven, 45
Volontaires Etrangers de la Marine, 44,
    45
Von Flottwell, E., 122
Von Schon, 122

Wachowski, Rev. J., 216
Wachtl, K. 149, 168, 183, 231, 261
Wagner, W., 40
Wainright, J. W., 205
Waldo, A. L., 21, 223
Walewski, F. C., 47
Walsh, S., 95
Walter, J., 223, 224
Waner, J. L., 97
Wankowicz, Lieut. L., 73
Wankowicz, M., 113
War of 1812, 33, 39, 47
Wardzinski, F., 61
Warka, Poland, 42
Warna, 8
Warnadowicz, F., 20
Warren Tavern, 41
Warsaw Conservatory of Music, 80, 209
Warsaw Opera, 80
Warsaw, Poland, 17, 47, 59, 80, 131, 179,
    260
Warsaw Society, 114
Warszawski, Dr. E. H., 89
Warwick, 72
Washington, 97
Washington, D. C., 21, 67, 100, 182, 197,
    203
Washington, G., 37-39, 46, 47, 54, 206
Washington Island, 246
Washington Rifles Company, 69
Wasp, 41
Wassell, F. F., 262, 270
Wawel Hill, 39
Wayne State University, 88, 288
Webster, D., 57
Wegrzynek, M., 273
Weiss, Dr. C., 89
Weitzel, G., 69
Wellesley, 31
Wengierski, A., 52, 61, 71
Werki, 135
Wertheimer, Z., 132
West Germany, 1
West India Company, 24, 25
West Point Academy, 36, 99, 168, 274

West Virginia, 84, 97, 220
Western Reserve College, 56
Westphalia, 129
Westphalians, 123
White, G., 82
White Russia, 134
Whitfield, F., 279
Whitman, W., 287
Whitton, Major F. E., 133
Wiadomosci Codzienne, 104
Wierusz, 279
Wierzbicki, F. P., 60
Wilkes-Barre, 203
Williamsburg, 72
Willink, 45
Wilno, 8, 135
Wilowski, C. E., 96
Wilski, 99
Winslow, E., 33
Wilson, Woodrow, 17, 98, 186, 187, 198, 206
Windmill Point, 71
Winook see Wunk
Wisconsin, 60-63, 75, 79, 97, 100-102, 104, 109, 129, 174, 198, 200, 210, 219, 220, 246, 266
Wisniewski, J., 96, 99
Wisniowiecki, M., 12
Witkowski, B., 93
Witkowski, J., 97
Witkowski, J. T., 96
Witnesses of Jehovah, 103
Witos, W., 143
Wittke, C., 37, 79, 104, 113, 120, 169, 194
Wloszczewski, Dr. S., 65, 283
Wojciechowski, 73
Wojciechowski, F., 60
Wojciechowski, Capt. F., 78
Wojciechowski, Z., 123
Wojcik, Rev. J., 188
Wojczynski, A., 173
Wojnarowski, F., 93
Wolanin, A. S., 218
Wolowska, H., 263
Wolski, C., 71
Wolynia, 5, 135
Women's National Loyal League, 55
Woolsey, L. H., 269
Worcester, 49, 100
Worcester Highland Military Academy, 58
World War I, 261
World War II, 260-275
Woytycha, C. J., 96, 97
Wozniak, D., 97
Wozniak, G., 96
Woznicki, Bishop S., 85, 90, 193
Wright, H., 269
Wright, T., 32
Wroblewski, D., 94
Wroclaw, 2, 5

Wraclawice, 39
Wuchang, 102
Wrotnowski, A., 69
Wunk, J., 63
Wyczolkowski, 279
Wyslouch, B., 143
Wyslouch, M., 143
Wyspianski, S., 181, 222
Wyszynski, E. 52
Wytrwal, J., 41, 51, 68, 82, 92, 93, 100, 221, 224, 243-245, 289
Wytrwal, W., 151

Yablonski, J., 97
Yale University, 30
Yalta Conference, 1, 265-270
Yanaletz, F., 42
Yasnaya Polyana, 81
Yeardley, Governor, 23
Yezierska, A., 113, 117
Yolles, P., 116, 192
Yorktown, 44, 62
Youngtown, 84

Zablocki, C. J., 96, 97
Zaborowski, 108
Zaborowski, J., 29
Zaborowski, O., 28, 29, 31
Zabriskie, Abraham, 30
Zabriskie, Albert, 29
Zabriskie, A. H., 96
Zabriskie, C. A., 30
Zabriskie, C. B., 30
Zabriskie, Chancellor, 31
Zabriskie, Col. J., 29, 61
Zabriskie, F. H., 30
Zabriskie, H. J., 30
Zabriskie, J., 42
Zabriskie, J. A., 70
Zabriskie, Dr. J. B., 30
Zabriskie, J. C., 30
Zabriskie, S. T., 30
Zabriskie, W. F., 60
Zabriskie, Y., 42
Zabrisky, J. C., 42
Zajaczek, 52
Zakrzewska, Dr. M., 55-57
Zakrzewski, A., 60
Zaleski, 144
Zaleski, Bishop A., 90, 102
Zalinski, Lieut. E. L. G., 69-70, 75
Zangwill, I., 244
Zawadzki, Dr. E. S., 89
Zawadzki, W., 46
Zawistowski, A., 52
Zawistowski, C., 52
Zawistowski, E., 52
Zawodooski, P., 42
Zborowski, E., 31
Zborowski, M., 30
Zborowski, Count W. E., 31

Zelherowicz, E., 97
Zenger, J. P., 109
Zeromski, 153, 284
Zgoda, 93, 94, 98, 105, 176, 202, 211,
    228
Zgierz, 107
Zglenicki, L., 186, 192, 201
Ziegfeld Follies, 82
Zielinski, General, 144
Zielinski, J., 41
Ziolkowski, Korczak, 92
Ziontz, A., 97
Znaniecki, F., 80, 112-114, 146, 156, 158,
    235, 276, 286

Znaniecki, V., 96
Zoltowski, A., 134, 135
Zrenica, K., 21
Zuboff, M., 58
Zubrzycki, J., 21, 31, 49
Zulawski, E. K., 70
Zurchin, General J. B., 120
Zwiazek Polek w Ameryce, 185, 242
Zwiazek Polskich Ksiezy w Ameryce,
    187-190
Zwicki, C., 74
Zwolinski, Dr. B., 89
Zybura, Rev. J. S., 90
Zychlinski, Capt. L., 69
Zygmunt, J. J., 99

## Date Due